SELF-DETERMINATION, STATEHOOD, AND THE LAW OF NEGOTIATION

From the Madrid Invitation in 1991 to the introduction of the Oslo process in 1993 to the present, a negotiated settlement has remained the dominant leitmotiv of peacemaking between Israel and the Palestinian people. That the parties have chosen negotiations means that either side's failure to comply with its obligation to negotiate can result in an internationally wrongful act and, in response, countermeasures and other responses. This monograph seeks to advance our understanding of the international law of negotiation and use this as a framework for assessing the Israeli–Palestinian dispute, with the Palestinian people's unsuccessful attempt to join the United Nations as a Member State in autumn 2011 and the successful attempt to join the same institution as a non-Member Observer State in November 2012 providing a case study for this. The legal consequences of these applications are not merely of historical interest; they inform the present rights and obligations of Israel and the Palestinian people. This work fills a significant gap in the existing international law scholarship on the Israeli–Palestinian dispute, which neither engages with this means of dispute settlement generally nor does so specifically within the context of the Palestinian people's engagements with international institutions.

Self-Determination, Statehood, and the Law of Negotiation

The Case of Palestine

Robert P. Barnidge, Jr.

•HART•

OXFORD • LONDON • NEW YORK • NEW DELHI • SYDNEY

HART PUBLISHING
Bloomsbury Publishing Plc
Kemp House, Chawley Park, Cumnor Hill, Oxford, OX2 9PH, UK

HART PUBLISHING, the Hart/Stag logo, BLOOMSBURY and the Diana logo are trademarks of Bloomsbury Publishing Plc
First published in Great Britain 2016

First published in hardback, 2016
Paperback edition, 2018

A catalogue record for this book is available from the British Library.

Library of Congress Cataloging-in-Publication Data

Barnidge, Robert P., Jr. author.
Self-determination, statehood, and the law of negotiation : the case of Palestine /
Robert P. Barnidge, Jr.
pages cm
Includes bibliographical references and index.
ISBN 978-1-84946-812-1 (hardback : alk. paper) 1. Self-determination, National—Palestine.
2. Mediation, International. 3. Palestine—International status. 4. Arab-Israeli conflict—History.
I. Title.
KZ4282.B36 2016 341.26—dc23
2015036601

ISBN: PB: 978-1-50992-119-5
HB: 978-1-84946-812-1

Typeset by Compuscript Ltd, Shannon

To the memory of my father, Robert P. Barnidge (1940–2010)

ACKNOWLEDGEMENTS

When I began this research in 2010, the International Court of Justice had just handed down its advisory opinion in *Accordance with International Law of the Unilateral Declaration of Independence in Respect of Kosovo*. As I complete it, International Criminal Court Prosecutor Fatou Bensouda is conducting a preliminary examination of the Palestinian situation. Some of the tactics that Israel and the Palestinian people have used in their dispute have changed, but the underlying clash, of two self-determination movements, remains the same. This multi-year research project has been as much about the past as it has been about the present.

The following colleagues were gracious enough to have read and commented upon earlier incarnations of this work: Sreeram Chaulia, Ronen A. Cohen, Matthew Craven, Lori Damrosch, Rohee Dasgupta, Joel Fishman, Sandy Ghandhi, Rotem Giladi, James A. Green, Anne Herzberg, Pasha Hsieh, Dino Kritsiotis, Charlotte Ku, Robert Lloyd, Swechha Malik, Marko Milanovic, William K. Morrison, Mordechai Nisan, Mutaz M. Qafisheh, Surabhi Ranganathan, J. Martin Rochester, Ron Schleifer, Ofira Seliktar, Sandesh Sivakumaran, Thomas W. Smith, Aldo Zammit-Borda, and Reuven (Ruvi) Ziegler.

I am grateful for the feedback that I received on presentations of this research at the 2011 and 2013 annual conferences of the Association for the Study of the Middle East and Africa, the Indian Law Institute, the Second Annual Junior Faculty Forum for International Law at the University of Nottingham, the Brandeis-Jindal Workshop on Israel Studies at O.P. Jindal Global University, the 2014 annual conference of the International Studies Association, the 2014 American Society of International Law's Midyear Meeting and Research Forum, the Department of Political Science at Belmont University, the Palestinian Academic Society for the Study of International Affairs, the College of Law at Hebron University, and the 2015 Legalities and Legacies: The Past, Present, and Future of the Palestine Mandate in International Law Conference in Jerusalem, which was co-sponsored by the Hebrew University Faculty of Law and Columbia Law School.

I also appreciate the substantive exchanges of views with Mahdi Abdul Hadi, Ahmad Azem, Alan Baker, David Bukay, Yoram Dinstein, Saeb Erakat, Avi Goldstein, Efraim Karsh, Eugene Kontorovich, Yossi Kuperwasser, B.C. Nirmal, Meital Nir-Tal, Doron Pely, Thomas Phillips, Robbie Sabel, Jonathan Schanzer, Malcolm Shaw, Assaf Shelleg, Achilles Skordas, Nathan Stock, and Uri Weiss, as well as with colleagues at the International Law, Foreign Law, and the United States Constitution Colloquium, which took place in 2015 thanks to the co-sponsorship of the Federalist Society for Law and Public Policy Studies and the Liberty Fund.

Speaking with International Court of Justice Judge Xue Hanqin and International Tribunal for the Law of the Sea Judge Gudmundur Eiriksson at the Fourth Biennial Conference of the Asian Society of International Law improved my understanding of the international law of negotiation as a means of dispute settlement.

Thanks to a £1,200 Undergraduate Research Opportunity Programme grant that I was awarded from the University of Reading, I was able to hire LLB student Chantelle Bacchus during the summer of 2012 to research "Self-Determination and 'Peoplehood' in International Law." Chantelle's assistance informed my findings on self-determination, and I am grateful to her. I also wish to thank Kevan Morshed for his research assistance at Webster University.

I would also like to acknowledge the Association for the Study of the Middle East and Africa for funding a research visit to Israel and the West Bank in 2015. I am grateful to Reading, Jindal, and Webster for providing research funding during this project.

During the summer of 2012, I was a fellow of the Schusterman Center for Israel Studies Summer Institute for Israel Studies at Brandeis University. I am thankful for what I learned on the fellowship, as well as for the continuing support and encouragement of S. Ilan Troen and others at the Schusterman Center.

Last, but certainly not least, I wish to thank my wife, Rachel. Thank you for bearing with me during the completion of my manuscript. I wish that I had your patience.

Part of this work have been previously published as: Robert P. Barnidge, Jr., *The Evolution of Palestinian Arab Proto-Self-Determination and "Peoplehood" During the Mandate for Palestine* (New York University Jean Monnet Working Paper No. 09/15, 2015); and Robert P. Barnidge, Jr., *The International Law of Negotiation as a Means of Dispute Settlement*, 36(3) Fordham Int'l L.J. 545 (2013).

TABLE OF CONTENTS

TABLE OF CASE LAW AND ARBITRAL AWARDS

TABLE OF LEGISLATION

United Nations General Assembly Resolutions

United Nations Security Council Resolutions

Israel Law

Political ideas make their own realities. Often in defiance of logic, they hold men and are in turn held by them, creating a world in their own image, only to play themselves out in the end, shackled by routine problems not foreseen by those who spun the myth, or living past their prime and ceasing to move people sufficiently. Or, political ideas turn to ashes and leave behind them a trail of errors, suffering and devastation.

Fouad Ajami (1945–2014)
The End of Pan-Arabism, 57(2) FOREIGN AFF. 355, 355 (1978)

1

Introduction

There are at least two potential understandings of "rights." Firstly, there is the moral claim of rights. Rights understood this way point to sets of behavior that are said to be morally desirable. This view typically overlaps with preferred policy outcomes and sees rights claims, rooted in a moral imperative, that aim at politically preferred outcomes. A second way of looking at rights would be to see them as claims that the law recognizes, even if it does so imperfectly in practice. To understand rights juridically is to insist upon a discourse that speaks the language of law, to acknowledge that it is through law that rights are both realized and rebuffed. It is through "rights talk,"[1] in other words, that lawyers lodge their claims, but it is important to point out that the "invisible college of international lawyers"[2] no longer monopolizes this conversation. Whole multitudes of actors have come to realize that they must articulate rights as legal claims, as a complement to their moral claims, if they are to be effective in "bringing rights home."[3]

The word "rights" also has a different meaning. "In all efforts for peace the overriding problem is to relate the sense of individual justice to the common good. The great tragedies of history occur not when right confronts wrong, but when two rights face each other."[4] When United States Secretary of State Henry Kissinger made these remarks at the Peace Conference on the Middle East in late December 1973, his words indicated a sense of competing justice claims. There is in this a discourse of contested narratives.[5] In the context of the Peace Conference on the Middle East, the narratives aligned against one another were Zionism (as the

[1] On this, see MARY ANN GLENDON, RIGHTS TALK: THE IMPOVERISHMENT OF POLITICAL DISCOURSE (1991).

[2] Oscar Schachter, *The Invisible College of International Lawyers*, 72(2) NW. U. L. REV. 217 (1977).

[3] To borrow a slogan of the United Kingdom Labour Party in the run-up to the adoption of the 1998 Human Rights Act. *See* Rights Brought Home: The Human Rights Bill, cmd. 3782 (1997).

[4] Addresses at the Opening Meeting of the Geneva Peace Conference, Dec. 21, 1973, *in* Israel's Foreign Relations: Volumes I–II: 1947–1974, http://mfa.gov.il/MFA/ForeignPolicy/MFADocuments/Yearbook1/Pages/21%20Addresses%20at%20the%20Opening%20Meeting%20of%20the%20Geneva.aspx. *See* AMOS OZ, HOW TO CURE A FANATIC (2010).

[5] For a conscious attempt to put forward the Zionist, Palestinian, and Arab narratives of the Arab–Israeli conflict without attempting to "take sides," *see* ARABS AND ISRAELIS: CONFLICT AND PEACEMAKING IN THE MIDDLE EAST (Abdel Monem Said Aly et al. eds., 2013). One of the purposes of *Arabs and Israelis: Conflict and Peacemaking in the Middle East*, Said Aly, Feldman, and Shikaki write, is to "convey that almost every important development in the history of the conflict was seen differently by each of the important parties and to show *how* differently these events were seen. Each of these parties *interpreted* these developments differently, each *explained* these developments differently and each *told* themselves and their neighbors *a different story* about what had happened." *Id.* at 2.

national liberation movement of the Jewish people) and Arab rights (in a predominantly Arab region of the world). The Palestinians remained, in effect, an afterthought of history, one of the reasons that the Palestine Liberation Organization (PLO) would have nothing to do with the proceedings in Geneva.[6] The Peace Conference on the Middle East did not represent the first attempt to settle a dispute framed largely in inter-State terms, but it was the first major initiative after the United Nations Security Council introduced a negotiation imperative in 1973.[7] It would be some time still, in September 1993, that this paradigm of peacemaking would expand to include a specifically bilateral element between Israel and the PLO.[8] Negotiation, first made imperative in 1973, continues to guide these peacemaking efforts as a matter of law.

This research aims to advance our understanding of the international law of negotiation and use this as a framework for assessing the Israeli–Palestinian dispute, with the Palestinian people's unsuccessful attempt to join the United Nations as a Member State in autumn 2011 and its successful attempt to join the same institution as a non-member observer State in autumn 2012 providing a case study for this. Over the decades, a variety of means have been used to settle the Israeli–Palestinian dispute, and the larger conflict between Israel and the Arab States within which it is embedded,[9] but negotiation has remained the dominant leitmotiv. That Israel and the PLO have channeled the settlement of their dispute through negotiation means that either party's failure to comply with this substantive obligation of law to negotiate can result in an internationally wrongful act and, in response, countermeasures and other responses by the victim party. The legal consequences of the Palestinian applications at the United Nations are not merely of historical interest; they inform the *present* rights and obligations of Israel and the Palestinian people. They must be taken seriously, furthermore, because they form part of a

[6] *See* Palestine Liberation Organization, Political Program, June 9, 1974, *in* ISRAEL IN THE MIDDLE EAST: DOCUMENTS AND READINGS ON SOCIETY, POLITICS, AND FOREIGN RELATIONS, PRE-1948 TO THE PRESENT 344, 345, ¶ 1 (Itamar Rabinovich & Jehuda Reinharz eds., 2d ed. 2008) ("reaffirm[ing] the Palestine Liberation Organization's previous attitude to Resolution 242 [...], which obliterates the national right of our people and deals with the cause of our people as a problem of refugees. The Council therefore refuses to have anything to do with this resolution at any level, Arab or international, including the Geneva Conference").

[7] *See* S.C. Res. 338, at ¶ 3, U.N. Doc. S/RES/338 (Oct. 22, 1973) ("*Decides* that, immediately and concurrently with the cease-fire, negotiations shall start between the parties concerned under appropriate auspices aimed at establishing a just and durable peace in the Middle East").

[8] *See* Israel–PLO Recognition: Exchange of Letters Between PM Rabin and Chairman Arafat (Sept. 9, 1993), http://unispal.un.org/unispal.nsf/9a798adbf322aff38525617b006d88d7/36917473237100e285257028006c0bc5?OpenDocument; Letter Dated 8 October 1993 from the Permanent Representatives of the Russian Federation and the United States of America to the United Nations Addressed to the Secretary-General, Annex at 4, U.N. Doc. A/48/486 (Oct. 11, 1993) (Declaration of Principles on Interim Self-Government Arrangements).

[9] Of the Arab States, only Egypt and Jordan have peace treaties with Israel. *See* Peace Treaty Between Israel and Egypt, Mar. 26, 1979, *in* ISRAEL IN THE MIDDLE EAST, *supra* note 6, at 383; Letter Dated 9 January 1995 from the Permanent Representatives of Israel, Jordan, the Russian Federation, and the United States of America to the United Nations Addressed to the Secretary General, Annex at 3, U.N. Doc. A/50/73 (Jan. 27, 1995) (Treaty of Peace Between the State of Israel and the Hashemite Kingdom of Jordan, Oct. 26, 1994, Arava/Araba).

coordinated effort by the Palestinian people to engage with international institutions in a way that may undermine the bilateral negotiation imperative.[10]

This is a work of five substantive chapters. It roots itself in legal doctrine but recognizes that interdisciplinary insights can bring texture, nuance, and depth to legal analysis. This is not to say that this work's sometimes interdisciplinarity obviates controversy or somehow makes its legal analysis more "objective": the "erudite and fiercely contested polemic on facts and questions concerning geography, ethnography, linguistics and, above all, history"[11] that International Court of Justice (ICJ) Judge de Castro identified in *Western Sahara* seems to be just as inescapable when grappling with the Israeli–Palestinian dispute. Yet, it is hoped that recognizing this complexity will enrich this work in a way that ignoring it could not. Multiple voices and actors have something valuable to contribute to one's understanding of a multi-faceted contest of rights and obligations such as the Israeli–Palestinian dispute. Indeed, there is a sense of modesty in "admit[ting] that one's political opponents are not monsters,"[12] and in acknowledging that their views deserve to be seriously considered rather than cavalierly dismissed.

The dispute between Jews and Arabs in Palestine has a history older than the United Nations itself. "The history of each case is not limited to the successive attempts of its peaceful settlement: it also comprises its *causes* and *epiphenomena*," ICJ Judge Cançado Trindade suggests, "which have likewise to be taken carefully into account."[13] Appreciating the wisdom of Judge Cançado Trindade's insight, Chapter 2 stresses the importance of the law's intersection with developments in Palestine between the First and Second World Wars. These years saw international law shift in focus away from what had been the accepted practice of acquiring territory by war, to one that focused on the Mandate system and its "sacred trust of civilization."[14] While the Mandate system was an important (formal) break from previous post-war dispensations, vestiges of colonialism did remain during the interwar years,[15] and it would be incorrect to see the Mandate system as reflecting

[10] For background to the "Palestine 194" effort at the United Nations, see JONATHAN SCHANZER, STATE OF FAILURE: YASSER ARAFAT, MAHMOUD ABBAS, AND THE UNMAKING OF THE PALESTINIAN STATE (2013). The present author reviewed Schanzer's *State of Failure: Yasser Arafat, Mahmoud Abbas, and the Unmaking of the Palestinian State* at: 5(1) J. MID. E. & AFR. 91 (2014). On Palestinian engagements with some of international law's most politically-sensitive treaties, ranging in subject matter from the law of the sea and the recognition and enforcement of foreign arbitral awards to international human rights law and international humanitarian law, *see* State of Palestine, Palestine Liberation Organization, Negotiations Affairs Department, Statement by PLO Executive Committee Member Dr. Saeb Erekat on Palestine's Accession to International Treaties (Dec. 31, 2014), http://unispal.un.org/UNISPAL.NSF/0/6AC31155 00C569E985257DC100552B95.

[11] Western Sahara, Advisory Opinion, 1975 I.C.J. 12, 139 (Oct. 16) (De Castro, J., separate).

[12] U.S. v. Windsor, No. 12-307, at 25 (2013) (Scalia, J., dissenting).

[13] Accordance with International Law of the Unilateral Declaration of Independence in Respect of Kosovo, Advisory Opinion, 2010 I.C.J. 403, 543 (July 22) (Cançado Trindade, J., separate).

[14] Covenant of the League of Nations Adopted by the Peace Conference at Plenary Session, Apr. 28, 1919, 13(2) AM. J. INT'L L. SUPP. 128, 137, art. 22(1) (1919).

[15] *See* R.P. Anand, *The Formation of International Organizations and India: A Historical Study*, 23(1) LEIDEN J. INT'L L. 5, 14 (2010) (stating that: "The League [of Nations (League)] had not accepted the principle of self-determination outside Europe. The mandate system of the League in India's view was nothing more than 'colonialism' and 'oppression' of the territories taken from Germany and Turkey and given to the imperialist powers, where conditions had further deteriorated").

more than a sense of proto-self-determination for the populations concerned. The idea of a distinct Palestinian Arab national sentiment was also *in statu nascendi* during this time. Chapter 2 examines the evolution of Palestinian Arab proto-self-determination and "peoplehood" during the Palestine Mandate and draws upon evidence that States gave to the United Nations Special Committee on Palestine in 1947 and other key primary documents on the Palestine question up to the 1948 War.

Chapter 3 begins in the wake of the 1948 War and the devastation that it caused to both Jews and Arabs in the region. Tragically, the United Nations Palestine Commission proved prescient in predicting, in a report dated February 16, 1948, that: "Powerful Arab interests, both inside and outside Palestine, are defying the resolution of the [United Nations] General Assembly [i.e., Resolution 181 (1947)] and are engaged in a deliberate effort to alter by force the settlement envisaged therein."[16] The General Assembly's call for "Independent Arab and Jewish States and the Special International Regime for the City of Jerusalem"[17] was not fulfilled. In the years that followed, the international community attempted a variety of means of dispute settlement with Israel and the Arab States, often in combination with one another: a form of inquiry, through the Security Council's Questionnaire of May 18, 1948; mediation, through the United Nations Mediator on Palestine; and conciliation, through the establishment of the United Nations Conciliation Commission for Palestine. Chapter 3 explores these disparate means of dispute settlement and traces their failure largely to the Arab world's rejectionist posture. It ends by showing how Resolution 338, which the United States and the Soviet Union introduced in the Security Council in late October 1973, fundamentally changed the nature of this debate with its call for "negotiations [...] between the parties concerned under appropriate auspices aimed at establishing a just and durable peace in the Middle East."[18] The paradigm had shifted, and negotiation had become the imperative means of dispute settlement.

At the same time that one can observe that international law moved squarely behind a negotiation imperative in 1973, one should also be careful not to overlook the PLO's juridical "absence" from this landscape. "[B]read and circuses"[19] was how one General Assembly delegation described the inter-State dispute settlement efforts in late 1974. Chapter 4 explores how the years after 1973 saw the gradual emergence of a specifically bilateral negotiation imperative between Israel

[16] Letter from the Chairman of the United Nations Palestine Commission to the President of the Security Council Dated 16 February 1948, Annex at 1, 3, U.N. Doc. S/676 (Feb. 16, 1948) (First Special Report to the Security Council: The Problem of Security in Palestine). The Arab Office had cautioned the Anglo-American Committee of Inquiry less than two years earlier "not [to] be influenced by such questions as who can make the most trouble. But if it is a question of degree of violence, the Arabs are prepared to break the record—and not only in Palestine." Public Hearings Before the Anglo-American Committee of Inquiry, Jerusalem (Palestine), Mar. 25, 1946, at 128 (Mr. Shykayri).

[17] G.A. Res. 181, at (I)(A)(3), U.N. Doc. A/RES/181 (Nov. 29, 1947).

[18] S.C. Res. 338, *supra* note 7, at ¶ 3.

[19] U.N. GAOR, at 659, U.N. Doc. A/PV.2267 (Oct. 14, 1974) (Dahomey).

and the PLO and the crystallization of Palestinian international legal personality and (an unfolding sense of) self-determination for the Palestinians. It identifies this shift roughly through three phases: the Arab world's recognition of the PLO as an independent actor rather than a tool that they could "tame," a negotiation effort in Geneva, and the establishment of diplomatic relations between Egypt and Israel in the late 1970s; the PLO's decision to afford Israel some measure of recognition in 1988; and the Oslo dialogue of the early 1990s that led to formal negotiations and an exchange of letters between Israel and the PLO. By September 1993, the Palestinian people's international legal personality had unquestionably crystallized, and a dispute settlement process rooted in bilateral negotiations had become entrenched.

Given that an inter-State negotiation imperative was ushered into law in 1973 and a bilateral negotiation imperative between Israel and the PLO was introduced in September 1993, it becomes critical to understand the international law of negotiation as a means of dispute settlement. Chapter 5 attempts to do this, conscious that "identification of principles and guidelines of relevance to international negotiations could contribute to enhancing the predictability of negotiating parties, reducing uncertainty and promoting an atmosphere of trust at negotiations."[20] International law understands negotiation as a process, but this does not imply that negotiations are devoid of legal regulation.[21] Chapter 5 begins by looking at the relationship between negotiation (as a diplomatic means of dispute settlement) and other means of dispute settlement (of both a diplomatic and legal nature). Secondly, it examines when it can be said as a matter of law that negotiation has been tried and has been exhausted. Chapter 5 sustains one leading commentator's conclusion that the test is, in essence, whether a "genuine attempt in good faith to settle by negotiations has been made and that there is no reasonable probability that continuation or resumption of the process would turn out to be successful."[22] The final section in Chapter 5 considers a victim party's options when its negotiating counterpart has committed an internationally wrongful act by violating a substantive obligation of law to negotiate with it.

Chapter 6 brings to bear the international law of negotiation to recent Palestinian engagements with the United Nations. What were, and are, the legal consequences of the Palestinian people's unsuccessful attempt to join the United Nations as a Member State in autumn 2011 and its successful attempt to join the same institution as a non-member observer State in autumn 2012? Chapter 6 begins by looking at the precise nature of the rights and obligations that adhered to Israel and the PLO between September 1993 and the events of autumn 2011 and autumn 2012. Although the instruments that the two sides agreed to during these

[20] G.A. Res. 53/101, at pmbl., U.N. Doc. A/RES/53/101 (Dec. 8, 1998).

[21] Indeed, the "question whether prior negotiations did take place and whether or not they have failed is an objective one, in both a factual and legal sense." Karel Wellens, Negotiations in the Case Law of the International Court of Justice: A Functional Analysis 181 (2014).

[22] *Id.* at 328.

years were by their nature *lex specialis*, the specificities that emerged from them seem to have largely mirrored the *lex generalis* of negotiation (and its emphasis on such considerations as good faith and meaningful engagement). After examining this complex matrix of law, Chapter 6 scrutinizes the texts associated with the two Palestinian applications and the reaction to them by diverse constellations of States. There appears to have been at least some degree of *prima facie* disconnect between the applications and the PLO's substantive obligation of law to negotiate with Israel, but the wrongfulness of the applications might nevertheless be precluded if one understands them as countermeasures in respect of an internationally wrongful act, actions taken in response to a material breach, or an expression of the legal principle *exceptio non adimpleti contractus* (the exception of non-performance). While the conclusions of Chapter 6 are tentative, it is hoped that they will encourage future scholars and practitioners to more readily engage with the international law of negotiation as a framework of legal evaluation, not only with respect to developments in the Israeli–Palestinian dispute since autumn 2012, but also more broadly for disputes that involve, *inter alia*, ongoing negotiations and competing self-determination claims.

Clarifying the law in this area can enhance the ability of parties to disputes that threaten the peace (or that risk doing so) to de-escalate their rhetoric and settle their differences on a more predictable and sustainable footing. But one should not exaggerate the case. Despite the claims of some international lawyers, international law only goes so far, and it is but one instrument of international relations. "[N]either a chimera nor a panacea," Brierly prefaced the first edition of his seminal *Law of Nations* (1928), international law is "just one institution among others which we have at our disposal for the building up of a saner international order."[23] One would do well neither to exaggerate nor underestimate its efficacy in world affairs.[24]

What must be appreciated, in summary, is that as much as it is desirable to clarify the international law of negotiation, interested parties must not neglect the existence of "divergent realities [between Israel and the Palestinian people]. Each side views the other as having acted in bad faith; as having turned the optimism of Oslo into the suffering and grief of victims and their loved ones."[25] The 2001 Sharm El-Sheikh Fact-Finding Committee Report made this observation in the wake of the outbreak of the second *intifada*, or "uprising," but it just as acutely describes the present moment. The enduring challenge is for international law to facilitate a productive reconciliation of these "divergent realities." This work seeks to equip the reader with some of the tools for doing this.

[23] Andrew Clapham, Brierly's Law of Nations: An Introduction to the Role of International Law in International Relations v (7th ed. 2014).

[24] *See id.* at v–vi.

[25] Report of the Sharm El-Sheikh Fact-Finding Committee, Apr. 30, 2001, http://unispal.un.org/unispal.nsf/9a798adbf322aff38525617b006d88d7/6e61d52eaacb860285256d2800734e9a?OpenDocument.

2

The Evolution of Palestinian Arab Proto-Self-Determination and "Peoplehood" During the Mandate for Palestine

I. Introduction

In an interview that she gave to the *Sunday Times* in 1969, two years after the 1967 War, Israeli Prime Minister Golda Meir was famously quoted as saying:

> There was no such thing as Palestinians ... It was not as though there was a Palestinian people in Palestine considering itself as a Palestinian people and we came and threw them out and took their country away from them. They did not exist."[1]

Prime Minister Meir went on to note that Palestine had in recent memory been either geographically southern Syria or the larger part of a geographical expanse including Transjordan, and that there had never been, as she put it, an "independent Palestinian people with a Palestinian State."[2] Although later years would see Prime Minister Meir seek to clarify her remarks,[3] the sentiments expressed in the original quotation raise two important issues that have hindered rapprochement between Jews and Arabs since the beginning of the Zionist project in Palestine: the question of what it means to be a "people" and the geographical spaces within which "peoples" can legitimately express their national aspirations.[4]

One reading of Prime Minister Meir's words would be that a non-Jewish, and specifically Arab, population did not exist in the physical sense when Jews began making *aliyah* to Palestine in large numbers during the late nineteenth century.

[1] Golda Meir, *Who Can Blame Israel?*, SUN. TIMES, June 15, 1969.

[2] *Id. See* Golda Meir, *Israel in Search of Lasting Peace*, 51(3) FOREIGN AFF. 447, 450 (1973) (noting the absence of a specifically Palestinian Arab nationalism at the time of the Mandate for Palestine).

[3] *See* Golda Meir, *On the Palestinians*, N.Y. TIMES, Jan. 14, 1976 (in which she states, regarding this view: "My actual words were: 'There is no Palestine people. There are Palestinian refugees'").

[4] The phrase "for a people without a land, a land without a people" raises almost identical issues as Prime Minister Meir's remarks. On this phrase and its origin, meaning, and uses and abuses, see Adam M. Garfinkle, *On the Origin, Meaning, Use and Abuse of a Phrase*, 27(4) MID. E. STUD. 539 (1991). On Prime Minister Meir's remarks, see *id.* at 541.

On this view, Zionist pioneers would have essentially been unfettered and free to have realized Herzl's dream of a Jewish State and to have done so, conveniently, on a *tabula rasa.*[5] While at the time many did comment upon the sparsely populated nature of the land,[6] the reality of an Arab population was well known to the *yishuv.* To take but one example, consider that Zionist intellectual Ahad Ha'am's seminal 1891 essay "Truth from Eretz Yisrael" clearly recognized, and made something of a premonition about, the Arab population in the following language: "if the time comes when the life of our people in Eretz Israel develops to the point of encroaching upon the native population [i.e., the Arabs of Palestine], they will not easily yield their place."[7] Increasing friction between Jews and Arabs during the final years of the Ottoman Empire and as the Palestine Mandate unfolded between the First and Second World Wars, particularly with the unrest of the late 1930s, would make it difficult to reasonably deny the physical presence of an Arab population whose numbers were both significant and increasingly hostile to the Zionist project of national redemption in *Eretz Israel*, the land of Israel.

This chapter traces the evolution of Palestinian Arab proto-self-determination and "peoplehood" during the Mandate for Palestine through what Skouteris calls a "positioned engagement with the past."[8] In doing so, it seeks to clarify what are two of the most controversial and emotive concepts in international legal discourse and popular imagination today, "Palestine" and "Palestinian," concepts that were understood quite differently during the time of the Mandate between the First and Second World Wars and until the 1948 War than they are today. This chapter begins by describing the Mandate system and the territorial dispensation

[5] *See* THEODOR HERZL, THE JEWISH STATE (2010).

[6] Mark Twain's account in *The Innocents Abroad* is a classic one. Reflecting on his journey to Palestine, he wrote of part of its expanse: "There is not a solitary village throughout its whole extent—not for thirty miles in either direction. There are two or three small clusters of Bedouin tents, but not a single permanent habitation. One may ride ten miles, hereabouts, and not see ten human beings." MARK TWAIN, THE INNOCENTS ABROAD 362 (2002). *See* Felix Frankfurter, *The Palestine Situation Restated*, 9(3) FOREIGN AFF. 409, 409–11 (1931). *See also* S. Ilan Troen, *Israeli Views of the Land of Israel/Palestine*, 18(2) ISR. STUD. 100, 106–108 (2013). "It is obvious to every passing traveller, and well-known to every European resident, that the country was before the War [i.e., World War I], and is now, undeveloped and under-populated." An Interim Report on the Civil Administration of Palestine, During the Period 1st July 1920–30th June 1921, *in* PALESTINE AND TRANSJORDAN ADMINISTRATION REPORTS: 1918–1948: VOLUME I: 1918–1924 169, 172 (R. Jarman ed., 1995).

[7] Alan Dowty, *Much Ado About Little: Ahad Ha'am's "Truth from Eretz Yisrael," Zionism, and the Arabs*, 5(2) ISR. STUD. 154, 162 (2000). *See* Alan Dowty, *"A Question That Outweighs All Others": Yitzhak Epstein and Zionist Recognition of the Arab Issue*, 6(1) ISR. STUD. 34 (2001). *See also* JACOB LASSNER & S. ILAN TROEN, JEWS AND MUSLIMS IN THE ARAB WORLD: HAUNTED BY PASTS REAL AND IMAGINED 325–26 (2007); Israel Kolatt, *The Zionist Movement and the Arabs, in* ESSENTIAL PAPERS ON ZIONISM 617 (Jehuda Reinharz & Anita Shapira eds., 1996). Jabotinsky was also under no illusions as to the physical presence of an Arab population in Palestine. Writing in 1923, he noted that the Arabs of Palestine were "not a rabble, but a living people. And when a living people yields in matters of such a vital character it is only when there is no longer any hope of getting rid of us, because they can make no breach in the iron wall." Zeev Jabotinsky, *The Ethics of the Iron Wall*, Jabotinsky Institute, Tel Aviv at 7, No. A1-7/14 (Nov. 4–Dec. 31, 1923).

[8] Thomas Skouteris, *Engaging History in International Law, in* NEW APPROACHES TO INTERNATIONAL LAW 99, 101 (J.M. Beneyto & D. Kennedy eds., 2012).

for Palestine that was secured within it. Taking the view that the Mandate system sought to secure some permutation of what one might understand as a type of proto-self-determination, it then assesses the extent to which one can reasonably conclude that a specifically Palestinian Arab "people" existed at the time in a juridical sense. This chapter's final substantive section draws upon evidence that States gave to the United Nations Special Committee on Palestine (UNSCOP) in 1947 and the United Nations' work on the question of Palestine up to the 1948 War. This chapter shows that rediscovering the evolution of Palestinian Arab proto-self-determination and "peoplehood" during the Palestine Mandate reveals the malleability of these concepts, something that remains the case, at least to a certain extent, today.

II. The Mandate System

The First World War was a war of empires, of great powers aligned against one another. Some of these empires would survive the war largely intact; others would not. The administrative core of the Ottoman Empire in Anatolia, for example, would remain together, but its outer territories would be placed on a track to eventual independence that would complete a process of secession and cession that had been taking place in the Ottoman Empire for decades.[9] As Attorney-General of the Palestine Government Norman Bentwich put it in 1929, "conditions in those areas [detached from what was to become the Turkish Republic] precluded immediate independence; principle precluded annexation; experience precluded internationalization."[10] It was the Mandate system that would channel the dispensation of these territories.[11]

Article 22 of the 1919 Covenant of the League of Nations (Covenant) set up the Mandate system and acted as the "supreme constitutional authority under which the mandates function[ed]."[12] Although it represented a striking break from the

[9] *See, e.g.*, Treaty of Peace with Turkey, Lausanne, July 24, 1923, art. 16. On this process, see Patrick Dumberry, *Is Turkey the "Continuing" State of the Ottoman Empire Under International Law?*, 59(2) NETH. INT'L L. REV. 235, 238–42 (2012). *See also* Peter Sluglett, *An Improvement on Colonialism? The "A" Mandates and Their Legacy in the Middle East*, 90(2) INT'L AFF. 413 (2014). United States President Woodrow Wilson's "Fourteen Points" envisaged that the Turkish core of the Ottoman Empire would retain its sovereignty but that the "other nationalities which are now under Turkish rule should be assured an undoubted security of life and an absolutely unmolested opportunity of autonomous development." Woodrow Wilson, Fourteen Points, Jan. 8, 1918.

[10] Norman Bentwich, *The Mandate for Palestine*, 10 BRIT. Y.B. INT'L L. 137, 143 (1929).

[11] On the particulars of the A Mandates for Mesopotamia, Syria, and Palestine, with discussion of Lebanon and Transjordan, see JOHN QUIGLEY, THE STATEHOOD OF PALESTINE: INTERNATIONAL LAW IN THE MIDDLE EAST CONFLICT 42–51 (2010). On Mandates and Trust Territories and Trusteeships, see JAMES CRAWFORD, THE CREATION OF STATES IN INTERNATIONAL LAW 565–601 (2d ed. 2007).

[12] Benjamin Akzin, *The Palestine Mandate in Practice*, 25(1) IOWA L. REV. 32, 48 (1939). On the San Remo Conference that would essentially operationalize article 22 in the Middle East, see GEORGE ANTONIUS, THE ARAB AWAKENING: THE STORY OF THE ARAB NATIONAL MOVEMENT 302–306 (1938).

law that had for centuries permitted victor States to annex conquered territories,[13] it is important to recognize that article 22 also reflected a number of Eurocentric and racialist assumptions. At the time, it will be recalled, large parts of Africa and Asia were colonies of the West, from (much of) Cape to Cairo and from the Atlas Mountains in the west through much of south and southeast Asia and onward to Oceania in the east. It should come as no surprise, then, that the States Parties to the Covenant were largely Western and that the treaty that established the League of Nations would have reflected certain of their prerogatives and interests.

The Covenant does not expressly state that the Mandate territories of the old German and Ottoman Empires were not sovereign, but this is article 22's clear implication. The territories are described as having "ceased to be under the sovereignty of the States which formerly governed them,"[14] and at no point can it be said that these territories had somehow (re)captured their sovereignty. Article 22, furthermore, describes these territories as being "inhabited by peoples not yet able to stand by themselves under the strenuous conditions of the modern world."[15] The position, then, is that the peoples in the Mandate territories were not modern, were perhaps pre-modern; certainly, they were not (yet) fit for modernity. As Anghie has put it, the view was that "the native's deficiency must in some way be remedied."[16]

The use of the passive voice in article 22(1), territories "which are inhabited by," suggests that the peoples in the Mandate territories were peoples who were acted upon from forces external to them, and indeed, from a juridical point of view, they were. This is confirmed by the subsequent use of the active voice in article 22(1): "there should be applied the principle that the well-being and development of such peoples form a sacred trust of civilization."[17] In other words, the Mandatories were to be the subjects, the peoples of the Mandate territories the objects. Bentwich, writing at the time in the *British Yearbook of International Law*, described the Mandates as "infant nations, and a new relation is set up in international law, like that in private law of tutor to ward."[18] Although clearly paternalistic, Bentwich's

[13] *See* International Status of South-West Africa, Advisory Opinion, 1950 I.C.J. 128, 131 (July 11) (noting that the two principles that were of "paramount importance" to the Mandate system were "the principle of non-annexation and the principle that the well-being and development of such peoples form 'a sacred trust of civilization'").

[14] Covenant of the League of Nations Adopted by the Peace Conference at Plenary Session, Apr. 28, 1919, 13(2) AM. J. INT'L L. SUPP. 128, 137, art. 22(1) (1919).

[15] *Id.*

[16] ANTHONY ANGHIE, IMPERIALISM, SOVEREIGNTY AND THE MAKING OF INTERNATIONAL LAW 156 (2007). *See also* R.P. ANAND, CONFRONTATION OR COOPERATION? INTERNATIONAL LAW AND THE DEVELOPING COUNTRIES 31–32 (2d rev. ed. 2011) (making a similar point).

[17] Covenant, *supra* note 14, at 137, art. 22(1).

[18] Norman Bentwich, *Mandated Territories: Palestine and Mesopotamia (Iraq)*, 2 BRIT. Y.B. INT'L L. 48, 48 (1921) (continuing two sentences later by stating that: "The League delegates the care of the minor to a Power who is termed the Mandatory; and lays down the terms of his charge in a Mandate; and the Mandatory is then responsible to the League as to a Court for the carrying out of the trust"). *Cf.* Akzin, *supra* note 12, at 33 (describing the Mandate system in similar terms).

language accurately reflected the Western view at the time of the Mandate system in general and article 22 of the Covenant in particular.[19]

Article 22(2) of the Covenant reflects Bentwich's tutor/ward characterization of the Mandate system in that it describes it as "tutelage,"[20] of "advanced nations who by reason of their resources, their experience, or their geographical position can best undertake this responsibility, and who are willing to accept it."[21] It was the advanced that were charged with taking care of the interests of the not (yet) advanced. Each Mandate was to be tailored to, *inter alia*, the "stage of the development of the people,"[22] and from this one can conclude that the peoples under Mandate were not (yet) wholly developed either. Rather, they were at various stages of development.[23]

Article 22(1)–(3) reflects the general framework of the Mandate system, but the Covenant placed those peoples of the Ottoman Empire who were not in what was to become the Turkish Republic in a special category. According to article 22(4), these peoples were at such a stage of development that their independence could be "provisionally recognized."[24] Although there is no sense in this that these peoples could at the time that the Covenant was adopted claim an entitlement to sovereign State status as such, it was hoped that this would be achieved in time. This was less the case, or at least not as obviously the case, for B and C Mandates.[25] The peoples of A Mandates were still in need of the advice and assistance of a Mandatory, however, "until such time as they are able to stand alone."[26] In the understanding of the Covenant, to "stand alone" meant, presumably, to be sovereign, and article 22(4)'s express language can lead to no other conclusion than that these peoples were not, in the view of the drafters, (yet) able to do so.[27] Certainly, in no sense could it be said that the peoples of what would become known as the A Mandates were sovereign in the Huberian sense, which was the abiding sense at the time, of

[19] *See* ANGHIE, *supra* note 16, at 144–46.

[20] Covenant, *supra* note 14, at 137, art. 22(2).

[21] *Id.*

[22] *Id.* at 137, art. 22(3).

[23] The precise difference between "advanced" (in art. 22(2)) and "develop[ed]" (in art. 22(3)) is unclear.

[24] *Id.* at 137, art. 22(4).

[25] *See* QUINCY WRIGHT, MANDATES UNDER THE LEAGUE OF NATIONS 530 (1930) (also noting that it was envisaged that B and C Mandates would move toward independence at a slower pace than A Mandates).

[26] Covenant, *supra* note 14, at 137, art. 22(4).

[27] *See* Quincy Wright, *Sovereignty of the Mandates*, 17(4) AM. J. INT'L L. 691 (1923). *See also* International Status, *supra* note 13, at 150 (McNair, J., separate) (famously describing sovereignty as being "in abeyance" in the Mandate system). On the Mandate system and the sovereignty question, with particular focus on South West Africa/Namibia, *see* JOHN DUGARD, THE SOUTH WEST AFRICA/NAMIBIA DISPUTE: DOCUMENTS AND SCHOLARLY WRITINGS ON THE CONTROVERSY BETWEEN SOUTH AFRICA AND THE UNITED NATIONS 75–82 (1973). *See also* RALPH WILDE, INTERNATIONAL TERRITORIAL ADMINISTRATION: HOW TRUSTEESHIP AND THE CIVILIZING MISSION NEVER WENT AWAY 161–67 (2008).

having "[i]ndependence in regard to a portion of the globe[, …] the right to exercise therein, to the exclusion of any other State, the functions of a State."[28]

Apart from the system of A Mandates in article 22(4), there were also B and C Mandates. As with A Mandates, special regimes applied to these Mandates that built upon the general framework for the Mandate system in article 22(1)–(3). The territories of B Mandates were to be administered with a general view to securing freedom of religion and conscience, prohibiting the slave trade and the trafficking of arms and intoxicating liquor, ensuring trading opportunities for all Members of the League of Nations on a non-discriminatory basis, and ensuring that the peoples of the B Mandates were kept in a militarily disadvantaged position vis-à-vis the Mandatory.[29] In many respects, the special regime for C Mandates in article 22(5) resembled annexation in that these territories could "be best administered under the laws of the Mandatory as integral portions of its territory,"[30] though this was "subject to the safeguards above mentioned in the interests of the indigenous population."[31] C Mandates could be distinguished from A and B Mandates on account of their small size and population, geographical contiguity to the Mandatory's territory, and "remoteness from the centers of civilization."[32] In summary, article 22 of the Covenant set forth the general framework of the Mandate system and distinguished between A, B, and C Mandates.[33]

In *Legal Consequences for States of the Continued Presence of South Africa in Namibia (South West Africa) Notwithstanding Security Council Resolution 276 (1970) (Namibia)*, the International Court of Justice (ICJ) had an opportunity to interpret article 22 of the Covenant and concluded that the "ultimate objective of the sacred trust was the self-determination and independence of the peoples concerned."[34] The ICJ delivered its advisory opinion in 1971, barely two

[28] Island of Palmas (Neth. v. U.S.) (1928), 2 R. Int'l Arb. Awards 829, 838 (1949). *See* Customs Regime Between Germany and Austria, Advisory Opinion, 1931 P.C.I.J. (ser. A/B) No. 41, at 46 (Sept. 5) (describing sovereignty in opposition to "any voluntary act […] which would cause it [i.e., a State] to lose its independence or which would modify its independence in that its sovereign will would be subordinated to the will of another Power or particular group of Powers, or would even be replaced by such will"). *But see* Quigley, *supra* note 11, at 24–27 (arguing that Class A Mandates were indeed States). Anghie views the focus on formal (political) sovereignty within the context of the Mandate system as a distraction from the reification of colonialism in the guise of neo-colonialism. *See* Anghie, *supra* note 16, at 115–95. On neocolonialism and international law, see Robert P. Barnidge, Jr, *Neocolonialism and International Law, With Specific Reference to Customary Counterterrorism Obligations and the Principle of Self-Defence*, 49(1) Indian J. Int'l L. 21 (2009).

[29] *See* Covenant, *supra* note 14, at 137, art. 22(5).

[30] *Id.* at 138, art. 22(6).

[31] *Id.* at 138, art. 22(6). Although C Mandates resembled annexation in many respects, the Mandate system precluded annexation. *See* International Status, *supra* note 13, at 131.

[32] Covenant, *supra* note 14, at 137, art. 22(6). All of the Mandates were subject to certain reporting and oversight requirements. *See id.* at 138, art. 22(7)–(9).

[33] *See generally* Norman Bentwich, The Mandates System 1–20 (1930). For an overview of British State practice as Mandatory, with particular focus on Palestine, see Wright, *supra* note 25, at 405–21.

[34] Legal Consequences for States of the Continued Presence of South Africa in Namibia (South West Africa) Notwithstanding Security Council Resolution 276 (1970), Advisory Opinion, 1971 I.C.J. 16, 31 (June 21). *See* Sovereignty over Pedra Branca/Pulau Batu Puteh, Middle Rocks and South Ledge (Malay./Sing.), 2008 I.C.J. 12, 128–29 (May 23) (Bennouna, J., declaration).

years after the adoption of the Vienna Convention on the Law of Treaties (VCLT) and almost ten years prior to its entry into force. Since the terms of the VCLT precluded the ICJ from retroactively applying it to article 22,[35] the ICJ focused its interpretation on article 22's "object and purpose."[36] Its application of this means of interpretation, however, was confused. On the one hand, the ICJ professed a "[m]indful[ness …] of the primary necessity of interpreting an instrument in accordance with the intentions of the parties at the time of its conclusion";[37] on the other hand, it read a half century of legal developments into article 22, a provision that the ICJ stated was not static but, rather, evolutionary in nature, and asserted that the States Parties to the Covenant had intended this, though without delving into the Covenant's *travaux préparatoires* to explain exactly how or why this was so.[38]

Although the ICJ's conclusion that one of article 22's "ultimate objective[s]" was self-determination can be defended as applied to the contemporary context of 1971, this conclusion should not be seen as somehow reflecting how article 22 was understood at the time that the Covenant was adopted in 1919, or for some not insignificant time thereafter. To begin with, and at the most basic level, nowhere in article 22 does the language "self-determination" appear. Quite simply, this is because the concept that features so markedly in the Charter of the United Nations (Charter), and that adheres to "peoples"[39] had not juridically crystallized by the time that the Covenant was adopted, a point that Vice President Ammoun made in his separate opinion appended to *Namibia*.[40] The principle of self-determination

[35] *See* Vienna Convention on the Law of Treaties (VCLT), Vienna, May 23, 1969, art. 4.

[36] *See, e.g.*, Namibia, *supra* note 34, at 30. The ICJ presumably did this because such an approach to treaty interpretation reflected customary international law at the time. *Cf.* VCLT, *supra* note 35, at art. 31(1) (stating that: "A treaty shall be interpreted in good faith in accordance with the ordinary meaning to be given to the terms of the treaty in their context and in the light of its object and purpose.")

[37] Namibia, *supra* note 34, at 31.

[38] *See id.* at 31–32. The ICJ could be criticized on this count for having succumbed to what it had referred to in an earlier case as the temptation of the "process of after-knowledge." South West Africa (Eth. v. S. Afr.; Liber. v. S. Afr.) (Second Phase), 1966 I.C.J. 6, 47 (July 18). It is worth noting, however, that: "Subsequent agreements and subsequent practice under articles 31 and 32 may assist in determining whether or not the presumed intention of the parties upon the conclusion of the treaty was to give a term used a meaning which is capable of evolving over time." Text of the Draft Conclusions and Commentaries Thereto Provisionally Adopted by the Commission at Its Sixty-Fifth Session, *in* Report of the International Law Commission, 65th Sess., May 6–June 7, July 8–Aug. 9, 2013, at 12, 24, draft concl. 3, U.N. Doc. A/68/10; GAOR, 68th Sess., Supp. No. 10 (2013).

[39] *See* U.N. Charter arts 1(2), 55.

[40] *See* Namibia, *supra* note 34, at 69 (Ammoun, V. Pres., separate). Indeed, as Weitz relates, the powerful States at the Paris Peace Conference "drew back from the term [self-determination], fearful of the popular demands that Wilson and Lenin had unleashed and the political fragmentation that might ensue if every self-proclaimed people, or at least the parties and movements that professed to embody them, actually achieved its own state." Eric D. Weitz, *Self-Determination: How a German Enlightenment Idea Became the Slogan of National Liberation and a Human Right*, 120(2) Am. Hist. Rev. 462, 486 (2015).

was, to be sure, *in statu nascendi* at the time and did feature in the argumentative strategies of aggrieved groups,[41] but it did not (yet) exist as *lex lata*.[42] Furthermore, article 22 does not have the terminological precision that one would expect in the articulation of such a consequential legal norm: "communit[y]," "nation[]," "people," and "population" are used with abandon, certainly with very little care for or sensitivity to the nuances in and differences between such concepts.

More broadly, it is doubtful that the principle of self-determination existed in general international law at the time that the Covenant was adopted. An International Commission of Jurists that the Council of the League of Nations established with Finnish and Swedish consent in the Aaland Islands Question was quite clear on the matter in its report of September 5, 1920 (First Aaland Islands Report):

> Positive International Law does not recognise the right of national groups, as such, to separate themselves from the State of which they form part by the simple expression of a wish, any more than it recognises the right of other States to claim such a separation.[43]

[41] *See, e.g.*, Lala Lajpat Rai, *Self-Determination for India, in* 7 The Collected Works of Lala Lajpat Rai 239 (B.R. Nanda ed., 2005); Marcus Garvey, *Declaration of the Rights of the Negro Peoples of the World, in* Selected Writings and Speeches of Marcus Garvey 16 (Bob Blaisdell ed., 2004). On the "pre-history" of self-determination, see Arnulf Becker Lorca, *Petitioning the International: A "Pre-History" of Self-Determination*, 25(2) Eur. J. Int'l L. 497 (2014). *See also* Weitz, *supra* note 40.

[42] Cassese refers to it as then being a "political postulate." *See* Antonio Cassese, Self-Determination of Peoples: A Legal Reappraisal 11–33 (2008). *See also* David Raič, Statehood and the Law of Self-Determination 197 (2002) (describing the principle of self-determination during the interwar years as being in the nature of a "gift or a favour. At the very most it was a political principle"); B.C. Nirmal, The Right to Self-Determination in International Law 46 (1999) (contending that, "[d]espite initial invocations, self-determination had very little legal significance during [the] inter-war period[]"); The Right of Self-Determination of the Palestinian People, at 3, U.N. Doc. ST/SG/SER.F/3 (1979) (stating that the principle of self-determination was part of a "new morality emerging in international relations" during the interwar years and that, "[i]n juridical terms, [...] the concept of the right of self-determination advanced little in the period between the wars"). Whelan argues that the principle of self-determination did not "reach[] full maturity, and the new power legal validity at the expense of the old, before the Second World War. But it is suggested that the peace settlement after the first great global war was largely responsible for this development, which formed part of a general (if limited) revolution in international relations in this century." Anthony Whelan, *Wilsonian Self-Determination and the Versailles Settlement*, 43(1) Int'l & Comp. L.Q. 99, 108 (1994). "[S]elf-determination as a general principle did not form part of the Covenant of the League of Nations and therefore was, for the duration of the League of Nations, a political rather than a legal concept." Daniel Thürer & Thomas Burri, *Self-Determination, in* Max Planck Encyclopedia of Public International Law ¶ 4 (last updated Dec. 2008). *See* Single German Nationality (Teso) Case (Case No. 2 BvR 373/83), 91 I.L.R. 211, 230 (1987) (1993) (stating that the principle of self-determination crystallized in law after the Second World War).

[43] Report of the International Committee of Jurists Entrusted by the Council of the League of Nations with the Task of Giving an Advisory Opinion upon the Legal Aspects of the Aaland Islands Question, L.N.O.J. 3, 5 (Special Supp. No. 3 1920). *Cf.* Charles Homer Haskins & Robert Howard Lord, Some Problems of the Peace Conference 10–21 (1920) (putting forth some of the considerations that went into self-determination at this time). A subsequent report on the Aaland Islands Question stated that the principle of self-determination was "not, [*sic*] properly speaking a rule of international law [...] It is a principle of justice and of liberty, expressed by a vague and general formula which has given rise to the most varied interpretations and differences of opinion." Report Presented to the Council of the League of Nations by the Commission of Rapporteurs, L.N. Doc. B7 21/68/106 (1921).

To recognize international legal regulation in this context, the report went on, would amount to an unlawful interference in each State's domestic jurisdiction and risk destabilizing the international system.[44] The First Aaland Islands Report denied as a general proposition that international law regulated the "rights of peoples to determine their political fate,"[45] but it made clear that this was only the case in *de jure* situations, or "under normal conditions,"[46] and that in *de facto* situations, that is, in situations in which it could not be said that the State at issue was "definitively constituted as a sovereign State and an independent member of the international community, and [...] continue[d] to possess these characteristics,"[47] account would have to be taken of the principle of self-determination in conjunction with the protection of minorities.[48]

This view was in line with the prevalent concern of international law at the time to accept, begrudgingly, accommodations for minority populations but not to acknowledge self-determination rights for peoples as such. While the examples of *de facto* situations that the First Aaland Islands Report gave, in particular those in which revolutions and war affect the functioning and constitution of a State,[49] might be said to describe a considerable number of States depending upon how one interprets these criteria, what is clear is that the First Aaland Islands Report reflects a general reluctance to view the principle of self-determination as anything but exceptional. Qureshi makes the point, in fact, that self-determination at the time was "not meant to challenge the predominant state centred legal order that had achieved universal status through the mystical violent foundations of [...] international law but rather was permissible only as long as it remained commensurate to it."[50]

Still, it would be correct to see article 22 of the Covenant as reflective of a type of proto-self-determination in that it foresaw what would later crystallize as *lex lata*, represented an important example of State practice, and would be frequently

[44] *See* First Aaland Islands Report, *supra* note 43, at 5. The subsequent League of Nations Commission of Rapporteurs on the Aaland Islands Question was even more blunt: "To concede to minorities, either of language or religion, or to any fractions of a population the right of withdrawing from the community to which they belong, because it is their wish or their good pleasure, would be to destroy order and stability within States and to inaugurate anarchy in international life; it would be to uphold a theory incompatible with the very idea of the State as a territorial and political unity." Second Aaland Islands Report, *supra* note 43.

[45] First Aaland Islands Report, *supra* note 43, at 6.

[46] *Id.* at 5.

[47] *Id.* at 5–6.

[48] *See id.* at 6.

[49] *See id.*

[50] Zainab Qureshi, *Self Determination, International Law & the Indigenous*, 1(3–4) PAK. J. INT'L L. 121, 123 (2011) (continuing by contending that: "The 'state' was thus the predominant and often the only repository of legal rights under international law; entities or populations including indigenous within the nation-state did not possess any claim that could in any way challenge national sovereignty"). On the Aaland Islands Question and self-determination, see CASSESE, *supra* note 42, at 27–31; CRAWFORD, *supra* note 11, at 108–12; RAIČ, *supra* note 42, at 198–99; M.K. Nawaz, *The Meaning and Range of the Principle of Self-Determination*, 14(1) DUKE L.J. 82, 86–88 (1965); Philip Marshall Brown, *The Aaland Islands Question*, 15(2) AM J. INT'L L. 268 (1921).

referred to in later years as one of the building blocks of self-determination as a legal norm.[51] Even as reflective of a type of proto-self-determination, however, the Mandate system in no way foresaw anything more than political self-government for the concerned populations, or, as Wright would describe it, self-determination as a "doctrine closely associated with the democratic thesis that government can only be justified by the consent of the governed."[52] More sweeping understandings of self-determination would develop in international legal discourse in the decades following the Second World War—Lenin had already begun to articulate an even more radical understanding of self-determination as the Bolsheviks took power in Russia[53]—with many of these discussions taking place in the United Nations General Assembly and among the socialist bloc and newly-independent States of the developing world.[54]

[51] *Cf.* Martti Koskenniemi, *National Self-Determination Today: Problems of Legal Theory and Practice,* 43(2) INT'L & COMP. L.Q. 241, 241 n.1 (1994) (referring to self-determination's "minimal version" in the Mandate system).

[52] Quincy Wright, *Recognition and Self-Determination*, 48 AM. SOC'Y INT'L L. PROC. 23, 27 (1954). *Cf.* ROBERT LANSING, THE PEACE NEGOTIATIONS: A PERSONAL NARRATIVE 96 (1921).

[53] *See, e.g.,* V.I. Lenin, *Socialism and War, in* LENIN ON WAR AND PEACE: THREE ARTICLES 1, 26–27 (1966). On Lenin and self-determination, see CASSESE, *supra* note 42, at 14–19. As Lenin saw it: "Complete equality of rights for all nations; the right of nations to self-determination; the unity of the workers of all nations—such is the national programme that Marxism, the experience of the whole world, and the experience of Russia, teach the workers." V.I. Lenin, *The Right of Nations to Self-Determination, in* THE LENIN ANTHOLOGY 153, 180 (Robert C. Tucker ed., 1975). *See also* G.I. TUNKIN, THEORY OF INTERNATIONAL LAW 7–14 (William E. Butler ed. & trans., 2003); G.I. TUNKIN, LAW AND FORCE IN THE INTERNATIONAL SYSTEM 220–25 (1985); G.I. Tunkin, *Coexistence and International Law, in* 95 COLLECTED COURSES OF THE HAGUE ACADEMY OF INTERNATIONAL LAW 1, 67 (1958).

[54] *See* KATHLEEN GALLAGHER CUNNINGHAM, INSIDE THE POLITICS OF SELF-DETERMINATION 11–12 (2014); KATJA L.H. SAMUEL, THE OIC, THE UN, AND COUNTER-TERRORISM LAW-MAKING: CONFLICTING OR COOPERATIVE LEGAL ORDERS? 338–45 (2013); Robert McCorquodale & Kristin Hausler, *Caucuses in the Caucasus: The Application of the Right of Self-Determination, in* CONFLICT IN THE CAUCASUS: IMPLICATIONS FOR INTERNATIONAL LEGAL ORDER 26, 27–34 (James A. Green & Christopher P.M. Waters eds., 2010); Reliance Natural Resources Ltd. v. Reliance Industries Ltd., 2010 7 S.C.C. 1, 102 (India); W. Ofuatey-Kodjoe, *Self-Determination, in* 1 UNITED NATIONS LEGAL ORDER 349 (Oscar Schachter & Christopher C. Joyner eds., 1995); S. Chowdhury, *The Status and Norms of Self-Determination in Contemporary International Law, in* THIRD WORLD ATTITUDES TOWARD INTERNATIONAL LAW: AN INTRODUCTION 87 (Frederick E. Snyder & Surakiart Sathirathai eds., 1987); AURELIU CRISTESCU, THE RIGHT TO SELF-DETERMINATION: HISTORICAL AND CURRENT DEVELOPMENT ON THE BASIS OF UNITED NATIONS INSTRUMENTS, U.N. Doc. E/CN.4/Sub.2/404/Rev.1 (1981); U.O. UMOZURIKE, INTERNATIONAL LAW AND COLONIALISM IN AFRICA 131–33 (1979); TUNKIN, LAW AND FORCE, *supra* note 53, at 103–106; R.P. Dhokalia, *International Recognition of the Human Right of Collective Self-Determination,* 11(1–2) BAN. L.J. 20 (1975); Manfred Lachs, *The Law in and of the United Nations (Some Reflections on the Principle of Self-Determination),* 1 INDIAN. J. INT'L L. 429 (1960); Milena Srnská, *On the Principle of Equal Rights and Self-Determination of Nations, in* THE LEGAL PRINCIPLES GOVERNING FRIENDLY RELATIONS AND CO-OPERATION AMONG STATES IN THE SPIRIT OF THE UNITED NATIONS CHARTER 115 (1966); R.L. Bobrov, *Basic Principles of Present-Day International Law, in* CONTEMPORARY INTERNATIONAL LAW 36, 51–55 (Grigory Tunkin ed., G. Ivanov-Mumjiev trans., 1969); Satpal Kaur, *Self-Determination in International Law,* 10 INDIAN J. INT'L L. 479 (1970); Rosalyn Higgins, *International Law and the Avoidance, Containment and Resolution of Disputes: General Course on Public International Law, in* 230 COLLECTED COURSES OF THE HAGUE ACADEMY OF INTERNATIONAL LAW 9, 154–74 (1991); Abdulqawi A. Yusuf, *The Role that Equal Rights and Self-Determination of Peoples Can Play in the Current World Community, in* REALIZING UTOPIA: THE FUTURE OF INTERNATIONAL LAW 375 (Antonio Cassese ed., 2012); IJAZ HUSSAIN, KASHMIR DISPUTE: AN INTERNATIONAL LAW PERSPECTIVE 141–52 (2d ed. 2004). For a critical third world perspective on internal self-determination, see Kalana Senaratne, *Internal Self-Determination in International Law: A Critical Third-World Perspective,* 3(2) ASIAN J. INT'L L. 305 (2013).

III. The Mandate for Palestine

The Council of the League of Nations adopted the Palestine Mandate, an A Mandate, on July 24, 1922, and "Palestine" thus came for the first time since the early Middle Ages to denote a distinct territory.[55] In doing so, the League Council effectively operationalized the Balfour Declaration in international law. The Balfour Declaration, which British Secretary of State for Foreign Affairs Lord Arthur Balfour conveyed to Zionist leader Lord Rothschild in 1917, stated that "His Majesty's Government view[ed] with favour the establishment in Palestine of a national home for the Jewish people, and will use their best endeavours to facilitate the achievement of this object,"[56] with the caveat that it was to be "clearly understood that nothing shall be done which may prejudice the civil and religious rights of existing non-Jewish communities in Palestine, or the rights and political status enjoyed by Jews in any other country."[57] With the adoption of the Palestine Mandate, the League of Nations tasked the Mandatory, in this case, the United Kingdom, with putting the Balfour Declaration into effect. This included positive obligations for the United Kingdom to create the political, administrative, and economic conditions that were best suited to establishing the Jewish national home in Palestine,[58] with the Jewish Agency to be a proto-State body that would assist it in this task.[59] Although, in practice, the United Kingdom took a number of steps that undermined the Palestine Mandate's primary concern to establish the Jewish national home in Palestine,[60] there can be no doubt that the Palestine Mandate sought a "dynamic regime aiming at large-scale colonization by a distinct national group, thus changing the ethnical character of the country."[61]

Read as a whole, it can be argued that the Mandate's concern to establish the Jewish national home in Palestine was its primary focus and that the Mandate's other obligations had to complement this. In other words, they had to be read so as to conform with the establishment of the Jewish national home. One example of this would be article 6, which required the "facilitat[ion of] Jewish immigration under suitable conditions and [... the] encourage[ment], in co-operation

[55] *See* Bernard Lewis, *Palestine: On the History and Geography of a Name,* 2(1) INT'L HIST. REV. 1, 7 (1980). On the geography of Palestine from antiquity to the present, see LASSNER & TROEN, *supra* note 7, at 43–63. *See also* Moshe Sharon, *Palestine in the Islamic and Ottoman Period, in* THE PALESTINIANS: PEOPLE, HISTORY, POLITICS 9 (Michael Curtis et al. eds., 1975). Technically, the Palestine Mandate entered into force on September 29, 1923. *See* British Mandate for Palestine, Minutes of Meeting of Council Held at Geneva on September 29th, 1923, Oct. 13, 1923, http://unispal.un.org/unispal.nsf/9a798adbf322aff38525617b006d88d7/554d2d5ebe5313d6052565f50053999b?OpenDocument.

[56] Balfour Declaration, Foreign Office, Nov. 2, 1917.

[57] *Id.*

[58] *See* British Mandate for Palestine, 17(3) AM. J. INT'L L. SUPP. 164, 165, art. 2 (1922) (1923).

[59] *See id.* at 165, art. 4. *See also* Mavrommatis Palestine Concessions, 1924 P.C.I.J. (ser. A) No. 2, at 21 (Aug. 30).

[60] *See* Akzin, *supra* note 12.

[61] *Id.* at 35.

with the Jewish agency referred to in Article 4, [of] close settlement by Jews on the land, including State lands and waste lands not required for public purposes," though this had to be done "while ensuring that the rights and position of other sections of the population are not prejudiced." Another would be article 2 and the United Kingdom's obligation to also "safeguard[] the civil and religious rights of all inhabitants of Palestine, irrespective of race and religion." Where, without undue difficulty, it was possible to read these secondary obligations in conformity with the primary Jewish national home focus of the Mandate, the Mandatory could easily comply with both obligations. In situations in which this would be difficult, then the United Kingdom, while continuing to be obliged to comply with both obligations as a formal matter, would have to interpret these obligations in a way that recognized the prevailing emphasis that the terms of the Mandate gave to realizing the Jewish national home, which, again, was the Mandate's primary focus.

Crucially, the Palestine Mandate's preamble recognized the Jewish people's "historical connection" with the land of Palestine and accepted the Zionist case for reestablishing the "[Jewish] national home in that country." In recognizing Zionism's "grounds for reconstituting their [i.e., the Jewish people's] national home in that country [i.e., Palestine],"[62] the Council of the League of Nations effectively endorsed the Zionist project in Palestine and reaffirmed the ancient Jewish connection to the land. Although the Council's reaffirmation of the Balfour Declaration and call to facilitate the "close settlement by Jews on the land, including state lands and waste lands not required for public purposes,"[63] were by far the most significant aspects of the Palestine Mandate, the Palestine Mandate also dealt with such matters as citizenship, antiquities, and rights of access to Holy Places.[64] It was an endorsement, in other words, of the merits and legitimacy of Zionism.

Understandably, Zionists celebrated the terms of the Palestine Mandate; by contrast, Arabs opposed it. The Mandate's reach remained largely in flux, however, on account of article 25.[65] Through the Privy Council's adoption of the Palestine Order in Council on August 10, 1922, the United Kingdom accepted the Mandate, though the Order in Council also empowered the High Commissioner for Palestine to disapply certain provisions of the Mandate to those parts of Palestine east of the Jordan River.[66] High Commissioner Herbert Samuel took advantage of this language less than a month later, on September 1, when he ordered the

[62] British Mandate for Palestine, *supra* note 58, at 164, pmbl.

[63] *Id.* at 165–66, art. 6.

[64] *See id.* at 166, art. 7, 167, arts 12–14, 169–70, art. 21.

[65] "In the territories lying between the Jordan and the eastern boundary of Palestine as ultimately determined, the Mandatory shall be entitled, with the consent of the Council of the League of Nations, to postpone or withhold application of such provisions of this mandate as he may consider inapplicable to the existing local conditions, and to make such provision for the administration of the territories as he may consider suitable to those conditions, provided that no action shall be taken which is inconsistent with the provisions of Articles 15, 16 and 18." *Id.* at 170, art. 25.

[66] *See* Palestine Order in Council, Aug. 10, 1922, § 86.

disapplication of the Jewish national home provisions to those parts of Palestine east of the Jordan.[67] While the Palestine Order in Council and Samuel's order were creatures of British municipal law, the Council of the League of Nations would shortly thereafter ratify this radical repositioning of the Mandate, that is, the exclusion of the Jewish national home provisions to the larger part of Palestine.[68] This was despite the fact that, as then British Secretary of State for the Colonies the Duke of Devonshire put it to Samuel in a confidential dispatch of late 1923, the Balfour Declaration's promise of a Jewish national home in Palestine "formed an essential part of the conditions on which Great Britain accepted the mandate for Palestine, and thus constitute[d] an international obligation from which there can be no question of receding."[69] This vesting of governance responsibilities in an Arab Emir in those parts of Palestine east of the Jordan took place despite the fact that the Mandate expressly prohibited any part of Palestine from being transferred in any way to a foreign power.[70] Might the exclusion of the Jewish national home provisions east of the Jordan and the creation of an Arab governing authority there that had an alien pedigree be seen as a constructive transfer of a part of Palestine to a foreign power?

The effect of this combination of events in mid 1922 was dramatic. The Jewish national home was truncated and, as one commentator would put it, "handed [...] to some foreign Arabs for a private pasturage."[71] While what was Transjordan, later to become Jordan, was, of course, not bereft of indigenous Arabs, the Hashemites, the "foreign Arabs" to which Ziff alludes in his critique, were neither from the area nor had any roots there. The British looked to the Sherifian clan,

[67] *See* Order of the High Commissioner for Palestine, Sept. 1, 1922.

[68] *See* Article 25 of the Palestine Mandate, Territory Known as Trans-Jordan, Note by the Secretary-General, Geneva, Sept. 23, 1922, 17(3) AM. J. INT'L L. SUPP. 171 (1922) (1923); Memorandum by the British Representative, 17(3) AM. J. INT'L L. SUPP. 172 (1922) (1923); Declaration Approved by the Council of the League of Nations, London, July 24, 1922, 17(3) AM. J. INT'L L. SUPP. 193 (1922) (1923). *See also* QUIGLEY, *supra* note 11, at 46–48; GIDEON BIGER, THE BOUNDARIES OF MODERN PALESTINE, 1840–1947 159–89 (2005); The Jewish National Home in Palestine, Committee on Foreign Affairs, U.S. House of Representatives, 78th Congress, 2d Sess., H. Res. 418 and H. Res. 419 1 (1944); Akzin, *supra* note 12, at 39–40; BENTWICH, *supra* note 33, at 43–46; Leonard Stein, *The Jews in Palestine,* 4(3) FOREIGN AFF. 415 (1926).

[69] Despatch from Secretary of State for the Colonies to High Commissioner, Palestine, No. 1223, Oct. 4, 1923, *in* FUTURE OF PALESTINE, app. 1 at 2, 2, No. CAB/24/162 (1923).

[70] *See* British Mandate for Palestine, *supra* note 58, at 165, art. 5. Ironically, the 1928 Agreement Between His Britannic Majesty and His Highness the Amir of Trans-Jordan contained a non-alienation clause worded almost exactly the same as the non-alienation clause in the Palestine Mandate. *See* Agreement Between His Britannic Majesty and His Highness the Amir of Trans-Jordan, *in* LEGISLATION OF TRANSJORDAN: 1918–1930, app. I. at 703, 708, art. 18 (C.R.W. Seton ed., 1931) (stating that: "No territory in Transjordan shall be ceded or leased or in any way placed under the control of any foreign power; this shall not prevent His Highness the Amir from making such arrangements as may be necessary for the accommodation of foreign representatives and for the fulfilment of the provisions of the preceding Articles"). On British policy with respect to the "Jewish national home" between November 1917 and July 1922, see Martin Gilbert, *"An Overwhelmingly Jewish State"—From the Balfour Declaration to the Palestine Mandate, in* ISRAEL'S RIGHTS AS A NATION-STATE IN INTERNATIONAL DIPLOMACY 23 (Alan Baker ed., 2011).

[71] WILLIAM B. ZIFF, THE RAPE OF PALESTINE 105 (1948).

with its historic connection to Muhammad and central role in the uprising against the Ottomans from its base in the Hijaz, as an obvious source of leadership for their Mandates in the Middle East and, along with the Council of the League of Nations, jettisoned the Jewish national project in the larger part of Palestine based upon these geopolitical considerations.[72] Many Zionists, particularly the revisionists, would see this as a gross betrayal and continue to insist, as Jabotinsky did before the Palestine Royal Commission (Peel Commission) in 1937, that "the idea is that Palestine on both sides of the Jordan should hold the Arabs, their progeny, *and* many millions of Jews."[73]

This truncation of the Jewish national home in Palestine, while an obvious disappointment to many Zionists and a coup for the Hashemites, should not be seen as altogether surprising when one considers what had transpired at the Middle East Conference in Cairo and Jerusalem in March 1921.[74] Over the course of just over two weeks, it was here that the British sought out the views of relevant stakeholders in the region about its policies in Aden and Somaliland, Mesopotamia, and Palestine. Specifically, then British Secretary of State for the Colonies Winston S. Churchill suggested that an Arab Emir should rule Palestine east of the Jordan under the supervision of the British High Commissioner for Palestine, with this Arab province remaining formally part of Palestine.[75] Emir Abdullah opposed this and proposed to Churchill that an Arab Emir should rule Palestine as a whole (under the supervision of the British High Commissioner for Palestine) just as an Arab Emir of the Hashemite dynasty, Feisal, would rule Mesopotamia (under the supervision of the British High Commissioner for Mesopotamia).[76] Alternatively, Abdullah suggested that Palestine east of the Jordan should be combined with Mesopotamia, thus ensuring Hashemite control over all of present-day Jordan and Iraq.[77] Churchill stressed to Abdullah, as a way of convincing the latter, that the former's suggestion of an Arab province in the larger part of Palestine under the supervision of the High Commissioner for Palestine would be hostile, so to speak, to Jews. Specifically, Churchill's offer to Abdullah of the disapplication of the Balfour Declaration to Palestine east of the Jordan would mean that, "therefore[,] the Zionist clauses of the mandate would not apply. Hebrew would not be made an official language in Trans-Jordania, and

[72] *See id.* at 105–108.

[73] Vladimir Jabotinsky, *Evidence Submitted to the Palestine Royal Commission (1937), in* The Zionist Idea: A Historical Analysis and Reader 559, 562 (Arthur Hertzberg ed., 1997).

[74] For the full report of the conference, with appendices, see Report on Middle East Conference Held in Cairo and Jerusalem, March 12th to 30th, 1921, With Appendices, No. CAB/24/126 (1921). *See also* Efraim Karsh, *Israel, the Hashemites and the Palestinians: The Fateful Triangle,* 9(3) Isr. Aff. 1, 2–3 (2003); Antonius, *supra* note 12, at 316–19.

[75] *See Trans-Jordania, in* Report on Middle East Conference, *supra* note 74, app. 19 at 107, 109.

[76] *See id.* Abdullah reiterated his proposal to the Woodhead Commission in May 1938. *See* Amir Abdallah, Proposal for the Solution of the Palestine Problem Submitted to the Woodhead Commission, May 1938, *in* 1 Documents on Palestine 357 (Mahdi Abdul Hadi ed., 2007).

[77] *See Trans-Jordania, supra* note 75, at 109.

the local Government would not be expected to adopt any measures to promote Jewish immigration and colonisation."[78]

One point that should be highlighted at this juncture is the prevalent sense among Arabs at the time that Zion, for the Jews, was not simply Palestine in its pre- or post-mid 1922 incarnations but, rather, that it expanded, or would be pushed to expand, considerably further afield. Writing in 1949, for example, the prominent Palestinian Arab lawyer Musa Alami claimed that the Zionist understanding was that "Palestine includes present-day Palestine, Transjordan, and large portions of Syria, Lebanon, and Egypt. They [i.e., the Zionists] dream of 'a greater Jewish state between the Nile and Euphrates.'"[79] Although there is biblical support for the idea of a geographically much more expansive Jewish polity,[80] this has never been recognized by international law. From an international law perspective, in other words, the Jewish national home was always to be limited to Palestine, truncated or not. There was simply no convincing legal case to the contrary.

The events of mid 1922 would see the formal realization of Churchill's vision in law, with the British remaining obliged to put into effect the Jewish national home provisions in Palestine west of the Jordan but with those same provisions being disapplied to the larger part of the Palestine Mandate.

IV. The Concept of a Palestinian Arab "People" During the Mandate for Palestine

Given that the (first) partition of Palestine in mid 1922 was the last structural change to the Mandate for well over two decades,[81] it is useful at this point to put all of this in a broader regional context. The United Kingdom and France were at the time administering their respective A Mandates at the periphery of Palestine, and these Mandates would emerge, in time, as the independent States of Iraq, Syria, and Lebanon. Of course, these Mandates were majority Arab, and mostly Muslim, with the most notable exception being the Maronites of the Eastern Rite and Orthodox Christians in what was to become the Republic of Lebanon. To a large extent, the borders between the A Mandates were arbitrary, which is to say, they were agreed upon by the Western powers, and confirmed by the League of

[78] *Id.* at 110.

[79] Musa Alami, *The Lesson of Palestine,* 3(4) MID. E. J. 373, 387 (1949). *Cf.* ADOLF HITLER, MEIN KAMPF 295 (2013); HAJ AMIN AL-HUSAYNI, *The Goal of the Zionist Movement: To Establish a Jewish State in Palestine and in the Neighbouring Arab Countries and to Build a Jewish Temple in Place of the Dome of the Rock at the al-Aqsa Mosque, in* THROUGH THE EYES OF THE MUFTI 98 (Zvi Elpeleg ed., Rachel Kessel trans., 2009).

[80] *See Genesis* 15:18–21 ("On that day the Lord made a covenant with Abram, saying, 'To your descendants I give this land, from the river of Egypt to the great river, the river Euphra'tes, the land of the Ken'ites, the Ken'izzites, the Kad'monites, the Hittites, the Per'izzites, the Reph'aim, the Amorites, the Canaanites, the Gir'gashites and the Jeb'usites'").

[81] *See also* Agreement, *supra* note 70.

Nations, primarily with geopolitical considerations in mind rather than out of a sense that the borders were somehow, or should somehow be, "natural" or that each of the Arab populations in each of the Mandates shared, or should share, an identity that marked it off as unique from Arab populations in surrounding Mandates.[82] Reflecting upon what he referred to as the "dismemberment of the Arab World" in the first half of the twentieth century, Arab scholar Fayez A. Sayegh would make the following lament in 1958: "the one nation [i.e., the Arab nation] was condemned to liv[e] separate lives in separate compartments."[83] Just a few years earlier, King Abdullah warned in his memoirs that: "To accept this division is to submit to an idea which the Arab nation has rejected and which exposes it to the ambitions of the Jews and their supporters in Palestine."[84]

On the identity issue, the position of Palestinian Arabs was particularly problematic, and it would remain so for the duration of the Mandate. The summarized remarks of then Secretary of State for the Colonies W.G.A. Ormsby-Gore before the League of Nations Permanent Mandates Commission in mid 1937, relay the following point: "[T]hese people [i.e., Palestinian Arabs] had not hitherto regarded themselves as 'Palestinians', but as part of Syria as a whole, as part of the Arab world."[85] In other words, the view conveyed is that the Arabs of Palestine did not view themselves as possessing a separate identity that set them off as a people distinct from Arabs elsewhere in the Levant.

The question of identity, of course, is a most intimate one, and it operates at the group level in addition to at the level of the individual. Given its complexity, it must be approached with care. How one defines oneself and identifies as part of a larger group, if one does, and how that larger group relates to international law generally and is regulated by it, if it is, can be consequential matters indeed. Although, as noted above, self-determination as *lex lata* did not exist during the interwar years, the proto-self-determination that did exist at the time required, first of all, the identification of beneficiaries. These beneficiaries were "peoples," though legal practice has been to use the words "peoples" and "nations" interchangeably.[86]

At the time of the Mandate, "peoplehood" was famously difficult to define, and this has remained the case to the present.[87] "What is a nation?" Renan famously

[82] *See* LASSNER & TROEN, *supra* note 7, at 16 (writing that the "potpourri of Arab nation-states created by colonial mapmakers has neither geographic nor demographic coherence").

[83] FAYEZ A. SAYEGH, ARAB UNITY: HOPE AND FULFILLMENT 42 (1958).

[84] *A Review of the Present Position of the Arab Countries, in* MEMOIRS OF KING ABDULLAH OF TRANSJORDAN, app. 1 at 243, 248–49 (Philip P. Graves ed., 1950).

[85] League of Nations, Permanent Mandates Commission, Minutes of the 32d (Extraordinary) Sess. (Aug. 13, 1937), http://unispal.un.org/unispal.nsf/9a798adbf322aff38525617b006d88d7/fd05535118aef0de052565ed0065ddf7?OpenDocument (continuing by stating that "[t]hey [, if transferred,] would be going literally only a comparatively few miles away to a people with the same language, the same civilisation, the same religion; and therefore the problem of transfer geographically and practically was easier even than the interchanges of Greeks and Turks between Asia Minor and the Balkans").

[86] *See* JAMES SUMMERS, PEOPLES AND INTERNATIONAL LAW: HOW NATIONALISM AND SELF-DETERMINATION SHAPE A CONTEMPORARY LAW OF NATIONS 1–3 (2007).

[87] For some of the debates in the academic literature, see KAREN KNOP, DIVERSITY AND SELF-DETERMINATION IN INTERNATIONAL LAW 51–65 (2008); SUMMERS, *supra* note 86, at 45–81; B.C. Nirmal, *The Right of Self-Determination of the Tibetan People, Approaches and Modalities, in* TIBETAN PEOPLE'S RIGHT

asked himself at the Sorbonne in March 1882, and his answer was that it is a "large-scale solidarity, constituted by the feeling of the sacrifices that one has made in the past and of those that one is prepared to make in the future";[88] in Anderson's understanding, the nation is an "imagined political community—and imagined as both inherently limited and sovereign."[89] Recognizing the contested nature of "peoplehood" in 2010 in his separate opinion in *Accordance with International Law of the Unilateral Declaration of Independence in Respect of Kosovo*, ICJ Judge Cançado Trindade stated that: "There is in fact no terminological precision as to what constitutes a 'people' in international law, despite the large experience on the matter."[90] As in 2010, there was certainly terminological imprecision as to the nature of "peoplehood" at the time of the Palestine Mandate.[91]

The present section does not pretend to be able to magically wish away the terminological imprecision that comes with the concept of "peoplehood" in

OF SELF-DETERMINATION 44, 44–49 (1996); PAUL J.I.M. DE WAART, DYNAMICS OF SELF-DETERMINATION IN PALESTINE: PROTECTION OF PEOPLES AS A HUMAN RIGHT 58–61 (1994); Robert McCorquodale, *Self-Determination: A Human Rights Approach*, 43(4) INT'L & COMP. L.Q. 857, 866–68 (1994).

[88] Ernest Renan, *What Is a Nation?*, in NATION AND NARRATION 8, 19 (Homi K. Bhabha ed., 2008).

[89] BENEDICT ANDERSON, IMAGINED COMMUNITIES: REFLECTIONS ON THE ORIGIN AND SPREAD OF NATIONALISM 6 (2006). Also on nations and nationalism, see GEORGE ORWELL, *Notes on Nationalism, in* ESSAYS 300 (2014); MARTIN BUBER, *Nationalism, in* A LAND OF TWO PEOPLES: MARTIN BUBER ON JEWS AND ARABS 47 (Paul Mendes-Flohr ed., 2005). For Gandhi, the "truest test of nationalism" was each "person['s] thinking not only of half a dozen men of his own family or of a hundred men of his own clan, but considering as his very own the interest of that group which he calls his nation." Mahatma Gandhi, *Speech at Public Meeting, Jaffna, in* 35 THE COLLECTED WORKS OF MAHATMA GANDHI (SEPTEMBER 1927–JANUARY 1928) 320, 321 (Publ'n Dep't, Gov't of India ed., 1969).

[90] Accordance with International Law of the Unilateral Declaration of Independence in Respect of Kosovo, Advisory Opinion, 2010 I.C.J. 403, 613 (July 22) (Cançado Trindade, J., separate). *See* Rupert Emerson, *Self-Determination,* 65(3) AM. J. INT'L L. 459, 462 (1971) (noting that "all commentators on self-determination have pointed out that neither 'people' nor 'nation' has any generally accepted meaning which can be applied to the diverse world of political and social reality"). Cristescu's seminal 1981 study on self-determination provides the most meticulous deconstruction of the concepts of "peoples," "nations," and "States," though he focuses exclusively on the United Nations era. *See* CRISTESCU, *supra* note 54, at 37–43. Cristescu suggests that there are three main elements of a "people," namely that it be a "social entity possessing a clear identity and its own characteristics," that it have a special relationship with a specific territory, and that it differ from ethnic, religious, or linguistic minority groups as these groups are understood within the context of the 1966 International Covenant on Civil and Political Rights. *Id.* at 41. *See* International Meeting of Experts on Further Study of the Concept of the Rights of Peoples, Final Report and Recommendations, at 7–8, SHS-89/CONF.602/7 (1990). For a flavor of the debates as to the meaning of "peoples," "nations," and "States" in the Charter's *travaux préparatoires*, see 18(2) DOCUMENTS OF THE UNITED NATIONS CONFERENCE ON INTERNATIONAL ORGANIZATION, SAN FRANCISCO, 1945 657–58 (1954); 6 DOCUMENTS OF THE UNITED NATIONS CONFERENCE ON INTERNATIONAL ORGANIZATION, SAN FRANCISCO, 1945 300 (1945). *See also* Kaur, *supra* note 54, at 483–85. *But see* Higgins, *supra* note 54, at 169–70 (arguing that "people" simply means a given territory's population writ large). *See also* RAIČ, *supra* note 42, at 244–47; Chowdhury, *supra* note 54, at 88–93; Yuval Shany, *Does International Law Grant the People of Crimea and Donetsk a Right to Secede? Revisiting Self-Determination in Light of the 2014 Events in Ukraine*, 21(1) BROWN J. WORLD AFF. 233, 234–37 (2014).

[91] Emerson suggests that the definition of "people" during the interwar years and during decolonization after the Second World War fundamentally differed. *See* Emerson, *supra* note 90, at 463–64. Whether this is a fundamental difference of definition or a fundamental difference of interpretation and application, on the whole, there is much to commend this line of reasoning.

international law, which it regards as inevitable in a dynamic and multicultural world, or to arrive at a definitive definition of "people" during the interwar years. Identities are multiple and often fluid, and one would do well to bear in mind Sen's call for a "clearer understanding of the pluralities of human identity, and [...] appreciation that they cut across each other and work against a sharp separation along one single hardened line of impenetrable division."[92] This section seeks to sketch the parameters of how the concept of "peoplehood" was juridically understood at the time of the Palestine Mandate and then to apply this understanding to the case of the Palestinian Arabs. One gets a good sense of how "peoplehood" was understood during the interwar years by looking at the Aaland Islands Question and the 1937 Palestine Royal Commission Report (Peel Report).

In the Aaland Islands Question, the League of Nations viewed self-determination as an equitable principle and only conceded it as an exceptional remedy. Even in those exceptional *de facto* situations in which self-determination could theoretically apply, however, the principle would have to be harmonized with and draw upon the existing law related to the protection of minorities.[93] The beneficiaries of these protections were the same, namely populations who could draw upon "old traditions or on a common language and civilization"[94] and had particular "social, ethnical or religious characteristics."[95] The Second Aaland Islands Report, which a Commission of Rapporteurs presented to the Council of the League of Nations in 1921, described States' duties with regard to the protection of minorities as follows: "It is just that the ethnical character and the ancient traditions of these minorities should be respected as much as possible, and that they should be specially authorised to practise freely their religion and to cultivate their language."[96] Thus, "ethnical character," "ancient traditions," "religion," and "language" were indicative of those beneficiaries who were entitled to minority protection as a matter of law. The Permanent Court of International Justice would give a similar understanding of "community" a decade later in Greco-Bulgarian "Communities,"[97] in which it expressly equated "community" and "minority."[98]

The Peel Report strongly reinforces the understanding of "people" in the Aaland Islands Question. The Peel Commission was established in 1936 to advise His Majesty's Government on the best way forward for the Mandatory amidst

[92] AMARTYA SEN, IDENTITY AND VIOLENCE: THE ILLUSION OF DESTINY xiv (2007).

[93] *See* First Aaland Islands Report, *supra* note 43, at 6.

[94] *Id.*

[95] *Id.*

[96] Second Aaland Islands Report, *supra* note 43.

[97] *See* Greco-Bulgarian "Communities," Advisory Opinion, 1930 P.C.I.J. (ser. B) No. 17, at 33 (July 31) (defining a "community" as a "group of persons living in a given country or locality, having a race, religion, language and traditions of their own, and united by the identity of such race, religion, language and traditions in a sentiment of solidarity, with a view to preserving their traditions, maintaining their form of worship, securing the instruction and upbringing of their children in accordance with the spirit and traditions of their race and mutually assisting one another"). *See also id.* at 21–23.

[98] *See id.* at 19.

increasing inter-communal violence in Palestine.[99] "The disease is so deep-rooted," the Peel Report would put it, "that, in our firm conviction, the only hope of a cure lies in a surgical operation."[100] A further partition of Palestine was the recommended "surgical operation,"[101] but whether because of subsequent events, or in spite of them, it was never implemented. The Peel Commission's particular understanding of "peoplehood" revolved around its description of the "force of circumstances" as the existence of a conflict between two nationalities, or nations.[102] In the Peel Report's words: "The Arab community is predominantly Asiatic in character, the Jewish community predominantly European. They differ in religion and in language. Their cultural and social life, their ways of thought and conduct, are as incompatible as their national aspirations."[103] These characteristics (race, religion, and language, cultural and social mores, thought and conduct) were what distinguished the Jews of Palestine from the Arabs of Palestine. It was what made them, so to speak, of different nations.[104] The Peel Report's typological description of nations was almost identical to the approach that had been taken almost two decades earlier in the Aaland Islands Question, and like the Aaland Islands Question, it teases out a broad and consistent, though admittedly still question-begging and context-specific, understanding of "people."

Approaching the question of whether the Arabs of Palestine constituted a "people" in the juridical sense at the time of the Palestine Mandate is obviously a complex one given the often nuanced and slippery nature of identity. Then, as now, the question of "peoplehood" raises what Koskenniemi has described as the "'onion problem' of nationalism: the problem that one's definition of the 'nation' depends on the perspective (the distance) from which one's vision is formed."[105] In sifting through the considerable body of material that can be drawn upon in an attempt to clarify the issue, one should be careful not to rely upon second-hand reports, uncorroborated evidence, or partisan or inaccurate testimony,[106] though such can sometimes be in the eye of the beholder and a matter of degree rather than of kind. Some of the material worth drawing upon in the Palestine context has

[99] Palestine Royal Commission Report, cmd. 5479 (1937). *See* Penny Sinanoglou, *The Peel Commission and Partition, 1936–1938*, in BRITAIN, PALESTINE AND EMPIRE: THE MANDATE YEARS 119 (Rory Miller ed., 2010); H.St.J.B. Philby, *The Arabs and the Future of Palestine*, 16(1) FOREIGN AFF. 156 (1937).

[100] Peel Report, *supra* note 99, at 368.

[101] *See id.* at 370–96.

[102] *See id.* at 370–76.

[103] *Id.* at 370.

[104] Ten years later, the UNSCOP's Report to the General Assembly would stress that the Jews and Arabs of Palestine had distinct cultural mores, outlooks, religions, languages, and aspirations. *See* United Nations Special Committee on Palestine, Report to the General Assembly: Volume I, at 41, U.N. Doc. A/364 (Sept. 3, 1947). *See also id.* at 45 (highlighting the two communities' spiritual and physical separation, separate ideals and aspirations, and different cultural mores).

[105] Koskenniemi, *supra* note 51, at 260. And the "perspective," or "distance," is enormously consequential: "Who they are, how the people is constituted, by what standards and criteria, determines whether or not an individual has access to rights." Weitz, *supra* note 40, at 496.

[106] *See* Armed Activities on the Territory of the Congo (Dem. Rep. Congo v. Uganda), 2005 I.C.J. 168, 225–26 (Dec. 19).

already been commented upon by other scholars; some has been ignored; some has been de-emphasized. Yet an examination of the terms of the Palestine Mandate and an appreciation for geopolitical developments and the official statements of Arab leaders and scholars at the time suggest that any distinct national identity for Palestinian Arabs *qua* Palestinian Arabs was, at best, *in statu nascendi* during the Mandate.

To begin with, one will recall that the Balfour Declaration and the subsequent reaffirmation of it by the Council of the League of Nations in the form of the Palestine Mandate only recognized national rights for the Jewish people. In other words, from the perspective of the League of Nations, which, in a juridical sense, "represented" the international community at the time, there were no other nations in Palestine. That the terms of the Mandate were never changed suggests that this formally remained the League's perspective until the Mandate ended in the wake of the Second World War.[107] To be sure, the Mandate acknowledged that there was a non-Jewish population in Palestine and variously referred to this population as "non-Jewish communities,"[108] "inhabitants of Palestine,"[109] and "other sections of the population,"[110] but it never did so in terms of national rights. Most of this non-Jewish population, of course, was Arab, and as a non-Jewish population under the Mandate, it was assured civil and religious rights.[111] Unsurprisingly, because the Palestine Mandate did not consider any parts of the non-Jewish population to be discrete nations, its terms did not recognize national rights for any of them, including Palestinian Arabs.

Geopolitical developments at the time are also important to consider when assessing the question of whether the Arabs of Palestine constituted a "people" in the juridical sense at the time of the Palestine Mandate. While one should be careful not to overlook the significance of truncating the Jewish national home in mid 1922, one should be equally cautious not to conclude from this that "Western Palestine" and "Transjordan" somehow emerged from this as "natural" territorial entities. Indeed, this was far from the case. From both Zionist and Arab perspectives, the (first) partition of Palestine was nothing more than an exercise in imperial decision-making designed to placate Abdullah. With his own "private pasturage," the British thought, the Arab Emir would surely quit meddling across Palestine's northern frontier in the French Mandate for Syria and the Lebanon.[112] London hoped to fashion a bridge of stability between British-controlled territory in Mesopotamia and French-controlled territory in the Levant and, by giving control of the larger part of Palestine to an Arab Emir, to dilute Arab opposition to the Zionist project. This dispensation was squarely rooted in geopolitics, not out of a

[107] The approval of the League Council was required for amendments to the Mandate. *See* British Mandate for Palestine, *supra* note 58, at 171, art. 27.

[108] *Id.* at 164, pmbl.

[109] *Id.* at 165, art. 2.

[110] *Id.* at 165, art. 6.

[111] *See, e.g., id.* at 165, art. 2.

[112] *See* Report on Middle East Conference, *supra* note 74, at 7–9.

concern to delineate separate Arab nations, and it was recognized for this at the time.[113] Reflecting upon these regional machinations decades later, former Arab Knesset Member Azmi Bishara, an anti-imperialist with little in the way of Zionist sympathies, made the following observation:

> I do not think there is a Palestinian nation, I think its [*sic*] a colonialist invention—Palestinian nation. When were there any Palestinians? Where did it come from? I think there is an Arab nation [...] I think that until the end of the 19th century, Palestine was the south of Greater Syria.[114]

Particularly within elite Arab circles, there was little sense that the borders between and within the British and French A Mandates in the Levant could last or were even desirable, much less that they somehow demarcated national allegiances.[115] Indeed, sentiment was quite to the contrary. As Arab Higher Committee (AHC) representative Jamal Husseini put it in a letter to the United Nations Assistant Secretary-General for Security Council Affairs in late May 1948, the Arab States surrounding Palestine were "linked to them [i.e., the Arabs of Palestine] by all the ties of nationality and had only been segregated from them by the imperialistic ambitions of foreign powers."[116] The AHC was the Arab equivalent of the Jewish Agency in Palestine, and it was recognized by the General Assembly as "representative of the views of the Arab population [of Palestine]."[117]

[113] As Nisan has put it, Transjordan, "founded by Arab aliens in association with British imperialists, represented no national idea or political ideal. From the start it was lacking in roots and values. We might describe it as an 'imagined kingdom' born on the edge of a desert, to deny the east bank to Zionism and southern Syria to Arab nationalism." MORDECHAI NISAN, ONLY ISRAEL WEST OF THE RIVER: THE JEWISH STATE AND THE PALESTINIAN QUESTION 117 (2011). *See* Mudar Zahran, *Jordan Is Palestinian*, 19(1) MID. E. Q. 3 (2012); Israeli Foreign Minister Abba Eban, Statement to the Knesset Regarding the "Legitimate Rights of the Palestinian People," Jerusalem, July 18, 1973, *in* 2 DOCUMENTS ON PALESTINE 403 (Mahdi Abdul Hadi ed., 2007); Mordechai Nisan, *The Palestinian Features of Jordan*, *in* JUDEA, SAMARIA, AND GAZA: VIEWS ON THE PRESENT AND FUTURE 191 (Daniel J. Elazar ed., 1982). Hupp describes it as a "Kingdom of Dreams." *See* CLEA LUTZ HUPP, THE UNITED STATES AND JORDAN: MIDDLE EAST DIPLOMACY DURING THE COLD WAR 9–30 (2014).

[114] Sam Sokol, *The Catastrophe Called Israel?*, JERUSALEM POST, May 10, 2012.

[115] Much of this can be explained, of course, by reference to the 1916 Sykes-Picot Agreement between the two powers. *See* Sykes-Picot Agreement (May 15–16, 1916), *in* THE ISRAEL–ARAB READER: A DOCUMENTARY HISTORY OF THE MIDDLE EAST CONFLICT 13 (Walter Laqueur & Barry Rubin eds., 7th ed. 2008).

[116] Letter Dated 18 May 1948 from the Assistant Secretary-General for Security Council Affairs Addressed to the Arab Higher Committee, and Reply Dated 24 May 1948 Addressed to the Secretary-General Concerning the Questions Submitted by the Security Council, at 5, U.N. Doc. S/775 (May 24, 1948). *See* Statement to the *Ad Hoc* Committee on the Palestinian Question by the Representative of the Arab Higher Committee, 29 September 1947, *in* THE ARAB-ISRAEL CONFLICT AND ITS RESOLUTION: SELECTED DOCUMENTS 57, 57 (Ruth Lapidoth & Moshe Hirsch eds., 1992) (noting that Arabs generally shared a "racial homogeneity" and "spoke one language, had the same history, tradition and aspirations").

[117] 1946–47 U.N.Y.B. 285. The General Assembly endorsed the First Committee's views to this effect. *See id.* at 286. As Husseini put it in his letter, the AHC "speaks in the name of the majority of the whole of Palestine." Letter Dated 18 May 1948, *supra* note 116, at 2 (also stating that the AHC was "exercising political authority over the overwhelming majority of the citizens of Palestine. The Committee is composed of members representing the different political Arab parties in the country. It thus forms a coalition, which expresses the Arab public opinion in Palestine. Whereas, Arabs are in majority in all

Two years earlier, Husseini had sent a blistering letter to British Prime Minister Clement Attlee in which he criticized the 1946 Report of the Anglo-American Committee of Inquiry and expressed the AHC's aversion to it in terms that unmistakably reflected Palestinian Arabs' sense of transboundary national allegiance.[118] The proposals, according to Husseini, "would threaten the existence and national life of the Arab nation."[119] In no uncertain terms, Husseini then expressed the AHC's view that Palestinian Arabs would resist the proposals not as a distinct people—there was little sense of this at the time—but, rather, as an indispensable part of the Arab people: "The Arab Higher Committee [...] confirms the Arab people's determination—in Palestine—to defend their country by all means in their power."[120]

Put differently, rather than a Palestinian Arab people as such, the "official" record suggests that the Arabs of Palestine tended to view themselves as part of a single, and singular, nation, the larger Arab nation. Valentine Dannevig, a Norwegian member of the Permanent Mandates Commission, noted during an extraordinary session of the Permanent Mandates Commission in the summer of 1937 that the self-representation of Palestinian Arabs had always consciously been as part of a larger Arab nation.[121] British Secretary of State for Foreign Affairs Anthony Eden reflected a perceptive sensitivity to this transboundary national dynamic in a November 1937 memorandum that noted that the Middle East

> is an organic whole. The frontiers between the Arab States as shown on the maps are largely artificial post-war creations, resting on no true national, geographical or ethnographical basis. Palestine's neighbour States are not "foreign" to Palestine in the European sense, and opinion or events in one produce quick reactions in another.[122]

Indeed, Arab scholars such as Sayegh were quick to criticize attempts to channel and understand Arab national sentiment according to accepted Western notions of the nation-State and national identity.[123] The Lebanese scholar Albert Hourani would note that the first four decades of the twentieth century were, for many

districts and sub-districts, save that of Jaffa, in which Tel Aviv is situated, the Arab Higher Committee, therefore, speaks in the name of the majority of the whole of Palestine"). *See* 2 A Survey of Palestine Prepared in December 1945 and January 1946 for the Information of the Anglo-American Committee of Inquiry 945–55 (1991); Henry Cattan, Palestine and International Law: The Legal Aspects of the Arab-Israeli Conflict 35 (2d ed. 1976); Shabtai Rosenne, Israel's Armistice Agreements with the Arab States 29 n.1 (1951).

[118] *See* Arab Reactions in Palestine to the Report of the Anglo-American Committee of Enquiry, June 6, 1946, No. CAB/129/10.

[119] *Id.* at 1 (continuing by asserting later in his letter that the "Arab nation will proceed in mobilising its national forces and preparing the means for the defence of itself, to resume the national movement fight. The Arab nation will not hesitate to adopt an attitude which will lead to the checking of the approaching danger and realise freedom and independence for them").

[120] *Id.*

[121] *See* League of Nations, Permanent Mandates Commission, Minutes of the 32d (Extraordinary) Sess. (Aug. 12, 1937), http://unispal.un.org/unispal.nsf/9a798adbf322aff38525617b006d88d7/fd05535118aef0de052565ed0065ddf7?OpenDocument.

[122] Palestine, at 3, No. CAB/24/237 (1937).

[123] *See* Sayegh, *supra* note 83, at 85–89.

Arabs of the Levant, a rejection of territorial-based nationalism in favor of a sense of unified allegiance across territory, with racial, cultural, and ethnic elements to it.[124]

To fully appreciate the position that Palestine held within this larger geographical conversation, it is helpful to turn to the rise of the General Syrian Congress and Emir Feisal's brief reign in Damascus. Feisal, who had been maneuvering for control of the Levant at the time, was proclaimed King of Syria by Resolutions adopted in Damascus on July 2, 1919,[125] Syria being understood to include, *inter alia*, Palestine.[126] According to Arab scholar George Antonius, the General Syrian Congress, which included representatives from Palestine, was truly representative: "its deliberations did reflect the fears and hopes of the vast majority of the population, and [...] the resolutions it passed may safely be taken as expressing those views and sentiments that were most widely held."[127] Antonius, describing the Resolutions as an "impressive display of patriotic fervour,"[128] wrote that the views as to the territorial integrity of the entirety of Syria were "echoed throughout the country."[129]

While it is probably impossible to verify the popularity of the General Syrian Congress' Resolutions of July 1919 within greater Syria, there seems to be little reason to doubt that they echoed widely among many Arabs in the Levant.[130] In fact, in recommending that Emir Feisal be installed as head of a united Syrian State, the King-Crane Commission, which United States President Woodrow Wilson had tasked with advising him on the post First World War dispensation, stated that:

> This [recommendation] is expressly and unanimously asked for by the representative Damascus Congress in the name of the Syrian people, and there seems to be no reason to doubt that the great majority of the population of Syria sincerely desire to have Amir Faisal as ruler.[131]

The General Syrian Congress, "reject[ing] the claims of the Zionists for the establishment of a Jewish commonwealth in that part of southern Syria which is known as Palestine, and [...] oppos[ing ...] Jewish immigration into any part of the country,"[132] called for the unity of all of Syria, expressly including Palestine and

[124] *See* Albert Hourani, *Near Eastern Nationalism Yesterday and Today*, 42(1) FOREIGN AFF. 123, 130 (1963).

[125] *See* Resolutions of the General Syrian Congress, *in* ANTONIUS, *supra* note 12, app. G at 440.

[126] *See id.* at 440, ¶ 1 (defining Syria's boundaries as, "on the north, the Taurus Range; on the south, a line running from Rafah to al-Jauf and following the Syria-Hejaz border below 'Aqaba; on the east, the boundary formed by the Euphrates and Khabur rivers and a line stretching from some distance east of Abu-Kamal to some distance east of al-Jauf; on the west, the Mediterranean Sea").

[127] ANTONIUS, *supra* note 12, at 293.

[128] *Id.* at 294.

[129] *Id.*

[130] On the General Syrian Congress' Resolutions of July 2, 1919, see *id.* at 292–94.

[131] Recommendations of the King-Crane Commission with Regard to Syria-Palestine and Iraq (Aug. 29, 1919), http://unispal.un.org/unispal.nsf/9a798adbf322aff38525617b006d88d7/392ad7eb009 02a0c852570c000795153?OpenDocument&Highlight=2,king-crane.

[132] Resolutions of the General Syrian Congress, *in* ANTONIUS, *supra* note 12, at 440, ¶ 7.

Lebanon within this understanding of Syrian territory.[133] This prevalent feeling of Palestine as part of Syria is further reinforced when one recalls that just a few months earlier, in March 1919, Feisal had written to Felix Frankfurter, then in Paris representing American Zionism at the Peace Conference, rejecting the suggestion that either Jewish nationalism or Arab nationalism was imperialist in nature and going on to state that "there is room in Syria for both of us."[134]

Khalidi has suggested that the sense among Palestinian Arabs that theirs was a territory that was naturally part of a greater Syria was but a three-year, context-specific aberration (between roughly 1917 and 1920),[135] but this view seems too unequivocal. While the events in Damascus were emblematic of the strong sense of pan-Arabism, and, more specifically, pan-Syrianism, that existed at the time, their effects would continue for some time thereafter, and the dominance of a pan-Syrian consciousness in the region would last well after France succeeded in wrestling power from Feisal in 1920.[136] The Peel Report, for example, the most significant report on Palestine of the interwar years, reflected this in no uncertain terms when it was published in 1937. Stating that "Palestine had virtually dropped out of history,"[137] the Peel Report nonetheless recognized that Palestinian Arabs oriented both their territorial compass and national allegiance to Palestine as an integral part of Syria, "poor and neglected though it was, to the Arabs who lived in it Palestine—or, more strictly speaking, Syria, of which Palestine had been a part since the days of Nebuchadnezzar—was still their country, their home, the land in which their people for centuries past had lived and left their graves."[138]

Elsewhere in its report, the Peel Commission recognized that the Arabs of Palestine and Syria were bitter at the divorce that the Mandate system had imposed upon them and sought to reverse its coerced effects.[139] Chief Secretary of the Palestine Government John Hathorn Hall noted shortly after the Peel Report's release that the idea of Palestine as part of the Arab world had been central to the Arabs since the beginning of the Palestine Mandate and that: "The Arab [...] was in the habit of referring to Palestine on political occasions as 'Southern Syria'. The union of sentiment between Palestine and the rest of Arabia was strongly developed [before the uprising of 1936]."[140]

[133] *See id.* at 440, ¶ 8.

[134] Charles A. Selden, *Prince of Hedjaz Welcomes Zionists*, N.Y. TIMES, Mar. 5, 1919. Feisal's memorandum to the Paris Peace Conference is a classic example of this plea for Arab unity. *See* Amir Faysal's Memorandum to the Paris Peace Conference, Jan. 1, 1919, *in* 2 THE ARAB STATES AND THE ARAB LEAGUE: A DOCUMENTARY RECORD 302 (Muhammad Khalil ed., 1962).

[135] *See* RASHID KHALIDI, PALESTINIAN IDENTITY: THE CONSTRUCTION OF MODERN NATIONAL CONSCIOUSNESS 162–75 (2010). *See also* As'ad Ghanem, *Palestinian Nationalism: An Overview*, 18(2) ISR. STUD. 11, 12–16 (2013).

[136] *See* JULIUS STONE, ISRAEL AND PALESTINE: ASSAULT ON THE LAW OF NATIONS 9–18 (1981). On the French bombardment of Damascus five years later, see Quincy Wright, *The Bombardment of Damascus*, 20(2) AM. J. INT'L L. 263 (1926).

[137] Peel Report, *supra* note 99, at 6.

[138] *See id.* at 25.

[139] *See id.* at 59 and 58–59.

[140] League of Nations, Permanent Mandates Commission, Minutes of the 32d (Extraordinary) Sess. (Aug. 6, 1937), http://unispal.un.org/unispal.nsf/9a798adbf322aff38525617b006d88d7/fd05535118aef0de052565ed0065ddf7?OpenDocument.

That the Peel Report articulated a shared sense of national identity among the Arabs of Palestine and Syria did not come as a surprise when the report was released in 1937. Indeed, the recognition of a shared sense of national identity formed the basis of many of the Recommendations of the King-Crane Commission with Regard to Syria-Palestine and Iraq in 1919 (King-Crane Recommendations).[141] The King-Crane Commission urged that any foreign administration of Syria-Palestine (as it tellingly referred to this geographical expanse) needed to conform with the spirit of article 22 of the Covenant and not be administered out of colonial ambition, that Syria-Palestine's unity be upheld and not undermined in any way, that the Zionist project of Jewish statebuilding in Palestine be done away with, and that, ideally, a single power, the United States, administer Syria-Palestine as an undivided Mandate.[142] In stressing the need to uphold Syria-Palestine's territorial integrity and the national imperatives of its Arab population, the King-Crane Recommendations did not make any fundamental distinctions within the Arab population, and one could reasonably have expected it to have done so had there been a discernible sense that groups within this larger Arab population, such as the Arabs of Palestine, were separate nations. In Syria-Palestine, the Arab population's "economic, geographic, racial and language unity [was] too manifest [...] The country is very largely Arab in language, culture, tradition, and customs."[143] Unity along such lines hardly gives one reason to postulate a separate "peoplehood" for the Palestinian Arabs at the time.

Even after the King-Crane Commission's concern not to compartmentalize the Arabs of Syria-Palestine had been jettisoned by subsequent events, Arabs would continue to admonish what they viewed as the arbitrary way in which the British and French had drawn the borders of their respective A Mandates in the Levant. Antonius, for example, reminded an audience at Chatham House in March 1934 that the land mass between the Taurus Mountains in the north and the Sinai Peninsula and Desert in the south and between the Mediterranean Sea in the west and the Syrian Desert in the east formed, historically, Syria, since the time of the Roman Empire.[144] The political difficulties that the Mandatories in the Levant were then experiencing were, according to him, a direct result of what he referred to as the Mandate system's "dismemberment of Syria."[145] Speaking for the people of historic Syria—one can assume here that he was referring to the Arab population alone—Antonius made the point as follows:

> [I]f I were to single out one point on which they were all united in discontent, I should say that it was the dismemberment of this rectangle of land, which is so obviously one from every point of view and which can only live and thrive by remaining one.[146]

[141] *See* King-Crane Recommendations, *supra* note 131.
[142] *See id.*
[143] *Id.*
[144] *See* George Antonius, *Syria and the French Mandate*, 13(4) INT'L AFF. 523, 523–25 (1934).
[145] *Id.* at 525.
[146] *Id.* at 526. Antonius went on to describe the "absurdity of having cut up this small territory into so many divisions."

He was quite clearly highlighting the unity of historic Syria as a political and national unit.

Antonius expanded upon this commonly held view that Palestine was but a sub-region of Syria, and an indispensable one at that, in his celebrated work *The Arab Awakening: The Story of the Arab National Movement*, which was originally published in 1938.[147] Decrying the partition of Syria, he noted that Syria as a whole shared much in common economically, culturally, and historically—indicative factors of distinct "peoplehood," one will recall—and that, "[i]n spite of the great diversity of its physical features, it was geographically one and formed a self-contained unit enclosed by well-defined natural frontiers."[148] "In the Arab view," Antonius put it, "Palestine was an Arab territory forming an integral part of Syria and, as such, was bound to remain in the area of Arab independence."[149] The AHC made a similar point in July 1937 when it described "Arab Palestine and Arab Syria [as …] two areas which are linked by bonds of blood and culture which make them inherently one."[150] In Jerusalem less than a decade later, the Arab Office would make a similar observation in evidence that it submitted to the Anglo-American Committee of Inquiry.[151]

Antonius, the AHC, and the Arab Office were far from alone in these views. The title of Arab historian Philip Hitti's monumental *History of Syria Including Lebanon and Palestine* of 1951 is itself indicative. Hitti criticized the very idea and operation of separate British and French A Mandates in the Levant. For him, the existence of the Palestine Mandate meant that the "southern part of Syria [was] amputated."[152] Writing about the possibility of union among the Arab States in 1943, he observed that Transjordan had a "Biblical name but no real historical existence."[153] Sayegh's careful and meticulous choice of words in his 1958 monograph *Arab Unity: Hope and Fulfillment* reflects the unfortunate sense in which the Arab nation had been "acted upon" from outside: "The western sector is geographical Syria, which in turn comprises the political entities which came to be known, after the First World

[147] See also Lawrence's colorful description of the peoples and geographies of Syria and its six main towns (Jerusalem, Homs, Aleppo, Damascus, Beirut, and Hama) in T.E. LAWRENCE, *Syria: The Raw Material, in* SECRET DESPATCHES FROM ARABIA AND OTHER WRITINGS 101 (Malcolm Brown ed., 1991) (Arab Bulletin, Mar. 12, 1917, Fragmentary Notes Written Early in 1915, But Not Circulated).

[148] ANTONIUS, *supra* note 12, at 352.

[149] *Id.* at 284.

[150] Memorandum Submitted by the Arab Higher Committee to the Permanent Mandates Commission and the Secretary of State for the Colonies, July 23, 1937, at 9. Interestingly, Philby predicted that the Arab State of Palestine as proposed by the Peel Report would inevitably unite with Syria. *See* Philby, *supra* note 99, at 164.

[151] "Geographically Palestine is part of Syria; its indigenous inhabitants belong to the Syrian branch of the Arab family of nations; all their culture and tradition link them to the other Arab peoples; and until 1917 Palestine formed part of the Ottoman Empire which included also several of the Arab countries." The Problem of Palestine, Evidence Submitted by the Arab Office, Jerusalem, to the Anglo-American Committee of Inquiry, March 1946, at 1 (1946).

[152] PHILIP K. HITTI, HISTORY OF SYRIA INCLUDING LEBANON AND PALESTINE 703 (1951).

[153] Philip K. Hitti, *The Possibility of Union Among the Arab States,* 48(4) AM. HIST. REV. 722, 727 (1943).

War, as Palestine, Transjordan, the Republic of Lebanon and the Republic of Syria proper."[154] Antonius, Hitti, and Sayegh were but three of the most important Arab scholars to present observations of the intimate territorial relationship of Palestine, and its Arabs, within Syria. They were uncontroversial at the time.[155]

As this section has shown, to the extent that one can identify a predominant national orientation, one is led to conclude that Palestinian Arabs tended to project a pan-Arab, and, more specifically, pan-Syrian, sense of national identity during the greater part of the Palestine Mandate, and any distinct national identity for Palestinian Arabs *qua* Palestinian Arabs was, at best, *in statu nascendi* at the time. This sense of national identity continued through the UNSCOP deliberations in 1947 and the United Nations' work on the question of Palestine up to the 1948 War. It is to these events that this chapter now turns.

V. The United Nations Special Committee on Palestine and the Drums of 1948

1945 saw the Second World War draw to a close and the United Nations replace the League of Nations as the world's foremost international organization. Two years later, head of the United Kingdom delegation to the United Nations Alexander Cadogan wrote to Victor Hoo, then Acting United Nations Secretary-General, about the Palestine question.[156] Cadogan promised an accounting of the United Kingdom's administration of the Mandate and asked that the General Assembly make recommendations for Palestine pursuant to article 10 of the Charter.[157] The General Assembly responded by meeting in special session and endorsed the British request while expounding upon certain particulars.

Adopted on May 15, 1947, General Assembly Resolution 106 created the UNSCOP, a special committee that would "have the widest powers to ascertain and record facts, and to investigate all questions and issues relevant to the problem of Palestine."[158] One of the most contentious issues during the drafting stage was the insistence by the Arab States that the UNSCOP not only be tasked with examining the situation in Palestine generally, but also that it needed to focus particular attention on the "termination of the mandate over Palestine and the declaration of

[154] SAYEGH, *supra* note 83, at 4 n.1.

[155] *See* DANIEL PIPES, GREATER SYRIA: THE HISTORY OF AN AMBITION 64–71 (1992).

[156] *See* 1946–47 U.N.Y.B. 276–77.

[157] *See id.* at 276. "The General Assembly may discuss any questions or any matters within the scope of the present Charter or relating to the powers and functions of any organs provided for in the present Charter, and, except as provided in Article 12, may make recommendations to the Members of the United Nations or to the Security Council or to both on any such questions or matters." U.N. Charter art. 10. On the thinking behind the United Kingdom's entreaty to the United Nations, see CONOR CRUISE O'BRIEN, THE SIEGE: THE SAGA OF ISRAEL AND ZIONISM 271–77 (1986).

[158] G.A. Res. 106, at ¶ 2, U.N. Doc. A/RES/106 (May 15, 1947).

its independence."[159] The Arab world had been united in this goal for some time, a point that the AHC made clear in its official reply to the United Kingdom's White Paper of May 17, 1939: "The Arab people have expressed their will and said their word in a loud and decisive manner, and they are certain that with God's assistance they will reach the desired goal: PALESTINE SHALL BE INDEPENDENT WITHIN AN ARAB FEDERATION AND SHALL REMAIN FOREVER ARAB."[160] Although the General Assembly's final text excluded this express language pointing to independence, in no sense did consideration of independence fall outside of the UNSCOP's broadly-phrased terms of reference.[161] In fact, the UNSCOP's Report to the General Assembly (UNSCOP Report) would call for the independence of Palestine, though, to the obvious frustration of the Arab States, as two States, one majority Jewish, one majority Arab, not one.

The UNSCOP conducted its work over several months on three continents (at Lake Success and in Palestine, Beirut, and Geneva).[162] It published its work in a five-volume compendium in the autumn of 1947: volume one is the UNSCOP Report; volume two contains twenty-one annexes, an appendix, and maps; volumes three and four are the records of, respectively, the public and private hearings that UNCSOP held; and volume five indexes the UNSCOP Report and its various annexes.[163] Apart from the UNSCOP Report's obvious legal importance and the role that it played in sustaining the Peel Commission's basic conclusion that partition was indeed the "least worst" option for Palestine, a close reading of the concerns that the AHC expressed in the General Assembly immediately prior to the founding of the UNSCOP and volumes two, three, and four of the UNSCOP's work give one a clear sense of the national sentiments of Palestinian Arabs at the time. This material also reveals how internally divided the UNSCOP actually was and demonstrates the fundamentally divergent perspectives of the Jewish and Arab leaders who submitted evidence to the UNSCOP and the intimate bond of the Arabs of Palestine with the larger Arab world.

The UNSCOP began its work in May 1947 by reflecting upon the various proposals that had by that time been put forward with a view to settling the Palestine question. These included plans that had been suggested by commissions and the

[159] 1946–47 U.N.Y.B. 277.

[160] Reply of the Arab Higher Committee for Palestine to the White Paper Issued by the British Government of May 17, 1939, at 15. On the United Kingdom's White Paper of May 17, 1939, see Nevill Barbour, *The White Paper of 1939, in* From Haven to Conquest: Readings in Zionism and the Palestine Problem Until 1948 461 (Walid Khalidi ed., 2005).

[161] On the drafting of what was to become Resolution 106, see UNSCOP Report, *supra* note 104, at 1–3; 1946–47 U.N.Y.B. 277–303. *See also* General Assembly, 1(3) Int'l Org. 488, 488–91 (1947).

[162] *See* UNSCOP Report, *supra* note 104, at 3–9.

[163] *See id.;* United Nations Special Committee on Palestine, Report to the General Assembly: Volume II: Annexes, Appendix and Maps, U.N. Doc. A/364/Add.I (Sept. 9, 1947); United Nations Special Committee on Palestine, Report to the General Assembly: Volume III: Annex A: Oral Evidence Presented at Public Meetings, U.N. Doc. A/364/Add.2 (1947); United Nations Special Committee on Palestine, Report to the General Assembly: Volume IV: Annex B: Oral Evidence Presented at Private Meetings, U.N. Doc. A/364/Add.3 (1947); United Nations Special Committee on Palestine, Report to the General Assembly: Volume V: Index to the Report and Annexes, U.N. Doc. A/364/Add.4 (Oct. 9, 1947).

United Kingdom and proposals for a single Jewish or Arab State that had been put forward by, respectively, Jewish and Arab organizations.[164] At this initial stage of its work, the UNSCOP rejected plans that would have entrenched a single Jewish or Arab State in Palestine and, because they were viewed as unworkable, binational and cantonal alternatives.[165] It then proceeded by unanimously agreeing that the Palestine Mandate should end and that independence should be declared as soon as practicable, that a transitional period should take place between the end of the Mandate and full independence and that the administering authority during this time should be accountable to the United Nations and act on its behalf, that holy places and interests of a religious nature should be preserved and kept safe and accessible, that an international initiative should resolve the issue of displaced European Jews, that the new State or States in Palestine should be democratic, dedicated to peaceful relations with other States, and protective of minority rights, that Palestine's economic unity should be preserved, that capitulations should cease, and that the population in Palestine should cooperate with the United Nations and refrain from violence.[166]

Of the UNSCOP's eleven members, Canada, Czechoslovakia, Guatemala, the Netherlands, Peru, Sweden, and Uruguay formed the majority supporting the partition of Palestine with economic union between the two proposed States.[167] The majority plan cast the conflict as a "clash of two intense nationalisms"[168] and contended that only by partition could "these conflicting national aspirations find substantial expression and qualify both peoples to take their places as independent nations in the international community and in the United Nations."[169] Boundaries were set for the two proposed States,[170] and Jerusalem, given its religious and political significance, was to remain outside the sovereign control of either State but within the economic union between the two States and was to be governed by an international civil servant appointed by the United Nations Trusteeship Council.[171]

India, Iran, and Yugoslavia formed the minority within the UNSCOP that supported a federal State solution.[172] Like the majority partition plan, the minority

[164] *See* UNSCOP Report, *supra* note 104, at 39–41.

[165] *See id.* at 42.

[166] *See id.* at 42–46. Guatemala and Uruguay were the only members of the UNSCOP that opposed a further recommendation to the effect that the UNSCOP's findings would not be considered a solution to what was described as "the Jewish problem in general." *Id.* at 46.

[167] *See id.* at 47–58.

[168] *Id.* at 47.

[169] *Id.* To the extent that they were meant in a legal sense, the words "peoples" and "nations" were not used here as carefully as they might have been. It is unclear whether the Arab "people[ ]" alluded to was meant to imply the existence of a discrete Palestinian Arab population in the sense of having an identity distinct from other Arab peoples; the use of the word "nations in the international community and in the United Nations" was likely meant to refer to the more juridically correct notion of "States."

[170] *See id.* at 53–56.

[171] *See id.* at 57–58.

[172] *See id.* at 59–64. Although serving on the UNSCOP, Australia refused to support either plan as a matter of principle. *See* United Nations Special Committee on Palestine, Report to the General Assembly, Volume II, *supra* note 163, at 23.

federal State plan cast the conflict as one of two nationalisms, but even though the UNSCOP minority shared this first principle with the UNSCOP majority, it took a fundamentally different approach to resolving the question of Palestine. Rather than proposing the partition of Palestine into a State with an Arab majority population and a State with a Jewish majority population, the UNSCOP minority argued that a federal plan would give the "most feasible recognition to the nationalistic aspirations of both Arabs and Jews, and [...] merge them into a single loyalty and patriotism which would find expression in an independent Palestine."[173] Interestingly, in recommending a transitional period of at most three years to precede the creation of the proposed federal State of Palestine, the UNSCOP minority noted that independence was a right of the "peoples of Palestine."[174] This suggests that the Jews and Arabs of Palestine were indeed distinct peoples, though it is important to recognize that this language does not as such imply that the Palestinian Arabs were a people distinct from the Arab people in the region at large. On the question of Jerusalem, the UNSCOP minority proposed that the city be administratively divided into two municipalities, with the Arab majority municipality to include the Old City and with both municipalities to together comprise the capital of Palestine.[175] An international commission was to be established to deal with the question of Jewish immigration to the Jewish sector of the proposed federal State, and such immigration would be permitted not as of right but, rather, on the basis of the "absorptive capacity of the Jewish state in the independent State of Palestine."[176] In the end, the General Assembly adopted Resolution 181, which rejected the federal State solution and accepted the plan for partition, with the United Nations Palestine Commission being established to facilitate the transition to independence.[177]

The AHC refused to cooperate with the UNSCOP.[178] Like the Arab States, it had wanted the General Assembly to have facilitated the independence of Palestine as a matter of utmost urgency rather than establish the UNSCOP to examine the question of Palestine *de novo.*[179] Even though it did not cooperate with the UNSCOP, the AHC issued *The Palestine Arab Case* in April 1947, a statement in which it noted that: "Neither at that juncture [i.e., the final days of the Ottoman Empire] nor before was Palestine a unit in itself."[180] "In those days, the name 'Palestine' was

[173] UNSCOP Report, *supra* note 104, at 59.

[174] *Id.* at 60.

[175] *See id.* at 63.

[176] *Id.* at 64.

[177] *See* G.A. Res. 181, U.N. Doc. A/RES/181 (Nov. 29, 1947). On the UNSCOP and partition, see Henry Cattan, *Recollections on the United Nations Resolution to Partition Palestine,* 4 PAL. Y.B. INT'L L. 260 (1987); Nabil Elaraby, *Some Legal Implications of the 1947 Partition Resolution and the 1949 Armistice Agreements,* 33(1) LAW & CONTEMP. PROBS. 97, 97–103 (1968).

[178] *See* United Nations Special Committee on Palestine, Report to the General Assembly, Volume II, *supra* note 163, at 5–6.

[179] *See id.* at 1–2.

[180] The Palestine Arab Case: A Statement by The Arab Higher Committee (The Body Representing the Palestine Arabs) 4 (1947).

never mentioned, nor was the country ever known by it. It was considered as a part of Syria from which, in fact, it was separated by no natural barriers whatever."[181] The AHC continued by deliberately obfuscating any distinctions that might otherwise be said to exist between Syrians, Lebanese, and Palestinians as Arabs, characterizing them as being essentially cosmetic. They were all one, indistinguishable, "united by practically indissoluble commercial, agricultural and industrial relations, not to mention the equally close ties of language, interests, customs, traditions, religion and blood that bound them together."[182] The Arab Office in London published a similar view in 1947, reaffirming the "profound national and historical unity"[183] of Syria, Lebanon, Palestine, and Transjordan and referring to Palestine (and its Arabs) as not being distinct as such but, rather, as merely being "part of the Arab world."[184]

Although it did not cooperate with the UNSCOP, the AHC did express its views in the General Assembly during the debates prior to the UNSCOP's creation, and these views are revealing. Henry Cattan, speaking for the AHC at the General Assembly's first special session just a few days prior to the adoption of Resolution 106, decried that "our national patrimony [is] in danger."[185] Cattan, one of the most eloquent and gifted Arab lawyers in Palestine at the time, went on to make the completely accurate and historically uncontroversial point that Palestine, as it then existed in 1947, had prior to the First World War been part of the Ottoman province of Syria.[186] The irony in this statement should not be lost. In arguing for the independence of Palestine as it then was as a geographical entity (with an Arab majority), Cattan was essentially arguing that what was by his own admission a small part (Palestine) of a larger geographical whole (Syria) was entitled to independence while at the same time refusing to countenance the possibility of a Jewish State in even a small part of that small part.

The evidence that the Arab States gave before the UNSCOP indicates that they did not consider the Arabs of Palestine to be a distinct people. Indeed, Palestinian Arabs were portrayed as being part of the larger Arab whole, the larger Arab nation. Lebanon, representing the Arab States during the public phase of the UNSCOP's oral hearings on July 22, 1947, spoke of the Zionist presence in Palestine as a foreign one intent on disturbing peace and human rights and portrayed it as that "method of pressing [...] claims on the basis of religious grounds and that theory of the lords of races who caused the most terrible war in history [i.e., the Second World War]."[187] An independent Jewish State in Palestine, Lebanon continued,

[181] *Id.*

[182] *Id.*

[183] ARAB OFFICE, THE FUTURE OF PALESTINE 3 (reprint 1976) (1947).

[184] *Id.* at 4.

[185] U.N. GAOR, U.N. Doc. A/C.1/PV.48 (May 7, 1947), http://unispal.un.org/UNISPAL.NSF/0/1343338D30D39DCF85256E5C00578E01.

[186] *See id.*

[187] United Nations Special Committee on Palestine, Report to the General Assembly, Volume III, *supra* note 163, at 241.

could simply not be countenanced for political, economic, cultural, and ethnic reasons.[188] In other words, Jews did not have a colorable claim to Palestine in any juridical sense as a people and could only be accommodated as one would accommodate a religious or ethnic minority.

The oral evidence that the Arab States gave to the UNSCOP at its private hearings showed a clear fear of Zionism and an insistence that Palestine could not be anything other than Arab, both as an entity (in the juridical sense, as a State) and as a people (the Arabs (of Palestine), as a majority). Iraq reiterated the point that the AHC had made in *The Palestine Arab Case* that Palestine and Syria were indistinguishable. Palestine, according to Iraq, was "only the southern part of the whole of natural and historical Syria. Nationally, the indigenous people of Palestine are one and the same people as those of Syria, and culturally and nationally united with the rest of the Arab world."[189] "Nationally," in other words, the Arabs of Palestine and the Arabs of Syria were the same "people," and in no sense could they be understood as being anything other than the same. At the same time that it dispelled any notion that Palestinian Arabs were distinct from their Arab brothers and sisters in the region, Iraq also denied the peoplehood of the Jews. Iraq further made the point that the nationalism of Palestinian Arabs was "directly connected with all the Arab world."[190] A few minutes earlier, Iraqi representative Fadel Jamali expressly stated that the Arabs of Iraq and the Arabs of Palestine formed "one nation."[191] As Jamali put it to the UNSCOP: "We consider Moslems, Christians and Jews as Arabs. We consider them all Arabs, all Iraqis."[192] While many Muslims and Christians would obviously identify themselves as Arab, few Jews, any more than Turks or Kurds, would do so, and to insist that Jews are Arabs is to also dispel the *raison d'être* of Zionism, that is, the national liberation movement of the Jewish people.

That these were the views of Iraq before the UNSCOP was hardly surprising, particularly given a very detailed memorandum explaining the Arab view that Iraqi General Nuri as-Sa'id had sent to the Rt. Hon. R.G. Casey, the British Minister of State in Cairo, just four years earlier. In that memorandum, Nuri stressed that Syria, Lebanon, Palestine, and Transjordan were "not distinguishable from each other."[193] As he put it, Syria was one, though the Mandate system had temporarily divided it into two halves, a northern (French-controlled) half and a southern (British-controlled) half. Nuri referred to the Mandate for Syria and the Lebanon as "Northern Syria" and to the Palestine Mandate (including Transjordan) as "Southern Syria," and Palestine was identified as one of Syria's

[188] *See id.* at 244.

[189] United Nations Special Committee on Palestine, Report to the General Assembly, Volume IV, *supra* note 163, at 50.

[190] *Id.* at 55.

[191] *Id.* at 51.

[192] *Id.* at 34.

[193] Nuri as-Sa'id, Arab Independence and Unity 1 (1943).

"integral part[s]."[194] To dispel the notion that nationalism in the Arab world could be sensibly understood as one might approach the question of national identity within the context of the European nation-State system, Nuri counseled his British colleague that nationalism in the Arab world was not confined to borders but, rather, transcended them.[195]

Unsurprisingly, Syria echoed the view that Palestine was but a geographical space within a larger Arab whole. As Syrian representative Emir Adel Arslan framed the issue in his evidence before the UNSCOP, the question of Palestine was, for Arabs, a question of "national dignity."[196] This, of course, points to a notion of the nation, for Arabs, that quite clearly transcends the borders of Palestine as a geographical space and makes it difficult to conclude that Palestinian Arabs existed as a people in the juridical sense except as mediated through Arabs outside of the Palestine Mandate. Less than three months earlier, Syria had made the point in the General Assembly that Syria was the "motherland of Palestine"[197] and that, based upon historical, geographical, religious, and racial links, "[t]here is no distinction whatever between the [Arab] Palestinians and the Syrians."[198] The similarity between the Arab view before the UNSCOP and Prime Minister Meir's as cited at the beginning of this chapter on the question of Palestinian Arab national identity could not be clearer.

Lebanon, again representing the Arab States, spoke before the UNSCOP on July 23, 1947. In response to a question about the viability of a Jewish State in Palestine, Foreign Minister Hamid Frangie denied that such a State would or could be viable. This was so, according to Frangie, because "[t]he surrounding Arab countries would never accept surrendering part of their territory for the creation of a Jewish State."[199] Clearly, this reflects a view of Palestine as Arab patrimony, as much a part of the Arab world and as Arab territory as the independent Arab States in the region were at the time. As Syria would put it just a few minutes later in the General Assembly, a Jewish State in all or part of Palestine would violate not the rights of the Palestinian Arabs as a people as such but, rather, the rights of the Arab States, "their rights, their aspirations, and their interests."[200]

In light of the fact that the Arab States were unanimous in their evidence before the UNSCOP that they did not consider the Arabs of Palestine to be a distinct

[194] *Id.* at 4.

[195] *See id.* at 8.

[196] United Nations Special Committee on Palestine, Report to the General Assembly, Volume IV, *supra* note 163, at 40. "All the Arab States consider that the establishment of the Jewish State in Palestine would constitute a violation of their rights, their aspirations, and their interests. Therefore it would be difficult, first of all, for them not to defend themselves, and further, to prevent an even more violent movement being the reaction." *Id.* at 41.

[197] U.N. GAOR, U.N. Doc. A/PV.78 (May 14, 1947), http://unispal.un.org/UNISPAL.NSF/0/0505FD58B778B90B852571D4004BF3E9.

[198] *Id.*

[199] United Nations Special Committee on Palestine, Report to the General Assembly, Volume IV, *supra* note 163, at 37.

[200] *Id.* at 41.

people and considering that the general tenor of the AHC's statements at the time are consistent with this sense of Arab national identity, it is difficult to understand the following sentence, inserted without deep explanation, in the UNSCOP Report: "Palestinian nationalism, as distinct from Arab nationalism, is itself a relatively new phenomenon, which appeared only after the division of the 'Arab rectangle' by the settlement of the First World War."[201] Firstly, the use of the word "Palestinian" to describe any type of "nationalism" during the Mandate is itself misleading given that Jews and Arabs in Palestine were both "Palestinian."[202] This sentence in the UNSCOP Report could conceivably be interpreted to mean that there was no discernible sense of nationalism of any sort among Palestinian Arabs prior to the Mandate. On this view, there would also clearly have been no sense of distinct national identity for Palestinian Arabs *qua* Palestinian Arabs at the time. Alami takes this view a step further in arguing that, as the events of 1947 led to 1948 and ensuing armed conflict between the Jewish State and its Arab neighbors, Palestinian Arabs only managed to organize themselves locally and without unity, with no general command structure or group effort,[203] hardly a convincing manifestation of a distinctly Palestinian Arab national identity or indicative of what Crossman refers to as the quintessential test of "nationhood": "war. The community must show that it is worthy of nationhood by fighting for its existence, even when the chances of survival are small."[204] Even if one accepts the accuracy of the

[201] UNSCOP Report, *supra* note 104, at 34.

[202] Needless to say, these groups had no discernible sense of shared Palestinian national identity. *See* Peel Report, *supra* note 99, at 120 (arguing that: "It is time, surely, that Palestinian 'citizenship' also should be recognized as what it is, as nothing but a legal formula devoid of moral meaning").

[203] *See* Alami, *supra* note 79, at 374. Similarly, Nasser's lament at Cairo's Officers' Club in late April 1959 criticized the Arab States that had intervened in Palestine for "not [being] under the unified flag of Arab nationalism, but torn by internal feuds, jealousies and rancour. We were seven armies fighting in Palestine under 6 or 7 different and separate commands. The great tragedy which befell the Arab nation was a direct result of the jealous ambitions between the different commands." Speech by President J. 'Abd an-Nasir at the Officers' Club, Cairo, Apr. 25, 1959, *in* 2 THE ARAB STATES AND THE ARAB LEAGUE, *supra* note 134, at 975, 977. Karsh argues that Palestinian Arab society collapsed at this time due to its "total lack of national cohesion or willingness to subordinate personal interest to the general good [...] There was no sense of an overarching mutual interest or shared destiny. Cities and towns acted as if they were self-contained units, attending to their own needs and eschewing the smallest sacrifice on behalf of other localities." EFRAIM KARSH, PALESTINE BETRAYED 239–40 (2011). *See* Efraim Karsh, *The Myth of Palestinian Centrality*, at 10–15 (Begin-Sadat Center for Strategic Studies Mideast Security and Policy Studies No. 108, 2014). *See also* Benny Morris, *The 1948 War Was an Islamic Holy War*, 17(3) MID. E. Q. 63, 68–69 (2010) (as regards 1948, noting that "National political awareness was then quite weak among the Palestinians, and this casts much doubt indeed on the credibility of the concept of the 'Palestinian people' in 1948. This was hardly something clear or palpable then, but it took hold later"). For a somewhat broader historical perspective, consider Lawrence's view, written early in 1915. *See* LAWRENCE, *supra* note 147, at 107 (Arab Bulletin, Mar. 12, 1917, Fragmentary Notes Written Early in 1915, But Not Circulated) (stating that: "There is no national feeling [in Syria, understanding Syria, as Lawrence did, as including the six main towns of Jerusalem, Homs, Aleppo, Damascus, Beirut, and Hama]. Between town and town, village and village, family and family, creed and creed, exist intimate jealousies, sedulously fostered by the Turks to render a spontaneous union impossible. The largest indigenous political entity in settled Syria is only the village under its sheikh, and in patriarchal Syria the tribe under its chief").

[204] RICHARD H.S. CROSSMAN, A NATION REBORN: A PERSONAL REPORT ON THE ROLES PLAYED BY WEIZMANN, BEVIN AND BEN-GURION IN THE STORY OF ISRAEL 86 (1960).

aforementioned sentence in the UNSCOP Report, it should be recognized that it does not imply that Palestinian Arabs identified themselves primarily as Palestinian Arabs, that is, that they identified themselves as Palestinian Arabs more than they did as part of the larger pan-Arab, and, more specifically, pan-Syrian, nation (if nationalism is itself an appropriate concept in this context). On balance, one should approach this isolated sentence with a degree of skepticism.[205]

VI. Conclusion

Writing in the wake of the rebirth of the Jewish State and the defeat of the Arabs, Alami observed: "The people are in great need of a 'myth' to fill their consciousness and imagination: a myth of which they dream in times of peace and in times of trouble, because it gives their life meaning and gives them self-respect and freedom."[206] Nationalism, or, more specifically, a group's sense that it possesses a distinct national identity, can indeed serve a "mythic" function. Whether understood as "national consciousness"[207] or "entity-consciousness,"[208] a group's sense of distinct national identity often reflects a yearning for a form of personality and recognition on the international plane. While a group purporting to be a "people" is free to claim, *proprio motu*, its "peoplehood," international law will not recognize it as such absent the international community's ratification of this claim. It is the merger of subjective belief and objective verification that a "people" makes.[209]

The Mandate system was an administrative arrangement peculiar to the inter-war years. As this chapter has attempted to show by reference to the terms of the

[205] Also not to be overlooked is the following observation by United Nations Mediator in Palestine, Count Folke Bernadotte, shortly before his assassination in September 1948: "The Palestine Arabs have at present no will of their own. Neither have they ever developed any specifically Palestinian nationalism. The demand for a separate Arab State in Palestine is consequently relatively weak. It would seem as though in existing circumstances most of the Palestinian Arabs would be quite content to be incorporated in Transjordan." FOLKE BERNADOTTE, TO JERUSALEM 113 (Joan Bulman trans., 1951).

[206] Alami, *supra* note 79, at 396.

[207] Leo Pinsker, *Auto-Emancipation: An Appeal to His People by a Russian Jew (1882), in* THE ZIONIST IDEA, *supra* note 73, at 181, 189.

[208] KHALIDI, *supra* note 135, at 172.

[209] Dinstein defines the subjective element as an existing state of mind or ethos and the objective element as the existence of an ethnic group with links of a common history. *See* Yoram Dinstein, *Collective Human Rights of Peoples and Minorities*, 25(1) INT'L & COMP. L.Q. 102, 104 (1976). *See also* Kevin Mgwanga Gunme et al. v. Cameroon, Afr. Comm'n Hum. & Peoples'Rts., at ¶ 179, No. 266/03 (2009); Tal Becker, *Self-Determination in Perspective: Palestinian Claims to Statehood and the Realty of the Right to Self-Determination*, 32(2) ISR. L. REV. 301, 326–27 (1998). It is useful to compare this with Skordas' conception of the "self," which he frames as the "clash between the existential political will of the group exercising the *pouvoir constituant*, and the negative or positive response of the various actors of the international community, that leads to the recognition or non-recognition of the self-determination unit or the new state." Achilles Skordas, *Self-Determination of Peoples and Transnational Regimes: A Foundational Principle of Global Governance, in* TRANSNATIONAL CONSTITUTIONALISM: INTERNATIONAL AND EUROPEAN MODELS 207, 209 (Nicholas Tsagourias ed., 2007).

Palestine Mandate and an appreciation for geopolitical developments and the official statements of Arab leaders and scholars at the time, the Mandate years saw little in the way of a distinct national identity for Palestinian Arabs *qua* Palestinian Arabs. This conclusion is further supported by evidence that States gave to the UNSCOP in 1947 and the United Nations' work on the question of Palestine up to the 1948 War. It seems reasonable to conclude, more or less, that the Mandate years were a period in which Palestinian Arabs' national identity was primarily pan-Arab, and, more specifically, pan-Syrian, in orientation. The next almost three-decade period, between the 1948 War and the 1973 War, would see little change in this regard, though this same period would witness, in 1973, the introduction of a negotiation paradigm.

3

From Disparate Means of Dispute Settlement to the Introduction of a Negotiation Imperative: 1948–1973

I. Introduction

Few observers were genuinely surprised when the broader Arab world made good on its threats of violence in the wake of United Nations General Assembly Resolution 181. The outrage was palpable, the threats to Jewish bodily integrity real. Shortly before the adoption of Resolution 181, Arab League Secretary-General Abdul Rahman Azzam predicted a "war of extermination and momentous massacre which will be spoken of like the Tartar massacre or the Crusader wars."[1] This did not seem altogether out of the question. After all, when the Jewish People's Council declared the establishment of the Jewish State a few months later, "by virtue of our natural and historic right and on the strength of the resolution of the United Nations General Assembly [i.e., Resolution 181],"[2] the response of Arab nationalists, *jihadists*, and the regular armed forces of a coalition of Arab States was to intervene in Palestine rather than accept the partition plan's call for two States for two peoples, one majority Jewish, one majority Arab. Certainly, the intervening Arab States had their own geopolitical interests in intervening in Palestine. In many respects, the *raison d'État* seemed to dictate asserting control of Palestine for their

[1] David Barnett & Efraim Karsh, *Azzam's Genocidal Threat*, 18(4) MID. E. Q. 85, 87 (2011) (citing Mustafa Amin, *A War of Extermination*, AKHBAR AL-YOM, Oct. 11, 1947). *See* Paul Seabury, *The League of Arab States: Debacle of a Regional Arrangement*, 3(4) INT'L ORG. 633, 637–39 (1949) (articulating the League of Arab States' position on the Palestine question). On the League of Arab States generally, see PHILIPPE SANDS & PIERRE KLEIN, BOWETT'S LAW OF INTERNATIONAL INSTITUTIONS 241–44 (6th ed. 2009).

[2] Declaration of the Establishment of the State of Israel, 14 May 1948, *in* THE ARAB-ISRAEL CONFLICT AND ITS RESOLUTION: SELECTED DOCUMENTS 61, 62 (Ruth Lapidoth & Moshe Hirsch eds., 1992) (capitals omitted). For a recent study that explores how Hersch Lauterpacht's (rejected) draft Israeli Declaration of Independence reflected an uneasy discourse of effectiveness and justice, see Eliav Lieblich & Yoram Shachar, *Cosmopolitanism at a Crossroads: Hersch Lauterpacht and the Israeli Declaration of Independence*, 84 BRIT. Y.B. INT'L L. 1 (2014).

own particular advantage.[3] Many of the Arab and Muslim fighters who streamed into Palestine had much more sinister and arguably genocidal intentions, however, since many of them were inspired by the sentiments then prevailing in Palestine's Arab press[4] and the call to force that Hassan al-Banna made in early August 1948: "If the Jewish state becomes a fact, and this is realized by the Arab peoples, they will drive the Jews who live in their midst into the sea."[5]

Fighting between Jews and Arabs continued from 1948 through hesitant truces into 1949 and would not end until Israel and Egypt, Lebanon, Jordan, and Syria signed a series of bilateral armistice agreements between February and July 1949.[6] United Nations Security Council Resolution 62 of November 16, 1948, ordered the directly involved parties to sign armistice agreements, as a vehicle for "permanent peace."[7] Even though the Arab States parties to these agreements were adamant that they should not in any way be construed as reflecting Arab recognition of Israel, there was no question that the agreements were subject to the law of treaties and had legally-binding force. The main objective of the armistice agreements was to freeze the opposing forces' existing positions on the ground, and there was no suggestion that these lines were to be permanent political borders between sovereign States. Indeed, the treaty language was quite expressly to the contrary,[8] and as United States Secretary of State John Foster Dulles observed in an address to the Council on Foreign Relations in 1955: "They were not designed to be permanent frontiers in every respect; in part, at least, they reflected the status of the fighting at the moment."[9] Clearly, the 1948 War showed that the United Nations'

[3] *See* Arab League, 2(2) INT'L ORG. 378 (1948). Immediately prior to the General Assembly's adoption of Resolution 186 on May 14, 1948, discussed *infra* (section III of this chapter), the Soviet delegate observed that: "For strange and somewhat obscure reasons, the representatives of the Arab States did not support the creation of an Arab State in Palestine." U.N. GAOR, at 38, U.N. Doc. A/PV.135 (May 14, 1948).

[4] *See* United Nations Palestine Commission, Excerpts from the Arab Press of Palestine, U.N. Doc. P/40 (Apr. 2, 1948). An editorial in *Ad-Difa'a* from March 3, 1948, is typical: "We are decisively determined finally to get rid of the Jewish danger—no state, no political existence, no immigration and nothing whatsoever. Our determination is decisive [...] We shall never reach a settlement with the Jews; the sole settlement we have decided to reach is the final elimination of the Jewish danger. This is the fact of all facts and this is what requires our utmost concern. There is no rest or future for us without it." *Id.* at 1–2.

[5] Dana Adams Schmidt, *Aim to Oust Jews Pledged by Sheikh; Head of Moslem Brotherhood Says U.S., British "Politics" Has Hurt Palestine Solution*, N.Y. TIMES, Aug. 2, 1948. Al-Banna was the influential founder and leader of the Muslim Brotherhood. *See generally* Joseph S. Spoerl, *Palestinians, Arabs, and the Holocaust*, 26(1–2) JEWISH POL. STUD. REV. 14 (2014). *See also Benny Morris: "The 1948 War Was an Islamic Holy War,"* 17(3) MID. E. Q. 63 (2010).

[6] For historical background, see SHABTAI ROSENNE, ISRAEL'S ARMISTICE AGREEMENTS WITH THE ARAB STATES 9–23 (1951). *See also* Nabil Elaraby, *Some Legal Implications of the 1947 Partition Resolution and the 1949 Armistice Agreements*, 33(1) LAW & CONTEMP. PROBS. 97, 104–108 (1968); TRYGVE LIE, IN THE CAUSE OF PEACE: SEVEN YEARS WITH THE UNITED NATIONS 174–98 (1954).

[7] S.C. Res. 62, U.N. Doc. S/RES/62 (Nov. 16, 1948).

[8] *See* Egyptian-Israeli General Armistice Agreement, Rhodes, Feb. 24, 1949, art. 5(2); Lebanese–Israeli General Armistice Agreement, Ras En Naqoura, Mar. 23, 1949, art. 2(2); Hashemite Jordan Kingdom–Israel: General Armistice Agreement, Rhodes, Apr. 3, 1949, art. 2(2); Israeli-Syrian General Armistice Agreement, Hill 232, Near Mahanayim, July 20, 1949, art. 2(2).

[9] U.S. Proposals for a Settlement of the Arab–Israeli Conflict: Address by Secretary Dulles to the Council on Foreign Relations, Aug. 26, 1955, *in* 2 THE ARAB STATES AND THE ARAB LEAGUE:

attempt to partition Palestine was, if not necessarily undesirable in principle, certainly ill-suited to the particular historical moment.

This chapter examines the various means of dispute settlement that were attempted between the 1948 War and the 1973 War. During this almost three-decade period, the international community encouraged Israel and the Arab States to settle their dispute using various means of dispute settlement, often in combination with one another: a form of inquiry, through the Security Council's Questionnaire of May 18, 1948; mediation, through the United Nations Mediator on Palestine; and conciliation, through the establishment of the United Nations Conciliation Commission for Palestine. Each of these methods is examined in the first three sections of this chapter. The final two sections look at the rejectionist posture of the Arab world during this same period and the introduction of a negotiation imperative in 1973. None of these attempts at dispute settlement resolved the Palestine question, but they clarified the positions of the parties and reflected unfolding understandings of the main issues between the sides.

II. The Onset of War in Palestine and the United Nations Security Council's Questionnaire of May 18, 1948

The previous chapter concluded that very little in the way of a distinct national identity for Palestinian Arabs *qua* Palestinian Arabs emerged during the Mandate years. This generally continued between the end of the 1948 War and the 1973 War, when the opposing parties to the conflict were consistently framed as Israel and the Arab States rather than also acknowledging the existence of a conflict between Israel and the Palestinians.[10] As Rabinovich writes, this period was one in which Palestinians were "absent from the Middle Eastern arena as an independent force. They were crushed, fragmented, and dispersed."[11] The traditional

A Documentary Record 638, 640 (Muhammad Khalil ed., 1962). *See* Stephen M. Schwebel, *What Weight to Conquest?*, 64(2) Am. J. Int'l L. 344, 347 n.8 (1970). Writing in 1981, Jordanian Crown Prince Hassan bin Talal made the point that the armistice lines, "sometimes erroneously referred to as 'borders', were temporary and military in nature and did not establish permanent borders." Hassan bin Talal, Palestinian Self-Determination: A Study of the West Bank and Gaza Strip 38 (1981). One does not risk conflict with the legal principle *lex retro non agit* when one quotes from a 1998 arbitral award with respect to armistice agreements generally: "Armistice agreements are instruments directed to stopping or containing hostilities and not to acknowledging or denying sovereign title." Territorial Sovereignty and Scope of the Dispute, Phase One (Eri./Yemen) (1998), 114 I.L.R. 1, 58 (1999).

[10] *See* Sari Nusseibeh, What Is a Palestinian State Worth? 40 (2011) (making this point with respect to the period between the 1948 War and the 1967 War). *See also* Herbert C. Kelman, *Some Determinants of the Oslo Breakthrough*, 2(2) Int'l Negot. 183, 184–89 (1997); Omar M. Dajani, *Stalled Between Seasons: The International Legal Status of Palestine During the Interim Period*, 26(1) Denv. J. Int'l L. & Pol'y 27, 40–41 (1997).

[11] Itamar Rabinovich, Waging Peace: Israel and the Arabs, 1948–2003 247 (2004). Rabinovich specifically demarcates this period as between 1949, when the armistice agreements were signed, and 1964, when the PLO was formed.

elites discredited, the younger generation of Palestinian activists subsumed their particularism within larger notions of Arab unity and redemption across borders.[12] Given that this was largely the national sentiment of Palestinian Arabs before the 1948 War, it is not altogether surprising that these trends would continue for some time after what Palestinians refer to as *al-Nakba*, or "catastrophe."

The 1948 War was really one that began in 1947, spanned approximately two years, and ended with the armistice agreements of 1949. Between roughly mid spring 1947 and mid spring 1948, it was largely confined to the borders of Palestine,[13] and it was during this time that it became the subject of repeated appeals for calm by the Security Council.[14] The 1948 War became internationalized right after Israel's declaration of independence on May 14, when a coalition of Arab States intervened in Palestine "on behalf of" its Arab population.[15] This was not wholly unexpected given the nature of Arab evidence before the United Nations Special Committee on Palestine (UNSCOP) less than a year earlier. And the Arab States were even clearer as to their intentions less than a month after the adoption of Resolution 181, issuing a statement that included the following language: "[T]he Arabs have firmly resolved to enter the battle which has been imposed upon them, and, God willing, to proceed with it to its successful end."[16]

The Arab League adopted a formal declaration of war on May 15.[17] This declaration conveyed a history of Palestine since Ottoman times that was one of utter betrayal by the United Kingdom, the League of Nations, and the United Nations, as well as Jewish duplicity.[18] Given that the Mandate had ended "without there being a legitimate constitutional authority in the country, which would safeguard the maintenance of security and respect for law and which would protect the lives and properties of the inhabitants,"[19] the declaration called for political power to immediately vest in Palestine's majority (Arab) population and warned that the

[12] *See id.* at 247–48.

[13] *But see* United Nations Palestine Commission, First Special Report to the Security Council: The Problem of Security in Palestine, at 4–9, U.N. Doc. A/AC.21/9 (Feb. 16, 1948).

[14] *See* S.C. Res. 42, U.N. Doc. S/RES/42 (Mar. 5, 1948); S.C. Res. 43, U.N. Doc. S/RES/43 (Apr. 1, 1948); S.C. Res. 46, U.N. Doc. S/RES/46 (Apr. 17, 1948); S.C. Res. 48, U.N. Doc. S/RES/48 (Apr. 23, 1948).

[15] For one of many accounts of the 1948 War, see EFRAIM KARSH, PALESTINE BETRAYED (2011).

[16] Statement by the Arab Governments Condemning the Palestine Partition Resolution, Dec. 17, 1947, *in* 2 THE ARAB STATES AND THE ARAB LEAGUE, *supra* note 9, at 550, 551. *See* Defending Palestine, Oct. 9, 1947, *in* 2 THE ARAB STATES AND THE ARAB LEAGUE, *supra* note 9, at 164.

[17] *See* Statement Issued by the Governments of the Arab League States on the Occasion of the Entry of the Arab Armies into Palestine, May 15, 1948, *in* 2 THE ARAB STATES AND THE ARAB LEAGUE, *supra* note 9, at 557. For background to this, see Paper by the Foreign Office Research Department, Sept. 30, 1948, FO 371/68382, *in* 6 THE ARAB LEAGUE: BRITISH DOCUMENTARY SOURCES: 1943–1963 153, 154–58 (Anita L.P. Burdett ed., 1995).

[18] *Cf.* Alexandria Protocol, Alexandria, Oct. 7, 1944, *in* 2 THE ARAB STATES AND THE ARAB LEAGUE, *supra* note 9, at 53, 55–56 (Special Resolution Concerning Palestine); Covenant of the League of Arab States, Cairo, Mar. 22, 1945, *in* 2 THE ARAB STATES AND THE ARAB LEAGUE, *supra* note 9, at 56, 61 (Special Appendix Relating to Palestine).

[19] Statement, *supra* note 17, at 559.

"aggressive intentions and the imperialistic designs of the Zionists"[20] had been exposed through grave disruption and disorder.[21] Chaos threatened to spread throughout the broader Arab world, furthermore, "where feeling is running high because of the events in Palestine."[22]

The Arab League's declaration described the situation as a "threat to peace and security in the area as a whole and (also) in each of them [i.e., the Arab States] taken separately"[23] and said that the Arab League constituted a regional arrangement in the sense of Chapter VIII of the Charter of the United Nations (Charter).[24] The declaration clarified that an Arab intervention in Palestine was necessary "solely in order to help its inhabitants restore peace and security and the rule of justice and law to their country, and in order to prevent bloodshed";[25] Palestinian independence had become an "accomplished fact."[26] At the end of its declaration, the Arab League emphasized that security in Palestine formed a "sacred trust in the hands of the Arab States."[27] This language recalls the language of article 22(1) of the Covenant of the League of Nations,[28] but just as importantly, and perhaps because of this, it shows that the centrality of Palestine as "sacred trust" to the broader Arab world and to the legitimacy of the Arab League itself could hardly be exaggerated.

Faced with escalating unrest in Palestine and no signs of rapprochement between the Arab and Jewish sides, the United Nations tried a number of different means to settle the dispute, or at least to pave the way for an eventual settlement of it. On May 18, 1948, the Security Council addressed a series of urgent questions to the Arab and Jewish sides.[29] The Arab States were asked whether their regular armed forces or sponsored irregular armed forces were operating in Palestine, if so, on what basis they were doing so and the nature of their military objectives, who was responsible for political functions in Arab majority areas of Palestine and whether such political representatives were negotiating with Jewish authorities, and whether Jewish forces had violated their, that is, the Arab States', international borders.[30] The Arab Higher Committee (AHC) was asked whether,

[20] *Id.* at 560.
[21] *See id.*
[22] *Id.*
[23] *Id.*
[24] *See* U.N. Charter arts 52–54. On Chapter VIII of the Charter of the United Nations, see Robert P. Barnidge, Jr, *The United Nations and the African Union: Assessing a Partnership for Peace in Darfur*, 14(1) J. Conflict & Sec. L. 93, 94–99 (2009).
[25] Statement, *supra* note 17, at 560.
[26] *Id.*
[27] *Id.*
[28] *See* Covenant of the League of Nations Adopted by the Peace Conference at Plenary Session, Apr. 28, 1919, 13(2) Am. J. Int'l L. Supp. 128, 137, art. 22(1) (1919) (stating as central to the Mandatory regime the "principle that the well-being and development of such peoples form a sacred trust of civilization").
[29] *See* Questions Addressed to the Governments of Egypt, Saudi Arabia, Transjordan, Iraq, Yemen, Syria and Lebanon, to the Arab Higher Committee and to the Jewish Authorities in Palestine Pursuant to the Decision of the Security Council Taken at the 295th Meeting Held on 18 May 1948, U.N. Doc. S/753 (May 18, 1948).
[30] *See id.* at 1.

with respect to areas of Palestine in which Arabs formed a majority, Jewish forces had asserted control, whether governmental functions related to public services and public order were in place, whether the AHC exercised political authority in Palestine, whether it had requested outside intervention and, if so, the reasons for this, and whether AHC representatives had been nominated to liaise with the Security Council Truce Commission for Palestine.[31] The Jewish side was asked eight questions, ranging from where its armed forces exercised control, whether in Jewish majority areas, Arab majority areas, or both, to whether it was negotiating with the Arab side, to whether an unconditional and immediate truce in Jerusalem and with respect to the Holy Places could be agreed to by the Jewish side.[32] The replies that the Arab and Jewish sides gave are instructive in that they reflected geopolitical developments on the ground and reveal the larger national trajectories within which all of the parties concerned understood the situation.

Firstly, consider the responses of the Arab States bordering Israel, which were also, of course, the same States that would go on to sign armistice agreements with the Jewish State during the first half of 1949. Egypt reaffirmed the Arab League's declaration of war and stated that it had intervened in Palestine to "put[] an end to the massacres perpetrated by the terrorist Zionist bands against Arabs and against humanity and of [*sic*] safeguard[] the lives and property of the inhabitants."[33] Cairo reaffirmed the unwavering Arab position in favor of a united Palestinian State and argued that Israel's declaration of independence as such "undoubtedly constitutes a menace to the security of Egypt and other Arab states neighbouring to Palestine."[34] Lebanon's reply held that the Arab League would not negotiate with the Zionists as long as they insisted upon a Jewish State and claimed that Lebanese armed forces were part of the larger Arab effort to "pacify Palestine."[35] According to Syria, Syrian troops had intervened to, *inter alia*, "restore law and order [... and] help their brethren, the Arabs of Palestine, in suppressing the armed insurrection of the Zionist bands of terrorists."[36] Syria, consistent with the nature of Arab evidence before the UNSCOP in July 1947, stressed that Palestine was in the nature of a national rather than an international concern for the Arab side. According to Damascus, Syria "consider[ed] Palestine an Arab territory linked with Syria and with the other Arab countries around it by all social, economic, political, racial,

[31] *See id.* at 1–2. Security Council Resolution 48 established the Security Council Truce Commission for Palestine on April 23. *See* S.C. Res. 48, U.N. Doc. S/RES/48 (Apr. 23, 1948).

[32] *See* Questions, *supra* note 29, at 2.

[33] Cablegram Dated 18 May 1948 from the President of the Security Council Addressed to the Foreign Minister of Egypt, and Reply Thereto Submitted by the Representative of Egypt at the Three Hundred and First Meeting of the Security Council, at 3, U.N. Doc. S/767 (May 22, 1948).

[34] *Id.* at 4.

[35] Cablegram Dated 18 May 1948 from the President of the Security Council Addressed to the Foreign Minister of Lebanon, and Reply Thereto Submitted by the Representative of Lebanon at the 301st Meeting of the Security Council, at 2, U.N. Doc. S/770 (May 22, 1948).

[36] Cablegram Dated 18 May 1948 from the President of the Security Council Addressed to the Foreign Minister of Syria, and Reply Thereto Submitted by the Representative of Syria at the 301st Meeting of the Security Council, at 2, U.N. Doc. S/768 (May 22, 1948).

geographical, linguistic and traditional inseparable links."[37] Transjordan refused to respond to the Security Council's questions out of protest at the body's failure to recommend its admission to the United Nations.[38] However, King Abdullah had cabled United Nations Secretary-General Trygve Lie on May 16 to justify Transjordan's entry into Palestine on the basis that it was protecting unarmed Arabs.[39]

Iraq, Saudi Arabia, and Yemen were the other Arab States to which the Security Council had addressed its questions. All of these States responded to the Security Council, though Yemen simply directed it to the Arab League.[40] Consistent with the Arab position that Palestine was *sine qua non* Arab and could not be conceived of otherwise or perceived in non-Arab terms, Iraq recoiled at how the Security Council's questionnaire had distinguished between Arab and Jewish areas of Palestine, since this was held to be presumptive and part of a "partitionist" mindset.[41] Iraq's military objectives were, according to Baghdad, the "suppression of lawless Zionist terrorism which was dangerously spreading all over the country, and the restoration of peace and order."[42] Iraq conveyed its refusal to negotiate "under threat of terrorism."[43] The Saudi response was along similar lines and identified Israel's declaration of independence as the root cause of the unrest in Palestine.[44]

The AHC confirmed that it had transferred and would continue to transfer all governmental functions related to public services and public order to the States of the Arab coalition as they entered Palestine.[45] The AHC described the Zionists as "invade[rs],"[46] "alien immigrants,"[47] "campaign[ers] of terrorism,"[48] and perpetrators of a "Jewish aggressive invasion of their [i.e., the Palestinians'] country."[49] This, of course, was the ultimate delegitimization of the presence of Jews as a

[37] *Id.*

[38] *See* Cablegram Dated 18 May 1948 from the President of the Security Council Addressed to the Foreign Minister of Transjordan, and Reply Thereto Dated 20 May 1948, U.N. Doc. S/760 (May 20, 1948). *See also* P.O. Humber, *Admission to the United Nations,* 24 Brit. Y.B. Int'l L. 90, 96 (1947).

[39] *See* Press Release, Transjordan Notifies UN of Armed Entry into Palestine, U.N. Doc. PAL/167 (May 16, 1948), http://unispal.un.org/unispal.nsf/9a798adbf322aff38525617b006d88d7/e2ab11675a195c3e85256a5700646474?OpenDocument.

[40] *See* Cablegram Dated 18 May 1948 from the President of the Security Council Addressed to the Foreign Minister of Yemen, and Reply Thereto Submitted by the Foreign Minister of Yemen on 23 May 1948, U.N. Doc. S/774 (May 24, 1948).

[41] *See* Cablegram Dated 18 May 1948 from the President of the Security Council Addressed to the Foreign Minister of Iraq, and Reply Thereto Submitted by the Representative of Iraq at the 301st Meeting of the Security Council, at 3, U.N. Doc. S/769 (May 22, 1948).

[42] *Id.*

[43] *Id.* at 6.

[44] *See* Cablegram Dated 18 May 1948 from the President of the Security Council Addressed to the Foreign Minister of Saudi Arabia, and Reply Thereto Submitted by the Representative of Saudi Arabia on 22 May 1948, at 3, U.N. Doc. S/772 (May 22, 1948).

[45] *See* Letter Dated 18 May 1948 from the Assistant Secretary-General for Security Council Affairs Addressed to the Arab Higher Committee, and Reply Dated 24 May 1948 Addressed to the Secretary General Concerning the Questions Submitted by the Security Council, at 2–3, U.N. Doc. S/775 (May 24, 1948).

[46] *Id.* at 4.

[47] *Id.*

[48] *Id.*

[49] *Id.* at 5.

"people," as opposed to a religious minority, in Palestine: without "peoplehood," to which and only to which the right of self-determination adheres, there could be no justification for a Jewish State.

The Arabs' replies to the Security Council reveal their justifications for intervening in Palestine and their understanding of how the conflict could be, indeed, should be, settled. Setting aside the argument that the Arab League in part seemed to justify its intervention on the basis of Chapter VIII of the Charter, the intervention could be seen, from the Arab perspective, as an assertion of collective self-defense. This view would seem to proceed on the basis that Palestine was a State, an Arab State, that had been attacked; that the AHC, on the basis that it was the *de jure* government of Palestine at the time,[50] had asked the Arab States for assistance in defending Palestine from the (creation of a) Jewish State in Palestine;[51] and that an Arab coalition had been assembled and entered Palestine on the basis of this request. Indeed, the AHC's language in a statement that it had submitted to Secretary-General Lie in February 1948 seemed to leave little doubt as to its self-defense rationale: the AHC "consider[ed] that any attempt by the Jews or any power or group of powers to establish a Jewish State in Arab territory is an act of aggression which will be resisted in self-defense by force."[52]

While it is true that the 1945 Covenant of the League of Arab States provides a mechanism for collective self-defense,[53] given the nature of article 103 of the Charter[54] and the fact that article 51 of the same instrument limits the "inherent right of individual or collective self-defense" to Member States of the United Nations and the fact that Palestine was not such a State, this justification for the use of force seems problematic. It is also questionable how the mere fact that Israel declared its independence and the Palestine Mandate ended could have qualified as an "armed attack," either singly or in combination, in the Charter sense of a "most grave form[] of the use of force."[55]

The Arab side also seemed to have viewed itself as engaging in a collective project of defense of (pseudo-)nationals (in the sense that Arab nationalism and Arab national identity penetrated the borders of Palestine), or perhaps even an

[50] *See* Covenant, *supra* note 18, at 61 (Special Appendix Relating to Palestine) (recognizing the *de jure* statehood of Palestine as an Arab majority State).

[51] *See* Letter, *supra* note 45, at 3 (informing the Security Council that it had made "recourse to the Arab League for assistance in the restoration of peace and order in the Holy Land").

[52] United Nations Palestine Commission, *supra* note 13, at 5. By contrast, Secretary-General Lie saw in the Arab intervention the "first armed aggression which the world had seen since the end of the war," LIE, *supra* note 6, at 174, something that elicited in the Security Council a "conspiracy of silence reminiscent of the most disheartening head-in-the-sand moments of the Chamberlain appeasement era." *Id.* at 175.

[53] *See* Covenant, *supra* note 18, at 58, art. 6. *See also id.* at 58, art. 5.

[54] "In the event of a conflict between the obligations of the Members of the United Nations under the present Charter and their obligations under any other international agreement, their obligations under the present Charter shall prevail." U.N. Charter art. 103.

[55] Military and Paramilitary Activities in and Against Nicaragua (Nicar. v. U.S.), 1986 I.C.J. 14, 101 (June 27). This analysis leaves aside the operation of self-defense under customary international law, which operates in parallel to the operation of article 51 of the Charter. *See id.* at 92–97.

early form of humanitarian intervention, during the 1948 War.[56] Certainly, given that force was used in Palestine rather than peaceful means of dispute settlement, the Arab intervention could hardly be seen as a form of diplomatic protection.[57] Transjordan justified its use of force on the basis that it had a "national duty towards Palestine in general and Jerusalem in particular and also Nazareth and Bethlehem."[58] Saudi Arabia said that the Arab fighters had entered Palestine to "help their brethren."[59] Egypt made clear that it did not view Palestinians as foreign, stating that Egyptians "do not regard Palestine Arabs as strangers, since they are from time immemorial strongly bound to them by many ties."[60] Reflecting the sense that an injury to Palestinians was an injury to Egyptians, Cairo went on to claim that: "Any aggression against Palestine Arabs and more particularly in the horrible and atrocious manner adopted by Zionist bands has its direct repercussion among the people of Egypt."[61] Iraq held a similar view.[62]

The AHC, too, did not seem to see the outside intervention as truly international. In a May 24 response to the Security Council, it reflected the Palestinian view that the Arabs in the Member States of the Arab League were "linked to them [i.e., the Palestinians] by all the ties of nationality and had only been segregated from them by the imperialistic ambitions of foreign powers."[63] The 1948 Progress Report of the United Nations Mediator on Palestine Submitted to the Secretary-General for Transmission to the Members of the United Nations (Progress Report) made a similar point about the justifications that the Arab States had given for their intervention in Palestine,[64] and resolutions had been adopted by the Arab

[56] *See* Two Memoranda Sent by the Political Committee of the Arab League to the U.N. Mediator (Bernadotte) and to the Security Council, Rejecting the Extension of the Truce, First Memorandum, July 8, 1948, *in* 2 The Arab States and the Arab League, *supra* note 9, at 563.

[57] In his comprehensive monograph on the subject, Amerasinghe distinguishes between a State's use of force abroad to protect its nationals and diplomatic protection, stressing that interventions that involve force with a view to protecting nationals abroad cannot "be regarded strictly as the exercise of diplomatic protection." Chittharanjan F. Amerasinghe, Diplomatic Protection 31 (2008). For the classic articulation of the law of diplomatic protection, see Mavrommatis Palestine Concessions, 1924 P.C.I.J. (ser. A) No. 2 (Aug. 30). For the International Law Commission's finished work product on the law of diplomatic protection, see Report of the International Law Commission, 58th Sess., May 1–June 9, July 3–Aug. 11, 2006, at 13-100, U.N. Doc. A/61/10; GAOR, 61st Sess., Supp. No. 10 (2006). *See also* Reuven (Ruvi) Ziegler, *Protecting Recognized Geneva Convention Refugees Outside Their States of Asylum,* 25(2) Int'l J. Refugee L. 235 (2013).

[58] Press Release, *supra* note 39.

[59] Cablegram, *supra* note 44, at 3.

[60] Cablegram, *supra* note 33, at 4.

[61] *Id.*

[62] *See* Cablegram, *supra* note 41, at 6 (claiming that: "Although there was no direct violation of Iraqi frontiers by Zionist bands yet the existing threat inside Palestine is not confined to the boundary of that country but extends to Iraq itself partly through the aggressive intentions of Zionism and partly through the fact that the Palestinians Arabs are an integral part of the Arab people in general").

[63] Letter, *supra* note 45, at 5. Compare this with an editorial in *Ad-Difa'a* from March 3, 1948, which stated: "Another fact is to open the way for our country to exercise its national life in conjunction with the Arab countries. No isolation, no separation; Palestine should share the great Arab caravan and procession in building the universe of the Arabs and their future." United Nations Palestine Commission, *supra* note 4, at 2.

[64] *See* Progress Report of the United Nations Mediator on Palestine Submitted to the Secretary-General for Transmission to the Members of the United Nations, at 15, U.N. Doc. A/648 (1948)

League in 1946 and 1947 giving a similar rationale for intervention.[65] Given the history, it is not particularly surprising that the Arab side framed its intervention in pan-Arab terms and continued to eschew the notion of a distinct Palestinian national identity.

For its part, of course, the Jewish side argued that it was acting in self-defense against an Arab invasion of land that Resolution 181 had partitioned and allocated to the Jewish people.[66] Military action was justified outside of Jewish majority territory in Palestine "[i]n order to repel aggression, and as part of our [i.e., the Jewish peoples'] essentially defensive plan, to prevent these areas being used as bases for attacks against the State of Israel."[67] The use of force in areas that had traditionally had a Palestinian Arab majority or in Jerusalem, where a Jewish majority was to have come under an international regime, was justified on the basis that the basic protections that Resolution 181 had envisaged for Jews in these areas had not been implemented.[68] The Jewish side's response to the Security Council conveyed a commitment to negotiate with the Arabs but only if this was done on the basis of Resolution 181's scheme of partition, a starting position that was clearly unacceptable to the Arabs.[69] One other noteworthy aspect of the Jewish response was the position that the State of Israel's *de jure* borders were those that Resolution 181 had stipulated for it even though Jewish forces were acting in areas that had traditionally had a Palestinian Arab majority, or in Jerusalem.[70]

From a dispute settlement point of view—and it need hardly be stressed that the Arab and Jewish sides had a legal dispute in the *Mavrommatis Palestine Concessions* sense of a "disagreement on a point of law or fact, a conflict of legal views or of interests between two persons"[71]—it is clear that the Arab side was unwilling to entertain a negotiated settlement with its Jewish counterparts, much less any other peaceful means of dispute settlement.[72] For the Arabs, Zionism was

(recognizing that the Arab States had justified their intervention on the basis that, Resolution 181 being, in the Arab view, unlawful, they had "come legitimately to the assistance of the Arabs of Palestine").

[65] *See* Jewish Terrorism in Palestine, Dec. 12, 1946, *in* 2 The Arab States and the Arab League, *supra* note 9, at 163; Defending Palestine, *supra* note 16.

[66] *See* Letter Dated 18 May 1948 from the Assistant Secretary-General for Security Council Affairs Addressed to the Jewish Agency for Palestine, and Reply Dated 22 May 1948 Addressed to the Secretary-General Concerning the Questions Submitted by the Security Council, U.N. Doc. S/766 (May 22, 1948).

[67] *Id.* at 4.

[68] *See id.*

[69] *See id.* at 5.

[70] *See id.* at 4 (implying this by stating that these Jewish forces were "outside the territory of the State of Israel [… but] under the control of the military authorities of the State of Israel" and noting that it, that is, the Jewish side, "consider[ed] the territory of Israel as a single unit with a Jewish majority. As indicated above, the Government of the State of Israel operates in parts of Palestine outside the territory of the State of Israel, parts which, with the notable exception of Jerusalem, formerly for the most part, contained Arab majorities. These areas have, however, been mostly abandoned by their Arab population. No area outside of Palestine is under Jewish occupation but sallies beyond the frontiers of the State of Israel have occasionally been carried out by Jewish forces for imperative military reasons, and as a part of an essentially defensive plan").

[71] Mavrommatis, *supra* note 57, at 11.

[72] *See* U.N. Charter art. 33(1).

the problem, the root cause, and Zionists' insistence upon statehood for the Jewish people was a non-starter. Syria was characteristically blunt on this point in a letter that it sent to the United Nations in late 1948: "Syrian Government thanks you for offer of good offices but could start negotiations with Jews only if accept and recognize establishment Arab State for whole Palestine and definitively renounce establish Jewish State in Palestine."[73] AHC representative Henry Cattan reflected broader Arab opinion in December 1948 when he stated the obvious, that Arabs would reject any attempt at conciliation of the question of Palestine that involved partition in Palestine.[74] That Cattan had said this was not surprising given that a little over a week earlier he had "observed that Arab opposition to the creation of a Jewish State in Palestine followed a law of nature which could be likened to the resistance of the human body to a cancerous growth. That opposition would continue until the cancer was destroyed."[75] With such a perspective engrained, it is not difficult to understand the "cancer patient's" determination and rejection of peaceful dialogue.

III. The Role of the United Nations Mediator on Palestine

Elsewhere at the United Nations, the General Assembly would make one of its most significant contributions to international peace and security at the time when, on May 14, 1948, it adopted Resolution 186.[76] This established the role of United Nations Mediator in Palestine (UNMP), who would assist the Truce Commission for Palestine and be tasked with mediating between the Arab and Jewish sides with respect to the protection of the Holy Places and public services and the promotion of a "peaceful adjustment of the future situation of Palestine."[77] Quite what "peaceful adjustment of the future situation of Palestine" meant, Resolution 186 left unclear, begging the question whether the General Assembly intended Resolution 181 to have remained the operative framework moving forward. The debates on point in the General Assembly did little to clarify this. Speaking just prior to the adoption of Resolution 186, for instance, Guatemala[78] and the Soviet

[73] Letter Dated 1 December 1948 from the Acting Mediator to the Secretary-General Transmitting a Communication from the Syrian Government Concerning the Security Council Resolution of 16 November (S/1080), at 2, U.N. Doc. S/1097 (Dec. 2, 1948).

[74] *See* U.N. GAOR, U.N. Doc. A/C.1/SR.220 (Dec. 1, 1948), http://unispal.un.org/unispal.nsf/9a798adbf322aff38525617b006d88d7/35b9b641f271dc0485256c72005d81be?OpenDocument.

[75] U.N. GAOR, U.N. Doc. A/C.1/SR.207 (Nov. 22, 1948), http://unispal.un.org/pdfs/AC1SR207.pdf.

[76] *See* G.A. Res. 186, U.N. Doc. A/RES/186 (May 14, 1948).

[77] *Id.* at ¶ 1.

[78] *See* U.N. GAOR, *supra* note 3, at 37 (arguing that: "Any attempt by the United Nations to depart from its function of mediation and conciliation, or to set up in Palestine a regime other than that proposed in the resolution of 29 November 1947, would be contrary to the principles of international law

Union,[79] which both spoke in favor of Resolution 181 remaining the operative framework moving forward, voted differently on the final text, with the former voting in favor and the latter voting against its adoption. The fact that all of the Arab Member States of the United Nations were both clearly opposed to partition in any form and chose to abstain from the vote might suggest a general ambivalence as to Resolution 186's potential to reinforce or rescind a scheme of partition in Palestine, of whatever scope, though this is admittedly speculative and unclear.

Much to the consternation of both the Arab and Jewish sides, Count Folke Bernadotte, the chosen UNMP, deliberately obfuscated on the question of whether Resolution 181 remained the operative framework moving forward. His Progress Report contradicted itself in that it stated that Resolution 181 had "already been outrun and irrevocably revised by the actual facts of recent Palestine history"[80] while at the same time Count Bernadotte acknowledged that:

> The *de jure* situation is that the resolution of 29 November of the General Assembly has not been annulled as a decision of that body, though the United Nations has not implemented it, and the United Nations Palestine Commission has been relieved of its responsibilities.[81]

Given that Count Bernadotte's proposed solution for Palestine was a partition scheme that differed in certain respects from that which Resolution 181 had envisaged, it was odd that he criticized Israel's "cherry picking" of Resolution 181 even though his Progress Report chose to do exactly this in light of developments since mid May 1948.[82]

Count Bernadotte completed his recommendations on September 16, 1948, the day before he and United Nations Observer Colonel Andre Serot were assassinated by the Stern Gang in a Jerusalem ambush.[83] The Progress Report upheld

and would constitute an act of intervention. The role of the United Nations representative in Palestine must be that of a mediator only [...] The delegation of Guatemala considered that the resolution of 29 November 1947 was still in force [...]").

[79] *See id.* at 38 (convinced that: "Even if the draft resolution was accepted, that would in no way affect the partition decision, which remained valid. Fearing that the opponents of the partition decision might take advantage of the provisions of the resolution to complicate the existing situation, the USSR delegation would vote against the resolution before the Assembly").

[80] Progress Report, *supra* note 64, at 5.

[81] *Id.* at 22 (continuing two sentences later by stating that Count Bernadotte did not consider himself bound by Resolution 181).

[82] *See id.* at 26 (criticizing Israel in this regard by stating that: "Whatever may be the precise legal significance and status of the 29 November resolution, it would seem quite clear to me that the situation is not of such nature as to entitle either party to act on the assumption that such parts of that resolution as may be favourable to it may be regarded as effective, while those parts which may, by reason of changes in circumstances, be regarded as unfavourable, are to be considered as ineffective").

[83] *See* Cablegram Dated 27 September 1948 from Ralph Bunche to the Secretary-General Transmitting Report Regarding the Assassination of the United Nations Mediator, U.N. Doc S/1018 (Sept. 28, 1948). *See also* Aage Lundström, *The Death of Count Folke Bernadotte, September 17, 1948, in* From Haven to Conquest: Readings in Zionism and the Palestine Problem Until 1948 789 (Walid Khalidi ed., 2005). Speaking for the United Nations, Secretary-General Lie reflected that the "enormity, the barbarism, the primeval stupidity of the act, were engulfing. And our grief was still more bitter." Lie, *supra* note 6, at 190.

the basic architecture of Resolution 181 in that it recommended that Palestine be partitioned to allow for a Jewish majority State. The Progress Report ended with both "basic premises" and "specific conclusions."[84] The basic premises were recognition that a Jewish State existed in Palestine and would continue to exist there, that peace should be restored to Palestine, that displaced persons should have a right to return or to compensation, that Jerusalem should be given special treatment, and that the Jewish State's borders should be fixed by agreement or, barring that, by the United Nations and that this should be done according to the "principle of geographical homogeneity and integration, which should be the major objective of the boundary arrangements, [… and] should apply equally to Arab and Jewish territories, whose frontiers should not, therefore, be rigidly controlled by the territorial arrangements envisaged in the resolution of 29 November."[85]

Count Bernadotte hoped that his specific conclusions would facilitate a "reasonable, equitable and workable basis for settlement."[86] His first specific conclusion called for perpetual peace between the Arab and Jewish sides: peace treaties if possible, or at least armistice agreements.[87] There would need to be "revisions in the boundaries broadly defined in the resolution of the General Assembly of 29 November in order to make them more equitable, workable and consistent with existing realities in Palestine."[88] This included transferring the Negev Desert to Arab hands, designating the Galilee as Jewish territory, ensuring that the port at Haifa and the airport at Lydda would be opened to all, and placing Jerusalem under "effective United Nations control with maximum feasible local autonomy for its Arab and Jewish communities, with full safeguards for the protection of the Holy Places and sites and free access to them, and for religious freedom."[89] That the Progress Report insisted that the borders needed to be made "more equitable, workable and consistent with existing realities in Palestine" implied that they were, if imposed exactly along the lines suggested by Resolution 181, less equitable, less workable, and less consistent with reality than they might otherwise be.

The Progress Report went on to say that whether an Arab majority State should be created west of the Jordan River would have to be decided by the Arab States "in full consultation with the Arab inhabitants of Palestine."[90] Although vague, the phrase "full consultation" would not seem to have required the Arab States to have granted a veto to the Palestinians, though it would assuredly have required all of the parties to have acted in good faith. The Progress Report counseled that there would be "compelling reasons for merging the Arab territory of Palestine with the territory of Transjordan, subject to such frontier rectifications regarding

[84] *See* Progress Report, *supra* note 64, at 17–19.
[85] *Id.* at 17. International guarantees based upon human rights protections were also suggested. *See id.*
[86] *Id.* at 18.
[87] *See id.*
[88] *Id.*
[89] *Id.*
[90] *Id.*

other Arab States as may be found practicable and desirable."[91] The "historical connexion and common interests of Transjordan and Palestine"[92] supported this presumption of merger between the two Arab territories, and one of these considerations, no doubt, was the basic fact that, as discussed in the previous chapter, the ruling Hashemites from the Hijaz were a distinct minority in what was then Transjordan. A merger between the Arab majority parts of the Palestine Mandate was not a novel idea and had been recommended, though never implemented, by the Palestine Royal Commission (Peel Commission) in 1937.[93]

With respect to displaced persons, the Progress Report's specific conclusion was much more detailed and one-sided than its equivalent basic premise. Specifically, whereas the basic premise referred vaguely to the "right of innocent people, uprooted from their homes by the present terror and ravages of war,"[94] the specific conclusion focused exclusively on the "right of the Arab refugees to return to their homes in Jewish-controlled territory at the earliest possible date [or receive compensation]."[95] This difference in language is significant because of what it excludes. Although the basic premise on the displaced persons issue would not on its face have seemed to have precluded sympathy for Jews displaced because of the 1948 War,[96] the specific conclusion is partial. For this reason, it arguably reflects something other than "pure" humanitarianism.

The final major aspect of Count Bernadotte's specific conclusions was the proposal for a conciliation commission to act as trustee for Jewish minority rights in Arab territory and for Arab minority rights in Jewish territory and to extend its good offices, at the invitation of Arab and Jewish authorities, to "any efforts toward exchanges of populations with a view to eliminating troublesome minority problems, and on the basis of adequate compensation for property owned."[97]

[91] *Id.*

[92] *Id.*

[93] *See* Palestine Royal Commission Report, at 381, cmd. 5479 (1937). *See also* CABINET, REPORT OF PALESTINE ROYAL COMMISSION, app. II at 7, 8, No. CAB/24/270 (1937) (Letter from Professor Reginald Coupland to the Secretary of State for the Colonies, June 23, 1937).

[94] Progress Report, *supra* note 64, at 17.

[95] *Id.* at 18.

[96] For a contemporary account of threats to Jews in Arab and Muslim lands at the time, see Mallory Browne, *Jews in Grave Danger in All Moslem Lands: Nine Hundred Thousand in Africa and Asia Face Wrath of Their Foes*, N.Y. TIMES, May 16, 1948. *See also* Shaul Bartal, *The Palestinian Refugee Problem Resolved*, 20(4) MID. E. Q. 29 (2013); Avi Beker, *The Forgotten Narrative: Jewish Refugees from Arab Countries*, 17(3–4) JEWISH POL. STUD. REV. 3 (2005); Andrew Kent, *Evaluating the Palestinians'* Claimed *Right of Return*, 34(1) U. PA. J. INT'L L. 149, 170–71 (2012). The Knesset recently approved a bill marking November 30 as a Day Marking the Exit and Deportation of Jews from Arab Lands and Iran. *See* Knesset, Final Approval: The Exit and Deportation of Jews from Arab Lands and Iran Day (June 24, 2014), http://knesset.gov.il/spokesman/eng/PR_eng.asp?PRID=11325. *See also* Israel Ministry of Foreign Affairs, Special Report on the Issue of Jewish Refugees from Arab Countries (Apr. 3, 2012), http://mfa.gov.il/MFA/ForeignPolicy/Peace/Guide/Pages/Jewish_refugees_from_Arab_and_Muslim_countries-Apr_2012.aspx.

[97] Progress Report, *supra* note 64, at 18. Twenty-first-century sensibilities might see in this language, to use an emotive if imprecise concept, a nod to the possibility of "ethnic cleansing" at the aegis of the United Nations, something that South Asia was experiencing around the same time during the

Count Bernadotte also envisaged that the conciliation commission would oversee and facilitate Arab displaced persons issues, promote friendly relations between the Arab and Jewish sides, and address related issues.[98] In other words, the conciliation commission was to have a fairly wide and flexible mandate.

The Arab and Jewish sides were both highly critical of Count Bernadotte's Progress Report, but it seems fair to say that the Arab side was intransigent. As before, the Arabs were unwilling to compromise with respect to, much less negotiate, any arrangement that would reify a Jewish State in Palestine. Two specific points are worth noting. Firstly, by classifying the Palestinians as the "original owners of the country"[99] and, thus, by impliedly contrasting them in this respect with the Jewish people, the Arab side continued to delegitimize Zionism and reject the "historical connection of the Jewish people with Palestine"[100] that the Palestine Mandate had recognized. Secondly, with respect to the proposed merger of the Arab majority parts of the Palestine Mandate, Secretary-General Azzam, on behalf of the Arab League, responded that this idea "not only exceed[ed] the terms of reference of mediation, but also constitute[d] a deliberate confirmation of the Zionists' false assertion that Palestine comprises the territories of that kingdom, an allegation which has never been conceded."[101] It is difficult to agree with the Arab side on this point given the breadth of Count Bernadotte's terms of reference, which extended, one will recall, to mediation with respect to the "peaceful adjustment of the future situation of Palestine." Furthermore, it is misleading to suggest, as Secretary-General Azzam did, that Palestine as Mandate did not also include the territory of Transjordan. It clearly did, and one need only recall that the disapplication of the Jewish national home provisions of the Palestine Mandate to the larger part of Palestine in mid 1922 did not formally sever what would become Transjordan from the Palestine Mandate.

The Jewish side appreciated two aspects of the Progress Report in particular. Firstly, there was Count Bernadotte's statement that it was unquestionable that the Arabs had made a "tragic mistake in employing force in Palestine."[102] This squarely blamed the Arab side for intervening in Palestine in mid May 1948. Had the Arab side refrained from using force in Palestine, in other words, and not placated the AHC's refusal to countenance a Jewish State in any part of Palestine, it is quite possible that an Arab majority State alongside a Jewish majority State could have emerged west of the Jordan at the time. The Jewish side also appreciated Count Bernadotte's unequivocal affirmation that the Jewish State was "here to stay." Not only was Israel described as a "living, solidly entrenched and vigorous reality,"[103]

partition of British India. For a fictionalized accounting of this, see KHUSHWANT SINGH, TRAIN TO PAKISTAN (2012). *See also* Kent, *supra* note 96, at 165–66.

[98] *See* Progress Report, *supra* note 64, at 18–19.

[99] *Id.* at 20.

[100] British Mandate for Palestine, 17(3) AM. J. INT'L L. SUPP. 164, 164, pmbl. (1922) (1923).

[101] Progress Report, *supra* note 64, at 20.

[102] *Id.* at 6.

[103] *Id.* at 5.

the Progress Report also praised the determination and grit of the Jewish people in asserting their self-determination: "In establishing their State within a semi-circle of gunfire, the Jews have given a convincing demonstration of their skill and tenacity."[104]

The Jewish side's main criticisms of the Progress Report centered around the question of displaced persons, territorial adjustments, and the status of Jerusalem. On the displaced persons issue, Israel's position was that Count Bernadotte's perspective was short-sighted in that it only addressed humanitarian aspects and failed to appreciate the larger context of equally pressing and persuasive considerations of an economic, military, and political nature.[105] The Jewish side was adamantly opposed to the Progress Report's suggested territorial adjustments. In light of the Arab world's intervention in Palestine and Count Bernadotte's suggestion that a single Arab State should straddle the Jordan next to the Jewish State, Israeli Minister for Foreign Affairs Moshe Shertok made clear that the Resolution 181 borders were an "irreducible minimum"[106] and, in fact, needed to be expanded in light of the Arabs' intervention and the situation considered as a whole.[107] The Jewish side felt particularly affronted by the Progress Report's view with respect to Jerusalem. Given, *inter alia*, the considerable damage that the Arab side had inflicted upon isolated Jewish population centers in Jerusalem during the 1948 War, and the fact that Resolution 181 was to have led to an internationalized Jerusalem, the mere reaffirmation of an internationalized dispensation premised upon United Nations guarantees and "local autonomy" was unacceptable to the Jewish side.[108] "It was proposed to demilitarize Jerusalem, but how could the Jews of Jerusalem who had saved their lives only by their own efforts be expected to give up their defensive arms and their military connexions with Israel and rely only on the name of the United Nations?"[109] Israel asked.

IV. The Establishment of the United Nations Conciliation Commission for Palestine

Between the publication of the Progress Report on September 16, 1948, and the adoption of Resolution 194 almost three months later,[110] Count Bernadotte's recommendations were discussed by the General Assembly, and many amendments and changes were made, and rejected, before the final text was adopted. There were

[104] *Id.*
[105] *See id.* at 27.
[106] *Id.* at 24.
[107] *See id.* at 24–25.
[108] *See id.* at 25.
[109] U.N. GAOR, *supra* note 74. *See* Statements of the Prime Minister David Ben-Gurion Regarding Moving the Capital of Israel to Jerusalem, http://www.knesset.gov.il/docs/eng/bengurion-jer.htm.
[110] G.A. Res. 194, U.N. Doc. A/RES/194 (Dec. 11, 1948).

few surprises when Shertok put forward the Israeli position on November 15.[111] One point that should not be overlooked is that even as the Arab States and the AHC continued to reject partition, it was the Jewish State that went on record expressing its strong preference for the "establishment of a separate independent Arab State corresponding, as far as practicable, to the provisions of the 29 November [1947] resolution, and [stating that it] would be ready to negotiate with it on mutual adjustments of boundaries, if such a State declared itself ready to enter into close alliance with Israel."[112]

Certainly, it was not the Arab side that was making the case for an Arab State west of the Jordan next to a Jewish State in Palestine. Indeed, Czechoslovakia lamented that few delegations in the General Assembly seemed at all concerned to work for an Arab State next to a Jewish State in Palestine.[113] The Soviets criticized the Progress Report on a number of grounds, mostly related to those aspects of it that deviated from Resolution 181, and they saw in Count Bernadotte's suggestion that a single Arab State should straddle the Jordan next to a Jewish State as an imperialistic maneuver meant to placate the United Kingdom and the United States.[114] Shertok was also critical of Count Bernadotte's merger proposal since, according to the Israelis, this would merely reward the aggression of the Arab side.[115]

Syria was by far the most active of the Arab States in proposing amendments and seeking to influence the drafts that were then making their way through the General Assembly at the time. It tabled two draft resolutions with respect to dispute settlement in Palestine. In its draft of November 26, Damascus reiterated Arab rejection of Resolution 181 and argued that it was Resolution 181, and its plan for partition, that had led to the unrest in Palestine.[116] This draft resolution fundamentally rejected Count Bernadotte's recommendations because they were based upon partition, and in any event, according to the Syrian draft, the General Assembly had been and would continue to be acting *ultra vires* in "mak[ing] imperative and compulsory recommendations for splitting countries."[117] There is some irony in this given that the Arab world would not long after the 1948 War become a leading force behind the adoption of General Assembly resolutions hostile to the Jewish State and be quite content to see the General Assembly assert a significant role on matters of international peace and security on the question of Palestine.[118] Syria's November 26 draft continued by describing Jews in Palestine

[111] *See* U.N. GAOR, at 640–47, U.N. Doc. A/C.1/SR.200 (Nov. 15, 1948).

[112] *Id.* at 645.

[113] *See* U.N. GAOR, at 965–70, U.N. Doc. A/PV.185 (Dec. 11, 1948).

[114] *See id.* at 981–84; U.N. GAOR, at 984–91, U.N. Doc. A/PV.186 (Dec. 11, 1948).

[115] *See* U.N. GAOR, *supra* note 74.

[116] *See* U.N. GAOR, at pmbl., U.N. Doc. A/C.1/402 (Nov. 26, 1948).

[117] *Id.*

[118] For an example of the former approach, see G.A. Res. 3379, U.N. Doc. A/RES/3379 (Nov. 10, 1975). *See* Bernard Lewis, *The Anti-Zionist Resolution*, 55(1) FOREIGN AFF. 54 (1976). *See also* Yehoshafat Harkabi, *Arab Positions on Zionism*, *in* ZIONISM AND THE ARABS 187, 190–91 (Shmuel Almog ed., 1983). On the latter tendency, see Legal Consequences of the Construction of a Wall in the Occupied Palestinian Territory, Advisory Opinion, 2004 I.C.J. 136, 148–52 (July 9).

as foreigners without even a colorable claim to sovereignty in any part of what for Zionists was Jewish sovereign space as a matter of right.[119]

The sole operative paragraph in Syria's draft resolution of November 26 called for the establishment of a commission of five United Nations Member States with a mandate to set forth plans for a single cantonal or federal State in Palestine.[120] One will recall that the UNSCOP had been unanimous at the initial stage of its work in 1947 in rejecting plans for a cantonal State of Palestine[121] and that the UNSCOP majority had rejected a federal State solution, with only India, Iran, and Yugoslavia supporting this option.[122] Furthermore, the fact that Resolution 186 had tasked the UNMP with the promotion of a "peaceful adjustment of the future situation of Palestine," a broadly-phrased mandate that would not have precluded Count Bernadotte from setting forth plans for a single cantonal or federal State in Palestine if he so chose, suggests that a single cantonal or federal State in Palestine would not, at least not maximally, have promoted the "peaceful adjustment of the future situation of Palestine." The General Assembly ultimately rejected Syria's draft of November 26.[123]

Syria tabled its second draft resolution with respect to dispute settlement at this time on November 30.[124] This second draft reiterated the main points that Damascus' earlier draft had made and recalled that United Nations Member States had expressed a number of concerns about the question of Palestine.[125] Syria's November 30 draft then requested the International Court of Justice (ICJ) to give an advisory opinion in light of this.[126] Like its earlier attempt to move its November 26 draft resolution through the General Assembly, Syria's efforts with respect to an advisory opinion also failed.[127] Even had it been adopted, however, the ICJ could very well have rejected the request given that the "legal question" being asked of it strained specificity.[128] The Syrian draft wanted the ICJ to speak to, *inter alia*, the "legal aspect involved in this problem [of Palestine]."[129] Although the ICJ has a practice of straining to entertain all manner of (legal) questions asked of it,[130] the exceedingly vague nature of the "legal question" would certainly

[119] *See* U.N. GAOR, *supra* note 116, at pmbl.

[120] *See id.* at ¶ 1.

[121] *See* United Nations Special Committee on Palestine, Report to the General Assembly: Volume I, at 42, U.N. Doc. A/364 (Sept. 3, 1947).

[122] *See id.* at 59–64.

[123] *See* 1948–49 U.N.Y.B. 171–72.

[124] *See* U.N. GAOR, U.N. Doc. A/C.1/405 (Nov. 30, 1948).

[125] *See id.* at pmbl.

[126] *See id.* at ¶ 1.

[127] *See* 1948–49 U.N.Y.B. 169.

[128] "The General Assembly or the Security Council may request the International Court of Justice to give an advisory opinion on any legal question." U.N. Charter art. 96(1).

[129] U.N. GAOR, *supra* note 124, at pmbl.

[130] *See, e.g.*, Wall, *supra* note 118, at 153–54 (stating that "lack of clarity in the drafting of a question does not deprive the Court of jurisdiction. Rather, such uncertainty will require clarification in interpretation, and such necessary clarifications of interpretation have frequently been given by the Court").

have provided a reasonable ground for the ICJ to have rejected the request on jurisdictional grounds.[131] Of course, this is merely speculative, however, since the resolution was never adopted.

The General Assembly moved to a vote, and on December 11, 1948, it adopted Resolution 194, with Pakistan, Afghanistan, Cuba, and the Soviet Bloc States joining the Arab States in voting against it.[132] The resolution did not wholeheartedly embrace the Progress Report, but neither did it scrap it in its entirety; in other words, it was a qualified endorsement. Resolution 194 adopted the Progress Report's idea of a conciliation commission for Palestine but gave what would become the United Nations Conciliation Commission for Palestine (UNCCP) a mandate that was as confused as it was vague. On the one hand, the General Assembly tasked the UNCCP with the mandate that Count Bernadotte had had, a mandate that included pondering, *inter alia*, the "peaceful adjustment of the future situation of Palestine." Wide as this was, and as indeterminate and question-begging, too, the UNCCP could jettison and modify this mandate, *proprio motu*, "in so far as it considers necessary in existing circumstances."[133] Resolution 194 specifically called for the UNCCP to assist the Arab and Jewish sides in negotiating with each other with a view to peacefully resolving their differences.[134] Palestine's Holy Places were to be placed under "effective United Nations supervision,"[135] but Jerusalem, which the General Assembly defined quite widely,[136] was to be internationalized.[137] Resolution 194 also called for the UNCCP to facilitate economic development and cooperation throughout Palestine.[138]

Like the United Nations Palestine Commission before it,[139] the UNCCP had little success,[140] and as before, Palestine continued to be seen by the Arabs as a national cause, with scant consideration for a distinct national identity for

[131] By way of historical context, it should be noted that the Arab States had earlier hoped to have the General Assembly request the ICJ to give an advisory opinion on various legal issues related to the United Nations Special Committee on Palestine's 1947 Report to the General Assembly. This attempt also failed. *See* VICTOR KATTAN, FROM COEXISTENCE TO CONQUEST: INTERNATIONAL LAW AND THE ORIGINS OF THE ARAB-ISRAELI CONFLICT, 1891–1949 148–51 (2009).

[132] There were thirty-five affirmative votes and eight abstentions. *See* U.N. GAOR, *supra* note 114, at 995–96.

[133] G.A. Res. 194, *supra* note 110, at ¶ 2(a). The UNCCP had other specified functions under Resolution 194, and its mandate could be further modified by the General Assembly or Security Council. *See id.* at ¶ 2(b)–(c).

[134] *See id.* at ¶¶ 5–6.

[135] *Id.* at ¶ 7.

[136] Resolution 194 defined the "Jerusalem area" as municipal Jerusalem and its surrounding towns and villages, from Shu'fat in the north to Bethlehem in the south, and from Ein Karim, including Motsa, in the west, to Abu Dis in the east. *See id.* at ¶ 8.

[137] *See id.* at ¶ 7. This presumes that "Jerusalem" (paragraph 7) and "Jerusalem area" (paragraph 8) mean the same thing and that a "permanent international regime" (paragraph 7) is identical in meaning to placement under "effective United Nations control" (paragraph 8).

[138] *See id.* at ¶ 10.

[139] Resolution 186 had relieved the United Nations Palestine Commission of its responsibilities. *See* G.A. Res. 186, *supra* note 76, at § 3.

[140] The UNCCP would be rendered terminally ineffectual by the mid 1950s. *See* Shabtai Rosenne, *Israel and the United Nations: Changed Perspectives, 1945–1976*, 78 AM. JEWISH Y.B. 3, 17–21 (1978).

Palestinian Arabs *qua* Palestinian Arabs. As the UNCCP recounted on June 3, 1949, in its Third Progress Report: "The Arab delegations have insisted from the beginning that the Palestine question is of equal concern to all the Arab States, and that the Commission therefore should look upon them as a single 'party', carrying on all discussions and negotiations with them en bloc."[141]

That the UNCCP did not fulfill its mandate despite due diligence came as little surprise.[142] As a progress report from 1951 noted with exasperation, the UNCCP had failed to make "substantial progress";[143] "neither side," the UNCCP reflected, "is now ready to seek that aim [i.e., stability in Palestine] through full implementation of the General Assembly resolutions under which the Commission is operating."[144] The displaced persons issue was but one example of the challenges that the UNCCP faced. Whereas Israel viewed the displaced Arabs as having at least some degree of culpability in that they "chose to leave through fear or in the hope of a speedy victory by the Arab armies,"[145] the Arabs compared the Zionists to Nazis who were "vying in horror with the methods of Hitler."[146] The opposing narratives from the Arab and Jewish sides were simply irreconcilable.

Resolution 194 endorsed Count Bernadotte's recommendation that displaced persons should have the option of return or compensation.[147] From the text of Resolution 194, it is not clear whether this was meant to benefit Arab or Jewish displaced persons, or perhaps both Arab and Jewish displaced persons. Paragraph 11 simply describes the intended beneficiaries as "refugees," not "Arab refugees," "Jewish refugees," or "Arab and Jewish refugees." Most delegations in the General Assembly presumed that it was Arab displaced persons who needed protection[148] or unhelpfully described the intended beneficiaries using the imprecise shorthand "Palestine refugees."[149] One delegation expressed its preference for "most generous compensation to all those who had been displaced, both Arabs and Jews."[150]

141 United Nations Conciliation Commission for Palestine, Third Progress Report to the Secretary-General of the United Nations (For the Period Extending from 9 April to 8 June 1949 Inclusive), U.N. Doc. A/927 (June 13, 1949), http://unispal.un.org/UNISPAL.NSF/0/AD7D4FE6D9F547CB8525750C00766FAB#sthash.tfKv67hE.dpuf.

142 "The Commission is of the opinion [...] that the present unwillingness of the parties fully to implement the General Assembly resolutions under which the Commission is operating, as well as the changes which have occurred in Palestine during the past three years, have made it impossible for the Commission to carry out its mandate, and this fact should be taken into consideration in any further approach to the Palestine problem." Progress Report of the United Nations Conciliation Commission for Palestine Covering the Period from 23 January to 19 November 1951, at 10, U.N. Doc. A/1985 (1951).

143 *Id.*

144 *Id.*

145 *Id.* at 18.

146 *Id.* at 20.

147 *See* G.A. Res. 194, *supra* note 110, at ¶ 11 ("*Resolves* that the refugees wishing to return to their homes and live at peace with their neighbours should be permitted to do so at the earliest practicable date, and that compensation should be paid for the property of those choosing not to return and for loss of or damage to property which, under principles of international law or in equity, should be made good by the Governments or authorities responsible").

148 *See, e.g.*, U.N. GAOR, at 945–46, U.N. Doc. A/PV.184 (Dec. 11, 1948) (France).

149 *See, e.g.*, *id.* at 953 (El Salvador).

150 U.N. GAOR, *supra* note 113, at 977 (New Zealand).

The Arabs voted against Resolution 194 for various reasons, but what can be said is that in doing so they were effectively voting against giving Arab displaced persons the option of return or compensation.

This is not the place to dwell upon paragraph 11 in any detail, though it is clear that it raises myriad issues that need to be clarified. There is, for example, the fundamental question of the legally-binding nature of General Assembly resolutions, and individual provisions within them.[151] There is the issue of how paragraph 11 is meant to operate within the larger context of the question of Palestine. Is there a broader tapestry within which international law requires this provision to be considered, or can it be, should it be, implemented in isolation? Is paragraph 11 a human rights provision? If so, in whom does this human right or rights vest? Can the option of return or compensation be negotiated? What of those who might "wish[] to return to their homes and live at peace with their neighbours" but who no longer have homes to which to return? A working paper that the United Nations Secretariat prepared for the UNCCP in May 1950 stated that there was "no doubt that in using this term [i.e., 'to their homes'] the General Assembly meant the home of each refugee, i.e., his house or lodging and not his homeland."[152] Count Bernadotte reported that "in many localities their [i.e., the Arab displaced persons'] homes had been destroyed, and their furniture and assets dispersed."[153] It need hardly be stressed that this reality has been amplified, exponentially, over the course of the almost seventy years since Count Bernadotte made this point.[154] These and other issues related to paragraph 11 and the displaced persons issue more generally need to be addressed and resolved.[155]

V. Arab Rejectionism and Boycotts of the Jewish State

Thus far, this chapter has shown how the years between the 1948 War and the 1973 War, and particularly the beginning of this period, involved, by the United

[151] *See* Marko Divac Öberg, *The Legal Effects of Resolutions of the UN Security Council and General Assembly in the Jurisprudence of the ICJ*, 16(5) EUR. J. INT'L L. 879, 883–84 (2005).

[152] Analysis of Paragraph 11 of the General Assembly's Resolution of 11 December 1948, at 3, U.N. Doc. W/45 (May 15, 1950).

[153] Progress Report, *supra* note 64, at 48.

[154] On these and related questions, see Shabtai Rosenne, *Directions for a Middle East Settlement—Some Underlying Legal Problems*, 33(1) LAW & CONTEMP. PROBS. 44, 64–66 (1968); Ruth Lapidoth, *Israel and the Palestinians: Some Legal Issues*, at 43–54 (Jerusalem Institute for Israel Studies Series No. 94, 2003).

[155] For two studies that discuss the displaced persons issue in considerable detail, see John Quigley, *Displaced Palestinians and a Right of Return*, 39(1) HARV. INT'L L.J. 171 (1998) (holding that repatriation of displaced Palestinians is required as a matter of international law); and Justus R. Weiner, *The Palestinian Refugees' "Right to Return" and the Peace Process*, 20(1) B.C. INT'L & COMP. L. REV. 1 (1997) (articulating a legal position that mirrors Israel's position and that sees the displaced persons issue as one among many that need to be resolved by the parties). *See also* Kent, *supra* note 96, and exhaustive biography at 152 n.3 supporting and denying the proposition that international law dictates a "right of return." For a working paper that the United Nations Secretariat prepared for the UNCCP in May 1950 that analyzes each clause of paragraph 11, see Analysis, *supra* note 152.

Nations, a number of means of dispute settlement. Palestine was unraveling at the very point in time when the General Assembly had hoped to see it peacefully transition to an Arab majority State and a Jewish majority State. While it would not exactly be correct to say that the United Nations had exhausted all of the peaceful means of dispute settlement that article 33(1) of the Charter lays out, if only because this article is one of perpetual possibility for parties to disputes, it is clear that many means had been tried, both singly and in combination. The United Nations Palestine Commission made way for the mediation of Count Bernadotte and his successor, Ralph J. Bunche, the Truce Commission for Palestine was tasked with securing truces between the Arab and Jewish sides and monitoring them and the armistice agreements that would follow therefrom,[156] and the UNCCP brought together the full machinery of the United Nations to prod the Arab and Jewish sides to arrive at a peaceful settlement. There was even a Syrian attempt to have the General Assembly request the ICJ to give an advisory opinion on the Palestine question in late 1948. None of these efforts succeeded. The dispute remained, unabated.

While the Jewish side fully engaged with these attempts at dispute settlement, the Arabs of Palestine and the Arab States refused to cooperate with any dispute settlement arrangement that could be perceived as countenancing a Jewish State in Palestine. Speaking for the then Mandatory power at the sixteenth meeting of the United Nations Palestine Commission in late January 1948, British representative Alexander Cadogan made the point that, for the Arabs of Palestine, "the killing of Jews now transcends all other considerations."[157] The AHC, which, it will be recalled, eschewed all manner of cooperation with the UNSCOP, remained intransigent. To the United Nations Palestine Commission in January 1948, it responded as follows: "'ARAB HIGHER COMMITTEE IS DETERMINED PERSIST IN REJECTION PARTITION AND IN REFUSAL RECOGNIZE UNO RESOLUTION THIS RESPECT AND ANYTHING DERIVING THEREFROM. FOR THESE REASONS IT IS UNABLE ACCEPT INVITATION.'"[158] This rejectionism demonstrates a fundamental aspect of international dispute settlement: unless the parties to a dispute are willing to attempt a settlement and, what is more, to do so in good faith, it is unlikely that they will be able to settle their dispute.

The Arabs of Palestine, of course, had a particular interest in the Zionist project, but their rejectionism was not unique to them. Indeed, it was pan-Arab in orientation and had the full backing of the Arab world in general and the Arab League in particular. In December 1946, for example, the Arab League adopted a resolution that committed itself to "spar[ing] no effort to do everything warranted by the

[156] *See* S.C. Res. 48, U.N. Doc. S/RES/48 (Apr. 23, 1948); S.C. Res. 73, U.N. Doc. S/RES/73 (Aug. 11, 1949).

[157] Summary Record of the Sixteenth Meeting of the United Nations Palestine Commission, at 10, U.N. Doc. A/AC.21/SR.16 (Jan. 21, 1948).

[158] United Nations Palestine Commission, Communication from the Representative of the Arab Higher Committee for Palestine, U.N. Doc. A/AC.21/6 (Jan. 19, 1948).

circumstances for maintaining the Arab character of Palestine and for considering it a vital part of the larger Arab homeland."[159] The Arabs' campaign of defiance was already well underway by then. A year earlier, the Arab League had called for a boycott of Jewish products and manufactured goods from Palestine and demanded that Jewish industry generally be opposed by "all possible means."[160] This boycott was strengthened in mid June 1946.[161] The rejection of dialogue that the boycott represented would, the Arab League hoped, become the "firm creed of every Arab which he may most enthusiastically preach to all and which he may defend faithfully and genuinely."[162] A year after the armistice agreements were signed, a resolution was adopted that forbade the transport of Arab cargo on ships that also had Jews seeking to immigrate to Israel or that carried Jewish products and manufactured goods from the newly formed Jewish State and Jewish industry generally.[163] When the Arab world and Jewish self-determination were concerned, *mare liberum* was to be no more, at least according to the Arab side.

Perhaps sensing that the United Nations era would be one that would see the proliferation of international organizations, specialized agencies, and regional arrangements, the Arab League adopted an approach to international diplomacy at this time that was ideologically consistent with its rejection of Zionism and the Jewish State. It called for the refusal of entry by Israelis to Arab States for the purpose of attending conferences, Arab delegates were forbidden to speak with Israeli delegates at all conferences, and, although there were some pragmatic exceptions, the general position was that conferences in which Israel would be represented were to be boycotted out of principle by the Arab States.[164] While not as such prohibiting Arab States from joining treaty regimes in which Israel would also be a State Party, the Arab League made clear that joining such treaty regimes could not be construed as bestowing recognition upon Israel or reflecting a willingness on the part of the Arab States to cooperate with it with respect to the particular treaties at issue.[165] Furthermore, the conference boycott applied to both Arab State functionaries and Arab non-governmental organizations.[166] In other words, the boycott was to be total and complete, bridging both the public and private realms of the Arab world.

[159] Rejection of Palestine Partition Plan, Dec. 12, 1946, *in* 2 THE ARAB STATES AND THE ARAB LEAGUE, *supra* note 9, at 164.

[160] The Boycott of Zionist Goods and Products, Dec. 2, 1945, *in* 2 THE ARAB STATES AND THE ARAB LEAGUE, *supra* note 9, at 161.

[161] *See* Boycott of Zionist Products and Goods, June 12, 1946, *in* 2 THE ARAB STATES AND THE ARAB LEAGUE, *supra* note 9, at 162.

[162] *Id.* at 163.

[163] *See* Ships Carrying Contraband Goods and Immigrants to Israel, Apr. 8, 1950, *in* 2 THE ARAB STATES AND THE ARAB LEAGUE, *supra* note 9, at 166.

[164] *See* The Attitude of the Arab States Towards International Conferences and Organizations in Which Israel Participates, May 19, 1951, *in* 2 THE ARAB STATES AND THE ARAB LEAGUE, *supra* note 9, at 168.

[165] *See id.* at 169.

[166] *See* Regional Conferences Attended by Israel, Sept. 23, 1952, *in* 2 THE ARAB STATES AND THE ARAB LEAGUE, *supra* note 9, at 171.

On August 11, 1949, the Security Council adopted Resolution 73, which noted its satisfaction that a series of bilateral armistice agreements had been signed between Israel and Egypt, Lebanon, Jordan, and Syria.[167] Resolution 73 also expressed the Security Council's hope that the armistice agreements would act as a springboard, either through negotiations by individual Arab States with Israel or by them with the assistance of the UNCCP, "at an early date [... to] achieve agreement on the final settlement of all questions outstanding between them [i.e., the Arab States and Israel]."[168] Fundamentally, however, there was a disconnect in this hope because the Arab States were not interested in making peace with the Jewish State: they wanted to destroy it and the Zionism that it represented.[169]

To say this is not to engage in hyperbole. The Arab League claimed a "common danger to which the League States have been exposed in (their) defence of Palestine and of themselves"[170] and forbade individual Arab States from "negotiat[ing] or actually conclud[ing] a separate peace (treaty) or any (other) political, military, or economic agreement with Israel."[171] Violation of this would serve as grounds for expulsion from the Arab League,[172] but the penalty would not stop there. According to a resolution that the Arab League adopted in April 1950, the Arab States would also be required to close their borders with the violating State, enact a full boycott of it, and sever all political and consular relations with the violating State.[173] In many ways, a violating State would be treated as the Arab States had committed themselves to treating Israel, as a State *non grata.*

From the 1950s and into the 1960s and still further into the future, the Arabs' unyielding rejectionism remained constant. Gamal Abdel Nasser, President of the United Arab Republic, was one of the most prominent exponents of the Arab stance, and few were surprised when he used his influence as host of the Second Conference of Heads of State or Government of Non-Aligned Countries in October 1964 to steer the conference to the Arab world's way of thinking. The final declaration that was adopted in Cairo, the Programme for Peace and International Co-operation, "(1) endorse[d] the full restoration of all the rights of the Arab people of Palestine to their homeland, and their inalienable right to self-determination; [and] (2) declare[d] their full support to the Arab people of Palestine in their

[167] *See* S.C. Res. 73, *supra* note 156, at pmbl.

[168] *Id.* at ¶ 1.

[169] Unsurprisingly, this was also the view of the AHC, which decried, in 1955, the "Jewish authorities in Occupied Palestine." Letter from the Higher Arab Committee for Palestine, Presented to the Heads of Arab Governments, Foreign Ministers, Secretariat-General of the Arab League, and to Leaders of Political Parties and Parliamentary Blocs, Concerning Mr. Eric Johnston's Scheme, Aug. 18, 1955, *in* 2 The Arab States and the Arab League, *supra* note 9, at 634, 635.

[170] Peace with Israel, Apr. 1, 1950, *in* 2 The Arab States and the Arab League, *supra* note 9, at 165.

[171] *Id.* at 165–66.

[172] *See id. See also* The Policy of the Arab States Towards the Question of Palestine, *in* 2 The Arab States and the Arab League, *supra* note 9, at 166; Separate Peace with Israel, Apr. 13, 1950, *in* 2 The Arab States and the Arab League, *supra* note 9, at 166.

[173] *See* Separate Peace, *supra* note 172, at 167.

struggle for liberation from colonialism and racism."[174] In effect, then, the Non-Aligned Movement endorsed Palestinian self-determination at the expense of Jewish self-determination; it rejected Jewish nationalism, that is, Zionism, in favor of an exclusive Palestinian nationalism. The declaration's references to "colonialism" and "racism" were clear harbingers of the General Assembly's adoption a little over a decade later of Resolution 3379, which claimed that "zionism is a form of racism and racial discrimination."[175] There was no reaffirmation in the Non-Aligned Movement's Cairo declaration of the peaceful means of dispute settlement that had been proffered until then on the Palestine question, means that remained available to all of the parties under article 33(1) of the Charter, much less was there any condemnation in the Cairo declaration of the legitimacy of violent means of dispute settlement by the Arabs. Indeed, by not limiting its endorsement to peaceful means of dispute settlement, the Non-Aligned Movement seemed to have impliedly endorsed violent means of dispute settlement through its "full support to the Arab people of Palestine in their struggle for liberation from colonialism and racism."

VI. Between 1967 and 1973: The Introduction of a Negotiation Imperative

Given this historical pattern of Arab rejectionism, the Arab League's Khartoum Resolution, which was adopted on September 1, 1967, was entirely consistent with past practice. The Khartoum Resolution reiterated the call for Israeli withdrawal from "Arab lands," though the Arab League somewhat confusedly stated that the "occupied lands are Arab lands"[176] and in a subsequent paragraph in the Khartoum Resolution described the lands at issue as "Arab lands which have been occupied since the [Israeli] aggression of June 5."[177] Given that the Arabs had since 1948 consistently decried Israel itself for existing on "Arab lands," be it within the borders that Resolution 181 had stipulated for the Jewish State or within the 1949 armistice lines, it is unclear exactly which "Arab lands" the Arab League was referring to; the Arabs certainly did not recognize that Israel existed on any lands that they did not authentically view as "Arab lands." The Khartoum Resolution reaffirmed that "Arab lands" would be recovered "within the framework of the main principles by which the Arab States abide, namely, no peace with Israel, no recognition of Israel, no negotiations with it, and insistence on the rights of the

[174] Letter Dated 28 October 1964 from the Permanent Representative of the United Arab Republic to the United Nations Addressed to the Secretary-General, at 10, U.N. Doc. A/5763 (Oct. 29, 1964).
[175] G.A. Res. 3379, *supra* note 118, at pmbl.
[176] League of Arab States, Khartoum Resolution, Sept. 1, 1967, at ¶ 2, http://unispal.un.org/unispal.nsf/9a798adbf322aff38525617b006d88d7/1ff0bf3ddeb703a785257110007719e7?OpenDocument.
[177] *Id.* at ¶ 3.

Palestinian people in their own country."[178] As United States President Lyndon B. Johnson related to King Faisal in a letter later that September, the Khartoum Resolution "states what the Arabs will not do but, except by indirection, is silent on what the Arabs may be willing to do."[179]

In many respects, the 1967 War was a reprise of the 1948 War in that a coalition of Arab States sought to effect a regime change in what they continued to regard as the usurped "Arab lands" upon which the Jewish State had been established in 1948. Full-scale war broke out on June 5 after a month of escalating tensions in the region. In a heated meeting of the Security Council on June 6, Israeli Minister of Foreign Affairs Abba Eban invoked article 51 of the Charter.[180] As he told it, Egyptian troops were amassing along with Algerian and Kuwaiti forces on Israel's western border prior to Israel's strike of June 5, and Jordanian, Iraqi, and Syrian troops were approaching Israel's eastern approaches.[181] President Nasser had expelled the United Nations Emergency Force from the Sinai Peninsula, the Strait of Tiran and the Gulf of Aqaba had been closed to ships sailing to and from Eilat, Israel continued to be denied a right of passage through the Suez Canal, and Jordan had just entered into a defense agreement with Cairo.[182] Israel, according to Eban, faced an "apocalyptic air of approaching peril [... and] a systematic, overt, proclaimed design at politicide, the murder of a State."[183]

The Security Council responded much as it had in 1948, by demanding an immediate ceasefire,[184] though it was clear that a ceasefire could not be sustained

[178] *Id.*

[179] Letter from President Johnson to King Faisal, Washington, September 25, 1967, *in* 19 FOREIGN RELATIONS OF THE UNITED STATES, 1964–1968 Doc. 447, 846, 846–47. Although not a Member State of the Arab League, it is worth mentioning that Pakistan remarked at the time that the Khartoum Resolution was "moderate and in favour of a peaceful solution." U.N. GAOR, at 11, U.N. Doc. A/PV.1584 (Oct. 10, 1967).

[180] *See* U.N. SCOR, at 15, U.N. Doc. S/PV.1348 (June 6, 1967). "Nothing in the present Charter shall impair the inherent right of individual or collective self-defense if an armed attack occurs against a Member of the United Nations, until the Security Council has taken the measures necessary to maintain international peace and security. Measures taken by Members in the exercise of this right of self-defense shall be immediately reported to the Security Council and shall not in any way affect the authority and responsibility of the Security Council under the present Charter to take at any time such action as it deems necessary in order to maintain or restore international peace and security." U.N. Charter art. 51.

[181] *See* U.N. SCOR, *supra* note 180, at 14.

[182] *See id.* at 14–19.

[183] *Id.* at 15. For Eban's extended defense of Israel in the fifth emergency special session of the General Assembly on June 19, see U.N. GAOR, at 7–16, U.N. Doc. A/PV.1526 (June 19, 1967). *See also* U.N. GAOR, at 13–19, U.N. Doc. A/PV.1566 (Sept. 25, 1967). For a "revisionist" perspective on the 1967 War, see JOHN QUIGLEY, THE SIX-DAY WAR AND ISRAELI SELF-DEFENSE: QUESTIONING THE LEGAL BASIS FOR PREVENTIVE WAR (2013). The present author reviewed Quigley's *The Six-Day War and Israeli Self-Defense: Questioning the Legal Basis for Preventive War* at: 1 J. USE FORCE & INT'L L. 190 (2014).

[184] *See* S.C. Res. 233, U.N. Doc. S/RES/233 (June 6, 1967); S.C. Res. 234, U.N. Doc. S/RES/234 (June 7, 1967); S.C. Res. 235, U.N. Doc. S/RES/235 (June 9, 1967); S.C. Res. 236, U.N. Doc. S/RES/236 (June 11, 1967); S.C. Res. 240, U.N. Doc. S/RES/240 (Oct. 25, 1967). On June 14, the Security Council called for all of the parties to the armed conflict to comply with international humanitarian law. *See* S.C. Res. 237, U.N. Doc. S/RES/237 (June 14, 1967). It also called for Israel to "facilitate the return of those inhabitants who have fled the areas since the outbreak of hostilities." *Id.* at ¶ 1.

in the absence of a willingness by all of the parties to the dispute to settle their underlying differences. For its part, Israel reaffirmed its commitment to negotiate with the Arab world,[185] but the Arab response was the by then standard position of rejectionism and delegitimization. Syria, for example, castigated the "terrorist and sabotage roots on which Israel as a State was founded"[186] and accused Israel of a genocidal war of conquest and intimidation.[187] Morocco criticized the "mistake" of 1948, which, in its understanding, was not the Arab world's rejection of the partition plan's call for two States for two peoples but, rather, the "amputation of the Arab territory in order to put people there who are free to go wherever they wish but who have evicted others who had lived there much longer than the oft-mentioned two thousand years."[188] Pakistan, though not an Arab State, expressed a similar view in the General Assembly, asserting that the "real roots of the conflict in the Middle East are the concomitants of Israel's creation."[189]

As summer 1967 turned to autumn, the Security Council remained deadlocked, unable to agree to anything other than a ceasefire between the parties. Ensuing months gave all of the sides further time to make their positions known. Jordan, which, it will be recalled, had occupied much of the land that Resolution 181 had designated for the envisaged Arab State of Palestine and the eastern part of what was intended to have become the *corpus separatum* of Jerusalem, adopted a common Arab tactic at the time of comparing the Jewish State to Nazi Germany.[190] The establishment of Israel in 1948 was itself said to be an act of "aggression[]."[191] On November 13, Amman called for the withdrawal of the Israel Defense Forces to the 1949 armistice lines[192] and the enforcement of the "inalienable right [of the Palestinians] to go back to their homes and regain their life and property [within these same lines]."[193] Given demographic realities, this was quite clearly a call to reverse the existing reality of a Jewish State in Palestine, something that Jordan assailed in the Security Council as a "mistake committed two decades ago."[194]

The Arabs were uncompromising in the debates in the United Nations, with Syria even alleging in the Security Council that Israel sought a "Greater Reich"[195] and later claiming that "Israel is very similar to the Nazis because it has blood on its hands and it cannot escape its guilt."[196] It was not a question of the Arab world

[185] *See* U.N. SCOR, *supra* note 180, at 18.
[186] *Id.* at 19.
[187] *See id.* at 21.
[188] *Id.* at 25.
[189] U.N. GAOR, *supra* note 179, at 11.
[190] *See, e.g.*, U.N. GAOR, at 4, U.N. Doc. A/PV.1575 (Oct. 2, 1967).
[191] *Id.*
[192] *See* U.N. SCOR, at 10, U.N. Doc. S/PV.1375 (Nov. 13, 1967).
[193] *Id.* at 11.
[194] *Id. Cf.* Henry Cattan, Palestine and International Law: The Legal Aspects of the Arab-Israeli Conflict 157 (1974) (recognizing that implementation of a "right of return" would "de-Judaize the present racist State of Israel").
[195] U.N. SCOR, at 13, U.N. Doc. S/PV.1377 (Nov. 15, 1967).
[196] *Id.* at 15. Syria had earlier informed the General Assembly that: "Zionism is following in the footsteps of Nazism, another philosophy based on intimidation, aggression, occupation and expulsion of peoples from their lands." U.N. GAOR, *supra* note 183, at 21 (1566th mtg.).

being willing to accommodate a Jewish State with territorial adjustments; the Arabs remained opposed, as they always had been, to a Jewish State of any kind. Saudi Arabia was quite clear in expressing the Arab consensus, "the Arab world cannot accommodate Zionism in our midst."[197] Zionism was not the national liberation movement of the Jewish people[198] but, as Riyadh put it, a "new form of colonialism,"[199] an ideology that had generated and continued to sustain an "artificial State."[200] According to the Saudis, those who were not unremittedly committed to Israel's destruction would be "liquidated by none other than the Arab people."[201] It need hardly be emphasized that an expressed will to live in peace and security with the Jewish State this was not. Lebanon made clear that even if Israel were to withdraw from territories beyond the 1949 armistice lines that the Arabs would refuse peace with it, refuse to recognize it, and refuse to negotiate with it.[202] In Beirut's reading, Israel was a colonial power, and the Arabs would continue to strive ever onward to their "liberation from colonialism in all its forms and manifestations."[203]

These same months also saw Israel make its case to the international community and convey its view as to how the underlying dispute should be settled. Its position was the opposite of the Arabs' view, the opposite of the Khartoum Resolution and its embodiment of Arab rejectionism. Eban put it thus in the Security Council on November 13: "Against the Khartoum policy of no recognition, no negotiation and no peace, Israel presents its policy: Recognition, negotiation, peace."[204] The bedrock position for Israel was Israeli–Arab peace based upon treaties of mutual recognition and grounded in security.[205] As it had consistently done since 1948, Israel continued to insist upon negotiations with the Arab States that would lead to a permanent settlement. Certainly, negotiations are usually seen as a means to an end, a means to settle a dispute, but to Eban, to insist upon a negotiated settlement with the Arab States was "not a matter of procedure. The issue is one of principle and substance. A refusal to negotiate is inherently identical with a refusal to live in peace."[206] Israel felt that the United Nations could play a constructive role in resolving the Israeli–Arab dispute to the extent that it promoted direct negotiations between the parties.[207]

India, a State with neither a significant Jewish population nor a significant Arab population, made a particularly noteworthy contribution to the debates then

[197] U.N. GAOR, *supra* note 183, at 17 (1526th mtg.).

[198] For an extended case in this direction, of Zionism as an anti-imperialist movement and national liberation struggle, see U.N. SCOR, at 7–9, U.N. Doc. S/PV.1747 (Oct. 21–22, 1973) (Israel).

[199] U.N. GAOR, *supra* note 183, at 17 (1526th mtg.).

[200] *Id.*

[201] *Id.*

[202] *See* U.N. GAOR, at 3, U.N. Doc. A/PV.1582 (Oct. 6, 1967).

[203] *Id.* at 4.

[204] U.N. SCOR, *supra* note 192, at 4.

[205] *See id.* at 3–4.

[206] U.N. GAOR, *supra* note 183, at 16 (1566th mtg.).

[207] *See id. See also* U.N. SCOR, *supra* note 192, at 8.

taking place in the United Nations. It co-sponsored a draft resolution with Mali and Nigeria that, though never brought to a vote, was appreciated for its insistence that the dispute between Israel and the Arab States needed to be settled by peaceful means. The three-Power draft resolution affirmed that peace needed to be achieved "within the framework of the Charter of the United Nations."[208] One of the bedrock principles of the United Nations is Member States' obligation to settle their disputes peacefully,[209] which precludes, of course, the threat or use of force as a means of dispute settlement.[210] The three-Power draft resolution went on to expressly call for Israel and the Arab States to "settle their international disputes by peaceful means,"[211] a reference that brings to mind the panoply of diplomatic and legal means of dispute settlement that are contained in Chapter VI of the Charter and that are available to parties to disputes. Much of this thinking would find its way into the final resolution that the Security Council adopted in the wake of the 1967 War.

The Security Council adopted Resolution 242 early on the morning of November 22 as a compromise resolution, and it has acted as the general framework for settling the Israeli–Arab dispute and for all mainstream peace initiatives since 1967.[212] Its preamble emphasizes article 2 of the Charter, article 2(3) of which expressly calls for Member States to settle their disputes peacefully. Paragraphs 1 and 2 of Resolution 242 reflect a "land for peace" formula and affirm certain other matters as priorities. Resolution 242 also calls for a Special Representative of the Secretary-General to the Middle East to engage with Israel and the Arab States in order to "promote agreement and assist efforts to achieve a peaceful and accepted settlement in accordance with the provisions and principles in this resolution."[213] In other words, Resolution 242 does not require a particular means of dispute settlement for the parties but does require them to settle their dispute peacefully and on the basis of consent. Ethiopia,[214] Brazil,[215] Canada,[216] and Bulgaria[217] expressed some support in the Security Council for a negotiated settlement, but the requirement to negotiate as such does not appear in Resolution 242 and cannot be said to have been intended by the Security Council as an exclusive means of dispute settlement for the parties.[218]

[208] U.N. SCOR, at ¶ 1, U.N. Doc. S/8227 (Nov. 7, 1967).

[209] *See* U.N. Charter art. 2(3).

[210] *See id.* at art. 2(4).

[211] U.N. SCOR, *supra* note 208, at ¶ 1(ii).

[212] *See* S.C. Res. 242, U.N. Doc. S/RES/242 (Nov. 22, 1967). The United Kingdom's Permanent Representative to the United Nations at the time, Lord Caradon, introduced the draft resolution that was to become Resolution 242. For his views on Resolution 242, see Lord Caradon, *An Interview with Lord Caradon*, 5(3–4) J. PAL. STUD. 142 (1976).

[213] S.C. Res. 242, *supra* note 212, at ¶ 3.

[214] *See* U.N. SCOR, at 4–5, U.N. Doc. S/PV.1382 (Nov. 22, 1967).

[215] *See id.* at 13.

[216] *See id.* at 14.

[217] *See id.* at 15.

[218] Less than a year later, Iraq would make the point that "the old position of direct negotiations [...] was expressly excluded from the resolution of 22 November 1967—excluded not by accident but

Like many legal texts, Resolution 242 opens itself to a variety of interpretations, and many of these can be arrived at in good faith. Indeed, in explaining their votes in favor of Resolution 242 in the Security Council, delegations themselves expressed disparate interpretations of a text that they had only a few minutes before unanimously adopted.[219] One thing that does seem clear, however, is that Resolution 242 is a profoundly inter-State instrument, in the sense that it positions the parties to the dispute as being the States in the region and only the States in the region. The instrument dismisses the Palestinians as one might dismiss a "non-people." Indeed, it does not even seem too strong to say that Palestinians *qua* Palestinians, in the juridical sense, "do not exist" in Resolution 242. A 1979 cable from the British Mission to the United Nations in New York observed that Resolution 242

> does not deal with the question of the Palestinians. It takes no account of their belief that they are a separate people with political rights which go well beyond their status as refugees, which was recognized in Resolution 242, a people distinct from the peoples of the countries where they now live.[220]

Syria was surely correct when it made the point that the Arabs of Palestine "are totally absent from the picture"[221] and that the British draft resolution that would shortly thereafter be adopted in the Security Council as Resolution 242 "ignores [...] the right of the Palestinian people to self-determination."[222]

That, in Resolution 242, the Palestinians possessed neither national rights nor the "peoplehood" upon which is predicated the exercise of self-determination was clear at the time. In a statement that it issued the day after Resolution 242 was adopted, the Palestine Liberation Organization (PLO) vehemently rejected the final text as "fundamentally and gravely inconsistent with the Arab character of Palestine, the essence of the Palestine cause and the right of the Palestinian people to their homeland."[223] Resolution 242 "disappoints the hopes of the Arab nation and ignores its national aspirations [... and] ignores the existence of the Palestinian people and their right of self-determination."[224] Tellingly, though consistent

deliberately excluded in the long weeks and months of discussions and deliberations that preceded the adoption of the resolution." U.N. SCOR, at 9, U.N. Doc. S/PV.1407 (Mar. 24, 1968).

[219] *See* U.N. SCOR, *supra* note 214, at 8–19. Justice Arthur J. Goldberg, the Permanent United States Representative to the United Nations at the time that Resolution 242 was adopted, stated that the final text's "ambiguities" were "purposeful and not unintended." Arthur J. Goldberg, *United Nations Security Council Resolution 242 and the Prospects for Peace in the Middle East,* 12(2) COLUM. J. TRANSNAT'L L. 187, 192 (1973). *See* Charles D. Smith, *The United States and the 1967 War, in* THE 1967 ARAB-ISRAELI WAR: ORIGINS AND CONSEQUENCES 165, 185 (William Roger Louis & Avi Shlaim eds., 2012) (referring to Resolution 242 as a "masterpiece of British ambiguity and obfuscation").

[220] Mansfield, Telegram Number 946 of 24 August 1979, *in* RECORDS OF THE PRIME MINISTER'S OFFICE: CORRESPONDENCE AND PAPERS, 1979–1997. MIDDLE EAST. SITUATION IN THE MIDDLE EAST; PART 1 at 38, 38, No. PREM/19/92 (1979) (capitals omitted).

[221] U.N. SCOR, *supra* note 214, at 1.

[222] *Id.* at 2.

[223] Statement Issued by the Palestine Liberation Organization Rejecting U.N. Resolutions [*sic*] 242, Cairo, 23 November, 1967, *in* THE ISRAELI-PALESTINIAN CONFLICT: A DOCUMENTARY RECORD: 1967–1990 290, 290 (Yehuda Lukacs ed., 1992).

[224] *Id.* at 291.

with the Arab stance according to which the existence of a Jewish State on any part of what had been the British Mandate for Palestine was itself illegitimate, the PLO's statement of rejection referred to the coast of the Gulf of Aqaba as being "occupied."[225] Israel was itself "occupation," in other words, by its very nature. As the Embassy of Israel in London put it in a "Background Paper" in August 1979, the PLO opposed Resolution 242 "not because this Resolution refers to the Palestinians as refugees but because it demands recognition of Israel, while the P.L.O. wants a state in place of Israel."[226] In fact, both reasons were sufficient cause for the PLO's rejection of Resolution 242, since Palestinian nationalism had not reconciled itself with a Jewish State.[227]

Others associated with Palestinian nationalism, jurists and activists alike, were of a similar mind as the PLO in seeing Resolution 242 as a betrayal of the idea of a Palestinian national identity. This much was clear to Cattan, for example, who had made the AHC's case against partition in the United Nations in 1947.[228] Edward W. Said also recognized that Resolution 242 "do[es] not have one word [...] about Palestinians, their rights, or aspirations."[229] Francis A. Boyle, a legal adviser to the PLO, made the point that the Palestinian people did not have legal rights as such under Resolution 242 and that it was Jordan, not the Palestinians, that had standing according to Resolution 242 to demand Israeli withdrawal from territories beyond the 1949 armistice lines, excepting, of course, the Gaza Strip.[230] In a letter that he published in the *Times* in November 1973, PLO representative Said Hammami also noted that Resolution 242's failure to mention the Palestinians as such, that is, the Palestinians as autonomous actors, as a "people" with "rights," was a "flagrant disregard of the human and national rights of a whole people."[231] If the aim of Resolution 242 was to "establish [...] a just and lasting peace in the Middle East,"[232] which it surely was, such a peace could be established, at least according to the United Nations principal organ charged with "primary responsibility for the

[225] *Id.*

[226] Embassy of Israel, Background Paper, Aug. 15, 1979, *in* RECORDS, *supra* note 220, at 62, 68. *See Self-Determination: The Case of Palestine*, 82 AM. SOC'Y INT'L L. PROC. 334, 339 (1988) (Yehuda Blum).

[227] The 1967 War was a seminal event in the development of Palestinian nationalism. As Pearlman relates it, the 1967 War "redefined the balance of power between Palestinian nationalist mobilization and Arab state action," Wendy Pearlman, *The Palestinian National Movement*, *in* THE 1967 ARAB-ISRAELI WAR, *supra* note 219, at 126, 138, and "confirm[ed] the Palestinian national movement as a distinct force in the Arab-Israeli conflict," *id.* at 148.

[228] *See* HENRY CATTAN, PALESTINE AND INTERNATIONAL LAW: THE LEGAL ASPECTS OF THE ARAB-ISRAELI CONFLICT 203–209 (2d ed. 1976).

[229] EDWARD W. SAID, PEACE AND ITS DISCONTENTS: GAZA-JERICHO 1993–1995 6 (1995). *See* EDWARD W. SAID, THE QUESTION OF PALESTINE 226 (1992) (stating that accepting Resolution 242 was to "deny the *national* dimension of the Palestinian question, for 242 spoke only of 'refugees'"). *See also* JAMES SUMMERS, PEOPLES AND INTERNATIONAL LAW: HOW NATIONALISM AND SELF-DETERMINATION SHAPE A CONTEMPORARY LAW OF NATIONS 363–64 (2007).

[230] *See* Francis A. Boyle, *The Interim Agreement and International Law*, 22(3) ARAB STUD. Q. 1, 8–9 (2000). *See also* Richard Falk, *Forty Years After 242: A "Canonical" Text in Disrepute?*, 37(1) J. PAL. STUD. 39, 41 (2007).

[231] Said Hammami, *The Palestinian Way to Middle East Peace*, TIMES, Nov. 16, 1973.

[232] S.C. Res. 242, *supra* note 212, at ¶ 1.

maintenance of international peace and security,"[233] without acknowledging the Palestinians as a "people."[234]

It was only on October 22, 1973, when the Security Council adopted Resolution 338, that the Security Council entrenched negotiation as the imperative means of dispute settlement for the Israeli-Arab dispute. The shuttle diplomacy of Gunnar V. Jarring, the appointed Special Representative of the Secretary-General to the Middle East, had by then proven itself unsuccessful. As a report from United Nations Secretary-General Kurt Waldheim frankly admitted in September 1972, "it has not been possible to make any substantial progress [...] an agreed basis for discussions under Ambassador Jarring's auspices does not seem to exist at the present time."[235] With the introduction of *détente* between the two superpowers, the United States and the Soviet Union seemed willing to cooperate more closely on the Palestine question and take a leadership role together in the Security Council. Reflective of this, the two States jointly sponsored a draft resolution on October 21, the text of which would become Resolution 338.[236]

Resolution 338 essentially had three aims. Firstly, it called for an immediate ceasefire.[237] Secondly, it called for all of the parties concerned, immediately after the ceasefire, to implement Resolution 242.[238] Thirdly, Resolution 338 decided that, "immediately and concurrently with the cease-fire, negotiations shall start between the parties concerned under appropriate auspices aimed at establishing a just and durable peace in the Middle East."[239] The three aims of Resolution 338 were to be sequenced such that the ceasefire was to be achieved immediately, or at least "no later than 12 hours after the moment of the adoption of this decision, in the positions they [i.e., the parties to the 1973 War] now occupy."[240] Implementation of Resolution 242 was to take place immediately after this (immediate) step, which perhaps suggests that the legally-binding effect of Resolution 242 was to be held "in abeyance" until the ceasefire came into (immediate) effect. Negotiations were to commence "immediately and concurrently with the cease-fire." Thus, one can say that Resolution 338 required the immediate implementation of both the ceasefire and negotiations, with the implementation of Resolution 242 to take

233 U.N. Charter art. 24(1).

234 Similarly, Peretz, writing in 1970, observed that "[n]either the principal antagonists nor the major powers officially acknowledge [the] existence of the Palestinians as a nation-party to the dispute." Don Peretz, *Arab Palestine: Phoenix or Phantom?*, 48(2) FOREIGN AFF. 322, 322 (1970). *See* Omar M. Dajani, *Forty Years Without Resolve: Tracing the Influence of Security Council Resolution 242 on the Middle East Peace Process*, 37(1) J. PAL. STUD. 24, 36 (2007) (criticizing Resolution 242 for its "complete inattention to the Palestinians' right of self-determination").

235 Report of the Secretary-General on the Activities of the Special Representative to the Middle East, U.N. Doc. A/8815 (Sept. 15, 1972). *See* Questionnaire by UN Special Representative Gunnar Jarring to the Governments of Egypt, Jordan, Israel, and Lebanon, With Replies, March 1969, *in* THE ISRAELI-PALESTINIAN CONFLICT, *supra* note 223, at 2.

236 *See* U.N. SCOR, U.N. Doc. S/11036 (Oct. 21, 1973).

237 *See* S.C. Res. 338, at ¶ 1, U.N. Doc. S/RES/338 (Oct. 22, 1973).

238 *See id.* at ¶ 2. Effectively, then, Resolution 338 reaffirmed Resolution 242's dismissal of the Palestinians as a "non-people."

239 *Id.* at ¶ 3.

240 *Id.* at ¶ 1.

place immediately after the ceasefire had been implemented and negotiations had commenced.

It was the third paragraph of Resolution 338—"immediately and concurrently with the cease-fire, negotiations shall start between the parties concerned under appropriate auspices aimed at establishing a just and durable peace in the Middle East"—that broke new ground. It did this by amending the approach that Resolution 242 had taken to dispute settlement and by enhancing the sense of urgency and engagement for all of the parties concerned. Quite what the "appropriate auspices" were under which negotiations were to take place, however, remained a point of debate. The United States suggested that this meant the joint good offices of it and the Soviet Union.[241] London interpreted "appropriate auspices" to mean the United Nations[242] while Paris viewed it as meaning the Security Council.[243] Kenya agreed with the British interpretation of paragraph 3, though it suggested that the Security Council also needed to be regularly updated on developments.[244] Javier Pérez de Cuéllar, who would later become United Nations Secretary-General, expressed the Peruvian view that the Secretary-General and the Security Council, working together, were the "appropriate auspices."[245] Saudi Arabia cynically asked: "What will prevent Israel from saying that the negotiations to start between the parties concerned should be at the same table? Who is going to say what 'under appropriate auspices' means?"[246] Israel, of course, continued to insist upon "free, direct, normal peace negotiations between Israel and its neighbours,"[247] though this was nothing new, and saw in paragraph 3 "important progress in international policy on this crucial point."[248]

Despite some ambiguities in the text, Resolution 338 represented a discernible shift in favor of the Israeli view as to how the dispute between Israel and the Arab States should be settled. The Arabs hoped that the "appropriate auspices" language would sufficiently distance them from Israel and allow them to continue with their traditional rejectionist stance, but the express inclusion in paragraph 3 of an obligation to negotiate belies this possibility. Paragraph 3 was also undoubtedly a Security Council "decision," meaning that it legally obligated the Arabs to accept and carry it out,[249] "it," in this case, being negotiations with Israel.

Resolution 338 was also a clear rejection of the Fourth Conference of Heads of State or Government of Non-Aligned Countries, which Algiers had hosted on September 5 to 9, 1973.[250] The official documents from that conference had called

241 *See* U.N. SCOR, *supra* note 198, at 2.

242 *See id.* at 6. This was also the Sudanese interpretation. *See id.* at 13.

243 *See id.* at 7.

244 *See id.* at 10.

245 *See id.* at 11.

246 *Id.* at 18.

247 *Id.* at 12.

248 *Id.*

249 *See* U.N. Charter art. 25.

250 For the official documents of the Algiers conference, see Letter Dated 22 November 1973 from the Permanent Representative of Algeria to the United Nations Addressed to the Secretary-General, U.N. Doc. A/9330 (Nov. 22, 1973).

for Zionism's "eradicat[ion],"[251] stressed the national rights of Palestinians,[252] described the Jewish State as "zionism settler-colonialism [that] has taken the form of a systematic uprooting of the Palestinian people from their homeland and [that] represents a very serious threat to their survival as a nation,"[253] demanded that States prevent their Jewish nationals from immigrating to anywhere in the former Palestine Mandate west of the Jordan, and called for a full boycott of Israel.[254] A declaration that Algeria had circulated to the Security Council on October 10 on behalf of the Non-Aligned Movement that reaffirmed the Algiers manifesto was also rejected by the Security Council.[255]

Of course, to say that the Rubicon had been crossed and that negotiation had become the imperative means of dispute settlement for Israel and the Arab States is not to suggest that the Arabs had accepted Israel as a legitimate sovereign. The Soviets had opined in the Security Council in March 1968 that an Israeli withdrawal to the 1949 armistice lines would mean that "there would be neither occupied territories nor any foreign population oppressed in those territories, and there would be no conflicts,"[256] but this was clearly not the Arabs' perception of the territories that were "occupied." At the same Security Council meeting in 1968, Morocco perceived that the Arabs' "liberation movement" had been "continuing without a let-up for the past twenty years."[257] 1948 was also quite obviously, for Jordan, the date of Israel's "continued occupation of territories belonging to Jordan, Syria, the United Arab Republic and *the Palestinian people*,"[258] and Iraq also traced Israel's "occupation" to 1948.[259] Of course, even though Resolutions 242 and 338 did not recognize the PLO as being a party to the Israeli–Arab dispute, it should also be recognized, given the succor and refuge that the Arab States gave to it, that the PLO also viewed 1948, and not 1967, as the date of Israel's "occupation" of "Arab lands," as evidenced by PLO constitutional documents both before and after the 1967 War.[260]

VII. Conclusion

The almost three-decade period between the 1948 War and the 1973 War unfolded, quite obviously, contrary to the General Assembly's intentions. By adopting

[251] *Id.* at 9.
[252] *See id.* at 11.
[253] *Id.* at 27.
[254] *See id.* at 35.
[255] *See* Letter Dated 10 October 1973 from the Permanent Representative of Algeria to the United Nations Addressed to the Secretary-General, U.N. Doc. S/11019 (Oct. 10, 1973).
[256] U.N. SCOR, *supra* note 218, at 4.
[257] *Id.* at 10.
[258] *Id.* at 14 (emphasis added).
[259] *See* U.N. SCOR, at 4, U.N. Doc. S/PV.1736 (Aug. 13, 1973). *See also* U.N. SCOR, at 4–5, U.N. Doc. S/PV.1744 (Oct. 9, 1973) (Syria).
[260] *See* National Covenant of the Palestine Liberation Organization, May 28, 1964, HAARETZ, May 14, 2002; The Palestine National Covenant, 1968, *in* THE ISRAELI-PALESTINIAN CONFLICT, *supra*

Resolution 181, which can now surely be regarded as having been naive and misplaced given geopolitical realities at the time, the General Assembly sought to reconcile the Arab and Jewish national movements with one another in the small piece of land west of the Jordan. The States that it had envisaged would be established were to have reflected the national prerogatives of the respective majority populations while simultaneously "[g]uaranteeing to all persons equal and non-discriminatory rights in civil, political, economic and religious matters and the enjoyment of human rights and fundamental freedoms, including freedom of religion, language, speech and publication, education, assembly and association."[261] This has been achieved, to a large extent, with respect to the Jewish State,[262] but a Palestinian State has yet to emerge as anticipated by Resolution 181. It was in Palestine that the Jewish and Arab national projects would collide and compete for recognition, and this would unfold, painfully and violently, in ensuing decades.

The Arab world no more recognized the legitimacy of Jewish self-determination at the end of this period, in 1973, than it did at the beginning, in 1948. From an Arab perspective, the Jews remained a religious minority in a land that was both foreign to them and where they were unwelcome, not a "people" with a right to self-determination. Palestinian poet laureate Mahmoud Darwish's 1988 poem "Those Who Pass Between Fleeting Words" makes the Arab view quite clear:

> Live wherever you like, but do not live among us
> It is time for you to be gone
> Die wherever you like, but do not die among us
> [...]
> So leave our country
> Our land, our sea
> Our wheat, our salt, our wounds
> Everything, and leave.[263]

It is not altogether surprising that such a worldview could do little to tempt the Arabs to engage with the various means of dispute settlement on offer during this period other than as half measures and with half a heart. By the end of 1973, however, Israel had succeeded in convincing the Security Council to entrench what it had always wanted, negotiation, as the imperative means of dispute settlement.

note 223, at 291. Israel made the point before the Security Council in August 1973 that "the objective of the Habashes and Arafats is not to bring about Israeli withdrawal from the cease-fire lines, but to eliminate Israel as a sovereign State and to annihilate its people. All are aware that Arab terrorism, aimed against the Jewish people's right to self-determination, began 50 years ago, and not in 1967." U.N. SCOR, *supra* note 259, at 9 (1736th mtg.).

[261] G.A. Res. 181, at (I)(B)(10)(d), U.N. Doc. A/RES/181 (Nov. 29, 1947).

[262] *See* Ruth Gavison, *The Jews' Right to Statehood: A Defense*, 15 AZURE 70 (2003). *See also* Asher Susser, *Partition and the Arab Palestinian Minority in Israel*, 14(2) ISR. STUD. 105 (2009).

[263] Mahmoud Darwish, Those Who Pass Between Fleeting Words, *in* INTIFADA: THE PALESTINIAN UPRISING AGAINST ISRAELI OCCUPATION 26, 27 (Zachary Lockman & Joel Beinin eds., 1989).

4

The Emergence of Palestinian International Legal Personality and the Bilateral Negotiation Imperative: 1973 to Oslo

I. Introduction

As the previous chapter showed, 1973 marked the crossing of the Rubicon after which negotiation became the imperative means of dispute settlement for the Israeli–Arab dispute. By adopting Resolution 338, the United Nations Security Council decided that negotiations under "appropriate auspices" were the most promising, and only acceptable, way forward. To be sure, there had never been any suggestion that the parties concerned could have used means other than peaceful ones to settle their dispute, but there was no question after this time that the dispute had to be settled through negotiation. Formally, of course, the dispute remained profoundly inter-State in orientation, with the Jewish State and the Arab States, which remained united as a bloc, being the only acknowledged parties to it. As with Security Council Resolution 242 before it, Resolution 338 showed little concern for Palestinian nationalism, and just as these resolutions saw the Palestine Liberation Organization (PLO) as dispensable to the dispute, so also did the Israeli side view the idea of dialogue with the PLO as inconceivable. Prime Minister Yitzhak Rabin put the matter thus in March 1977: "Le dialogue avec l'O.L.P. n'est possible que sur le champ de bataille."[1]

Many States found the juridical "absence" of the Palestinians to be quite unacceptable. Consider the debates in late 1974 that preceded the United Nations General Assembly's decision to allow the PLO to participate in its work on the Palestine question.[2] Tunisia, for example, lamented that the General Assembly was only then, and for the first time in over a quarter of a century, considering the

[1] *M. Rabin: Le Dialogue Avec l'O.L.P. n'est Possible que Sur le Champ de Bataille*, LE MONDE, Mar. 22, 1977.

[2] *See* G.A. Res. 3210, U.N. Doc. A/RES/3210 (Oct. 14, 1974).

"national and international identity of a people,"[3] and Benin (or Dahomey as it was then known) struck out in defense of the Palestinians' rejection of "bread and circuses."[4] When PLO Chairman Yasser Arafat addressed the General Assembly in mid November 1974, he framed Palestinian self-determination as being inherently hostile to Zionism, seeing in Zionism nothing but colonialism, neo-colonialism, imperialism, and racism.[5] Chairman Arafat's rejection of Jewish self-determination in Israel—he referred to the Jewish national home as an inferno that offered Jews "perpetual bloodshed, endless war and continuous thraldom"[6]—was consistent with the broader Arab view, but it effectively ensured that the Palestinian national movement would remain politically powerless on the ground for some time to come. Over time, however, the PLO's strategy would become less "radical," more "politically palatable," and enter the "mainstream" of international politics and notions of legality. Put simply, the PLO would come to afford some measure of recognition to the State of Israel.

This chapter explores how the negotiation imperative that was ushered into being in 1973 evolved to include a specifically bilateral negotiation imperative between Israel and the PLO, and the crystallization of Palestinian international legal personality and (an unfolding sense of) self-determination for the Palestinians. This was an uneven process that took place gradually and involved the input, acts, and omissions of a variety of State and non-State actors, in various fora and at different levels. It unfolded in roughly three phases, each of which this chapter examines in detail. The first phase took place in the aftermath of Resolution 338, when the Arab world recognized the PLO as the sole legitimate representative of the Palestinian people, the United States and the Soviet Union led a negotiation effort in Geneva, and Egypt and Israel established diplomatic relations at the end of the 1970s. During the second phase, peace plans, at least those that had the backing of the United States (and hence the Security Council), continued to exclude the PLO, but with the PLO's decision to afford some measure of recognition to Israel in 1988, this would change. The third phase began in the early 1990s and saw the PLO negotiate with Israel as a distinct international legal person in a dispute settlement process that had come to involve the creation of specific rights and obligations. It is only by closely engaging with this complex matrix of law that the international law of negotiation can thereafter be applied as a framework for assessing the Israeli–Palestinian dispute discussed in Chapter 6 of this work.

[3] U.N. GAOR, at 662, U.N. Doc. A/PV.2267 (Oct. 14, 1974).
[4] *Id.* at 659.
[5] *See* U.N. GAOR, at 861, U.N. Doc. A/PV.2282 and Corr. 1 (Nov. 13, 1974).
[6] *Id.* at 868.

II. In the Aftermath of United Nations Security Council Resolution 338 (1973): From Algiers to Rabat, and Geneva to Camp David

The Security Council invited the PLO to participate in its work on Palestine in a procedural vote that it took in mid January 1976.[7] In addressing the Security Council immediately after the vote, the PLO's Farouk Khaddoumi put forward what was then an accurate depiction of the Palestinians' juridical position. The question of Palestine "had become," Khaddoumi lamented, "either one of displaced persons or a matter of disputed frontiers between the adjacent Arab States and Israel."[8] As Chairman Arafat put it to the General Assembly just two years earlier, the Palestinians were seen as "disembodied spirits, fictions without presence, without traditions or future."[9] This state of affairs surely raised questions of humanitarian concern and charity, but not (at least not necessarily) Palestinian rights vested in law. Much to their disappointment, the Palestinians remained at the margins of a dispute that continued to be seen as one between, to quote Resolution 242, "every *State* in the area."[10]

At this time, a large measure of international law's reluctance to afford a distinct role to the Palestinians can be traced to the fate of the already existing "Palestinian" Arab State in the region.[11] Jordan, it will be recalled, had been forged out of key events in mid 1922, when the Palestine Mandate's Jewish national home provisions were disapplied to the larger part of Palestine east of the Jordan River.[12] During the 1948 War, Amman gained control of the eastern sector of Jerusalem, which the General Assembly had intended to have formed part of a *corpus separatum* administered by the United Nations under a special international regime,[13] and territory that would thereafter come to be known as the West Bank (of the

[7] *See* U.N. SCOR, U.N. Doc. S/PV.1870 (Jan. 12, 1976). The United States was alone in voting against this procedural motion, with France, Italy, and the United Kingdom abstaining.

[8] *Id.* at 19 (continuing by stating: "Such a depiction of the question of Palestine was a blatant attempt to ignore the existence of the Palestinian people, its national rights, its right to self-determination, independence and sovereignty, and even the resolutions of the United Nations—unjust as some of these were").

[9] U.N. GAOR, *supra* note 5, at 863.

[10] S.C. Res. 242, at ¶ 1(ii), U.N. Doc. S/RES/242 (Nov. 22, 1967) (emphasis added). The same could be said for Resolution 338, which "set the seal on 242 without allowing for any alterations or additions to meet the Palestinian question directly." MADIHA RASHID AL MADFAI, JORDAN, THE UNITED STATES AND THE MIDDLE EAST PEACE PROCESS, 1974–1991 180 (2007).

[11] On this, see Eugene Rostow, *"Palestinian Self-Determination": Possible Futures for the Unallocated Territories of the Palestine Mandate*, 5 YALE STUD. WORLD PUB. ORD. 147 (1979). *See also* Yehuda Blum, *Self-Determination: The Case of Palestine*, 82 AM. SOC'Y INT'L L. PROC. 334, 338–41 (1988); JULIUS STONE, ISRAEL AND PALESTINE: ASSAULT ON THE LAW OF NATIONS 22–25 (1981).

[12] See Chapter 2, 17–21.

[13] *See* G.A. Res. 181, 17–21 at pt. 3, U.N. Doc. A/RES/181 (Nov. 29, 1947).

Jordan). Effectively, this meant that a large proportion of Palestinians fell under Arab control for the first time.[14]

Even though it was unclear how long Jordan intended to hold onto this territory or what its precise intentions were, Amman's presence west of the Jordan was effectively regularized when a joint session of both Houses of Parliament met on April 24, 1950, to proclaim the "complete unity between the two sides of the Jordan and their union into one state."[15] The joint resolution justified this union on the basis of self-determination, "natural aspirations,"[16] the *de facto* position of Jordan and Palestine, and the two territories' "national, natural and geographic unity and their common interests and living space."[17] In opening Parliament on April 24, King Abdullah hailed the voice of its delegates (from both banks of the Jordan) as together representing the "will of one people and one country with identical aspirations."[18]

In one sense, the annexation of 1950 was an internal Jordanian concern, a creature of Jordanian constitutional law, but it cannot be denied that it also echoed much more widely from a geopolitical perspective.[19] This was because the joint resolution contained a "without prejudice" clause with respect to Palestinian national rights. Essentially, these were held "in abeyance," though, in truth, how Palestinian rights were meant to have played out in the medium to long term given the reality of Jordan's annexation is speculative. Rival bodies, purporting to speak for the Palestinians, held sway in the Gaza Strip and Jericho around this time, the former under the control of the League of Arab States, the latter under Amman's influence.[20] Although short-lived, these experiments in Palestinian expressionism raised the question of who, or what, represented the Palestinians. This question would only be resolved, from an Arab perspective, in the early 1970s.

[14] *See* Michael Karayanni, Conflicts in a Conflict: A Conflict of Laws Case Study on Israel and the Palestinian Territories 14–16 (2014) (also relating how Egypt gained control of the Gaza Strip during the 1948 War and would hold onto it until the 1967 War). *See also* Raja Shehadeh, From Occupation to Interim Accords: Israel and the Palestinian Territories 77–79 (1997). When, on October 13, 2014, the House of Commons voted in favor of a motion that resolved that "the Government should recognise the state of Palestine alongside the state of Israel, as a contribution to securing a negotiated two state solution" (by a vote of 274 to 12), Robert Halfon MP made the historically accurate point to his colleagues in Westminster that, in a sense, "Jordan is Palestine." *See* 586(40) Hansard, at cols. 105–107 (Oct. 13, 2014).

[15] Benjamin Shwadran, Jordan: A State of Tension 297 (1959).

[16] *Id.* at 296.

[17] *Id.*

[18] *Id.* On the annexation of (Arab) Palestine, see *id.* at 272–99. *See also* al Madfai, *supra* note 10, at 5–7; Anis F. Kassim, *Legal Systems and Developments in Palestine*, 1 Pal. Y.B. Int'l L. 19, 27–28 (1984); Hassan bin Talal, Palestinian Self Determination: A Study of the West Bank and Gaza Strip 40–41 (1981).

[19] It also caused considerable controversy within the League of Arab States itself. *See* Hussein A. Hassouna, The League of Arab States and Regional Disputes: A Study of Middle East Conflicts 33–45 (1975).

[20] *See* Shwadran, *supra* note 15, at 279–83. On the All-Palestine Government in Gaza, see Avi Shlaim, *The Rise and Fall of the All-Palestine Government in Gaza*, 20(1) J. Pal. Stud. 37 (1990).

At its Algiers summit in late November 1973, the Arab League pivoted against Jordan on the question of Palestinian representation. In addition to adopting the view that the PLO alone represented Palestinian aspirations, the Arabs reiterated their rejection of the Jewish State and called for Israel's withdrawal from Arab land, including Jerusalem (in this understanding), and the "restoration of the national rights of the Palestinian people."[21] This pledge to Arab national liberation in Palestine was to be "according to the decisions of the Palestine Liberation Organization, as the sole representative of the Palestine nation."[22] Jordan objected to this language because it undermined Amman's authority in the territories (land that it continued to hope it would eventually recapture from Israel).[23] Also in Algiers, the Arab League reiterated its traditional rejectionism and calls for boycotts of the Jewish State, and by endorsing the PLO's armed struggle, it continued to oppose peaceful means of dispute settlement in general and the negotiation imperative that the Security Council had sought to entrench a month earlier with Resolution 338. Needless to say, Israel vehemently opposed this Arab rejectionism.[24]

It was only at its Rabat summit a year after Algiers that the Arabs unanimously endorsed the PLO as the "sole legitimate representative of the Palestinian people."[25] What al-Shuaibi describes as the "open battle for Palestinian representation"[26] was decided decisively in favor of the PLO.[27] While this was clearly an important victory for Chairman Arafat and his comrades, this did not mean that the PLO derided any role for Amman in Palestinian national affairs as such. Indeed, in early June 1974, the Palestinian National Council (PNC), the PLO's most senior decision-making body, resolved that it would "[s]truggle along with the Jordanian national forces to establish a Jordanian-Palestinian national front whose aim will be to set up in Jordan a democratic national authority in close contact with the Palestinian entity that is established through the struggle."[28] Quite what precise

[21] League of Arab States, Sixth Arab Summit Conference, Algiers, Overview and Resolutions, Nov. 28, 1973, *in* ISRAEL IN THE MIDDLE EAST: DOCUMENTS AND READINGS ON SOCIETY, POLITICS, AND FOREIGN RELATIONS, PRE-1948 TO THE PRESENT 334, 335, ¶ 3 (Itamar Rabinovich & Jehuda Reinharz eds., 2d ed. 2008).

[22] *Id.*

[23] To be sure, King Hussein envisaged that the Palestinians would play a key role in determining the status of the territories. He put the matter thus to Italian journalist Oriana Fallaci in April 1972: "When the time comes, I'll ask the Palestinians of the West Bank to decide whether they want to remain with Jordan or become independent. I'll say to them: Decide your future for yourselves. Then I'll accept what they've decided." ORIANA FALLACI, *Hussein of Jordan, in* INTERVIEW WITH HISTORY 140, 148 (John Shepley trans., 1977).

[24] *See* Israel Knesset Statement, Prime Minister, Yitzhak Rabin, Following the Rabat Conference, 5 November, 1974 [Excerpts], *in* THE ISRAELI-PALESTINIAN CONFLICT: A DOCUMENTARY RECORD, 1967–1990 188 (Yehuda Lukacs ed., 1992) (though not referring to the Algiers declaration by name).

[25] League of Arab States, Seventh Arab Summit Conference, Rabat Resolutions, Oct. 29, 1974, *in* ISRAEL IN THE MIDDLE EAST, *supra* note 21, at 342, 343, ¶ 3.

[26] Issa Al-Shuaibi, *The Development of Palestinian Entity Consciousness: Part III*, 9(3) J. PAL. STUD. 99, 111 (1980).

[27] On the Rabat declaration in geopolitical context, see AL MADFAI, *supra* note 10, at 21–25. *See also* 20 KEESING'S CONTEMPORARY ARCHIVES 26813–15 (1974).

[28] Palestine Liberation Organization, Political Program, June 9, 1974, *in* ISRAEL IN THE MIDDLE EAST, *supra* note 21, at 344, 345, ¶ 5.

legal relationship "in close contact" envisaged was left textually unclear. It could have meant re-establishing the union arrangements of 1950, though this was perhaps unlikely given that these had been decidedly Amman-centric; the PNC may have been making a nod to King Hussein's federation plan of March 1972 (or some permutation thereof);[29] or it could have been pointing to an Arab confederation along the lines of that which King Hussein and Chairman Arafat would agree to a little over a decade later.[30]

1974, then, saw the Arab League move unanimously behind the PLO in its struggle against the Jewish State.[31] The General Assembly had already been moving in this direction. In mid December 1969, for example, it adopted Resolution 2535, which "[r]eaffirm[ed] the inalienable rights of the people of Palestine."[32] General Assembly Resolution 3210, of October 14, 1974, recognized the PLO as "the representative of the Palestinian people,"[33] with the definite article "the" before "representative" having the same exclusive meaning as "sole" did in the Arab League's unanimously-adopted Rabat declaration. The General Assembly would invite the PLO to participate in its work as an Observer in Resolution 3237 (1974).[34] It was from this time onwards that de Waart credits the General Assembly with no longer "r[unning] away from its responsibility by leaving the matter to the parties themselves and to the superpowers."[35]

As political statements, the General Assembly's resolutions supporting the PLO and its claim to speak for the Palestinian people clearly challenged the Security Council's approach, which continued to frame the dispute as profoundly inter-State in orientation. Yet, from a legal perspective, there is some need for caution when engaging with these resolutions, as with the general proposition that international law, through the "United Nations," had recognized Palestinian national rights as early as 1969.[36] The "dream of coexistence in a democratic society"[37]

[29] *See* King Hussein's Plan for a Federation, 15 Mar. 1972, *in* THE ARAB-ISRAEL CONFLICT AND ITS RESOLUTION: SELECTED DOCUMENTS 143 (Ruth Lapidoth & Moshe Hirsch eds., 1992).

[30] *See* Jordanian-Palestinian Accord, Amman, 11 February, 1985, *in* THE ISRAELI-PALESTINIAN CONFLICT, *supra* note 24, at 488.

[31] The Organization of Islamic Cooperation (or the Organization of the Islamic Conference as it was then known), also affirmed in 1974 that the PLO was the "sole legitimate representative of the Palestinian Nation in its just struggle." OIC Res. 1/2-IS, Lahore, at ¶ 3 (Feb. 22–24, 1974). On the Second Islamic Summit Conference, in Lahore, at which this resolution on the Middle East and the Palestine Cause was adopted, see 20 KEESING'S CONTEMPORARY ARCHIVES 26423 (1974).

[32] G.A. Res. 2535(B), at ¶ 1, U.N. Doc. A/RES/2535 (Dec. 10, 1969) (italics omitted).

[33] G.A. Res. 3210, *supra* note 2, at pmbl.

[34] *See* G.A. Res. 3237, U.N. Doc. A/RES/3237 (Nov. 22, 1974). On this, see PHILIPPE SANDS & PIERRE KLEIN, BOWETT'S LAW OF INTERNATIONAL INSTITUTIONS 561–63 (6th ed. 2009).

[35] PAUL J.I.M. DE WAART, DYNAMICS OF SELF-DETERMINATION IN PALESTINE: PROTECTION OF PEOPLES AS A HUMAN RIGHT 95 (1994).

[36] *See* M. Cherif Bassiouni & Eugene M. Fisher, *The Arab-Israeli Conflict—Real and Apparent Issues: An Insight into Its Future from the Lessons of the Past*, 44(3) ST. JOHN'S L. REV. 399, 447 (1970) (making such a claim). *See also* W. Thomas Mallison & Sally V. Mallison, *The National Rights of the People of Palestine*, 9(4) J. PAL. STUD. 119 (1980).

[37] U.N. GAOR, at 1078, U.N. Doc. A/PV.2296 (Nov. 22, 1974).

that the PLO declared in the General Assembly immediately after the adoption of Resolution 3237 pointed to a dispute to be settled at the expense of Jewish self-determination,[38] and there is an argument to be made that these General Assembly resolutions, since they reaffirmed the "exclusionist" self-determination program of the PLO and did not reaffirm the Jewish people's self-determination, conflicted with self-determination as a *jus cogens* norm.[39] Analogizing to article 53 of the 1969 Vienna Convention on the Law of Treaties (VCLT),[40] public interest considerations would "cut against" the persuasive value of such resolutions from the perspective of law.

Another reason to exercise some degree of caution when understanding these resolutions is more basic: as resolutions of the General Assembly, they do not have the legal effect that Security Council Resolutions do by virtue of article 25 of the Charter of the United Nations.[41] As the International Court of Justice noted in *South West Africa*, while the "persuasive force of [General] Assembly resolutions can indeed be very considerable, [...] this is a different thing. It operates on the political not the legal level: it does not make these resolutions binding in law."[42] This is to say, at the very least, that General Assembly resolutions do not have dispositive legal effect[43] and that, as Crawford has put it, "each [General Assembly] resolution must be assessed in the light of all the circumstances, including other available evidence of the states' opinions on the point or points in issue."[44]

Back in the Security Council, the United States and the Soviet Union were leading efforts to launch the Peace Conference on the Middle East (Geneva Conference). Shortly after the adoption of Resolution 338, the two superpowers invited United Nations Secretary-General Kurt Waldheim to play a supporting role in their efforts, and it immediately became clear that the question of representation

[38] *See, e.g.* U.N. GAOR, U.N. Doc. A/AC.183/2 (Mar. 9, 1976) (Palestine Liberation Organization).

[39] It is at least arguable that self-determination is a *jus cogens* norm. *See* ALEXANDER ORAKHELASHVILI, PEREMPTORY NORMS IN INTERNATIONAL LAW 51–53 (2008) (making such a case). *See also* Res. 19/15, *in* Report of the Human Rights Council on Its Nineteenth Session 44, 45, pmbl., U.N. Doc. A/HRC/19/2 (May 24, 2013) (describing self-determination as a *jus cogens* norm and stating that it is a "basic condition for achieving a just, lasting and comprehensive peace in the region of the Middle East"). The present author has expressed some skepticism about *jus cogens* norms generally. *See* Robert P. Barnidge, Jr, *Questioning the Legitimacy of* Jus Cogens *in the Global Legal Order*, 38 ISR. Y.B. HUM. RTS. 199 (2008). For a recent study that frames *jus cogens* within the context of the persistent objector rule and international human rights law, see James A. Green, *Persistent Objector Teflon? Customary International Human Rights Law and the United States in International Adjudicative Proceedings, in* ADJUDICATING INTERNATIONAL HUMAN RIGHTS: ESSAYS IN HONOUR OF SANDY GHANDHI 167 (James A. Green & Christopher P.M. Waters eds., 2015).

[40] Vienna Convention on the Law of Treaties, Vienna, May 23, 1969, art. 53 (defining such a norm as one that is "accepted and recognized by the international community of States as a whole as a norm from which no derogation is permitted and which can be modified only by a subsequent norm of general international law having the same character").

[41] "The Members of the United Nations agree to accept and carry out the decisions of the Security Council in accordance with the present Charter." U.N. Charter art. 25.

[42] South West Africa (Eth. v. S. Afr.; Liber. v. S. Afr.) (Second Phase), 1966 I.C.J. 6, 50–51 (July 18).

[43] *See* Michael Curtis, *International Law and the Territories*, 32(2) HARV. INT'L L.J. 457, 485–86 (1991).

[44] JAMES CRAWFORD, BROWNLIE'S PRINCIPLES OF PUBLIC INTERNATIONAL LAW 42 (6th ed. 2012).

would pose the greatest challenge and have to be addressed early on in Geneva.[45] The United States and Israel could not conceive that a "just and durable peace in the Middle East"[46] would be possible if the PLO participated in the discussions because the group remained ideologically opposed to Jewish self-determination, expressed through a Jewish State, in any part of what had been the Palestine Mandate and because the PLO refused to renounce its armed struggle.[47] Even had it been invited to Geneva in late December 1973, however, the PLO, for its part, would have refused to participate as a matter of principle, for the simple reason that the Geneva Conference took as its premise the need to implement Resolutions 242 and 338.

It will be recalled that Resolutions 242 and 338 refrained from casting blame on either Israel or the Palestinians and the Arab States for the unrest in the region and left the process of dispute settlement to unfold organically and, perhaps somewhat naively, through peaceful means. The PLO's position remained that Resolution 242 "obliterate[d] the national right of our [i.e., the Palestinian] people and deal[t] with the cause of our people as a problem of refugees."[48] In the sense that Resolution 242 did not deal with Palestine as a "national question," there is truth to this, though it should also be pointed out that there was nothing as such that would have precluded Resolution 242 from being creatively interpreted in time to accommodate (an unfolding sense of) Palestinian self-determination. The only Arab States to join Israel in Geneva were Egypt and Jordan; Syria refused to participate.[49]

The Geneva Conference did not achieve its goal of implementing Resolutions 242 and 338, and it is generally regarded as having been a failure.[50] There were later attempts to resurrect the process, but they also faltered.[51] This was mainly because the United States and the Soviet Union continued to hold fundamentally irreconcilable views with respect to whether Resolutions 242 and 338, read strictly, remained the operative framework moving forward. To include the PLO in these discussions would have effectively meant "conceding" Palestinian national rights, rights that the PLO continued to articulate at the expense of Jewish national rights and that Resolutions 242 and 338 did not obviously, or at least expressly,

[45] *See* Letter Dated 18 December 1973 from the Secretary-General to the President of the Security Council, U.N. Doc. S/11161 (Dec. 18, 1973). *See also* S.C. Res. 344, U.N. Doc. S/RES/344 (Dec. 15, 1973).

[46] S.C. Res. 338, at ¶ 3, U.N. Doc. S/RES/338 (Oct. 22, 1973).

[47] *See, e.g.*, Memorandum of Agreement Between the United States and Israel Regarding the Geneva Peace Conference, Sept. 17, 1975, *in* ISRAEL IN THE MIDDLE EAST, *supra* note 21, at 348.

[48] Palestine Liberation Organization, *supra* note 28, at 345, ¶ 1.

[49] *See* Report of the Secretary-General Submitted in Pursuance of Security Council Resolution 344 (1973), U.N. Doc. S/11169 (Dec. 24, 1973).

[50] It is important to note, however, that the Geneva Conference did lead to a series of bilateral disengagement agreements between Israel and, respectively, Egypt and Syria. *See* ALAN DOWTY, ISRAEL/PALESTINE 130 (3d ed. 2012); AL MADFAI, *supra* note 10, at 18–19. *See also* 20 KEESING'S CONTEMPORARY ARCHIVES 26317–21, 26565–67 (1974).

[51] *See* Report of the Secretary-General, U.N. Doc. A/31/270 (Oct. 18, 1976).

recognize.[52] In a response to the Secretary-General during a move to resurrect Geneva in early 1976, the Soviets argued for an "additional" Palestinian State west of the Jordan, and they saw it as imperative that the Palestinians be allowed to "leave the refugee camps, free themselves from oppression by the invaders and build their own State in their homeland."[53]

This reference to a right of three million Palestinians to return[54] did little to reassure those committed to Jewish self-determination, however, since it was at best unclear whether such an Arab-dominated State would exist in peace and harmony with the Jewish State, or at its expense. The PLO, of course, continued to frame its national project in terms of the latter.[55] Casting some doubt on the Soviets' claim to even-handedness, it should be noted that the Soviet Union had less than a year earlier voted in favor of General Assembly Resolution 3379, which determined that "zionism is a form of racism and racial discrimination."[56]

While it is impossible to know whether PLO participation would have led to a breakthrough in Geneva, or would perhaps have exacerbated tensions in the region even more, the General Assembly certainly thought that barring the group from peace-making efforts, even given the PLO's unwillingness to "sell out" its maximalist goal of eradicating Zionism, was mistaken. The General Assembly had hinted at the desirability of PLO participation when it adopted Resolution 3236 in late November 1974,[57] a resolution that Chairman Arafat viewed as "compris[ing] the liquidation of Zionist existence, since the Palestinian homeland is Palestine, and Palestine at present is Israel."[58] The General Assembly was even clearer a year later when it called for the PLO, "the representative of the Palestinian people, to participate in all efforts, deliberations and conferences on the Middle East which are held under the auspices of the United Nations, on an equal footing with other parties, on the basis of resolution 3236 (XXIX)."[59]

[52] The United States recognized the Palestinians' "legitimate interests," Letter Dated 20 February 1976 from the Chargé d'Affairs a.i. of the Permanent Mission of the United States of America to the United Nations Addressed to the Secretary-General, at 2, U.N. Doc. A/31/54 (Feb. 23, 1976), a concept that fell short of (vested) national rights, and certainly not the type of Palestinian national rights that the PLO had in mind.

[53] Letter Dated 29 April 1976 from the Permanent Representative of the Union of Soviet Socialist Republics to the United Nations Addressed to the Secretary-General, Annex at 1, 3, U.N. Doc. A/31/84 (Apr. 29, 1976).

[54] *See id.* at Annex at 1.

[55] *See, e.g.,* Letter Dated 31 August 1977 from the Permanent Representative of Israel to the United Nations Addressed to the Secretary General, Annex I at 1, U.N. Doc. A/32/202 (Aug. 31, 1977) (Statement Issued After a Meeting of the Palestinian Central Council, Held at Damascus on 25 and 26 August 1977); *id.* at Annex II at 1 (Fifteen-Point Programme Adopted at the Thirteenth Session of the Palestinian National Council, Held at Cairo from 12 to 20 March 1977).

[56] G.A. Res. 3379, at pmbl., U.N. Doc. A/RES/3379 (Nov. 10, 1975).

[57] *See* G.A. Res. 3236, at ¶ 7, U.N. Doc. A/RES/3236 (Nov. 22, 1974).

[58] U.N. GAOR, at 634, U.N. Doc. A/PV.2390 (Nov. 3, 1975) (Israel) (quoting Chairman Arafat in *Al Balagh*).

[59] G.A. Res. 3375, at ¶ 2, U.N. Doc. A/RES/3375 (Nov. 10, 1975). *See* G.A. Res. 3414, U.N. Doc. A/RES/3414 (Dec. 5, 1975).

By embracing the PLO and its particular agenda of Palestinian self-determination in the way that it did, the General Assembly, through this series of resolutions, did nothing to reaffirm Jewish self-determination. In fact, it would be more accurate to say that it effectively endorsed Palestinian self-determination at the expense of Jewish self-determination, thus jettisoning the carefully balanced approach to Jewish and Arab rights and obligations that the Security Council had achieved with Resolution 242. General Assembly Resolution 3414, for example, stated that a final settlement would need to "ensure[] complete Israeli withdrawal from all the occupied Arab territories as well as full recognition of the inalienable national rights of the Palestinian people and the attainment of those rights."[60] This, of course, amounted to a wholesale rejection of Resolution 242's "land for peace" formula in favor of a "land" formula that insisted upon Palestinian "inalienable national rights" even though Resolution 242 did not endorse Palestinian national rights, inalienable or not. One cannot but respond affirmatively to O'Brien's rhetorical question: "Did not the proceedings of the General Assembly in 1974—which included the passage of an impeccably pro-P.L.O. resolution—reverse the earlier verdict of world opinion, and *de*legitimize the State of Israel?"[61] The same question could be asked with respect to developments in 1975, including with respect to Resolution 3414, with the same affirmative reply.

The General Assembly's approach to these matters also challenged the Security Council's "primary responsibility for the maintenance of international peace and security"[62] within the United Nations system since it quite clearly undermined the Security Council's efforts to broker a carefully crafted settlement. To be sure, while some delegations in the General Assembly at the time did call for the reciprocal recognition of rights and expressed various degrees of concern that the General Assembly was not also simultaneously reaffirming Jewish self-determination,[63] these more moderate views did not ultimately prevail in the General Assembly.

The process that the United States and the Soviet Union had initiated in Geneva had run its course by the mid 1970s and was essentially spent. Few saw cause for optimism. Reporting to the Security Council in February 1977, Secretary-General Waldheim lamented that the main issues "remain[ed] intractable and extremely difficult to deal with."[64] Many doubted that a comprehensive peace could be achieved, and some cautioned in favor of deterrence as a more realistic long-term strategy. This perception would dramatically change, however, when Egyptian President Anwar el-Sadat announced his commitment to making peace with

[60] G.A. Res. 3414, *supra* note 59, at ¶ 4.

[61] Conor Cruise O'Brien, The Siege: The Saga of Israel and Zionism 486 (1986).

[62] U.N. Charter art. 24(1).

[63] *See, e.g.*, U.N. GAOR, *supra* note 37, at 1059–60 (Argentina), 1073 (Iceland).

[64] Report of the Secretary-General Submitted Under General Assembly Resolution 31/62 Concerning the Peace Conference on the Middle East, at 5, U.N. Doc. S/12290 (Feb. 28, 1977) (though stating his belief in "an increasing consciousness in the area that an opportunity now exists to resume negotiations in a meaningful way and that, if this opportunity is not seized, there are grave dangers that the situation will deteriorate once again, with incalculable consequences not only for the Middle East but for the international community as a whole"). *See* Al Madfai, *supra* note 10, at 33–45.

Israel. In early November 1977, before the People's Assembly in Cairo, he declared his "read[iness] to go to the ends [of the earth,] and Israel will be amazed to hear me say that we do not refuse them—I am prepared to go to their very home, to the Knesset itself and discuss things with them."[65]

This was the same President Sadat, of course, who had used force against Israel on Yom Kippur just a few years earlier and who had written in *Foreign Affairs* on the eve of the 1973 War that all of Palestine west of the Jordan, from the river to the sea, was "occupie[d]."[66] And this was the same Egypt that had voted in favor of delegitimizing the Jewish State through its support of General Assembly Resolution 3379 in mid November 1975.

In pivoting away from the traditional Arab posture of rejectionism and calls for boycotts of the Jewish State, President Sadat did not view himself as acting alone, even though he was clearly the only Arab leader who was making such radical entreaties to Israel at the time and was roundly condemned for doing so.[67] Rather, he saw Egypt as facilitating a larger process that would lead to a comprehensive settlement between Israel and the Arab world, including on the question of Palestine. President Sadat's address to the Knesset in late November 1977 was clear: "I have not come here for a separate agreement between Egypt and Israel. This is not part of the policy of Egypt."[68] As Cairo saw it, Egypt's actions fully accorded with the "Arab consensus," and President Sadat was merely acting as the Arab world's chief protagonist in an unfolding drama, at a particular moment in history, "not speaking for myself but for this [Arab] strategy in its principles."[69] The Egyptian–Israeli dialogue that began in 1977 grounded itself in Resolutions 242 and 338 and the commitment of both parties, Egypt and Israel, to perform their obligations under those two instruments.

The treaties that Egypt and Israel entered into during this process, the 1978 Framework for Peace in the Middle East (Camp David Accords)[70] and the 1979 Peace Treaty Between Israel and Egypt (Israeli–Egyptian Peace Treaty),[71] were, juridically speaking, "separate agreement[s]."[72] In the sense that only Egypt and

[65] President Sadat's Address to the Egyptian Parliament, Nov. 9, 1977, *in* Peace in the Making: The Menachem Begin-Anwar el Sadat Personal Correspondence 4, 6 (Harry Hurwitz & Yisrael Medad eds., 2011).

[66] Anwar el-Sadat, *Where Egypt Stands*, 51(1) Foreign Aff. 114, 119 (1972) (stating that "Israel now occupies all of Palestine, the part allotted to her by the 1947 resolution and all the part allotted by the same resolution to the Palestinian people").

[67] *See, e.g.*, Letter Dated 5 December 1977 from the Permanent Representative of the Libyan Arab Jamahiriya to the United Nations Addressed to the Secretary-General, U.N. Doc. A/32/411 (Dec. 6, 1977).

[68] Sadat Addresses the Knesset in Jerusalem, Nov. 20, 1977, *in* Peace in the Making, *supra* note 65, at 15, 20.

[69] Ismailia Summit, Dec. 26, 1977, *in* Peace in the Making, *supra* note 65, at 51, 57.

[70] *See* Camp David Accords, Sept. 17, 1978, *in* Israel in the Middle East, *supra* note 21, at 376.

[71] *See* Peace Treaty Between Israel and Egypt, Mar. 26, 1979, *in* Israel in the Middle East, *supra* note 21, at 383.

[72] Prime Minister Begin shared President Sadat's view to the contrary. *See, e.g.*, Sadat Receives an Honorary Degree, May 26, 1979, *in* Peace in the Making, *supra* note 65, at 146, 149.

Israel were States Parties to them, the treaties were certainly bilateral in nature.[73] This meant that, according to the VCLT, the treaties created neither rights nor obligations for third States absent their consent,[74] and one can assume that the same rule would apply, by analogy, to the Palestinians (the only non-State actor referred to in the Camp David Accords).[75] Certainly, the Camp David Accords foresaw—indeed, very much welcomed—the engagement of other actors, in particular Jordan and the Palestinians, and had these other actors consented to the creation of rights and obligations under the treaty, then they could be said to have been "bandwagoned" into the agreement.

From the perspective of Palestinian rights, the Camp David Accords were more significant than the Israeli–Egyptian Peace Treaty. Section A of the Camp David Accords addressed the question of Palestinian rights.[76] It set forth a negotiation framework involving Egypt, Israel, Jordan, and what was described as "the representatives of the Palestinian people"[77] to satisfy the "legitimate rights of the Palestinian people and their just requirements"[78] and secure the Palestinians' "full autonomy"[79] and "self-government."[80] During a transitional period of no longer than five years, a self-governing authority, or administrative council, would administer Palestinian affairs in the territories, and the Israel Defense Forces would withdraw from all but "specified security locations."[81] This latter move would arguably have satisfied Israel's obligation under Resolution 242 to effectuate the "[w]ithdrawal of Israel armed forces from territories occupied in the recent conflict."[82] Prime Minister Menachem Begin recognized an Israeli sovereign right to Judea and Samaria and Gaza but disclaimed any intention to annex these territories, determined, as he was, to separate the territorial question from the question of governance.[83]

Given this chapter's focus on the evolution of a specifically bilateral negotiation imperative between Israel and the PLO in the years after 1973, the Camp David Accords were clearly an important development. They also held the potential to lead to a negotiated settlement between Israel and the Palestinians, and between Israel and the Arab world more generally. A number of options seemed

[73] The United States, through President Jimmy Carter, acted as a witness to the Camp David Accords.

[74] *See* VCLT, *supra* note 40, at art. 34.

[75] Because Israel is not a State Party to the VCLT, this chapter refers to particular provisions in the treaty on the assumption that they reflect obligations of a customary nature.

[76] *See* Camp David Accords, *supra* note 70, at 377–78.

[77] *Id.* at 377.

[78] *Id.* at 378.

[79] *Id.* at 377.

[80] *Id.*

[81] *Id.*

[82] S.C. Res. 242, *supra* note 10, at ¶ 1(i).

[83] *See* Begin Addresses Jewish Leaders in New York, Sept. 20, 1978, *in* PEACE IN THE MAKING, *supra* note 65, at 83, 88 (arguing that the "question of sovereignty [should] be left open. And let us deal with the human beings. With the peoples on both sides. Let us give the Palestinian Arabs autonomy and the Palestinian Jews security, and we shall live together in human dignity, in equality of rights, in human progress. There will be justice. And we shall together advance").

to present themselves at the time, ranging from a territorial compromise or a variety of potential non-territorial settlements (involving either autonomy schemes or federal schemes, confederal schemes or condominial schemes) to a settlement involving Palestinian representatives other than the PLO or an Israeli–Arab settlement that would bypass the Palestinians altogether, and there always remained, of course, the possibility of continued non-settlement, with or without an Israeli withdrawal from the territories.[84] To be sure, the Camp David Accords did not refer to the PLO or include the group, and since Israel did not regard the PLO as "the representatives of the Palestinian people," it was not as such bound to negotiate with the group under the terms of Camp David. Still, it is juridically significant that the Camp David Accords reflected Israeli recognition of the "Palestinian people" in a collective sense, though not necessarily in a national sense; rather, the treaty "simply" acknowledged that the "Palestinian people" had "legitimate rights" and "just requirements."

Sayegh, writing in the *Journal of Palestine Studies* at the time, rhetorically asked: "Where indeed is the line of demarcation to be drawn, as between the 'legitimate' and the 'not-so-legitimate' or perhaps 'illegitimate' rights of the Palestinian people?"[85] The answer, of course, was that the line of demarcation on these and other questions was to be drawn through a negotiation process that, it was hoped, would develop organically between the parties concerned.[86] In this respect, it is not particularly surprising that Egypt and Israel interpreted "legitimate rights" and "just requirements" differently.[87] President Sadat approximated these to self-determination rights, writing to Prime Minister Begin in August 1980 to ask: "What are these rights if they do not include the fundamental right to self-determination which is part of the *jus cogens* of the contemporary world?"[88] By contrast, Prime Minister Begin rejected this interpretation and pointed out that "not one word about self-determination (which, of course, means a state), or

[84] *See* Mark A. Heller, A Palestinian State: The Implications for Israel 21–54 (1983). *See also* Ruth Lapidoth, *The Peace Process, in* Israel, The Middle East, and the Great Powers 197 (Israel Stockman-Shomron ed., 1984) (discussing the concept of autonomy within the context of the Camp David Accords). *Cf.* Ruth Lapidoth, Autonomy: Flexible Solutions to Ethnic Conflicts 49–58 (1997) (describing autonomy arrangements involving federal systems, decentralized arrangements, self-government, associate statehood, and forms of self-administration).

[85] Fayez A. Sayegh, *The Camp David Agreement and the Palestine Problem*, 8(2) J. Pal. Stud. 3, 28 (1979). *See* Mirko Aksentijević, *Reflections on the Palestinian Resistance*, 2(1) J. Pal. Stud. 111, 111 (1972) (making the point in 1972 that, "although one hears almost daily tributes paid to the 'rights' of the Palestinian people from the United Nations, governments and international organizations, the precise content of the concept of 'Palestinian rights' is uncertain and capable of a great variety of interpretations").

[86] On some of these other questions, see Lapidoth, *supra* note 84, at 155–56; Mayer Gabay, *Legal Aspects of the Camp David Framework for Peace in Relation to the Autonomy Proposal, in* Models of Autonomy 255 (Yoram Dinstein ed., 1981). *See also* Karayanni, *supra* note 14, at 31–32.

[87] *Cf.* al Madfai, *supra* note 10, app. B at 222 (Jordan-US Exchange of Questions and Answers on the Camp David Accords, September 1978) (giving the United States' responses to fourteen technical questions from Jordan about the Camp David Accords).

[88] Letters Following Begin's Hospitalization, Aug. 2–27, 1980, *in* Peace in the Making, *supra* note 65, at 186, 212.

about an independent (Palestinian) state appears in any one of the pages, paragraphs, sections, sub-sections etc. of the Camp David agreement."[89] Certainly, this was on its face true, in the sense that nothing in the Camp David Accords required extending self-determination rights to the Palestinians, but neither did the language preclude reading self-determination rights into the treaty.[90]

Where Prime Minister Begin erred, however, was in suggesting that self-determination (necessarily) implies statehood. A few years before the Camp David Accords, the International Court of Justice (ICJ) had articulated the notion of self-determination in its *Western Sahara* advisory opinion as the "free and genuine expression of the will of the people[ ],"[91] and just a few years before *Western Sahara*, the General Assembly noted that there were a variety of modes through which the right of self-determination could be implemented and that not all of them involved the creation of a new State.[92] This seems to imply that factors such as territorial integrity and perhaps also considerations of regional security need

[89] *Id.* at 200. Interestingly, Jordanian Crown Prince Hassan bin Talal agreed with Prime Minister Begin that autonomy rights did not extend to self-determination rights. *See* HASSAN, *supra* note 18, at 89–95.

[90] *Cf.* Robert Kolb, *Principles as Sources of International Law (With Special Reference to Good Faith)*, 53(1) NETH. INT'L L. REV. 1, 25–27 (2006).

[91] Western Sahara, Advisory Opinion, 1975 I.C.J. 12, 68 (Oct. 16). Permutations of the *Western Sahara* notion of self-determination have played out in the General Assembly on multiple occasions since the ICJ articulated it in 1975. A recent example involved the question of Ukraine's territorial integrity, in late March 2014. *See* U.N. GAOR, at 3, U.N. Doc. A/68/PV.80 (Mar. 27, 2014) (Russia) ("voluntary choice"), 5 (European Union) (the Ukrainian people's "right to choose their own future"), 9 (Costa Rica) ("To be genuine, self-determination must be preceded by open debate based on clear rules accepted by all parties, impartial authorities and the presenting of real options to the people. Furthermore, self-determination must be exercised without exclusion, influence or intimidation."), 18 (Guatemala) (stressing the importance of an "open and inclusive electoral process, which fully respects the country's ethnic, cultural and regional diversity, opening the way to a plural Government which would seek friendly relations with all its neighbours"), 21 (Democratic People's Republic of Korea) (noting approvingly that the "reunification of Ukraine [*sic*] with Russia has been undertaken in a legitimate manner by means of a referendum based on the voluntary wishes of the people of Ukraine [*sic*] in line with the right to self-determination set forth in the Charter of the United Nations"), 22 (Moldova) (making reference to the "free will and aspirations of all Ukrainians themselves, without any outside influence"). The General Assembly adopted Resolution 68/262 on March 27, 2014. *See* G.A. Res. 68/262, U.N. Doc. A/RES/68/262 (Mar. 27, 2014). For Russia's legal justification in this case, see Permanent Delegation of the Russian Federation to UNESCO, Legal Argumments [*sic*] for Russia's Position on Crimea and Ukraine (Nov. 7, 2014), http://russianunesco.ru/eng/article/1637. For a Ukrainian perspective, see Anna Stepanowa, *International Law and Legality of Secession in Crimea*, CAMBRIDGE J. INT'L & COMP. L. ONLINE, Apr. 20, 2014, http://cjicl.org.uk/2014/04/20/international-law-legality-secession-crimea/. *See also* Sergey Sayapin, *The United Nations General Assembly Resolution 68/262 in the Context of General International Law*, 2(1) EUR. POL. & L. DISC. 19 (2015). *Western Sahara* has also been relied upon in ways unintended, as, for example, by the "Supreme Court of Bophuthatswana." *See* S. v. Banda (1989) (Bop.), 82 I.L.R. 388, 416–17 (1990).

[92] *See* G.A. Res. 2625, Annex, U.N. Doc. A/RES/2625 (Oct. 24, 1970) (Declaration on Principles of International Law concerning Friendly Relations and Co-operation Among States in Accordance with the Charter of the United Nations) (stating that the "establishment of a sovereign and independent State, the free association or integration with an independent State or the emergence into any other political status freely determined by a people constitute modes of implementing the right of self-determination by that people"). *See also* Katangese Peoples' Congress v. Zaire, Afr. Comm'n Hum. & Peoples' Rts., at ¶ 4, No. 75/92 (1995).

to be considered in the balance when engaging with self-determination claims.[93] Within the context of Camp David, the question became whether, assuming that the parties agreed to extend self-determination rights to the Palestinians, "the representatives of the Palestinian people" referred to in the Camp David Accords, could be regarded as sufficiently "authentic" under international law such that it could be said that they could convey the "free and genuine expression of the will of the [Palestinian] people[]."

Rapprochement between Egypt and Israel was condemned by the General Assembly,[94] and it was also met with overwhelming hostility in the region, so much so that Prime Minister Begin's claim that President Sadat showed courage in the face of the "pack of wolves all around, from Damascus to Baghdad!,"[95] did not seem an exaggeration. Mid November 1978 saw the PLO circulate to Iraq, which then sent to Secretary-General Waldheim, seven declarations from within Palestinian civil society that condemned the Egyptian–Israeli dialogue in no uncertain terms.[96] The Camp David Accords were described as a "surrenderist agreement [… and] a *de facto* sanctification of the occupation with a new guise."[97] Another declaration decried the attempt to foster Palestinian governance in the territories through a Palestinian-run administration as a "very filthy project among the politically naive and the opportunists among our fellow citizens."[98] A declaration circulated clandestinely among the Palestinian leadership of municipalities and

[93] *Cf.* John F. Murphy, *Beyond Camp David*, 74 AM. SOC'Y INT'L L. PROC. 117 (1980) (making this point within the context of the Camp David Accords). It has been argued that "self-determination is not the ultimate value. Self-determination must be exercised in a context where the rights of other people to self-determination are respected also, and where the right of a people in the region to live in peace is respected." *Self-Determination: The Case of Palestine, supra* note 11, at 349 (Allan Gerson). *See* Robert McCorquodale & Kristin Hausler, *Caucuses in the Caucasus: The Application of the Right of Self-Determination, in* CONFLICT IN THE CAUCASUS: IMPLICATIONS FOR INTERNATIONAL LEGAL ORDER 26, 33–34 (James A. Green & Christopher P.M. Waters eds., 2010). Becker makes the case for a doctrine of "relative self-determination." *See* Tal Becker, *Self-Determination in Perspective: Palestinian Claims to Statehood and the Realty of the Right to Self-Determination*, 32(2) ISR. L. REV. 301 (1998). *See also* Solon Solomon, *The Quest for Self-Determination: Defining International Law's Inherent Interstate Limits*, 11(2) SANTA CLARA J. INT'L L. 397 (2013). Klabbers understands self-determination as a "right to be taken seriously." Jan Klabbers, *The Right to Be Taken Seriously: Self-Determination in International Law*, 28(1) HUM. RTS. Q. 186, 189 (2006).

[94] *See* G.A. Res. 34/65(B), U.N. Doc. A/RES/34/65(B) (Nov. 29, 1979).

[95] Begin Addresses the Knesset on the Peace Treaty, Mar. 21, 1979, *in* PEACE IN THE MAKING, *supra* note 65, at 117, 125.

[96] *See* Note Verbale Dated 15 November 1978 from the Permanent Representative of Iraq to the United Nations Addressed to the Secretary-General, at app. I–VII, U.N. Doc. A/33/380 (Nov. 20, 1978) (Declaration Concerning the Israeli "Self-Rule" Plan, Signed in Mid August; Declaration by the Administrative Board of the Arab Graduates' Union, Jerusalem, 21 September 1978; Declaration from the Professional Unions, Jerusalem, 24 September 1978; Declaration from the Occupied Territories (Circulated Clandestinely During the Last Week of September 1978); Declaration by the Arab Graduates' Union, Jerusalem, 28 September 1978; Declaration by the Conference of the Popular Organizations in the Occupied Land, Held at Beit Hanina (Jerusalem) on 1 October 1978; and Declaration Submitted on 3 October 1978 to the Ramallah Municipality by the Students of the UNRWA Men's Teachers' Training Centre in Support of the Resolution Adopted at the Meeting on 1 October at Jerusalem).

[97] *Id.* app. II at 3, 3 (Declaration by the Administrative Board of the Arab Graduates' Union, Jerusalem, 21 September 1978).

[98] *Id.* app. I at 2, 2 (Declaration Concerning the Israeli "Self-Rule" Plan, Signed in Mid August).

village councils, non-governmental organizations, and private individuals from late September 1978 criticized President Sadat's "capitulationist road,"[99] which, it was said, amounted to "nothing but the granting of a legal character and consecration of the action of occupying our land and swallowing it."[100] The viscerally negative reaction from within Palestinian civil society that the Camp David Accords engendered, challenged the organic project of Palestinian self-administration that Egypt and Israel had sought, in one form or another, to usher into being.

The Arab League shared this viscerally negative reaction.[101] Acknowledging that its "conflict with the Zionist enemy goes beyond the struggle of the countries whose territories were occupied in 1967 and involves the entire Arab nation,"[102] the Arab League's condemnation at its Baghdad conference in early November 1978 was total and uncompromising. A year after Baghdad, the Arab League met in Tunis and reiterated its denunciation of Egypt.[103] The clash between the Arab world and Israel was framed in almost eschatological terms. It was said to be one in which the forces of Arab nationalism were aligned against Jewish nationalism in an unending struggle that could not admit of compromise, a "battle of destiny and of civilization [, … a] fateful struggle [requiring assistance] from all the forces of peace and justice throughout the world."[104]

The attempt by Egypt and Israel, then, to facilitate a larger process that would lead to a comprehensive settlement between Israel and the Arab world, including on the question of Palestine, was firmly rejected by much of Palestinian civil society and the Arab League.

III. The Second Phase: From Exclusion to the Beginnings of Begrudging Inclusion

The period between 1973 and the adoption of the Israeli–Egyptian Peace Treaty in 1979 was one of uneven paradox for the Palestinians. During this time, the PLO

[99] *Id.* app. IV at 6, 6 (Declaration from the Occupied Territories (Circulated Clandestinely During the Last Week of September 1978)).

[100] *Id.* (Declaration from the Occupied Territories (Circulated Clandestinely During the Last Week of September 1978)).

[101] *See* AL MADFAI, *supra* note 10, at 46–61 (touching upon this viscerally negative reaction, with particular focus on the Jordanian response).

[102] Letter Dated 8 November 1978 from the Permanent Representative of Iraq to the United Nations Addressed to the Secretary-General, Annex at 1, 1, U.N. Doc. A/33/400 (Nov. 29, 1978) (Statement Dated 6 November 1978 Issued by the Ninth Arab Summit Conference) (continuing by stating that this was "in view of the military, political, economic and cultural danger which the Zionist enemy represents to the entire Arab nation, its fundamental nationalist interests, its civilization and destiny").

[103] *See* Letter Dated 3 December 1979 from the Permanent Representative of Tunisia to the United Nations Addressed to the Secretary-General, Annex at 1, U.N. Doc. A/34/763 (Dec. 10, 1979) (Final Declaration of the Tenth Arab Summit Conference).

[104] *Id.* at 1 (Final Declaration of the Tenth Arab Summit Conference). The Organization of the Islamic Conference similarly condemned Egyptian–Israeli dialogue and suspended Egypt from within its ranks. *See* OIC Final Declaration, Fez (May 8–12, 1979).

achieved a monopoly of representative authority—as the "sole legitimate representative of the Palestinian people" by the Arab League, as "the representative of the Palestinian people" by the General Assembly—and thereby gained a diplomatic edge in its campaign against the Jewish State. As Chairman Arafat explained to the General Assembly, this reflected a "faith in political and diplomatic struggle as complements, as enhancements of our [i.e., the PLO's] armed struggle."[105] The negotiation imperative that Resolution 338 had ushered into being in 1973 had been tried but had failed in Geneva, and had been tried and had succeeded but was then roundly condemned by the Arab world, including the PLO, when Egypt and Israel made peace at the end of the 1970s. For the first time in a legally-binding instrument and even before the Security Council would do so in such express language, Israel recognized that the Palestinians had "legitimate rights" and "just requirements." The PLO, by contrast, refused to renounce its armed struggle, much less would it entertain engaging in a dispute settlement process that would not displace Jewish national rights in favor of Palestinian national rights.

If the negotiation imperative that was ushered into being in 1973 and that would evolve to include a specifically bilateral negotiation imperative between Israel and the PLO unfolded in roughly three phases, the most consequential year during the second of these three phases was undoubtedly 1988. It was during this year that the PLO afforded some measure of recognition to Israel. Before one can fully appreciate the significance of 1988, however, it is necessary to reflect upon the fact that Jordan continued to play the role of "spoiler" during this second phase. In other words, "acceptable" Palestinian expressionism remained wedded to Jordan's "moderate" ways.[106]

Jordan had accepted the PLO's monopoly of representative authority since Rabat, but its unique position as the larger part of what had been the Palestine Mandate and the fact that a demographic majority of its population was Palestinian meant that Amman's influence west of the Jordan lingered on after 1974. As King Hussein put it to the PNC in late November 1984, Jordan and Palestine had a "special relationship[, …] a relationship forged by purely objective factors of history, geography and demography, which have placed the two brotherly countries and peoples, since the beginning of the century, in the same boat of suffering and hope, of interest and harm, of history and destiny."[107] To be sure, King Hussein had advocated Palestinian self-determination since 1974, but there was always a sense

[105] U.N. GAOR, *supra* note 5, at 863.

[106] As an example, consider United States President Ronald Reagan's 1982 plan (Reagan Plan), which declared that "self-government by the Palestinians of the West Bank and Gaza in association with Jordan offer[ed] the best chance for a durable, just and lasting peace." The Reagan Peace Plan—U.S. Involvement in Mideast Peace Effort, "A Moral Imperative." President Ronald Reagan, 1 September, 1982, *in* THE ISRAELI-PALESTINIAN CONFLICT, *supra* note 24, at 72, 76. On the Reagan Plan, see AL MADFAI, *supra* note 10, at 100–10. *See also* Crown Prince Hassan bin Talal of Jordan, *Palestine: Might Versus Rights*, TIMES, Sept. 3, 1982.

[107] Address by King Hussein to the 17th Session of the Palestine National Council, Amman, 22 November, 1984 [Excerpts], *in* THE ISRAELI-PALESTINIAN CONFLICT, *supra* note 24, at 485, 486.

that these rights, when expressed, would inevitably take into account Jordanian interests.

As an example of this dynamic, consider a confidential record of King Hussein's meeting with British Prime Minister Margaret Thatcher at 10 Downing Street in late September 1979, which made clear that the focus for the future, from the Arab perspective, lay squarely with the Palestinians.[108] King Hussein aligned himself with Palestinian self-determination and put Jordan on record as being willing to defer to the PLO's decision-making in this regard.[109] Sherif Abdul Hamid Sharaf of the Jordanian delegation went on to state at this meeting that the Jordanians were "willing to consider any relationship with whatever entity resulted from the free choice of the Palestinian people."[110] This understanding of self-determination, as "free choice," almost exactly mirrored the ICJ's articulation of self-determination in *Western Sahara.*

For most of the 1980s, the PLO welcomed Jordan's support, much as it had done before.[111] Indeed, the PLO went as far as agreeing that Palestinian self-determination would be expressed within the context of "proposed confederated Arab states of Jordan and Palestine."[112] This call for confederation, according to the terms of a bilateral agreement that the PLO and Jordan signed in mid February 1985 (Jordanian–Palestinian Accord), also proposed a joint delegation of PLO and Jordanian representatives that would participate together in future international conferences on the Palestine question.[113]

It is important to point out that the Jordanian–Palestinian Accord reflected neither PLO nor Jordanian reconciliation with the Jewish State.[114] This was because, *inter alia*, the Jordanian–Palestinian Accord called for the "termination of Israeli occupation of the occupied Arab territories, including Jerusalem,"[115] thus remonstrating as suspect Israel's control of or sovereign claim to any part of Jerusalem, including its western sector; and because the Jordanian–Palestinian Accord called for the "[r]esolution of the problem of Palestinian refugees in accordance with

[108] *See* Record of a Discussion Between the Prime Minister and King Hussein of Jordan at 10 Downing Street on 20 September 1979 at 1800 Hours, *in* Records of the Prime Minister's Office: Correspondence and Papers, 1979–1997, No. PREM/19/92 4 (1979).

[109] *See id.*

[110] *Id.* at 5.

[111] *See, e.g.*, Palestine National Council, Political Program, 12 January, 1973, *in* The Israeli-Palestinian Conflict, *supra* note 24, at 303, 305–306 (discussing, in considerable detail, the modalities of the "Jordanian-Palestinian national front" that would, it was hoped, liberate both banks of the Jordan).

[112] Jordanian–Palestinian Accord, *supra* note 30, at 489, ¶ 2.

[113] *See id.* at 489, ¶ 5.

[114] The same could be said for the Arab League's Fez Plan (1982). This plan reaffirmed the PLO and, by extension, its political program, a political program that continued to advocate Palestinian self-determination at the expense of Jewish self-determination. By doing so, the Fez Plan aimed for the dispute to be settled in a way that would undermine the legitimacy of the Jewish State and its long-term viability. *See* Letter Dated 3 December 1982 from the Permanent Representative of Morocco to the United Nations Addressed to the Secretary-General, U.N. Doc. A/37/696 (Dec. 15, 1982).

[115] Jordanian–Palestinian Accord, *supra* note 30, at 489, pmbl.

United Nations resolutions,"[116] which the PLO and Jordan both understood as requiring the implementation of paragraph 11 of General Assembly Resolution 194 (1948) in such a way that, given demographic realities, would have effectively reversed the existing reality of a Jewish State in Palestine.[117] In the event, the Jordanian–Palestinian Accord broke down between the parties and was never implemented.[118]

Juridically, it is important to recognize that the PLO's international legal personality at this time remained limited. This was because its particular program of Palestinian self-determination conflicted with the self-determination of the Jewish people and because international law is loath to recognize situations, or attach benefits of law to political projects, that seek to eviscerate *jus cogens* norms.[119] With this in mind, the United States' veto of a draft resolution that Tunisia submitted to the Security Council in late April 1980 that would have affirmed that the Palestinian people, "in accordance with the Charter of the United Nations, should be enabled to exercise its inalienable national right of self-determination, including the right to establish an independent State in Palestine,"[120] should be seen as reflecting not a rejection of Palestinian self-determination as such but, rather, a rejection of the PLO's particular program of Palestinian self-determination that sought expressionism at the expense of Jewish self-determination.[121] What was needed, from the perspective of both international legality and practical politics, were mutually complimentary self-determination projects for two distinct peoples, one Jewish, the other Palestinian.[122] In any event, even had the United States not vetoed the Tunisian draft, the resolution would arguably have been invalid as a matter of law because it would have conflicted with the *jus cogens* norm of self-determination (for the Jewish people).[123]

As noted above, the PLO afforded some measure of recognition to Israel in 1988, and it did so by adopting a Political Communiqué and Declaration of Independence at the PNC's nineteenth extraordinary session in Algiers in mid November

[116] *Id.* at 489, ¶ 3.

[117] *See* G.A. Res. 194, at ¶ 11, U.N. Doc. A/RES/194 (Dec. 11, 1948) ("*Resolves* that the refugees wishing to return to their homes and live at peace with their neighbours should be permitted to do so at the earliest practicable date, and that compensation should be paid for the property of those choosing not to return and for loss of or damage to property which, under principles of international law or in equity, should be made good by the Governments or authorities responsible").

[118] *See* AL MADFAI, *supra* note 10, at 151–90.

[119] *See supra* note 39.

[120] U.N. SCOR, at ¶ 1(a), U.N. Doc. S/13911 (Apr. 28, 1980).

[121] France, Norway, Portugal, and the United Kingdom abstained in the vote. Voting in favor were Bangladesh, China, the German Democratic Republic, Jamaica, Mexico, Niger, the Philippines, the Soviet Union, Tunisia, and Zambia.

[122] The Philippines and Norway, though ultimately voting differently on the Tunisian draft, made this point in the Security Council. *See* U.N. SCOR, at 13–14, U.N. Doc. S/PV.2220 (Apr. 30, 1980) (Philippines), 14–15 (Norway).

[123] *Cf.* Application of the Convention on the Prevention and Punishment of the Crime of Genocide (Bosn. & Herz. v. Serb. & Mont.) (Provisional Measures) (Order), 1993 I.C.J. 325, 439–41 (Sept. 13) (Lauterpacht, J., separate) (making a similar argument with respect to Security Council Resolution 713 (1991) and its call for an arms embargo to Yugoslavia).

of that year.[124] The Spokesman for United Nations Secretary-General Javier Pérez de Cuéllar hailed these developments as "fresh opportunities [...] for progress towards peace."[125] Certainly, these developments were significant in the sense that the PLO sought to inject a "new reckoning" into international peace efforts. Its moves certainly resonated with the international community generally, but they were as significant and relevant for the United States as they were for Israel.[126] Given its leadership position in the Western bloc, its veto power in the Security Council, and its close alliance with the Jewish State, the United States remained the key to the PLO's entry into "respectable politics." Washington was uniquely placed to pressure Israel to accept the PLO as a party in peace negotiations, if not immediately or on its own, then certainly, incrementally, as part of a Jordanian-led delegation.

Because so much would come to rest upon the Political Communiqué and Declaration of Independence, it is important to engage with the language of these two instruments separately, and in considerable detail. Firstly, consider the Political Communiqué. The PLO was meeting in Algiers at a time when the *intifada*, or "uprising," had been raging in the territories for almost a year, and the group was desperate to assert itself from exile in Tunis. It was within the context of this "revolutionary symphony among the children of the rocket-propelled grenades (RPGs) and the children of the sacred stones, both inside and outside our [i.e., Palestinian] occupied land,"[127] that the PLO decided to act.

The most significant part of the Political Communiqué is that, in it, the PLO, for the first time, called for an international conference based upon Resolutions 242 and 338.[128] Given the group's previous opposition to Resolutions 242 and 338 on the basis that they eviscerated Palestinian national rights,[129] it is not altogether surprising that the Political Communiqué then went on to insist upon Palestinian

[124] *See* Letter Dated 18 November 1988 from the Permanent Representative of Jordan to the United Nations Addressed to the Secretary-General, U.N. Doc. A/43/827 (Nov. 18, 1988). *See also* Edward W. Said, *From Intifadah to Independence,* (158) MID. E. REP. 12 (1989). For a debate as to whether the PNC's nineteenth extraordinary session in Algiers had the effect of creating the State of Palestine, see Francis A. Boyle, *The Creation of the State of Palestine*, 1(1) EUR. J. INT'L L. 301 (1990); James Crawford, *The Creation of the State of Palestine: Too Much Too Soon?*, 1(1) EUR. J. INT'L L. 307 (1990).

[125] Press Release, Secretary-General Says Reported Statements by Palestine National Conference Offer "Fresh Opportunities for Progress Towards Peace," U.N. Doc. SG/SM/4219 (Nov. 15, 1988), http://unispal.un.org/unispal.nsf/9a798adbf322aff38525617b006d88d7/faeae6340e419d6c85256bcf0079b3de?OpenDocument.

[126] A month after the Algiers session, the General Assembly adopted a resolution changing the PLO's designation in the United Nations system from "PLO" to "Palestine." *See* G.A. Res. 43/177, U.N. Doc. A/RES/43/177 (Dec. 15, 1988). *See also* G.A. Res. 52/250, U.N. Doc. A/RES/52/250 (July 7, 1998). On the status, privileges, and immunities under international law of the Permanent Observer Mission of Palestine to the United Nations, see Status, Privileges, and Immunities Under International Law of the Permanent Observer Mission of Palestine to the United Nations (May 5, 2000), 2000 U.N. Jurid. Y.B. 359, U.N. Doc. ST/LEG/SER.C/38.

[127] Letter, *supra* note 124, at Annex I at 3, 4 (Political Communiqué).

[128] *See id.* at Annex I at 7 (Political Communiqué).

[129] See Chapter 3, 67–76.

self-determination and statehood.[130] In this sense, the PLO's acceptance of Resolutions 242 and 338 did not eviscerate Palestinian national rights. Rather, it was hoped that acceptance would play an instrumental role and help the PLO achieve self-determination and statehood.

Yet, even if the Political Communiqué "salvaged" the national project of the Palestinian people at the same time that the PLO for the first time called for an international conference based upon Resolutions 242 and 338, still, it was by no means clear that the PLO's national project was meant to accommodate, alongside it, the Jewish national project. For example, the Political Communiqué described the PLO's "national program" as "advocat[ing] defeat of the occupation, the right to return, self-determination and the independent State."[131] To take but one aspect of this "national program," the PLO's "absolutist" interpretation of Resolution 194[132] cast some doubt on whether it was advocating mutually complimentary self-determination projects for two distinct peoples, one Jewish, the other Palestinian, or whether the PLO was seeking the demographic displacement of the Jewish State through an influx of Palestinians to Israel.

The Political Communiqué expressly called for an international conference to be "convened on the basis of Security Council resolutions 242 (1967) and 338 (1973),"[133] but only on the most "charitable" reading of it could it be said that the Political Communiqué reflected begrudging acceptance of the State of Israel. The Jewish State, for example, was described as a "colonialist, racist, Fascist State based on the seizure of Palestinian land, extermination of the Palestinian people and, in addition, threats, aggression and expansionism in neighbouring Arab territories."[134] The Political Communiqué went on to refer to the same State as genocidal, a "Fascist threat,"[135] and the protagonist of threats of "individual and collective expulsion of our [i.e., the Palestinian] people from its homeland [i.e., Palestine]."[136]

These statements were hardly a convincing olive branch to the Jewish State,[137] and the United States, for one, agreed. Although Washington would authorize a "substantive dialogue with PLO representatives"[138] by the end of 1988,[139] it remained unconvinced immediately after Algiers. It welcomed the reference

130 *See* Letter, *supra* note 124, at Annex I at 7–8 (Political Communiqué).

131 *Id.* at Annex I at 5 (Political Communiqué).

132 *See* G.A. Res. 194, *supra* note 117.

133 Letter, *supra* note 124, at Annex I at 7 (Political Communiqué).

134 *Id.* at Annex I at 5 (Political Communiqué).

135 *Id.* at Annex I at 10 (Political Communiqué).

136 *Id.* (Political Communiqué).

137 *See* Curtis, *supra* note 43, at 465–66; *International Law and Solutions to the Arab-Israeli Conflict*, 83 Am. Soc'y Int'l L. Proc. 121, 130–33 (1989) (Malvina Halberstam).

138 Statement by President Ronald Reagan on Relations with the PLO, 14 December, 1988, *in* The Israeli-Palestinian Conflict, *supra* note 24, at 120, 120.

139 *See* al Madfai, *supra* note 10, at 191–98. *See also* Mahmoud Abbas (Abu Mazen), Through Secret Channels: The Road to Oslo: Senior PLO Leader Abu Mazen's Revealing Story of the Negotiations with Israel 19–35 (1995).

to Resolutions 242 and 338 but said that the PNC's statement was "ambiguous both in its placement in the text and its meaning. Possibly implied or indirect reference to Israel's right to exist is not sufficient. Recognition must be clear and unambiguous."[140]

The Declaration of Independence followed the Political Communiqué. It began by defending Palestinian national identity and framed it as a constant through the ages. The most consequential part of the Declaration of Independence was undoubtedly its reference to the General Assembly's partition plan of 1947. Suddenly, that which the Palestinians had previously seen as a "criminal act perpetrated upon them [i.e., the Palestinians] by the United Nations,"[141] became the lodestar of legitimacy, and it was said to "continue[] to attach conditions to international legitimacy that guarantee the Palestinian Arab people the right to sovereignty and national independence."[142]

It is worth noting that the Declaration of Independence expressly used the words "Jewish State"[143] when referring to General Assembly Resolution 181 (1947). Although this was not inadvertent, the significance of this language should perhaps not be exaggerated. This is because the PLO was undoubtedly using the phrase as a statement of fact (as to what Resolution 181 had intended to have ushered into being) rather than with a view to bestowing legitimacy upon the State of Israel as a self-described Jewish State.

There is some irony in the fact that the PLO, in declaring the independence of the State of Palestine in 1988 in the way that it did, staked its claim to independence on grounds that were identical to those that the Jewish People's Council had made over forty years earlier when it declared the establishment of the Jewish State. The PLO justified itself on the basis of the "natural, historical and legal right of the Palestinian Arab people."[144] By comparison, the Jewish People's Council had done so "by virtue of our natural and historic right and on the strength of the resolution of the United Nations General Assembly [i.e., Resolution 181]."[145]

That the PLO went on in Algiers to advocate for a confederal relationship between Palestine and Jordan[146] is particularly significant given the constitutional

[140] Statement by State Department Spokesman Charles Redman on the Resolutions of the 19th Palestine National Council, 16 November, 1988, *in* THE ISRAELI-PALESTINIAN CONFLICT, *supra* note 24, at 115, 115.

[141] *International Law and Solutions to the Arab-Israeli Conflict, supra* note 137, at 123 (Francis Boyle).

[142] Letter, *supra* note 124, at Annex II at 13, 13–14 (Declaration of Independence). *See* Mohammed Hussain K.S., *Palestine and International Law: An Overview, in* ESSAYS ON CONTEMPORARY ISSUES IN INTERNATIONAL LAW 129, 167–68 (Asian–African Legal Consultative Org. ed., 2009) (contending that this signaled a "genuine desire by the Palestinian people to transcend the past forty years of history and to reach an historic accommodation with Israel on the basis of a two-state solution").

[143] Letter, *supra* note 124, at Annex II at 13 (Declaration of Independence).

[144] *Id.* at Annex II at 14 (Declaration of Independence).

[145] Declaration of the Establishment of the State of Israel, 14 May 1948, *in* THE ARAB-ISRAEL CONFLICT AND ITS RESOLUTION, *supra* note 29, at 61, 62 (capitals omitted).

[146] *See* Letter, *supra* note 124, at Annex I at 8 (Political Communiqué) (which was to be on the basis of "free and voluntary choice by the two fraternal peoples, in corroboration of the historical ties and vital common interests which link them").

changes that King Hussein had made respecting the West Bank of his Kingdom less than four months earlier.[147] On July 31, 1988, King Hussein dismantled all legal and administrative links that the East Bank maintained with the West Bank. He felt that casting the destiny of the West Bank to the PLO alone would shift the focus away from Jordan to the Palestinians themselves. As he put it in his disengagement address, this would "enhance Palestinian national orientation and highlight Palestinian identity."[148] Disengagement would also allow Amman to consolidate, or at least attempt to consolidate, the sense of a cohesive Jordanian national identity east of the Jordan.[149] Even though King Hussein insisted that "Jordan is not Palestine,"[150] there was no doubting the considerable "Palestinian" features of Jordan,[151] something that would continue to be a source of tension in the Hashemite Kingdom of Jordan.

Although developments in Algiers led the United States to open contacts with the PLO, these contacts remained only of a bilateral nature, and the international conference that all sides in principle favored remained a distant ambition. There was simply no agreement with respect to such an undertaking, only consensus that there should be an "international framework for the negotiation of a just and lasting settlement."[152] Many of the same obstacles from Geneva remained, ranging from what the mandate for such an international conference should be and the question of representation, that is, which parties would be invited to participate, to the powers and nature of such a conference.[153] In a report that he released in 1988 less than two months before Algiers, Secretary-General Pérez de Cuéllar drew attention to the positions of the PLO and the Arab States bordering Israel, which were largely the same and stressed the importance of a united Arab front, the need for the PLO to be afforded equal participation, and the national rights of the Palestinian people,[154] and contrasted these with Israel's position, which stressed that an international conference needed to support, rather than substitute for, direct negotiations between the parties concerned and not impose a solution, and reaffirmed the Jewish State's view that the PLO, "which does not accept the aforementioned Security Council resolutions [i.e., Resolutions 242 and 338], continues to resort to violence and terrorism and rejects the reality of the State of Israel as well as its legitimate security concerns, cannot be considered a partner to peace negotiations."[155]

[147] *See* Address by King Hussein on Jordan's Disengagement from the West Bank, 31 July, 1988, *in* The Israeli-Palestinian Conflict, *supra* note 24, at 520.

[148] *Id.* at 520.

[149] King Hussein referred to this sense of Jordanian national identity as one of "constructive plurality." *Id.* at 524.

[150] *Id.* at 523.

[151] *See Self-Determination: The Case of Palestine, supra* note 11, at 340 (Yehuda Blum).

[152] Report of the Secretary-General, at 8, U.N. Doc. A/43/691 (Sept. 30, 1988).

[153] *See id.*

[154] *See id.* at 3–8.

[155] *Id.* at 5.

The end of the Cold War and the success of the United States-led coalition in Iraq in early 1991[156] changed this, leading to the most significant multilateral initiative on the Israeli–Arab dispute in general and the Israeli–Palestinian dispute in particular since Geneva. New geopolitical realities opened up new geopolitical possibilities, or so it was hoped. As the then United States Secretary of State James A. Baker III put it in his memoirs, the "ultimate scenario [had arrived]: once Saddam's overriding threat to regional instability was removed, all the parties would feel more comfortable in taking risks for peace."[157] The result was the Middle East Peace Conference in Madrid (Madrid Conference).[158]

Like the Geneva Conference before it, the Madrid Conference was co-sponsored by the United States and the Soviet Union. Also like the Geneva Conference, it was based upon Resolutions 242 and 338, with two tracks for two disputes: one for the dispute between Israel and the Arab States, the other for the dispute between Israel and the Palestinians. "[R]eal peace"[159] was to be the conference's object, something that was surely as vague as Resolution 338's negotiations under "appropriate auspices" language. Although, as the United States made clear at Madrid's opening session, "[n]o one can say with any precision what the end result will be,"[160] it was clear that any agreements reached, because they would be consensual, would have to be "package deals."

The sequencing of events in Madrid proved to be particularly sensitive because the co-sponsoring States needed to balance Israel's preference for bilateral negotiations with the long-standing Arab concern to maintain a united front against the Jewish State. What was needed was what Secretary Baker, the architect of the Madrid Conference, called a "calculated exercise in creative ambiguity."[161] A series of delicately sequenced bilateral and multilateral negotiations was envisaged between the parties. The Arab Maghreb Union, the European Community, Egypt, the Gulf Cooperation Council, Israel, Lebanon, Syria, and the United Nations sent delegations to Madrid; a joint Jordanian–Palestinian delegation represented the interests of Jordan and the Palestinians.[162]

[156] *See* S.C. Res. 678, U.N. Doc. S/RES/678 (Nov. 29, 1990). *See also* S.C. Res. 687, U.N. Doc. S/RES/687 (Apr. 3, 1991).

[157] James A. Baker, III, The Politics of Diplomacy: Revolution, War and Peace: 1989–1992 426 (1995).

[158] For a detailed account of the United States' shuttle diplomacy in the months leading up to Madrid, see generally *id.*

[159] United Nations Division for Palestinian Rights, Approaches Towards the Settlement of the Arab-Israeli Conflict and the Question of Palestine, no. 7 (Oct. 1991) (Text of the Invitation to the Middle East Peace Conference, Oct. 18, 1991), http://unispal.un.org/unispal.nsf/9a798adbf322aff38525617b006d88d7/f952a47244aa95da852560ef0068e15f?OpenDocument.

[160] *Id.* (Statement Made at the Opening Session of the Middle East Peace Conference, Madrid, Oct. 30, 1991, United States President George H. Bush).

[161] Baker, *supra* note 157, at 416.

[162] The invitation stated: "Palestinians will be invited and attend as part of a joint Jordanian-Palestinian delegation." United Nations Division for Palestinian Rights, *supra* note 159 (Text of the Invitation to the Middle East Peace Conference, Oct. 18, 1991). For the proceedings of the Madrid Conference, see generally United Nations Division for Palestinian Rights, *supra* note 159.

Notably absent from Madrid, of course, was the PLO. Although Washington had opened contacts with the PLO by the end of 1988, Israel continued to maintain its hard line against the group. As Palestinian delegation head Haider Abdul Shafi lamented, the Palestinians at the Madrid Conference had been "denied the right to publicly acknowledge our [i.e., Palestinian] loyalty to our leadership [i.e., the PLO] and system of government."[163] This was, as it turned out, the price of Palestinian participation. Yet, as Secretary Baker described it, "Israel privately understood that any Palestinian delegation would have the tacit acquiescence of the PLO, but [that] a visible PLO was [, or would be,] unacceptable [in Madrid]."[164] In effect, this meant that the PLO was indeed "represented," in all but name, and this was quite despite Prime Minister Yitzhak Shamir's categorical insistence shortly before Madrid that "at no stage will the PLO, the terrorist organization, have a foothold in the peace process."[165]

In other words, it was clear that the Palestinians in the joint Jordanian–Palestinian delegation had the imprimatur of the PLO. Chairman Arafat acknowledged this shortly after the Madrid Conference when he lauded the Palestinians who had participated in the proceedings as "*our* Palestinian delegation [...] at the negotiating table."[166] They "enjoy[ed] their [i.e., the Palestinian people's] trust and that of their leadership—the PLO"[167]—and were "excellent peers in all respects."[168] Both sides, then, Israel and the Palestinians, deliberately obfuscated on the representation issue, adopting something approaching a willful blindness to reality, under a facade of formalities.[169]

[163] Address of the Palestinian Delegation to the Madrid Middle East Peace Conference, Presented by Dr. Haider Abdul Shafi, Head of the Palestinian Delegation, Oct. 31, 1991, 6 PAL. Y.B. INT'L L. 296, 297 (1990). Abdul Shafi went on to laud the PLO, by obvious inference, as the "symbol of our national identity and unity, the guardian of our past, the protector of our present and the hope of our future." *Id.*

[164] BAKER, *supra* note 157, at 464. *See* MAHMOUD ABBAS (ABU MAZEN), *supra* note 139, at 85–89.

[165] United Nations Division for Palestinian Rights, *supra* note 159 (Excerpts from the Address of Prime Minister Itzhak Shamir to the Knesset, Jerusalem, Oct. 7, 1991) (continuing by stating that: "The Palestinian component in the Jordanian-Palestinian delegation must be agreed upon in advance with Israel, and if the representatives at any stage declare that they were appointed by the PLO terror organization, or that they represent it, Israel will not sit with them").

[166] United Nations Division for Palestinian Rights, Approaches Towards the Settlement of the Arab-Israeli Conflict and the Question of Palestine, no. 8 (Nov. 1991) (Excerpts from the PLO Chairman's Address Concerning the Intifadah and the Middle East Peace Conference, Nov. 9, 1991), http://unispal.un.org/unispal.nsf/9a798adbf322aff38525617b006d88d7/60ec74ed8a22b175852560f20062faa2?OpenDocument (emphasis added).

[167] *Id.* (Excerpts from the PLO Chairman's Address Concerning the Intifadah and the Middle East Peace Conference, Nov. 9, 1991).

[168] *Id.* (Excerpts from the PLO Chairman's Address Concerning the Intifadah and the Middle East Peace Conference, Nov. 9, 1991). The Palestinians in the joint Jordanian–Palestinian delegation, according to Chairman Arafat, "affirmed their allegiance to their national movement—the PLO—leader of their struggle, guardian of their history and heritage, and forger of the future of our generations." *Id.* (Excerpts from the PLO Chairman's Address Concerning the Intifadah and the Middle East Peace Conference, Nov. 9, 1991).

[169] In the 1993 Declaration of Principles on Interim Self-Government Arrangements, furthermore, discussed *infra* section IV in this chapter, the Palestinian side was described as the "P.L.O. team (in the Jordanian-Palestinian delegation to the Middle East Peace Conference (the 'Palestinian Delegation')."

Did the Palestinians possess international legal personality, and the "peoplehood" upon which is predicated self-determination, at the time of the Madrid Conference? Speaking before delegates in Madrid, Abdul Shafi argued that the Palestinians did not "stand before you [i.e., the attending delegations] as supplicants, but rather as the torch bearers who know that in our world of today, ignorance can never be an excuse."[170] "[S]upplicants" versus "torch bearers," "objects" versus "subjects": between these two extremes lies the distinction in international law between "non-personality" and "personality."[171] To have international legal personality is to have rights and obligations, but law's subjects are "not necessarily identical in their nature or in the extent of their rights, and their nature depends upon the needs of the community."[172]

It seems that the "needs of the community," for the (international) community assembled in Madrid, did not require the recognition of Palestinian "peoplehood," certainly not in a sense that was (fully) independent of Jordan. Those that accepted the conference invitation, including the Palestinians, were effectively consenting to a process of dispute settlement that did not as such entrench Palestinian rights, of self-determination or otherwise, since the conference invitation did not mention any such rights or in any way necessitate their realization. Of course, nothing prevented the juridical landscape from changing over time to accommodate such rights, but such were not the contours of the landscape at the time of Madrid.

If international law recognizes populations as "peoples" because doing so furthers their claims to self-determination and if "peoplehood" is meant to propel particular self-determination projects, it seems that Palestinian international legal personality remained conditional at the time of Madrid, conditioned by the dynamics of the process initiated in the Spanish capital. In other words, the international legal personality of the Palestinians *as a people* was at this time of a "qualified" nature or, put another way, *in statu nascendi.*[173]

Letter Dated 8 October 1993 from the Permanent Representatives of the Russian Federation and the United States of America to the United Nations Addressed to the Secretary-General, Annex at 4, 4, pmbl., U.N. Doc. A/48/486 (Oct. 11, 1993) (Declaration of Principles on Interim Self-Government Arrangements).

[170] Abdul Shafi, *supra* note 163, at 296.

[171] This binary understanding of international legal personality is not without its critics, of course. *See* Robert McCorquodale, *The Individual and the International Legal System, in* International Law 280, 280–84 (Malcolm D. Evans ed., 4th ed. 2014).

[172] Reparation for Injuries Suffered in the Service of the United Nations, Advisory Opinion, 1949 I.C.J. 174, 178 (Apr. 11). On the *Reparation for Injuries Suffered in the Service of the United Nations* advisory opinion, see Roland Portmann, Legal Personality in International Law 99–110 (2010).

[173] This is all the more clear when one contrasts Madrid's terms of reference with Resolution 46/75, which the General Assembly adopted on December 11, 1991, and which hailed the PLO as an equal party to the conflict and the Palestinian people as entitled to self-determination rights and put forth a concrete peace proposal that conflicted with the open-ended nature of the Madrid process. *See* G.A. Res. 46/75, U.N. Doc. A/RES/46/75 (Dec. 11, 1991).

IV. To Oslo

The Madrid Conference created a space for dialogue that had not existed previously. Israel, the Arab States, and the Palestinians could settle their differences peacefully, at multilateral and bilateral level, and with the support of the two superpowers. Secretary Baker was surely correct that the conference's "enduring legacy was simply that it happened at all,"[174] but his further suggestion that, "[l]ike the walls of Jericho, the psychological barriers of a half century came tumbling down with resounding finality that clear fall morning [in Madrid],"[175] reflected an optimism bordering on naiveté. Even though few observers predicted that a final settlement would be reached in Madrid (or even in its immediate aftermath), the fact remains that only one of the Arab delegations that took part in the Madrid Conference, Jordan, has entered into a peace treaty with Israel since 1991. Israel and Jordan, furthermore, agreed to leave the question of the Palestinians and the status of the territories to be resolved another day. Specifically, the 1994 Treaty of Peace Between the State of Israel and the Hashemite Kingdom of Jordan is "without prejudice to the status of any territories that came under Israeli military government control in 1967."[176]

Israel, the Arab States, and the Palestinians made little progress in the months (and months) after Madrid. In early summer 1992, the twelfth Knesset, which Prime Minister Shamir led, came to a close. Elections were held, the Labor Party cobbled together a coalition government in their wake, and Rabin again became prime minister. In his inaugural address to the thirteenth Knesset, the new premier sought to inject a new spirit of urgency into the process that began in Madrid. Admonishing the Palestinians in the territories to "forswear stones and knives and await the results of the talks that may well bring peace to the Middle East,"[177] Prime Minister Rabin called for an interim autonomy regime along the lines of Camp David. He reaffirmed the government's continued support for settlements in the territories that enhanced Israel's security and the exercise of Jewish

[174] BAKER, *supra* note 157, at 512.

[175] *Id.*

[176] Letter Dated 9 January 1995 from the Permanent Representatives of Israel, Jordan, the Russian Federation, and the United States of America to the United Nations Addressed to the Secretary General, Annex at 3, 6, art. 3(2), U.N. Doc. A/50/73 (Jan. 27, 1995) (Treaty of Peace Between the State of Israel and the Hashemite Kingdom of Jordan, Oct. 26, 1994, Arava/Araba). The Israeli–Egyptian Peace Treaty contained a similar clause with respect to Gaza. *See* Israeli–Egyptian Peace Treaty, *supra* note 71, at 384, art. 2 ("The permanent boundary between Egypt and Israel is the recognized international boundary between Egypt and the former mandated territory of Palestine, as shown on the map at Annex II, without prejudice to the issue of the status of the Gaza Strip. The Parties recognize this boundary as inviolable. Each will respect the territorial integrity of the other, including their territorial waters and airspace").

[177] Address to the Knesset by Prime Minister Rabin Presenting his Government, July 13, 1992, 13–14 Documents on the Foreign Policy of Israel (1992–94), http://mfa.gov.il/MFA/ForeignPolicy/MFADocuments/Yearbook9/Pages/1%20%20Address%20to%20the%20Knesset%20by%20Prime%20Minister%20Rabin.aspx.

property rights in all parts of Jerusalem, the "eternal capital of Israel."[178] Earlier in 1992, the Palestinians in the joint Jordanian–Palestinian delegation had also proposed an interim self-government arrangement, the Palestinian Interim Self-Government Authority (PISGA), but discussions on this were predicated upon two conditions that Israel could not, and would not, countenance: the extension of the PISGA's jurisdiction to all parts of the territories that Israel gained control of in 1967, including the eastern sector of Jerusalem, and what was vaguely described as the "total cessation of all settlement activities."[179] The chasm between the parties remained, unbridged.

The real "breakthrough" came on September 9, 1993, when Prime Minister Rabin and Chairman Arafat exchanged letters of reciprocal recognition (Exchange of Letters).[180] On behalf of the PLO, Chairman Arafat recognized the "right of the State of Israel to exist in peace and security,"[181] accepted Resolutions 242 and 338 without qualification, committed the Palestinian side to the peace process that began in Madrid, agreed to settle all permanent status issues through negotiation, and renounced those articles in the 1968 Palestinian Covenant that conflicted with these commitments and that denied Israel's "right to exist."[182] Chairman Arafat also committed the PLO to "renounce[] the use of terrorism and other acts of violence and [...] assume responsibility over all PLO elements and personnel in order to assure their compliance, prevent violations and discipline violators."[183] This series of commitments provided the assurances that Israel had found lacking in the PLO's Political Communiqué and Declaration of Independence of late 1988. The Jewish State responded to Chairman Arafat's moves by "recogniz[ing] the PLO as the representative of the Palestinian people and commenc[ing] negotiations with the PLO within the Middle East peace process."[184]

The Exchange of Letters laid the framework for the Declaration of Principles on Interim Self-Government Arrangements (Declaration of Principles), which the two sides signed on the White House lawn less than a week later, on

[178] *Id.*

[179] United Nations Division for Palestinian Rights, Approaches Towards the Settlement of the Arab-Israeli Conflict and the Question of Palestine, no. 10 (Jan. 1992) (Text of Draft "Outline of Model of the Palestinian Interim Self-Government Authority (PISGA)," Washington, DC, Jan. 14, 1992), http://unispal.un.org/unispal.nsf/9a798adbf322aff38525617b006d88d7/38b561cd9ba767e6852560f2006a150a?OpenDocument#sthash.93kvWqh8.dpuf.

[180] *See* Israel-PLO Recognition: Exchange of Letters Between PM Rabin and Chairman Arafat (Sept. 9, 1993), http://unispal.un.org/unispal.nsf/9a798adbf322aff38525617b006d88d7/36917473237100e285257028006c0bc5?OpenDocument.

[181] *Id.* (Letter from Yasser Arafat to Prime Minister Rabin).

[182] *See id.* (Letter from Yasser Arafat to Prime Minister Rabin). On the 1968 Palestinian Covenant, see Yehoshafat Harkabi, *The Palestinian Covenant and Its Meaning, in* Israel, The Middle East, and the Great Powers, *supra* note 84, at 219.

[183] Exchange of Letters, *supra* note 180 (Letter from Yasser Arafat to Prime Minister Rabin).

[184] *Id.* (Letter from Prime Minister Rabin to Yasser Arafat). In a letter to Norwegian Foreign Minister Johan Jørgen Holst on September 9, 1993, Chairman Arafat committed the PLO to "encourage[] and call[] upon the Palestinian people in the West Bank and Gaza Strip" to support the unfolding peace process. *Id.* (Letter from Yasser Arafat to Norwegian Foreign Minister).

September 13.[185] The Declaration of Principles began by expressing both sides' recognition of "mutual legitimate and political rights."[186] What is striking about this preambular language is that it is phrased in terms of the reciprocal recognition of "rights" between the "Government of the State of Israel" and the PLO, "representing the Palestinian people." This is striking because international law recognizes that international legal persons, not governments as such (in this case, the government of the State of Israel), possess rights (and bear obligations). It could perhaps be argued that the PLO was here recognizing the sovereign rights of the Israeli State as represented by its government. The PLO does not seem to have been recognizing the self-determination of the Jewish people as such, nor Israel as a "Jewish and democratic state."[187] Similarly, the Declaration of Principles did not commit Israel to the recognition of Palestinian self-determination as such, though it certainly did not exclude this interpretation from being brought to bear on the phrase "mutual legitimate and political rights":[188] self-determination, in any event, is itself an imprecise concept, something that has been said to be "loaded with dynamite."[189] What both sides did seem to be recognizing, however, and legally committing themselves to, was an unfolding process that would "concretize" the precise meaning of these rights. Much was obfuscated, here as elsewhere in the Declaration of Principles, for the sake of reaching rudimentary agreement between the sides.[190]

An important part of the Declaration of Principles was the call to establish the Palestinian Interim Self-Government Authority (Council) for Palestinians in the West Bank and Gaza. The Council was meant to be part of a transitional arrangement, not to exist for more than five years, which would lead to a "permanent settlement based on Security Council resolutions 242 (1967) and 338 (1973)."[191]

[185] *See* Letter, *supra* note 169, at Annex at 4 (Declaration of Principles on Interim Self-Government Arrangements). The United States and Russia witnessed the signing of the Declaration of Principles by Israel and the PLO.

[186] Letter, *supra* note 169, at Annex at 4, pmbl. (Declaration of Principles on Interim Self-Government Arrangements). *See* Yehuda Z. Blum, *From Camp David to Oslo*, 28(2–3) Isr. L. Rev. 211 (1994) (comparing and contrasting the terms of the Camp David Accords and the Declaration of Principles with respect to the Palestinians).

[187] Isr. Basic Law: Freedom of Occupation § 2 (1994); Isr. Basic Law: Human Dignity and Liberty § 1 (1992). *Cf.* Prime Minister's Office, At the Cabinet Meeting (Nov. 23, 2014), www.pmo.gov.il/English/MediaCenter/SecretaryAnnouncements/Pages/govmes231114.aspx?. On the Jewish Nation-State bill, see Joel Fishman, *The Jewish Nation-State Bill: Is There a Contradiction Between Judaism and Democracy?*, 26(1–2) Jewish Pol. Stud. Rev. 6 (2014).

[188] Dajani concedes that the Palestinians "surrendered one of their few bargaining chips as the price of commencing the Oslo process, recognizing Israel in 1993 without obtaining reciprocal recognition of their own right to self-determination." Omar M. Dajani, *Forty Years Without Resolve: Tracing the Influence of Security Council Resolution 242 on the Middle East Peace Process*, 37(1) J. Pal. Stud. 24, 33 (2007).

[189] Robert Lansing, The Peace Negotiations: A Personal Narrative 97 (1921).

[190] Shlaim describes the Declaration of Principles as containing "so many ambiguities and contradictions that it is open to widely differing interpretations." Avi Shlaim, *The Oslo Accord*, 23(3) J. Pal. Stud. 24, 38 (1994).

[191] Letter, *supra* note 169, at Annex at 4, art. 1 (Declaration of Principles on Interim Self-Government Arrangements). *Cf.* Camp David Accords, *supra* note 70, at 377–78.

Overall, this was a decidedly less ambitious project for the PLO than its 1988 Political Communiqué. Unlike the earlier instrument, the Declaration of Principles saw the PLO agree to Resolutions 242 and 338 but then not at the same time insist upon Palestinian self-determination and statehood.[192] The five-year transitional period that the Declaration of Principles anticipated would begin with the redeployment of the Israel Defense Forces from Gaza and the Jericho Area,[193] and the Palestinians' powers at this time would extend, at a minimum, to the spheres of tourism, education and culture, social welfare, health, and direct taxation.[194]

Although not phrased as such, a key aim of the Declaration of Principles was internal self-determination for the Palestinians in the territories.[195] The Palestinians would, according to its terms, "govern themselves according to democratic principles,"[196] with a Palestinian police force to ensure law and order during "direct, free and general political elections."[197] Although the Declaration of Principles thus acknowledged internal self-determination rights for the Palestinians in the territories, in no way did it extend external self-determination rights to them at the outset and absent an agreed final settlement.[198] In fact, it reaffirmed Israel's continued authority over external matters and security at the perimeters and with respect to Israelis and settlements in the territories.[199]

The two sides agreed to negotiate the final status of the territories, Jerusalem, security, settlements, refugees, and other issues of common concern during permanent status negotiations,[200] with what they would ultimately decide with respect to these issues depending upon economic, political, psychological, and

[192] *See* Letter, *supra* note 124, at Annex I at 7 (Political Communiqué) (framing the PLO's acceptance of Resolutions 242 and 338 within the larger context of, *inter alia*, assurance of the "legitimate national rights of the Palestinian people, first and foremost among which is the right to self-determination").

[193] *See* Letter, *supra* note 169, at Annex at 5, art. 5(1) (Declaration of Principles on Interim Self-Government Arrangements).

[194] *See id.* at Annex at 5, art. 6(2) (Declaration of Principles on Interim Self-Government Arrangements). Further particulars with respect to the Council were to be set forth in the Interim Agreement. *See id.* at Annex at 6, art. 7 (Declaration of Principles on Interim Self-Government Arrangements).

[195] *See* Antonio Cassese, *The Israel-PLO Agreement and Self-Determination*, 4(1) Eur. J. Int'l L. 564, 568–69 (1993). On internal self-determination, see Accordance with International Law of the Unilateral Declaration of Independence in Respect of Kosovo, Advisory Opinion, 2010 I.C.J. 403 (July 22) (Cançado Trindade, J., separate), (Yusuf, J., separate). *See also* General Recommendation 21, *in* Report of the Committee on the Elimination of Racial Discrimination 125, 125, ¶ 4, U.N. Doc. A/51/18 (Sept. 30, 1996).

[196] Letter, *supra* note 169, at Annex at 4, art. 3(1) (Declaration of Principles on Interim Self-Government Arrangements).

[197] *Id.* at Annex at 4, art. 3(1) (Declaration of Principles on Interim Self-Government Arrangements).

[198] *See* U.N. Hum. Rts. Comm., at ¶¶ 18–20, U.N. Doc. CCPR/C/SR.1675 (July 21, 1998) (Israel); U.N. Hum. Rts. Comm., at ¶ 14, U.N. Doc. CCPR/C/SR.1676 (Sept. 28, 1998) (Israel). *See also* Cassese, *supra* note 195, at 569. On external self-determination, see Kosovo, *supra* note 195 (Cançado Trindade, J., separate), (Yusuf, J., separate). *See also* General Recommendation 21, *supra* note 195, at 125, ¶ 4.

[199] *See* Letter, *supra* note 169, at Annex at 6, art. 8 (Declaration of Principles on Interim Self-Government Arrangements).

[200] *See id.* at Annex at 5, art. 5(3) (Declaration of Principles on Interim Self-Government Arrangements).

military elements and the persistence of will.[201] Indeed, it may not even be too strong to say that the Declaration of Principles no more precluded, or required, the eventual annexation of the territories by Israel than it precluded, or required, the creation of a Palestinian State west of the Jordan.[202] Malanczuk puts it thus, in reference to the Declaration of Principles (and subsequent arrangements between Israel and the PLO):

> As long as these arrangements remain legally in effect and are not suspended or terminated on a valid ground under the law of treaties, the highly controversial notion of self-determination, its precise meaning in international law and its exact legal consequences are not of practical relevance for the peace process.[203]

And PLO negotiator Mahmoud Abbas, who would go on to become Palestinian President, admitted that the PLO "d[id] not [even] claim that we [i.e., the PLO] signed an agreement that created an independent Palestinian State; none of the provisions in the Declaration of Principles make such a claim."[204]

Aust suggests that the use of the phrase the "two sides" in the Declaration of Principles means that the instrument cannot be regarded as a treaty.[205] Inasmuch as the VCLT defines a treaty in strictly inter-State terms[206] and given that the PLO was an international legal person at the time that the Declaration of Principles was adopted and that Palestine was not a State,[207] this is surely correct.[208] But that the

[201] *See* Cassese, *supra* note 195, at 571. For a particularly helpful introduction to many of the key international law issues related to the events of September 1993, see Eyal Benvenisti, *The Israeli-Palestinian Declaration of Principles: A Framework for Future Settlement*, 4(1) Eur. J. Int'l L. 542 (1993); Raja Shihadeh, *Can the Declaration of Principles Bring About a "Just and Lasting Peace"?*, 4(1) Eur. J. Int'l L. 555 (1993); Cassese, *supra* note 195. *See also The Oslo Agreement: An Interview with Nabil Shaath*, 23(1) J. Pal. Stud. 5 (1993).

[202] *Cf.* Richard Falk, *Some International Law Implications of the Oslo/Cairo Framework for the PLO/Israeli Peace Process, in* Human Rights, Self-Determination and Political Change in the Occupied Palestinian Territories 1, 14 (Stephen Bowen ed., 1997) (contending that, "[t]hroughout the agreements, there is no acknowledgement whatsoever of Palestinian sovereignty over West Bank, Gaza, and Jerusalem areas, and no implication that the Palestinian Authority is a vehicle for emerging Palestinian statehood").

[203] Peter Malanczuk, *Some Basic Aspects of the Agreements Between Israel and the PLO from the Perspective of International Law*, 7(4) Eur. J. Int'l L. 485, 493–94 (1996) (referring to Peter Malanczuk, *Minorities and Self-Determination: Reflections on International Law in General, Including Some Recent Developments in Ethiopia, in* Naar een Nieuwe Interpretatie van het Recht op Zelfbeschikking 169 (Neri Sybesma-Knol & Jef van Bellingen eds., 1995), and continuing on 494 by stating that: "At any rate, it is also an exercise of the right to self-determination that the PLO, as representative of the Palestinian people, has decided to pursue the specific course of the negotiations with Israel").

[204] Mahmoud Abbas (Abu Mazen), *supra* note 139, at 218.

[205] *See* Anthony Aust, Modern Treaty Law and Practice 58–59 (3d ed. 2013).

[206] *See* VCLT, *supra* note 40, at art. 2(1)(a) (defining a treaty as an "international agreement concluded between States in written form and governed by international law, whether embodied in a single instrument or in two or more related instruments and whatever its particular designation").

[207] *See* Ungar v. Palestine Liberation Organization and Palestinian Authority, 402 F.3d 274 (1st Cir. 2005). *See also* Klinghoffer v. *SNC Achille Lauro*, 937 F.2d 44, 47–49 (2d Cir. 1991) (making the same point in the wake of the PLO's Political Communiqué and Declaration of Independence of 1988).

[208] On the treaty-making power and capacity of non-State actors other than international organizations and the European Union, see Tom Grant, *Who Can Make Treaties? Other Subjects of International Law, in* The Oxford Guide to Treaties 125 (Duncan B. Hollis ed., 2012). *See also* International Law

Declaration of Principles is not a treaty is not because it used the phrase the "two sides" rather than, for example, the "two States": the test for whether the law of treaties applies is whether the instrument at issue qualifies as a treaty, an objective test that focuses on the nature of the instrument, "whatever its particular designation,"[209] and questions of substance.[210]

The more important point to make in this context is that the Declaration of Principles inaugurated a legal relationship between Israel and the PLO that both parties intended to be governed by international law. Even if, as Aust notes, the law of treaties does not apply *stricto sensu* to the Declaration of Principles, one can draw reasonable analogies from this body of law when engaging with the Declaration of Principles because, as the Special Tribunal for Lebanon has suggested, treaty law's rules of interpretation apply to any legally-binding international instrument, "whatever its normative source[, ...] because such rules translate into the international realm general principles of judicial interpretation that are at the basis of any serious attempt to interpret and apply legal norms consistently."[211]

Given that the PLO had consistently denounced Resolutions 242 and 338 as denigrations of Palestinian national rights, the group's acceptance of them in September 1993 opened it to charges that it was undermining the Palestinian people's claim to self-determination. Edward W. Said, for example, who had served on the PNC until 1991, condemned the Declaration of Principles as an "instrument of Palestinian surrender, a Palestinian Versailles,"[212] a "modified Allon Plan."[213] He charged the PLO with collaboration and likened the Palestinian regime that would be established in the territories to that of Marshall Pétain's in Vichy France, which obviously situated the Israelis as its Nazi overlords.[214]

Association, Sofia Conference Report: Non-State Actors, at 4 (2012) (discussing the treaty-making capacity of non-State actors within the context of the International Law Association's work on non-State actors); Geoffrey R. Watson, The Oslo Accords: International Law and the Israeli-Palestinian Peace Agreements 91–102 (2000) (noting the existence of legally-binding agreements between State and non-State actors, with particular reference to indigenous peoples, national liberation movements, mandates and trusteeships, colonies or subdivisions of federal States, and political units within federal States); John Quigley, *The Israel-PLO Interim Agreements: Are They Treaties?*, 30(3) Cornell Int'l L.J. 717 (1997) (highlighting a variety of non-State agreements).

209 VCLT, *supra* note 40, at art. 2(1)(a).

210 *Cf.* United Nations, Treaty Handbook, at 30, § 5.3.2, U.N. Sales No. E.12.V.1 (rev. ed. 2012) (stating that the "title and form of a document submitted to the Secretariat for registration are less important than its content in determining whether it is a treaty or international agreement"). Dajani's suggestion that the Declaration of Principles is not legally-binding because it is not a treaty misses the larger point. *See* Burhan Dajani, *The September 1993 Israeli-PLO Documents: A Textual Analysis*, 23(3) J. Pal. Stud. 5, 18 (1994).

211 Interlocutory Decision on the Applicable Law: Terrorism, Conspiracy, Homicide, Perpetration, Cumulative Charging, 2011 STL-11-01/I, at ¶ 26 (Feb. 16) (citing relevant jurisprudence on point of international courts and tribunals).

212 Edward W. Said, Peace and Its Discontents: Gaza-Jericho 1993–1995 5 (1995).

213 *Id. See* Dajani, *supra* note 210, at 21. On the Allon Plan, the Labor Party's preferred dispensation for the territories in the years after the wars of 1967 and 1973, see Yigal Allon, *Israel: The Case for Defensible Borders*, 55(1) Foreign Aff. 38 (1976).

214 *See* Said, *supra* note 212, at 35, 172.

Said would go on to castigate Chairman Arafat for entering into a dispute settlement process with Israel that would see the PLO leader "sign tens of documents that erase with the stroke of a pen many of the inalienable rights of the Palestinian people, including their right to independence."[215]

That the Declaration of Principles reflected an "agreement to disagree" on such issues as sovereignty in the territories is not without precedent when one takes into account the broader context of competing territorial claims. Consider, for example, the 1960 Indus Waters Treaty[216] and the *Indus Waters Kishenganga* arbitration, which Pakistan initiated against India in 2010.[217] The Indus Waters Treaty regulates the use by the two South Asian States of the Indus system of rivers in Jammu and Kashmir. It distinguishes between questions as to the treaty's interpretation or application, differences, and disputes, with each of these reflecting an increasing sense of seriousness, and the Indus Waters Treaty dictates that settlement is to take place through the combined workings of the Permanent Indus Commission, a Neutral Expert, negotiation, mediation, and arbitration.[218] In *Indus Waters Kishenganga*, Pakistan alleged, *inter alia*, that India had violated its obligations under the Indus Waters Treaty with respect to the Kishenganga Hydro-Electric Project, a dam project that was meant to divert waters on the Kishenganga/Neelum River.[219]

The Indus Waters Treaty addresses an issue of common concern for India and Pakistan, namely the use by the States of the Indus system of rivers in Jammu and Kashmir, but leaves the question of sovereignty in Jammu and Kashmir untouched.[220] It only acknowledges rights and obligations with respect to the use of the Indus system of rivers[221] and expressly eschews the notion that the treaty could constitute "recognition or waiver (whether tacit, by implication or otherwise) of any rights or claims whatsoever of either of the Parties other than those rights or claims which are expressly recognized or waived in this Treaty."[222]

[215] *Id.* at 180. *Cf.* Francis A. Boyle, *The Interim Agreement and International Law*, 22(3) ARAB STUD. Q. 1, 44 (2000) (cautioning the PLO against agreeing to a "very elegant and clever series of legal chains by which to enslave your [i.e., the Palestinian] People for the rest of history"). *But see* ICJ Commemorative Speech: ICJ Lead Attorney Vaughan Lowe, Speech on the Occasion of the First Anniversary of the International Court of Justice's Advisory Opinion on Israel's Wall (July 9, 2005), www.nad-plo.org/print.php?id=204 (arguing that "Palestine and Palestinians do not simply have claims and interests over which they must negotiate with Israel. They have legal rights. They do not have to bargain for those rights. They do not have to make concessions in return for the recognition of those rights. They have those rights now and they are entitled to have those rights observed").

[216] Indus Waters Treaty, Karachi, Sept. 19, 1960.

[217] *See* Indus Waters Kishenganga Arbitration (Pak. v. India), www.pca-cpa.org/showpageb106.html?pag_id=1392. On the *Indus Waters Kishenganga* arbitration, see Jawad Ahmad, *The Indus Waters Kishenganga Arbitration and State-to-State Disputes*, 29(3) ARB. INT'L 507 (2013).

[218] *See* Indus Waters Treaty, *supra* note 216, at art. 9.

[219] *See* Indus Waters Kishenganga Arbitration (Pak. v. India), Partial Award, at ¶¶ 126–27 (Feb. 18, 2013).

[220] *Cf.* Agreement Between the Government of India and the Government of the Islamic Republic of Pakistan on Bilateral Relations, Simla, July 2, 1972, art. 4(II).

[221] *See* Indus Waters Treaty, *supra* note 216, at art. 11(1)(a).

[222] *Id.* at art. 11(1)(b).

The court of arbitration's 2013 Partial Award in *Indus Waters Kishenganga* acknowledged this plain language of the Indus Waters Treaty and upheld the view that a legally-binding international instrument can regulate something that is intimately associated with territories in dispute, in the case of the Partial Award, the use of the Indus system of rivers in Jammu and Kashmir, without implication for competing territorial claims to the same territories.[223] As the Partial Award put it, the Indus Waters Treaty represents a "conscious effort to reach a definitive apportionment of the use of the waters of the Indus system of rivers, while avoiding entirely the matter of sovereignty over the areas through which those waters flow."[224]

"[A]voiding entirely the matter of sovereignty" also lay at the heart of the Declaration of Principles, and just as the *Indus Waters Kishenganga* Partial Award analyzed the Indus Waters Treaty's text, read in context and in light of its object and purpose, and found that its preambular language was "emblematic of [...] intent,"[225] so also does it prove useful to engage with the Declaration of Principles' preamble to ascertain the intent of the parties with respect to sovereignty in the territories. This language reflects Israeli and PLO agreement to end "decades of confrontation and conflict, recognize their mutual legitimate and political rights, and strive to live in peaceful coexistence and mutual dignity and security and achieve a just, lasting and comprehensive peace settlement and historic reconciliation through the agreed political process."[226] Nowhere in this, or anywhere else in the Declaration of Principles, is the question of sovereignty addressed, either expressly or by implication. Both parties reserved their rights, rather, their respective *claims*, with respect to sovereignty in the territories, in their entirety or with respect to particular parts of them.[227]

Another way to look at the sovereignty issue in the Declaration of Principles would be to borrow language that the ICJ uses with respect to requests for the indication of provisional measures.[228] The ICJ has adopted a test for such requests according to which rights asserted are assessed according to their "plausibility."[229] For example, in its Order of March 8, 2011, in response to Costa Rica's request for the indication of provisional measures in *Certain Activities Carried Out by Nicaragua in the Border Area*, the ICJ held that San José's claim of sovereign title to certain

[223] *See* Indus Waters Kishenganga, *supra* note 219, at ¶¶ 359–66.

[224] *Id.* at ¶ 360.

[225] *Id.* at ¶ 365.

[226] Letter, *supra* note 169, at Annex at 4, pmbl. (Declaration of Principles on Interim Self-Government Arrangements).

[227] As India and Pakistan did in article 11 of the Indus Waters Treaty, the Declaration of Principles also contained a "without prejudice" clause to protect the parties' concerns in this respect. *See id.* at Annex at 5, art. 5(4) (Declaration of Principles on Interim Self-Government Arrangements).

[228] *See* I.C.J. Stat. art. 41.

[229] *See* Questions Relating to the Obligation to Prosecute or Extradite (Belg. v. Sen.) (Provisional Measures) (Order), 2009 I.C.J. 139, 151 (May 28) (introducing this term in the ICJ's jurisprudence).

territory that Managua also claimed was "plausible."[230] It also referred to the territory at issue as "disputed territory,"[231] which is to say, territory to which Costa Rica had (at least) colorable, though not dispositive, title, and contrasted this with territory "over which it [i.e., Costa Rica and Nicaragua, separately,] unquestionably holds sovereignty."[232] Thus, a contrast can be drawn between a plausible claim to sovereign title to territory (territory that can also be said to be disputed territory) and territory to which a particular State's claim to sovereign title cannot reasonably be questioned.

In one sense, the Indus Waters Treaty's approach to the question of Indian/ Pakistani sovereignty in Jammu and Kashmir and the ICJ's approach to territory claimed simultaneously by both Costa Rica and Nicaragua reflect two sides of the same coin. The first is neutral, neutral in the sense that it takes no position with respect to sovereign title. The latter, by contrast, reflects a positive stance, positive in the sense that the ICJ takes an affirmative position, on grounds of plausibility, with respect to a particular State's claim to sovereign title (and also, according to two of the separate opinions appended to the ICJ's Order of March 8, 2011, "equalizing" the claim of another State, in that case, Nicaragua, to the same territory.)[233]

Similarly, the Declaration of Principles is neutral with respect to whether Israel or the PLO has sovereign title to the territories. By delaying the final status of the territories to permanent status negotiations, furthermore, it made both sides' claims to sovereign title seem equally plausible. It was through the consent of Israel and the PLO *embodied in and made manifest through* the Declaration of Principles that the two sides recognized the colorable claims of the other to the territories (and with respect to other permanent status issues): this was the price of a "seat at the table." As Said conceded, much to his consternation, the PLO thus rendered Israel's claim to the territories at least equal to that of the Palestinians'.[234]

It is not particularly surprising that Israel and the PLO agreed to settle the most intractable and problematic aspects of their dispute during permanent status negotiations. As Jordanian Crown Prince Hassan bin Talal remarked in a 1981 study on Palestinian self-determination, these issues (of self-determination, security, self-defense, and refugees) are, "in legal terms, unique. There are as many legal opinions on these disputed issues as there are jurists who have written about

[230] *See* Certain Activities Carried Out by Nicaragua in the Border Area (Costa Rica v. Nicar.) (Provisional Measures) (Order), 2011 I.C.J. 6, 19–20 (Mar. 8). The use of a plausibility standard was itself subject to considerable division in the opinions appended to the Order of March 8, 2011. For general support of the standard, see *id.* at 47–48 (Greenwood, J., declaration), 61–63 (Dugard, J. *ad hoc*, separate). For skepticism bordering on hostility, see *id.* (Koroma, J., separate), 36–38 (Sepúlveda-Amor, J., separate). The ICJ made no (provisional) finding as to Nicaragua's sovereign claim, as it was not at issue in this phase of the proceedings. *See id.* at 19.

[231] Border Area, *supra* note 230, at 19.

[232] *Id.* at 25.

[233] *See id.* at 55 (Guillaume, J., declaration) (stating his "read[]y acknowledge[ment] that both claims can be supported, and that they are both 'plausible'"), (Dugard, J. *ad hoc*, separate) (expressing concern that the ICJ's Order of March 8, 2011, juridically framed as equal two sovereign claims to territory that were actually of disparate weight).

[234] *See* SAID, *supra* note 212, at 8–9.

them."[235] It was hoped that the five-year transitional period that the Declaration of Principles set forth would create the trust and political will that both sides needed to settle their dispute peacefully, and to finality.

In such a multiple "exchange" process of negotiation, it was not surprising that the law would come to clash with politics, and that Israel and the PLO would find themselves engaged in "constant explicit and implicit communication about its [i.e., the Declaration of Principles'] meaning, application and, sometimes, its adaptation to unforeseen circumstances (or, at least, to circumstances which one of the parties did not—or subsequently says it did not—foresee)."[236] An intense discourse of law and politics did indeed unfold in the years after September 1993, but for a variety of reasons, it did not lead to the permanent settlement between Israel and the PLO (and between Israel and the Arab States, with the exception of Jordan in 1994) that the two sides had hoped for on the White House lawn.

V. Conclusion

The period between 1973 and 1993 was a remarkable one for the Palestinians. They went from being juridically "absent" from a profoundly inter-State dispute settlement process to inhabiting a central role with Israel and the Arab States. At a formal level (at least), the PLO's acceptance of bilateral negotiations with Israel reversed its traditional posture of rejectionism. It will be recalled that Arab Higher Committee representative Henry Cattan had "observed [in late November 1948] that Arab opposition to the creation of a Jewish State in Palestine followed a law of nature which could be likened to the resistance of the human body to a cancerous growth. That opposition would continue until the cancer was destroyed."[237] By September 1993, it seemed that the patient had stabilized or that the "ailment" that she had been convinced was "cancerous" no longer existed (if it had existed in the first place), or that it was, at worst, a "benign tumor."

[235] Hassan, *supra* note 18, at 111. More generally, it should be noted that, as the arbitral tribunal in *Affaire du Lac Lanoux* did: "pour qu'une négociation se déroule dans un climat favorable, il faut que les Parties consentent à suspendre, pendant la négociation, le plein exercice de leurs droits. Il est normal qu'elles prennent des engagements à cet effet. Si ces engagements devaient les lier inconditionnellement jusqu'à la conclusion d'un accord, elles perdraient, en les signant, la faculté meme de négocier; cela ne saurait être présumé." Affaire du Lac Lanoux (Spain v. Fr.) (1957), 12 R. Int'l Arb. Awards 281, 311 (1963).

[236] W. Michael Reisman, *The Diversity of Contemporary International Dispute Resolution: Functions and Policies*, 4(1) J. Int'l Disp. Settlement 47, 50 (2013) (making this point within the context of commercial disputes).

[237] United Nations General Assembly First Committee Debate, Summary Record, U.N. Doc. A/C.1/SR.207 (Nov. 22, 1948), http://unispal.un.org/pdfs/AC1SR207.pdf.

As Palestinian international legal personality crystallized along with (an unfolding sense of) self-determination for the Palestinians, a series of legal instruments emerged to regulate the relationship between Israel and the PLO. These texts would provide international law's reference point for assessing the Israeli–Palestinian dispute. Of both a procedural and substantive nature, the rights and obligations that these instruments reflected root themselves in the international law of negotiation. Because any attempt to understand the Israeli–Palestinian dispute from the perspective of international law must engage with this body of law, it is to the international law of negotiation as a means of dispute settlement that this work now turns.

5

The International Law of Negotiation as a Means of Dispute Settlement

I. Introduction

In the 1924 case *Mavrommatis Palestine Concessions* (*Mavrommatis*), the Permanent Court of International Justice (PCIJ) famously defined a "dispute" as a "disagreement on a point of law or fact, a conflict of legal views or of interests between two persons."[1] *Mavrommatis* hinged upon whether there was a dispute between the United Kingdom and Greece and, if so, whether the United Kingdom, as the then Mandatory of Palestine, had violated certain of its international legal obligations related to concessions that had been granted to Greek national Mavrommatis in Mandatory Palestine. In his dissenting opinion, Judge Moore built upon the PCIJ's understanding of the nature of a dispute by describing it as a "pre-existent difference, certainly in the sense and to the extent that the government which professes to have been aggrieved should have stated its claims and the grounds on which they rest, and that the other government should have had an opportunity to reply, and if it rejects the demands, to give its reasons for so doing."[2] The *Mavrommatis* test for determining whether a disagreement *simpliciter* can be regarded as a legally cognizable dispute is usually seen as reflecting general international law.[3] The existence of a dispute, of course, is a prerequisite for the application of the international law of dispute settlement.

Once a disagreement rises to the lecvel of a dispute, then the international law of dispute settlement will apply. The cornerstone of this body of law is that disputes must be settled peacefully, "in such a manner that international peace

[1] Mavrommatis Palestine Concessions (Greece v. U.K.), 1924 P.C.I.J. (ser. A) No. 2, at 11 (Aug. 30).

[2] *Id.* at 61 (Moore, J., dissenting).

[3] *See* Application of the International Convention on the Elimination of All Forms of Racial Discrimination (Geor. v. Russ.) (Preliminary Objections), 2011 I.C.J. 70, 84–85 (Apr. 1). *See also* Questions Relating to the Obligation to Prosecute or Extradite (Belg. v. Sen.), 2012 I.C.J. 422, 442 (July 20). "A dispute may be defined as a specific disagreement concerning a matter of fact, law or policy in which a claim or assertion of one party is met with refusal, counter-claim or denial by another." J.G. MERRILLS, INTERNATIONAL DISPUTE SETTLEMENT 1 (5th ed. 2011).

and security, and justice, are not endangered,"[4] and in the absence of the threat or use of force.[5] Like its corresponding articles in the Covenant of the League of Nations before it,[6] article 33 of the Charter of the United Nations (Charter) recognizes various means of dispute settlement.[7] In addition to such diplomatic means of dispute settlement as negotiation, enquiry, mediation, and conciliation, article 33(1) lists arbitration and judicial settlement, both of which channel the parties, upon agreement, to resolve their dispute through, ultimately, the reaching of a legally-binding agreement.[8] Hersch Lauterpacht captured the essential difference between diplomatic and legal means of dispute settlement well when, writing in 1930, he noted that parties that choose a diplomatic means of dispute settlement over a legal means of dispute settlement are effectively "substitut[ing] a series of attempts at settlement for a settlement proper."[9] Although it would not be correct to say that the law plays no role in diplomatic means of dispute settlement, or that political considerations do not inform legal means of dispute settlement, it is true that these dichotomies have classically been put forward as the key distinguishing factors between diplomatic and legal means of dispute settlement.[10]

To better understand the bilateral negotiation imperative between Israel and the Palestinian people, this chapter sets forth what can best be described as the international law of negotiation. Although the forms of negotiation are varied and diverse, that negotiation as a substantive obligation of law necessarily embeds itself within a framework of legal evaluation means that a party's failure to comply with its obligations can result in an internationally wrongful act and, in response, countermeasures and other responses by the victim party. This chapter proceeds in three sections. Firstly, it looks at the relationship between negotiation and other means of dispute settlement, both diplomatic and legal. Secondly, it explores the

[4] U.N. Charter art. 2(3).

[5] *See id.* at art. 2(4).

[6] *See* Covenant of the League of Nations Adopted by the Peace Conference at Plenary Session, Apr. 28, 1919, 13(2) AM. J. INT'L L. SUPP. 128, 132, art. 12 (1919); *id.* at 132–33, art. 13; *id.* at 133, art. 14; *id.* at 133–34, art. 15; *id.* at 134–35, art. 16; *id.* at 135–36, art. 17.

[7] On Chapter VI of the Charter, with particular reference to article 33, see Rosalyn Higgins, *International Law and the Avoidance, Containment and Resolution of Disputes: General Course on Public International Law, in* 230 COLLECTED COURSES OF THE HAGUE ACADEMY OF INTERNATIONAL LAW 9, 225–28 (1991). *See also* K.J. Keith, *Resolving International Disputes: The Role of the Courts,* 7 N.Z. Y.B. INT'L L. 255 (2009); G.A. Res. 60/1, at 21, U.N. Doc. A/RES/60/1 (Sept. 16, 2005); Anne Peters, *International Dispute Settlement: A Network of Cooperational Duties,* 14(1) EUR. J. INT'L L. 1, 4–9 (2003); Manfred Lachs, *The Law and the Settlement of International Disputes, in* DISPUTE SETTLEMENT THROUGH THE UNITED NATIONS 283 (K. Venkata Raman ed., 1977). *Cf.* EMER DE VATTEL, THE LAW OF NATIONS 448–67 (Béla Kapossy & Richard Whatmore eds., 2008) (discussing the "Mode of Terminating Disputes Between Nations").

[8] Article 33(1) also states that the parties to a dispute can have recourse to "regional agencies or arrangements" and "other peaceful means of their own choice," though it does so without specifying whether these must be diplomatic or legal in nature. Presumably, they could be either, appropriately tailored by the parties to the particular facts and circumstances of the dispute at issue.

[9] Hersch Lauterpacht, *The Absence of an International Legislature and the Compulsory Jurisdiction of International Tribunals,* 11 BRIT. Y.B. INT'L L. 134, 138 (1930).

[10] *See* D.W. Bowett, *Contemporary Developments in Legal Techniques in the Settlement of Disputes, in* 180 COLLECTED COURSES OF THE HAGUE ACADEMY OF INTERNATIONAL LAW 169, 177–78 (1983).

modalities that govern when it can be said as a matter of law that negotiation has been tried and has been exhausted. Finally, it turns to the not uncommon situation of a negotiation that has broken down due to the commission of an internationally wrongful act by one of the parties under the law of negotiation and the potential for the victim party to adopt countermeasures and other responses to facilitate compliance with law and the vindication of rights.[11]

II. The Relationship Between Negotiation and Other Means of Dispute Settlement

Negotiation is undoubtedly the oldest means of dispute settlement. In their dissenting opinions in *Mavrommatis*, Judges Moore and Pessôa referred to it as, respectively, the "legal and orderly administrative process by which governments, in the exercise of their unquestionable powers, conduct their relations one with another and discuss, adjust and settle, their differences"[12] and as "debate or discussion between the representatives of rival interests, discussion during which each puts forward his arguments and contests those of his opponent."[13] Like consultation within the context of the World Trade Organization's dispute settlement system, negotiation allows the parties to a dispute to exchange information, assess their respective cases, and attempt to reach a mutually agreed upon understanding.[14] Negotiation serves to focus disagreements and make disputes more "concrete," with a view to settlement.[15] It can involve tactics that are tough and challenging, and it often does. As such, International Court of Justice (ICJ) Judge Lachs' view that negotiation can "no longer be viewed as a chess game in

[11] This chapter does not cover the regime of lawful responses known as retorsion since these measures do not involve an internationally wrongful act. On retorsion, see JAMES CRAWFORD, STATE RESPONSIBILITY: THE GENERAL PART 676–78 (2014); Thomas Giegerich, *Retorsion*, *in* MAX PLANCK ENCYCLOPEDIA OF PUBLIC INTERNATIONAL LAW (last updated Mar. 2011). This chapter does not cover unilateral coercive measures either, in part because this is a relatively new concept but also because it has been couched in unduly vague and politicized language. *See* Research-Based Progress Report of the Human Rights Council Advisory Committee Containing Recommendations on Mechanisms to Assess the Negative Impact of Unilateral Coercive Measures on the Enjoyment of Human Rights and to Promote Accountability, at 5, U.N. Doc. A/HRC/28/74 (Feb. 10, 2015) (defining unilateral coercive measures as "the use of economic, trade or other measures taken by a State, group of States or international organizations acting autonomously to compel a change of policy of another State or to pressure individuals, groups or entities in targeted states to influence a course of action without the authorization of the Security Council").

[12] Mavrommatis, *supra* note 1, at 62–63 (Moore, J., dissenting).

[13] *Id.* at 91 (Pessôa, J., dissenting).

[14] *See* Appellate Body Report, Mexico—Anti-Dumping Investigation of High Fructose Corn Syrup (HFCS) from the United States, at ¶ 54, No. WT/DS132/AB/RW (Oct. 22, 2001).

[15] *See* J.G. Merrills, *The Mosaic of International Dispute Settlement Procedures: Complementary or Contradictory?*, 54(2) NETH. INT'L L. REV. 361, 366 (2007).

which one party steers the other into a checkmate position"[16] seems to overshoot the mark. Negotiation is most assuredly a "chess game in which one party steers the other into a checkmate position." Although there are (legal) rules as to how the "chess game" can be played, it would be a rare party to a dispute indeed that would not seek to maximize its advantage through negotiation.

In its purest form, negotiation does not involve third-party intervention,[17] and it can be relatively informal in nature.[18] As a diplomatic means of settling disputes, it has the advantage of, *inter alia*, giving notice to the parties as to the existence and scope of a dispute and providing an opportunity to settle their dispute consensually, on the basis of mutual consent.[19] It tends to favor parties that can leverage their greater attributes of power, be these military, political, economic, or otherwise, to influence the discussions, though it is also important to point out that the law does not require the weaker party to come to a legally-binding agreement with the stronger party. The PCIJ made this clear in 1931 when, in rejecting Poland's argument that Lithuania was bound to negotiate with it until a legally-binding agreement had been reached, it stated that although the law of negotiation requires that the parties to a negotiation "pursue them [i.e., negotiations] as far as possible, with a view to concluding agreements[, …] an obligation to negotiate does not imply an obligation to reach an agreement."[20] To be sure, there is ultimately a "floor" to negotiation, but this will vary in each case and depend upon the particular facts and circumstances of the dispute at issue.[21]

The text of article 33 of the Charter does not as such indicate whether the parties to a dispute must choose diplomatic or legal means of dispute settlement, much less does it suggest that there is a hierarchy of means, that is, whether international law privileges particular means of dispute settlement over others. This is

[16] Lachs, *supra* note 7, at 289.

[17] *See* Michael Waibel, *The Diplomatic Channel*, *in* THE LAW OF INTERNATIONAL RESPONSIBILITY 1085, 1090 (James Crawford et al. eds., 2010). *But see* Bowett, *supra* note 10, at 177 (articulating a rather broader understanding of negotiation that can admit of third-party involvement).

[18] Waibel notes that this informality means that negotiation can take place at, *inter alia*, informal meals and in casual conversation. *See* Waibel, *supra* note 17, at 1087.

[19] *See* Georgia, *supra* note 3, at 124–25.

[20] Railway Traffic Between Lithuania and Poland, Advisory Opinion, 1931 P.C.I.J. (ser. A/B) No. 42, at 12 (Oct. 15).

[21] On negotiation generally as a means of dispute settlement, see W. Michael Reisman, *The Diversity of Contemporary International Dispute Resolution: Functions and Policies*, 4(1) J. INT'L DISP. SETTLEMENT 47, 49–52 (2013); MERRILLS, INTERNATIONAL DISPUTE SETTLEMENT, *supra* note 3, at 1–25; Waibel, *supra* note 17; JOHN COLLIER & VAUGHAN LOWE, THE SETTLEMENT OF DISPUTES IN INTERNATIONAL LAW: INSTITUTIONS AND PROCEDURES 20–24 (2000); Antonio Cassese, *The Israel-PLO Agreement and Self-Determination*, 4(1) EUR. J. INT'L L. 564, 567 n.7 (1993); HANDBOOK ON THE PEACEFUL SETTLEMENT OF DISPUTES BETWEEN STATES, at 9–24, U.N. Doc. OLA/COD/2394 (1992). *See also* G.A. Res. 53/101, U.N. Doc. A/RES/53/101 (Dec. 8, 1998); G.A. Res. 37/10, Annex, U.N. Doc. A/RES/37/10 (Nov. 15, 1982) (Manila Declaration on the Peaceful Settlement of International Disputes); G.A. Res. 2625, Annex, U.N. Doc. A/RES/2625 (Oct. 24, 1970) (Declaration on Principles of International Law concerning Friendly Relations and Co-operation Among States in Accordance with the Charter of the United Nations). On the Manila Declaration on the Peaceful Settlement of International Disputes, see Vladimir-Djuro Degan, *The Value of the Manila Declaration on International Dispute Settlement in a Case in Which the Philippines is a Party*, 11(1) CHIN. J. INT'L L. 5 (2012).

because, generally speaking, it does not. Rather, the general aim of article 33 is to facilitate the peaceful settlement of disputes, and the means that the parties can choose to achieve this can be used either singly or in combination. The Charter leaves the choice of means largely to the parties themselves,[22] and they can arrive at the choice of means *ad hoc*, that is, as particular disputes arise, or this can be determined in advance, through a compromissory clause in a treaty that dictates particular means and modalities of dispute settlement.[23]

While it is clear that the Charter does not as such indicate whether the parties to a dispute must choose diplomatic or legal means of dispute settlement or suggest a hierarchy of means, international law can "direct" that particular disputes be settled through particular means of dispute settlement to the exclusion of others.[24] A typical example of this would be when the United Nations Security Council "recommends" that the parties settle their dispute through particular means but does so without adopting a legally-binding enforcement measure under Chapter VII of the Charter.[25] Of course, should the situation require it, the Security Council can also "decide" to require the parties to settle their dispute through particular means and can do so through the adoption of a legally-binding enforcement measure under Chapter VII of the Charter. This, of course, would then require the parties to settle their dispute through the mandated means of dispute settlement to the exclusion of others, pursuant to States' Charter obligation to "accept and carry out the decisions of the Security Council in accordance with the present Charter."[26]

Reference to the ICJ's handling of a dispute in the mid 1970s between Greece and Turkey that involved the delimitation of the continental shelf in the Aegean Sea, is helpful to illustrate this interplay. In exercise of its "primary responsibility for the maintenance of international peace and security,"[27] the Security Council adopted Resolution 395, which, *inter alia*, "[*c*]*all*[*ed*] *upon* the Governments of Greece and Turkey to resume direct negotiations over their differences and appeal[ed] to them to do everything within their power to ensure that these negotiations will result in mutually acceptable solutions."[28] Through this Resolution, the Security Council

[22] *See* Aerial Incident of 10 August 1999 (Pak. v. India) (Jurisdiction), 2000 I.C.J. 12, 33 (June 21).

[23] *See, e.g.*, United Nations Convention on the Law of the Sea, Montego Bay, Dec. 10, 1982, arts 279–99.

[24] *See* Merrills, *Mosaic, supra* note 15, at 366–69, 389–92. *Cf.* Treaty Between Australia and the Democratic Republic of Timor-Leste on Certain Maritime Arrangements in the Timor Sea, Sydney, Jan. 12, 2006, art. 4(7) (presenting the rather less common situation of an international treaty regime that expressly "precludes" any semblance of legal obligation to settle a dispute through a particular means of dispute settlement, in this case, through negotiation).

[25] *See* U.N. Charter arts 33(2), 36(1).

[26] *Id.* at art. 25.

[27] *Id.* at art. 24(1).

[28] S.C. Res. 395, at ¶ 3, U.N. Doc. S/RES/395 (Aug. 25, 1976). For another of the Security Council's "callings upon" to negotiation involving another dispute in the eastern Mediterranean with obvious implications for Greece and Turkey, see S.C. Res. 1250, at ¶ 7, U.N. Doc. S/RES/1250 (June 29, 1999) (Cyprus).

sought to channel the settlement of this dispute through a particular means of dispute settlement, negotiation, and when the dispute reached the ICJ, the ICJ expressed some reluctance to indicate provisional measures on the basis of this.[29] Two years later, in 1978, the ICJ rejected Greece's application on the basis that it lacked jurisdiction.[30] It did so on technical grounds, however, grounds that were unrelated to the fact that Resolution 395 had expressed a preference for a negotiated settlement between Greece and Turkey.[31] As the ICJ put it, "the fact that negotiations are being actively pursued during the present proceedings is not, legally, any obstacle to the exercise by the Court of its judicial function."[32] The basic idea here seems to be that international law's overriding concern with facilitating the peaceful settlement of disputes militates in favor of a multi-pronged strategy.[33]

Conceivably, of course, a court with jurisdiction *could* delay rendering a judgment or even use its discretion to refuse to render a judgment *tout court* when a dispute is being settled, with whatever measure of success, through a diplomatic means of dispute settlement such as negotiation. The PCIJ suggested just such a possibility in its 1929 order in *Free Zones of Upper Savoy and the District of Gex*,[34] and more recently, Judge Xue and Judge *ad hoc* Roucounas showed considerable sensitivity to the wisdom and prejudicial potential of rendering a judicial decision alongside an ongoing negotiating process in their respective dissenting opinions appended to the ICJ's 2011 judgment in *Application of the Interim Accord of 13 September 1995* (*Interim Accord*).[35] Nonetheless, a court with jurisdiction would be under no such obligation as a matter of law, a point that the ICJ most recently reiterated in *Interim Accord*.[36] From the ICJ's perspective, the question is whether there are "compelling reasons"[37] for it to use its discretion so as to stay proceedings and refuse to proceed to the merits despite the presence of *prima facie* jurisdiction over a dispute.[38]

[29] *See* Aegean Sea Continental Shelf (Greece v. Turk.) (Interim Measures), 1976 I.C.J. 3, 13 (Sept. 11).

[30] Aegean Sea Continental Shelf (Greece v. Turk.), 1978 I.C.J. 3 (Dec. 19).

[31] *See id.* In paragraph 4, Resolution 395 also "[*i*]*nvit*[*ed*] the Governments of Greece and Turkey [...] to continue to take into account the contribution that appropriate judicial means, in particular the International Court of Justice, are qualified to make to the settlement of any remaining legal differences which they may identify in connexion with their present dispute."

[32] Aegean Sea Continental Shelf, *supra* note 30, at 12. *See id.* at 52–53 (Lachs, J., separate).

[33] *See* Waibel, *supra* note 17, at 1094–95. *See also* Bola A. Ajibola, *Dispute Resolution by the International Court of Justice*, 11(1) Leiden J. Int'l L. 123 (1998) (stressing that the ICJ can act as part of the negotiation process and as a catalyst for negotiations).

[34] *See* Free Zones of Upper Savoy and the District of Gex, Order, 1929 P.C.I.J. (ser. A) No. 22, at 13 (Aug. 19) (stating that it had a "facilitat[ive]" role as regards "direct and friendly settlement," though only "so far as is compatible with its Statute").

[35] *See* Application of the Interim Accord of 13 September 1995 (Maced. v. Greece), 2011 I.C.J. 644, 718 (Dec. 5) (Xue, J., dissenting), 727 (Roucounas, J. *ad hoc*, dissenting). *Cf.* Peters, *supra* note 7, at 15 (suggesting that a court in such circumstances might be inclined to view this as an abuse of process).

[36] *See* Interim Accord, *supra* note 35, at 664–65. *See also* Legal Consequences of the Construction of a Wall in the Occupied Palestinian Territory, Advisory Opinion, 2004 I.C.J. 136, 159–60 (July 9).

[37] Judgments of the Administrative Tribunal of the ILO Upon Complaints Made Against the UNESCO, Advisory Opinion, 1956 I.C.J. 77, 86 (Oct. 23).

[38] *See* Judgment No. 2867 of the Administrative Tribunal of the International Labour Organization upon a Complaint Filed Against the International Fund for Agricultural Development, Advisory Opinion, 2012 I.C.J. 10, 24–25 (Feb. 1).

III. The International Law of Negotiation

Prior to its 2011 rejection of Georgia's application against Russia during the preliminary objections phase of *Application of the International Convention on the Elimination of All Forms of Racial Discrimination* (*Georgia*),[39] the ICJ had spoken only generally about what international law requires for a negotiation to qualify as such as a means of dispute settlement.[40] A notable exception to this occurred in 1969, when the ICJ rendered judgment in conjoined cases that involved a dispute about the delimitation of the continental shelf in the North Sea, the *North Sea Continental Shelf* cases.[41] In these cases, it found that both the 1958 Geneva Convention on the Continental Shelf did not apply against the Federal Republic of Germany because the State was not a party to the treaty and also that the equidistance principle did not apply as a matter of customary international law.[42] Instead, the ICJ held that the States at issue, the Federal Republic and Denmark, and the Federal Republic and the Netherlands, were required to enter into negotiations to settle their disputes and that these negotiations had to be purposeful, "with a view to arriving at an agreement, and not merely to go through a formal process of negotiation as a sort of prior condition for the automatic application of a certain method of delimitation in the absence of agreement,"[43] as well as "meaningful, which will not be the case when either of them insists upon its own position without contemplating any modification of it."[44] Although the ICJ articulated these legal parameters for negotiation as a means of dispute settlement within the particular context of the delimitation of the continental shelf, it seemed to have also been articulating the *lex generalis* of negotiation.[45]

The ICJ handed down its judgment rejecting Georgia's application against Russia during the preliminary objections phase in April 2011. It had previously, in October 2008, ordered provisional measures against both States, though it did acknowledge in its provisional measures order that it "need not finally satisfy itself, before deciding whether or not to indicate such [provisional] measures, that it has jurisdiction on the merits of the case, yet it may not indicate them unless the provisions invoked by the Applicant appear, prima facie, to afford a basis on which

[39] Georgia, *supra* note 3. *See* Phoebe Okowa, *The International Court of Justice and the Georgia/Russia Dispute*, 11(4) Hum. Rts. L. Rev. 739 (2011).

[40] For a fairly thorough articulation of the international law of negotiation outside the context of the ICJ prior to Georgia, see Agreement on German External Debts (Greece v. F.R.G.) (1972), 47 I.L.R. 418, 451–62 (1974).

[41] North Sea Continental Shelf (F.R.G./Den.) (F.R.G./Neth.), 1969 I.C.J. 3 (Feb. 20).

[42] *See id.* at 46.

[43] *Id.* at 47.

[44] *Id.*

[45] *See id.* at 47–48. *See also* Interim Accord, *supra* note 35, at 684–85; Pulp Mills on the River Uruguay (Arg. v. Uru.), 2010 I.C.J. 14, 67 (Apr. 20); Fisheries Jurisdiction (F.R.G. v. Ice.), 1974 I.C.J. 175, 201–202 (July 25); Fisheries Jurisdiction (U.K. v. Ice.), 1974 I.C.J. 3, 31–33 (July 25).

the jurisdiction of the Court might be founded."[46] In its 2011 judgment, the ICJ ultimately held that it did not have jurisdiction to proceed to the merits because, upholding the second of Russia's four preliminary objections, the terms of article 22 of the 1965 International Convention on the Elimination of All Forms of Racial Discrimination (CERD) had not been satisfied.[47] Thus, the case was dismissed.

Georgia is a key development in the international law of negotiation because the ICJ articulated a three-part understanding for this means of dispute settlement and, in doing so, not only spoke about negotiation within the framework of the CERD, which would be *lex specialis*, but also expanded its discussion to pronounce upon negotiation under international law generally.[48] It set forth the modalities that govern when it can be said as a matter of law that negotiation has been tried and has been exhausted. Specifically, the ICJ approached the condition predicate of negotiations by examining "what constitutes negotiations; [...] their adequate form and substance; and [...] to what extent they should be pursued before it can be said that the precondition has been met."[49] It is worth examining the ICJ's analysis here in some detail.

As to "what constitutes negotiations," the ICJ contrasted them with "mere protests or disputations."[50] "[M]ore than the plain opposition of legal views or interests between two parties, or the existence of a series of accusations and rebuttals, or even the exchange of claims and directly opposed counter-claims,"[51] a negotiation requires a "genuine attempt by one of the disputing parties to engage in discussions with the other disputing party, with a view to resolving the dispute."[52] A negotiation can be said as a matter of law to have been tried and to have been exhausted once the negotiating process experiences "failure [... or] become[s] futile or deadlocked."[53] Although it may seem obvious, the ICJ also felt compelled

[46] Application of the International Convention on the Elimination of All Forms of Racial Discrimination (Geor. v. Russ.) (Provisional Measures) (Order), 2008 I.C.J. 353, 377 (Oct. 15). On the October 2008 order, see Sandy Ghandhi, *The International Court of Justice and the Provisional Measures Order in the* Georgia v. Russian Federation *Case, in* CONFLICT IN THE CAUCASUS: IMPLICATIONS FOR INTERNATIONAL LEGAL ORDER 80 (James A. Green & Christopher P.M. Waters eds., 2010).

[47] *See* Georgia, *supra* note 3, at 120–40. "Any dispute between two or more States Parties with respect to the interpretation or application of this Convention, which is not settled by negotiation or by the procedures expressly provided for in this Convention, shall, at the request of any of the parties to the dispute, be referred to the International Court of Justice for decision, unless the disputants agree to another mode of settlement." International Convention on the Elimination of All Forms of Racial Discrimination, New York, Dec. 21, 1965, art. 22.

[48] *See* Georgia, *supra* note 3, at 132–33. *Cf.* Mavrommatis Palestine, *supra* note 1, at 13. Wellens accurately describes Georgia as a "landmark case on the interpretation of compromissory clauses in general and the precondition of prior negotiations more in particular." KAREL WELLENS, NEGOTIATIONS IN THE CASE LAW OF THE INTERNATIONAL COURT OF JUSTICE: A FUNCTIONAL ANALYSIS 5 (2014).

[49] Georgia, *supra* note 3, at 132.

[50] *Id.*

[51] *Id.*

[52] *Id.*

[53] *Id.* at 133 (citations omitted). In its July 2012 judgment in *Questions Relating to the Obligation to Prosecute or Extradite*, the ICJ clarified that it could be said that negotiation had been tried and

to state that a negotiation must also relate to the subject matter of the dispute.[54] What is absolutely clear from this is that, according to the ICJ, when the parties to a dispute are required to channel the settlement of their dispute through negotiation, neither party can credibly claim that it need not even attempt to negotiate or that the mere factual existence of a dispute suffices as a matter of law to show that negotiation has been tried and has been exhausted.[55]

As stated above, the ICJ in *Georgia* upheld Russia's preliminary objection that the terms of article 22 of the CERD had not been satisfied and, thus, held that there was no jurisdiction to proceed to the merits. There was not unanimity on this point, however. A joint dissenting opinion by President Owada, Judges Simma, Abraham, and Donoghue, and Judge *ad hoc* Gaja, for example, contended that the majority had set the "bar" for negotiation "too high."[56] According to this view, negotiation can be said as a matter of law to have been tried and to have been exhausted when there is no longer, if there ever was, a "reasonable possibility of settling the dispute by negotiation."[57] The joint dissent stated that the crux of the majority's analysis should have been more firmly rooted in matters of substance and a realistic assessment of the particular facts and circumstances of the dispute at issue rather than what it stated to be a formalistic or procedural perspective.[58] More radically, Judge Cançado Trindade's dissenting opinion dismissed the very relevance of article 22 of the CERD as a condition predicate to the ICJ's exercise of jurisdiction in *Georgia*, criticizing it for being a "groundless and most regrettable obstacle to justice."[59]

Implicit in all of this, of course, is the idea that negotiation must be conducted in good faith.[60] Although this legal principle is admittedly one that can seem irredeemably vacuous and question-begging *in abstracto*, it is, as the ICJ has noted,

had been exhausted when the "basic positions [... of the parties to a dispute had] not subsequently evolved." Prosecute or Extradite, *supra* note 3, at 446.

[54] *See* Georgia, *supra* note 3, at 133.

[55] Hence, the ICJ rejected Georgia's argument in its memorial that, "under Article 22 of the 1965 Convention, there is no affirmative obligation for the Parties to have attempted to resolve the dispute through negotiations (or through the procedures established by the Convention). All that is required is that, as a matter of fact, the dispute has not been so resolved." Memorial of Georgia, Application of the International Convention on the Elimination of All Forms of Racial Discrimination (Geor. v. Russ.), vol. 1, 2009 I.C.J., at 304 (Sept. 2).

[56] Georgia, *supra* note 3 (Owada, Pres. et al., dissenting).

[57] *Id.* at 145 (Owada, Pres. et al., dissenting).

[58] *See id.* at 158–61 (Owada, Pres. et al., dissenting). *Cf.* South West Africa (Eth. v. S. Afr.; Liber. v. S. Afr.) (Preliminary Objections), 1962 I.C.J. 319, 346 (Dec. 21) (de-emphasizing form and focusing on the "attitude and views of the Parties on the substantive issues of the question involved").

[59] Georgia, *supra* note 3, at 321 (Cançado Trindade, J., dissenting). "The Court cannot keep on embarking on a literal or grammatical and static interpretation of the terms of compromissory clauses enshrined in those treaties, drawing 'preconditions' therefrom for the exercise of its jurisdiction, in an attitude remindful of traditional international arbitral practice. When human rights treaties are at stake, there is need, in my perception, to overcome the force of inertia, and to assert and develop the compulsory jurisdiction of the ICJ on the basis of the compromissory clauses contained in those treaties." Id. at 320 (Cançado Trindade, J., dissenting).

[60] *Cf.* Reference re Secession of Quebec, [1998] 2 S.C.R. 217, at ¶ 104 (Can.) (articulating a notion of "principled negotiations").

"[o]ne of the basic principles governing the creation and performance of legal obligations, whatever their source,"[61] and international law has consistently reaffirmed the centrality of good faith to the law of negotiation.[62] It is a primary law obligation that focuses mainly, though not exclusively, on process considerations, and when a treaty requires that the parties to a dispute settle their dispute by negotiation, good faith "kicks in" by virtue of article 26 of the 1969 Vienna Convention on the Law of Treaties (VCLT).[63] This is, to quote Judge Greenwood in his separate opinion appended to the ICJ's 2010 judgment in *Pulp Mills on the River Uruguay*, "implicit,"[64] and the fact that some treaties qualify a duty to negotiate with the phrase "good faith" is reaffirmative rather than imposing a "new" obligation as such.[65] In this context, it is worth noting that *M/V "Louisa"*'s rejection of the view that article 300 of the 1982 United Nations Convention on the Law of the Sea (UNCLOS)[66] provided an independent ground of jurisdiction hinged not

[61] Nuclear Tests (Austl. v. Fr.), 1974 I.C.J. 253, 268 (Dec. 20); Nuclear Tests (N.Z. v. Fr.), 1974 I.C.J. 457, 473 (Dec. 20). *See* Application Instituting Proceedings of Marshall Islands, Obligations Concerning Negotiations Relating to Cessation of the Nuclear Arms Race and to Nuclear Disarmament (Marsh. Is. v. India), 2014 I.C.J., at 20–21 (Apr. 24); Application Instituting Proceedings of Marshall Islands, Obligations Concerning Negotiations Relating to Cessation of the Nuclear Arms Race and to Nuclear Disarmament (Marsh. Is. v. Pak.), 2014 I.C.J., at 18–19 (Apr. 24); Application Instituting Proceedings of Marshall Islands, Obligations Concerning Negotiations Relating to Cessation of the Nuclear Arms Race and to Nuclear Disarmament (Marsh. Is. v. U.K.), 2014 I.C.J., at 32–34 (Apr. 24). *See also* Steven Reinhold, *Good Faith in International Law* (Bonn Research Paper on Public International Law No. 2/2013, 2013); Mohammed Bedjaoui, Keynote Address at Good Faith, International Law, and Elimination of Nuclear Weapons Conference, Geneva, at 18–20 (May 1, 2008), http://lcnp.org/disarmament/2008May01eventBedjaoui.pdf; Robert Kolb, *Principles as Sources of International Law (With Special Reference to Good Faith)*, 53(1) NETH. INT'L L. REV. 1 (2006).

[62] *See, e.g.*, Articles on Prevention of Transboundary Harm from Hazardous Activities, With Commentaries, *in* International Law Commission, 2(2) Y.B. Int'l L. Comm'n 148, 160–61, U.N. Doc. A/CN.4/SER.A/2001/Add.1 (Part 2) (2001). On six consequences of the good faith principle within the context of international dispute settlement's duty to cooperate, see Peters, *supra* note 7, at 15–16.

[63] *See* Pulp Mills, supra note 45, at 67. *See also* ANTHONY AUST, MODERN TREATY LAW AND PRACTICE 160–62 (3d ed. 2013). "Every treaty in force is binding upon the parties to it and must be performed by them in good faith." Vienna Convention on the Law of Treaties, Vienna, May 23, 1969, art. 26.

[64] Pulp Mills, *supra* note 45, at 223 (Greenwood, J., separate). *See* Interim Accord, *supra* note 35, at 684.

[65] *See, e.g.*, Treaty on the Non-Proliferation of Nuclear Weapons, London/Moscow/Washington, DC, July 1, 1968, art. 6 (stating that: "Each of the Parties to the Treaty undertakes to pursue negotiations in good faith on effective measures relating to cessation of the nuclear arms race at an early date and to nuclear disarmament, and on a treaty on general and complete disarmament under strict and effective international control"). *See also* WELLENS, *supra* note 48, at 43–44. *But see* Bedjaoui, *supra* note 61, at 21. "With this mention in a treaty concerning a domain as crucial as that of global nuclear disarmament, good faith acquires a more imperative connotation than ever before, since its task thus becomes to protect the fundamental values of *the entire international community* and to reinforce *the international public order.*" *Id.* at 22. On article 6 of the 1968 Treaty on the Non-Proliferation of Nuclear Weapons (NPT), see Legality of the Threat or Use of Nuclear Weapons, Advisory Opinion, 1996 I.C.J. 226, 263–65 (July 8). For some perspective on this obligation in light of the NPT's negotiating history, see Edwin Brown Firmage, *The Treaty on the Non-Proliferation of Nuclear Weapons*, 63(4) AM. J. INT'L L. 711, 732–37 (1969). *See also* DANIEL H. JOYNER, INTERPRETING THE NUCLEAR NON-PROLIFERATION TREATY 95–108 (2011).

[66] "States Parties shall fulfil in good faith the obligations assumed under this Convention and shall exercise the rights, jurisdiction and freedoms recognized in this Convention in a manner which would

upon the permissibility of bad faith or abuse of rights as such, a point that the International Tribunal for the Law of the Sea made clear in paragraph 155 of its judgment, but, rather, upon the technical determination that St. Vincent and the Grenadines had invoked this provision in such a manner as to have amounted to an impermissible "new claim."[67]

The 1925 arbitral award in the *Tacna-Arica Question* (*Tacna-Arica*)[68] gives some texture to this legal principle of good faith within the context of negotiation.[69] *Tacna-Arica*, which United States President Calvin Coolidge decided as arbitrator, involved a dispute between Chile and Peru over the provinces of Tacna and Arica.[70] After the War of the Pacific in the late nineteenth century, Chile and Peru agreed that the former State would possess Tacna and Arica for ten years, after which time, according to article 3 of the Treaty of Ancon, a plebiscite would "'decide by popular vote whether the territory of the above-mentioned provinces is to remain definitely under the dominion and sovereignty of Chile or is to continue to constitute a part of Peru.'"[71] What is relevant for present purposes is the award's view as to how good faith should operate when a legal framework, in this case, the Treaty of Ancon, indicates an end result, the holding of a plebiscite, without stipulating the modalities and time frame that should govern the manner in which this end result should be reached.[72]

Given that the Treaty of Ancon on this point was merely an "agreement to agree with no time specified and no forfeiture provided,"[73] President Coolidge framed the question as a matter of good faith. Clearly, Chile and Peru had to negotiate in good faith, and this was an obligation for both States equally unless one of the States demonstrated a "wilful refusal [...] so to do."[74] In their negotiation, both States were free to propose and counter-propose conditions that each hoped would ultimately govern the holding of the plebiscite, and it could not be said that either State had violated the obligation to negotiate in good faith provided that

not constitute an abuse of right." United Nations Convention on the Law of the Sea, *supra* note 23, at art. 300.

[67] *See* M/V "Louisa" (St. Vincent v. Spain), 2013 I.T.L.O.S., at ¶¶ 126–50 (May 28).

[68] Tacna-Arica Question (Chile/Peru) (1925), 2 R. Int'l Arb. Awards 921 (1949).

[69] *Interim Accord* cited *Tacna-Arica* as reflecting customary international law on this point. *See* Interim Accord, *supra* note 35, at 685.

[70] For background to the dispute, see Ronald Bruce St. John, *Chile, Peru and the Treaty of 1929: The Final Settlement*, 8(1) Boundary & Sec. Bull. 91 (2000); Quincy Wright, *The Tacna-Arica Arbitration*, 10(1) Minn. L. Rev. 28 (1925).

[71] Tacna-Arica, *supra* note 68, at 926. Article 3 of the Treaty of Ancon also stipulated that the State that would ultimately annex Tacna and Arica after the plebiscite would have to pay a sum of money to the other State and that the two States would have to agree to a special protocol before the plebiscite could be held. *See id.*

[72] *See id.* at 927–44. President Coolidge also decided on the conditions of the plebiscite and some questions related to the northern and southern boundaries of Tacna and Arica. *See id.* at 944–57.

[73] *Id.* at 928.

[74] *Id.* at 929. Other potential indicia of bad faith include delayed responses, demands of an extreme nature, nominal concessions, and referrals to unauthorized actors. *See* Edy Glozman et al., *False Negotiations: The Art and Science of Not Reaching an Agreement*, 59(4) J. Conflict Resol. 671, 691 (2015).

it had at all times maintained the required, so to speak, *mens rea*. Put differently, neither State could show an "intent to frustrate the carrying out of the provisions of Article 3 with respect to the plebiscite; that is, not simply the refusal of a particular agreement proposed thereunder, because of its terms, but the purpose to prevent any reasonable agreement for a plebiscite."[75] A violation of the good faith obligation "should not be lightly imputed."[76] A sustainable case *could*, however, be made on the basis of circumstantial evidence, though not on the basis of "disputable inferences but[, rather,] by clear and convincing evidence which compels such a conclusion."[77]

An important point to note in relation to the international law of negotiation is that the *duration* of the process is not dispositive when it comes to determining whether it can be said as a matter of law that negotiation has been tried and has been exhausted. As the ICJ put it in its 1971 advisory opinion in *Legal Consequences for States of the Continued Presence of South Africa in Namibia (South West Africa) Notwithstanding Security Council Resolution 276 (1970) (Namibia)*: "In practice[,] the actual length of negotiations is no test of whether the possibilities of agreement have been exhausted."[78] Similarly, the arbitral tribunal in *Kuwait v. American Independent Oil Company* framed negotiation's temporal dimension as follows: "good faith as properly to be understood; sustained upkeep of the negotiations over a *period appropriate to the circumstances*; awareness of the interests of the other party; and a persevering quest for an acceptable compromise."[79] These are questions that must be decided by the parties in good faith, on a case-by-case basis, and with due regard to considerations of reasonableness and equity.[80] The international law of negotiation does not focus on temporal concerns as such; these are secondary. Rather, it looks at good faith and related considerations. In a word, the focus is on whether, considering all of the facts and circumstances at issue, the negotiation is, or can be said to have been, "meaningful."[81] The concern

[75] Tacna-Arica, *supra* note 68, at 930.

[76] *Id.*

[77] *Id.* On circumstantial evidence and adverse inferences in the ICJ's jurisprudence, see Michael P. Scharf & Margaux Day, *The International Court of Justice's Treatment of Circumstantial Evidence and Adverse Inferences*, 13(1) CHI. J. INT'L L. 123 (2012).

[78] Legal Consequences for States of the Continued Presence of South Africa in Namibia (South West Africa) Notwithstanding Security Council Resolution 276 (1970), Advisory Opinion, 1971 I.C.J. 16, 44 (June 21) (continuing by stating that "it may be sufficient to show that an early deadlock was reached and that one side adamantly refused to compromise"). *See* Mavrommatis, *supra* note 1, at 13 (stating that: "Negotiations do not of necessity always presuppose a more or less lengthy series of notes and despatches; it may suffice that a discussion should have been commenced, and this discussion may have been very short; this will be the case if a dead lock is reached, or if finally a point is reached at which one of the Parties definitely declares himself unable, or refuses, to give way, and there can therefore be no doubt that *the dispute cannot be settled by diplomatic negotiation*").

[79] Kuwait v. Amer. Indep. Oil Co. (1982), 66 I.L.R. 518, 578 (1984) (emphasis added).

[80] *See* Interpretation of the Agreement of 25 March 1951 Between the WHO and Egypt, Advisory Opinion, 1980 I.C.J. 73, 96 (Dec. 20).

[81] Interim Accord, *supra* note 35, at 685.

is with conduct, not result, on process, not conclusive resolution.[82] It is a question of due diligence, as well.[83]

Of course, while the general international law position is that duration is not dispositive, special rules of law can change this analysis.[84] A *lex specialis* norm within the context of a particular negotiation can "elevate" the relevance of duration and make it, if not the sole criterion, certainly a more consequential criterion than would otherwise be the case under general international law. The most obvious example of this would be when the underlying law requires the parties to reach a negotiated settlement within a fixed period of time.[85] Articles 74(2) and 83(2) of the UNCLOS would be a less straightforward example. These articles call for States with opposite or adjacent coasts to reach agreement with each other as regards the delimitation of, respectively, the exclusive economic zone and the continental shelf within a "reasonable period of time."[86] While there are no "hard and fast" rules as regards the meaning of a "reasonable period of time," each case having to be assessed on the basis of particular facts and circumstances, it is worth noting that the tribunal in the 2006 arbitral award in *Barbados/Trinidad and Tobago* found that negotiations over the course of roughly twenty-five years that failed to result in an agreement between the States satisfied the criterion of a "reasonable period of time."[87]

Finally, there is an important distinction to be made between negotiation as a precondition to jurisdiction, as was the case in *Georgia*, and negotiation as a substantive obligation of law (the violation of which would amount to an internationally wrongful act). While the ICJ's finding in *Georgia* that the terms of article 22 of the CERD had not been satisfied meant that it did not have jurisdiction to proceed to the merits, there was no suggestion that Georgia had committed an internationally wrongful act by its acts and omissions: the ICJ was simply saying that it did not have jurisdiction, and nothing else. Still, the contours of negotiation as a means of dispute settlement seem to be similar, if not identical,

[82] *See id.*

[83] On the due diligence principle generally under international law, see Robert P. Barnidge, Jr, *The Due Diligence Principle Under International Law*, 8(1) INT'L CMTY. L. REV. 81 (2006). *See, e.g.*, Responsibilities and Obligations of States with Respect to Activities in the Area, Advisory Opinion, 2011 I.T.L.O.S. 10 (Feb. 1).

[84] *See* Articles on Responsibility of States for Internationally Wrongful Acts, With Commentaries, *in* 2(2) Y.B. Int'l L. Comm'n, *supra* note 62, at 30, 139–41.

[85] *See, e.g.*, Ahmadou Sadio Diallo (Guinea v. Dem. Rep. Congo), 2010 I.C.J. 639, 691–92 (Nov. 30). For a view supporting the ICJ's ordering of a negotiated settlement as to reparation within a fixed period of time in its November 2010 judgment in *Ahmadou Sadio Diallo* (*Diallo*), see Sandy Ghandhi, *Human Rights and the International Court of Justice: The* Ahmadou Sadio Diallo *Case*, 11(3) HUM. RTS. L. REV. 527, 551–53 (2011). In the wake of *Diallo*, Guinea and the Democratic Republic of the Congo failed to reach agreement on compensation within the six-month period of time that the ICJ had stipulated for them for a negotiated settlement. The ICJ ended up awarding $85,000 for Diallo's non-material injury and $10,000 for the material injury to his personal property. *See* Ahmadou Sadio Diallo (Guinea v. Dem. Rep. Congo) (Compensation), 2012 I.C.J. (June 19).

[86] United Nations Convention on the Law of the Sea, *supra* note 23, at arts 74(2), 83(2).

[87] *See* Delimitation of the Exclusive Economic Zone and the Continental Shelf (Barb./Trin. & Tobago) (2006), 27 R. Int'l Arb. Awards 147, 204 (2008).

in both situations. Put differently, there does not seem to be reason to distinguish between the modalities that govern when it can be said that negotiation has been tried and has been exhausted (when negotiation operates as a precondition to jurisdiction) and the law that applies when this same means of dispute settlement operates as a substantive obligation of law (the violation of which would amount to an internationally wrongful act).

IV. When Negotiation Breaks Down: Countermeasures and Other Responses

Negotiation as a means through which the parties to a dispute can peacefully settle their differences does not usually have all of the trappings and formalities of, for example, arbitration or judicial settlement. As has been shown above, however, there is nonetheless a framework of legal norms against which the acts and omissions of the negotiating parties can be assessed, and a party to a dispute is theoretically no more (or less) likely to commit (or not) an internationally wrongful act within the context of a negotiation than it is within the context of a different means of dispute settlement, be it diplomatic or legal. Although this is true in theory, in practice, it can be "difficult to tell a false negotiator masquerading as a tough one from a sincere negotiator who was merely behaving competitively."[88] To quote the ICJ, when the parties to a dispute have established a legal relationship in which negotiation acts as a substantive obligation of law, "a party which disowns or does not fulfil its own obligations cannot be recognized as retaining the rights which it claims to derive from the relationship."[89] With the possibility of an internationally wrongful act comes the entire panoply of the law of international responsibility. The victim party can potentially take countermeasures and other responses to facilitate compliance with law and the vindication of rights.

It might be thought that the absence of third-party intervention in negotiation (in its purest form) and its relatively informal nature mean that a party to a dispute is left without recourse if the other party violates its obligations under the international law of negotiation. This, however, is not the case. One of the responses that a victim party can take is countermeasures, and these, it must be said, "hover disconsolately on the Stygian waters which divide the imperfectly held terrain of

[88] Glozman et al., *supra* note 74, at 690.

[89] Namibia, *supra* note 78, at 46. *See* Waibel, *supra* note 17, at 1093. As Rogoff has stated it, "[t]here are situations where the failure of a state to honor a consensual or customary obligation to negotiate would allow the aggrieved state to take certain legal action that would otherwise be legally impermissible, such as the termination of a treaty relationship or acting in a manner otherwise prohibited." Martin A. Rogoff, *The Obligation to Negotiate in International Law: Rules and Realities*, 16(1) MICH. J. INT'L L. 141, 174 (1994).

international law from the uncontrolled terrain of extralegal anarchy."[90] Within the context of negotiation, countermeasures are meant to facilitate, not obstruct, a negotiated settlement, to restore equality and symmetry between the parties.[91] As the arbitral tribunal in the 1978 *Case Concerning the Air Service Agreement of 27 March 1946 Between the United States of America and France* (*Air Service Agreement*) defined them, countermeasures are "contrary to international law but justified by a violation of international law allegedly committed by the State against which they are directed."[92]

The *Air Service Agreement* arbitral award involved a dispute between the United States and France concerning American-designated planes undertaking changes of gauge in the United Kingdom on flights between the West Coast of the United States and France, French grounding of a Pan American World Airways (Pan American) flight to Paris Orly Airport and the suspension by it of future Pan American flights to France, and, in response, the United States Civil Aeronautics Board requiring French companies Union de Transports Aériens and Air France to file with it existing and future flight schedules related to flights to and from the United States.[93] The second of two questions that the arbitral tribunal had to address was the issue of the lawfulness of the United States' response to France's actions against Pan American.[94]

While the arbitral tribunal in *Air Service Agreement* ultimately found in favor of the United States on the countermeasures issue, what is more broadly interesting than the specific dispute in that case is the reasoning that was used in assessing the contours of permissible countermeasures. The arbitral tribunal noted that, in taking countermeasures, a victim party essentially "affirm[s] its rights"[95] and can

[90] Julius Stone, *International Conflict Resolution, in* INTERNATIONAL ENCYCLOPEDIA OF THE SOCIAL SCIENCES (1968), http://www.encyclopedia.com/doc/1G2-3045000590.html. *See* Michael N. Schmitt, *"Below the Threshold" Cyber Operations: The Countermeasures Response Option and International Law*, 54(3) VA. J. INTL L. 697 (2014); CRAWFORD, *supra* note 11, at 684–706; AUST, *supra* note 63, at 316–19; Hubert Lesaffre, *Circumstances Precluding Wrongfulness in the ILC Articles on State Responsibility: Countermeasures, in* THE LAW OF INTERNATIONAL RESPONSIBILITY, *supra* note 17, at 469; Patricia Tarre Moser, *Non-Recognition of State Immunity as a Judicial Countermeasure to* Jus Cogens *Violations: The Human Rights Answer to the ICJ Decision on the* Ferrini *Case*, 4(3) GOETTINGEN J. INT'L L. 809, 816–27 (2012); ELENA KATSELLI PROUKAKI, THE PROBLEM OF ENFORCEMENT IN INTERNATIONAL LAW: COUNTERMEASURES, THE NON-INJURED STATE AND THE IDEA OF INTERNATIONAL COMMUNITY 68–76 (2010); David J. Bederman, *Counterintuiting Countermeasures*, 96(4) AM. J. INT'L L. 817 (2002); Oscar Schachter, *International Law in Theory and Practice: General Course in Public International Law, in* 178 COLLECTED COURSES OF THE HAGUE ACADEMY OF INTERNATIONAL LAW 9, 167–87 (1982).

[91] *See* Case Concerning the Air Service Agreement of 27 March 1946 Between the United States of America and France (1978), 18 R. Int'l Arb. Awards 417, 444–45 (1980).

[92] *Id.* at 444. The contemporary law related to countermeasures finds its roots in the notion of reprisals. *See* Oscar Schachter, *Dispute Settlement and Countermeasures in the International Law Commission*, 88(3) AM. J. INT'L L. 471, 471–72 (1994). For the classic definition of reprisals, see Responsabilité de l'Allemagne à Raison des Dommages Causés dans les Colonies Portugaises du Sud de l'Afrique (Port. v. Germ.) (1928), 2 R. Int'l Arb. Awards 1011, 1025–26 (1949).

[93] *See* Air Service Agreement, *supra* note 91, at 419–23.

[94] *See id.* at 441–46.

[95] *Id.* at 443.

only do so as a matter of proportionate response.[96] Obviously, proportionality is not an exact science, here as elsewhere in the law. According to the arbitral tribunal, what is involved is "some degree of equivalence"[97] and "very approximative appreciation."[98] In addition to the question of proportionality, the victim party's "hand" is potentially "strengthened" in that it can also account for issues of principle arising from the alleged violation of international law by the other party, not simply the material injury that may have been caused.[99] To this, it might be pointed out, arbitrator Reuter's dissenting opinion added consideration of "probable effects."[100] It is also crucial to note that the arbitral tribunal in *Air Service Agreement* acknowledged the permissibility of countermeasures by a victim party within the context of an ongoing negotiation as long as the dispute at issue is *sub judice*.[101]

Gabčíkovo-Nagymaros Project (*Gabčíkovo-Nagymaros*) is the seminal ICJ case dealing with countermeasures.[102] As its name suggests, this case involved the Gabčíkovo-Nagymaros Project, a complex project of locks along the River Danube between Hungary and Slovakia. Slovakia's purported countermeasure was a plan that became known as "Variant C," and this involved the unilateral diversion of the Danube, the construction of an overflow dam and levee, and some ancillary works.[103] In rejecting Slovakia's argument that Variant C was a permissible countermeasure, the ICJ spelled out four criteria that must be satisfied for any countermeasure to be considered permissible under international law: it must be responsive and directed at the wrongdoer; it must have followed an attempt to have the wrongdoer cease its internationally wrongful act or make reparation for it; there must be commensurability between the internationally wrongful act and the injury suffered, all rights considered; and the countermeasure must be reversible so as to facilitate what might be regarded as the *sine qua non* of any countermeasure, that is, to induce the wrongdoer to comply with its (violated) international legal obligation.[104]

[96] *See id.* On proportionality of countermeasures generally under international law, see Katselli Proukaki, *supra* note 90, at 260–76; Thomas M. Franck, *On Proportionality of Countermeasures in International Law*, 102(4) Am. J. Int'l L. 715 (2008).

[97] Air Service Agreement, *supra* note 91, at 443.

[98] *Id.* at 444.

[99] *See id.* at 443.

[100] *Id.* at 448 (Reuter, Arb., dissenting).

[101] *See* Air Service Agreement, *supra* note 91, at 445–46. *See also* Yuji Iwasawa & Naoki Iwatsuki, *Procedural Conditions, in* The Law of International Responsibility, *supra* note 17, at 1149, 1152–54. *Cf.* Articles on State Responsibility, *supra* note 84, at 131, art. 50(2)(a).

[102] Gabčíkovo-Nagymaros Project (Hung./Slovk.), 1997 I.C.J. 7 (Sept. 25).

[103] *See id.* at 25.

[104] *See id.* at 55–57. *Cf.* Louis Henkin, *International Law: Politics, Values and Functions: General Course on Public International Law, in* 216 Collected Courses of The Hague Academy of International Law 9, 85 (1989). For affirmation of the *Gabčíkovo-Nagymaros* criteria as reflecting the customary international law of countermeasures, see Archer Daniels Midland Co. and Tate & Lyle Ingredients Americas, Inc. v. Mex., at ¶¶ 124–33, I.C.S.I.D. Case No. ARB(AF)/04/05 (2007).

Two of the opinions appended to the majority's judgment in *Gabčíkovo-Nagymaros* are worth examining to better appreciate the texture of countermeasures under international law. In his separate opinion, Judge Bedjaoui agreed with the majority that Variant C did not qualify as a permissible countermeasure because it was, *inter alia*, disproportionate and irreversible.[105] He argued, however, that the majority should have made more of the (illicit) possibility of premeditation and calculated response by Slovakia as regards Variant C.[106] Judge Vereshchetin, in his dissenting opinion, accepted much of what the majority had held as to the black-letter law of countermeasures, but he disagreed with the application of these criteria to Variant C. According to him, the majority should have been more searching and critical in looking at the gravity and effect of Variant C on the particular facts and circumstances of the dispute at issue.[107] Within the context of Variant C, according to Judge Vereshchetin, these included economic, financial, and environmental considerations.[108] The respective opinions of Judges Bedjaoui and Vereshchetin, then, reinforce rather than undermine the majority's articulation of the *lex generalis* of countermeasures.

On August 9, 2001, almost four years after the ICJ had handed down its judgment in *Gabčíkovo-Nagymaros*, the International Law Commission (ILC) adopted the Articles on Responsibility of States for Internationally Wrongful Acts (Articles on State Responsibility).[109] The Articles on State Responsibility reflect the inevitability, if not the desirability, of countermeasures in contemporary international law, and they build upon the contours of permissible countermeasures set forth in *Air Service Agreement* and *Gabčíkovo-Nagymaros*. Given previous State practice, it is unsurprising that the Articles on State Responsibility preclude the wrongfulness of a victim party's conduct when it amounts to a permissible countermeasure in response to a previous or ongoing internationally wrongful act by the responsible party, though this is without prejudice to the possibility of compensation for material loss caused by the countermeasure.[110] Articles 49 and 51 mirror the criteria in the *Gabčíkovo-Nagymaros* test for permissible countermeasures, and the proportionality calculus, in a nod to *Air Service Agreement*, allows the victim party to consider the "purely 'quantitative' element of the injury suffered [... and] also 'qualitative' factors such as the importance of the interest protected by the rule infringed and the seriousness of the breach."[111] Of course, countermeasures must

[105] *See* Gabčíkovo-Nagymaros, *supra* note 102, at 134 (Bedjaoui, J., separate).
[106] *See id.* (Bedjaoui, J., separate).
[107] *See id.* at 224 (Vereshchetin, J., dissenting).
[108] *See id.* (Vereshchetin, J., dissenting).
[109] Articles on State Responsibility, *supra* note 84. For an historical overview of the International Law Commission's decades' long State responsibility project, see James Crawford, *Introduction* to THE INTERNATIONAL LAW COMMISSION'S ARTICLES ON STATE RESPONSIBILITY: INTRODUCTION, TEXT, AND COMMENTARIES 1 (James Crawford ed., 2003).
[110] *See* Articles on State Responsibility, *supra* note 84, at 75, art. 22, 85, art. 27.
[111] *Id.* at 135.

end when the responsible party's underlying internationally wrongful act, which triggered the privilege of countermeasures in the first place, ends.[112]

The Articles on State Responsibility largely reaffirm the *Gabčíkovo-Nagymaros* criteria for permissible countermeasures, but they also go a step further in that they expressly forbid countermeasures that "affect" article 2(4) of the Charter, obligations that protect "fundamental human rights," obligations of a humanitarian nature related to reprisals, and *jus cogens* norms.[113] The majority in *Gabčíkovo-Nagymaros* completely avoided referring to these or any other such considerations, though it might be argued that some such considerations were implied in the judgment, at least to an extent.[114] Dictated largely by policy considerations, these are the permissible limits beyond which countermeasures must not transgress, and the ILC's final incarnation of them in its 2001 draft is clearer than the corresponding provision in its 1996 Draft Articles on State Responsibility Provisionally Adopted on First Reading.[115] Article 50(b) of the earlier draft, for example, sought to prohibit, in exceedingly vague language, "[e]xtreme economic or political coercion designed to endanger the territorial integrity or political independence of the State which has committed the internationally wrongful act."[116]

Although the four limits beyond which permissible countermeasures must not transgress as articulated in the Articles on State Responsibility arguably improve upon the 1996 draft of the State responsibility project, they are still far from unproblematic. Indeed, they leave much to be desired and arguably beg more questions than they answer. For example, countermeasures must not affect, according to article 50(1)(b) of the Articles on State Responsibility, "fundamental human rights," but what is it precisely that makes a human right "fundamental" as opposed to, one might suppose, a "garden variety" human right? Do "*fundamental* human rights" impose greater obligations upon victim parties with respect to countermeasures than do, to use the corresponding language in the 1996 draft of

[112] *See id.* at 85, art. 27(a), 135, art. 52(3)(a), 137, art. 53.

[113] *See id.* at 131, art. 50(1). *See, e.g.,* Award in the Arbitration Regarding the Delimitation of the Maritime Boundary Between Guyana and Suriname (Guy./Surin.) (2007), 30 R. Int'l Arb. Awards 1, 126–27 (2012) (dismissing Suriname's argument that its actions amounted to a permissible countermeasure on the basis that they involved the threat of force). In its second paragraph, article 50 in the Articles on State Responsibility goes on to note that: "A State taking countermeasures is not relieved from fulfilling its obligations: (a) under any dispute settlement procedure applicable between it and the responsible State; (b) to respect the inviolability of diplomatic or consular agents, premises, archives and documents." *Cf.* Omer Yousif Elagab, The Legality of Non-forcible Counter-measures in International Law 96–135 (1988) (discussing and analyzing, in 1988, a number of countermeasures' "collateral constraints").

[114] Only Judge Vereshchetin, in his dissenting opinion, expressly recognized permissible limits to countermeasures. In his view, they were not at issue with Variant C, but they were, and are, "the threat or use of force, extreme economic or political coercion, infringement of the inviolability of diplomatic agents, derogations from basic human rights or norms of *jus cogens*)." Gabčíkovo-Nagymaros, *supra* note 102, at 222 (Vereshchetin, J., dissenting).

[115] *See* Draft Articles Provisionally Adopted by the Commission on First Reading, *in* International Law Commission, 2(2) Y.B. Int'l L. Comm'n 58, 64, art. 50, U.N. Doc. A/CN.4/SER.A/1996/Add.l (Part 2) (1996).

[116] *Id.* at 64, art. 50(b).

the State responsibility project, "*basic* human rights"?[117] If so, how, precisely, and in what way?

That countermeasures must not affect *jus cogens* norms seems unsurprising as a general principle, but the definition of a *jus cogens* norm contained in article 53 of the VCLT surely does not "interpret itself."[118] Even if one were to assume agreement on a definitive list of *jus cogens* norms, when could it be said that a countermeasure "affect[s]" such a norm?[119] Does "affect" mean the same as "breach"? One reading might be that the former verb would seem to potentially implicate more conduct than the latter verb. Are these questions of substance or process, and who, or what, is to answer them? Most importantly, how is a victim party reasonably to be expected to answer these questions in a measured manner without increasing the risk that it will be inadvertently engaging in an impermissible countermeasure, perhaps even entailing a violation of a *jus cogens* norm?

In addition to countermeasures *stricto sensu*, a party to a dispute that has suffered an injury under the international law of negotiation can potentially respond on the basis of the legal principle *exceptio non adimpleti contractus.*[120] *Exceptio*

[117] *Id.* at 64, art. 50(d) (emphasis added).

[118] VCLT, *supra* note 63, at art. 53 (defining such a norm as one that is "accepted and recognized by the international community of States as a whole as a norm from which no derogation is permitted and which can be modified only by a subsequent norm of general international law having the same character"). The ILC is currently studying this and other questions related to *Jus Cogens*, http://legal.un.org/ilc/summaries/1_14.shtml.

[119] *Cf.* Wall, *supra* note 36, at 214 (Higgins, J., separate) (critiquing the majority in the advisory opinion for concluding that the separation barrier, rather than the reaching of a negotiated settlement between Israelis and Palestinian Arabs, is what has complicated, or, one might say in the context of countermeasures, "affect[ed]," the exercise of the right to self-determination).

[120] As the United Kingdom Supreme Court put it in 2010: "Where a plaintiff sues to enforce performance of an obligation which is conditional upon performance by himself of a reciprocal obligation owed to the defendant, then the performance by him of this latter obligation (or, in cases where they are not consecutive, the tender of such performance) is a necessary prerequisite of his right to sue and should be pleaded by him. Conversely in such a case the defendant may raise as a defence, known as the *exceptio non adimpleti contractus*, the fact that the plaintiff has failed to perform, or in the appropriate case, tender performance of, his own reciprocal obligation." Inveresk PLC v. Tullis Russell Papermakers Ltd., 2010 U.K.S.C. 106, 122 (citing ESE Financial Services (PTY) Ltd. v. Cramer, 1973 (2) S.A. 805, 809 (Corbett, J.)). *See* Danae Azaria, Treaties on Transit of Energy via Pipelines and Countermeasures 151–52 (2015) (describing *exceptio non adimpleti contractus* as "permit[ting] the performance of an obligation to be withheld, if the other party has failed to perform the same or a related obligation"); Filippo Fontanelli, *The Invocation of the Exception of Non-Performance: A Case-Study on the Role and Application of General Principles of International Law of Contractual Origin*, 1(1) Cambridge J. Int'l & Comp. L. 119, 123 (2012) (characterizing *exceptio non adimpleti contractus* as the principle according to which a "refusal to perform by one party which would be objectively wrongful under the terms of the contract may be lawful in light of the previous conduct of the other party"); James Crawford & Simon Olleson, *The Exception of Non-Performance: Links Between the Law of Treaties and the Law of State Responsibility*, 21 Austl. Y.B. Int'l L. 55, 56 (2000) (casting a definition of *exceptio non adimpleti contractus* in general terms as the "principle that performance of an obligation may be withheld if the other party has itself failed to perform the same or a related obligation"). *See also* Chae Chan Ping v. U.S., 130 U.S. 581, 601 (1889) (reflecting the essence of *exceptio non adimpleti contractus* in a pre-VCLT setting by stating: "Neglect or violation of stipulations on the part of the other contracting party [to a treaty] may require corresponding action on our part. When a reciprocal engagement is not carried out by one of the contracting parties, the other may also decline to keep the corresponding engagement"). Klabbers concludes that the principle "may serve as something of a sanction, but is naturally of limited

non adimpleti contractus can best be understood within the context of reciprocal legal obligation. In his separate opinion appended to *Interim Accord*, Judge Simma, though presuming to have presided over the funeral of the principle and to have "declared [it] dead,"[121] nicely captured this notion of reciprocity. "Reciprocity," according to him, "constitutes a basic phenomenon of social interaction and consequently a decisive factor also behind the growth and application of law."[122] It is Janus-headed, both constructive and destructive, reinforcing stability and licensing instability, both, according to Judge Simma, "a propelling force in the making and keeping of the law and [...] a trigger in the breakdown of legal order."[123] One can scarcely think of a means of dispute settlement in which reciprocity plays a more pronounced role than negotiation. Under the international law of negotiation, the obligations of the parties to the dispute are often innately (inter)dependent. Indeed, without the "give and take" that negotiation requires, few negotiated settlements could be reached.

The ICJ had a chance to clarify the contours of *exceptio non adimpleti contractus* in December 2011, in *Interim Accord*, but it only dealt with it *arguendo* and expressly refused to even acknowledge the existence of the principle in contemporary international law.[124] Of course, this is far from fatal for the existence of this subsidiary means of redress, and this is so for a number of reasons. Firstly, the ICJ only refused to comment upon the status of *exceptio non adimpleti contractus* within the context of treaty law, specifically, in that case, the Interim Accord of 13 September 1995. Thus, it left wholly untouched the principle's status in contexts *other than or only in* treaty law, that is, in contexts in which the legal obligation said to have been violated roots itself other than or only in straight application of a treaty norm.[125] Secondly, it could be said that the fact that the ICJ even dealt with

scope, applying first and foremost to bilateral treaty relations, and even then only in fairly rare circumstances." JAN KLABBERS, INTERNATIONAL LAW 167 (2013). *See* CRAWFORD, *supra* note 11, at 678–82. For the contours of *exceptio non adimpleti contractus* in South African contract law, see Smith v. Van den Heever, Case No. 136/10 (2011) (S. Afr.). In Ibero-American law, see Edgardo Muñoz, *Right to Withhold Performance Under Ibero-American Law*, 1 CUADERNOS DE LA MAESTRÍA EN DERECHO 379 (2011).

[121] Interim Accord, *supra* note 35, at 706 (Simma, J., separate). Relying upon Judge Simma's separate opinion appended to Interim Accord with respect to *exceptio non adimpleti contractus*, see Energy Charter Treaty (Hully Enter. Ltd. (Cyprus) v. Russ.), Final Award, at ¶ 1360 (July 18, 2014); Energy Charter Treaty (Veteran Petroleum Ltd. (Cyprus) v. Russ.), Final Award, at ¶ 1360 (July 18, 2014); Energy Charter Treaty (Yukos Universal Ltd. (Isle of Man) v. Russ.), Final Award, at ¶ 1360 (July 18, 2014). *Cf.* Joe Verhoeven, *The Law of Responsibility and the Law of Treaties*, *in* THE LAW OF INTERNATIONAL RESPONSIBILITY, *supra* note 17, at 105, 108 (stating that the material breach regime of article 60 of the VCLT incorporates *exceptio non adimpleti contractus*); Commission on Human Rights Sub-Commission on the Promotion and Protection of Human Rights, Summary Record of the 14th Meeting, at 4, U.N. Doc. E/CN.4/Sub.2/2004/SR.14 (Aug. 11, 2004) (Mr. Bossuyt) (conflating *exceptio non adimpleti contractus* with the material breach regime of article 60 of the VCLT).

[122] Interim Accord, *supra* note 35, at 699 (Simma, J., separate).

[123] *Id.* (Simma, J., separate). Also on reciprocity, see Andreas Paulus, *Whether Universal Values Can Prevail over Bilateralism and Reciprocity*, *in* REALIZING UTOPIA: THE FUTURE OF INTERNATIONAL LAW 89, 91–97 (Antonio Cassese ed., 2012).

[124] *See* Interim Accord, *supra* note 35, at 680–92. *Cf.* SHABTAI ROSENNE, BREACH OF TREATY 118 (1985).

[125] *Cf.* Crawford & Olleson, *supra* note 120, at 62–63 (articulating an understanding of *exceptio non adimpleti contractus* that could conceivably exist outside of international treaty law).

the principle *arguendo* lends credence to it, and not simply within the context of treaty law.[126] To exaggerate the argument within the context of *Interim Accord*, if Greece had sought to justify its conduct on a clearly prohibited normative basis, such as a "need" to engage in genocide, the ICJ would clearly have condemned this justification as having no place in contemporary international law. That it refused to do so vis-à-vis *exceptio non adimpleti contractus* in *Interim Accord* reflects, at the very least, a colorable claim within the context of treaty law, and again, this is to say nothing of the principle's operation in contexts in which the legal obligation said to have been violated roots itself other than, or only, in straight application of a treaty norm. Finally, to grapple with the question of *exceptio non adimpleti contractus*' existence in contemporary international law as if it were a "yes" or "no" proposition, that is, that the principle must either "exist" or "not exist," may itself be an unduly simplistic approach. Indeed, it may be more appropriate to inquire as to the "scope" of the principle rather than whether or not it is "recognized" as such.[127]

Some of the opinions appended to *Interim Accord* provide further support for the existence of *exceptio non adimpleti contractus* in contemporary international law, in particular the declaration and dissenting opinion of, respectively, Judge Bennouna and Judge *ad hoc* Roucounas. Judge Bennouna cast the principle within the broader context of reciprocity and went on to positively affirm its existence "under a strict construction of reciprocity in the implementation of certain international obligations, where the implementation of one is inconceivable without the other. These are obligations of a strictly interdependent nature."[128] One senses in this an acknowledgement that *exceptio non adimpleti contractus* exists in international law generally, irrespective of the particular source of law at issue. In his dissenting opinion, Judge *ad hoc* Roucounas rejected Judge Simma's view that article 60 of the VCLT had somehow "displaced" *exceptio non adimpleti contractus.*[129] Indeed, for Judge *ad hoc* Roucounas, the nature of the principle and the constant overlap that exists between general international law and international treaty law mean that, "[a]s a defence to the non-performance of an obligation, it is a general

[126] *Cf.* Military and Paramilitary Activities in and Against Nicaragua (Nicar. v. U.S.), 1986 I.C.J. 14, 98 (June 27) (stating that, "If a State acts in a way prima facie incompatible with a recognized rule, but defends its conduct by appealing to exceptions or justifications contained within the rule itself, then whether or not the State's conduct is in fact justifiable on that basis, the significance of that attitude is to confirm rather than to weaken the rule").

[127] *See* Interim Accord, *supra* note 35, at 709 (Bennouna, J., declaration) (stating that "the issue is not about determining whether or not a given theory is recognized by general international law, but rather of ascertaining the scope, in general international law, of the principle of reciprocity, presented as *exceptio non adimpleti contractus*, with regard to the obligations of the Parties under the Interim Accord and, specifically, Article 11 thereof"). *See also* Serena Forlati, *Reactions to Non-Performance of Treaties in International Law*, 25(3) Leiden J. Int'l L. 759 (2012).

[128] Interim Accord, *supra* note 35, at 709 (Bennouna, J., declaration).

[129] *See* Interim Accord, *supra* note 35, at 745–46 (Roucounas, J. *ad hoc*, dissenting). *Cf.* Appeal Relating to the Jurisdiction of the ICAO Council (India v. Pak.), 1972 I.C.J. 46, 128 n.1 (Aug. 18) (De Castro, J., separate).

principle of law, as enshrined in Article 38, paragraph 1(c), of the Statute of the Court."[130] Judge de Castro used almost identical language in describing *exceptio non adimpleti contractus* in his separate opinion appended to *Namibia*.[131]

This view supporting the existence of *exceptio non adimpleti contractus* in contemporary international law was also affirmed in *Klöckner Industrie-Anlagen GmbH & Others v. Cameroon*[132] and has scholarly support.[133] Indeed, as ILC Special Rapporteur James Crawford noted in the Third Report on State Responsibility in 2000, it is recognized in law by a "respectable body of international authority and opinion."[134] It is also worth noting that in acknowledging the existence of *exceptio non adimpleti contractus* in contemporary international law in its 2002 award in *La Aplicación del "Imesi" (Impueso Específico Interno) a la Comercialización de Cigarrillos*, an *ad hoc* Mercado Común del Sur tribunal effectively recognized that the circumstances that can justify the use of this legal principle are different than those under the material breach regime of article 60 of the VCLT: a "violación sustancial; [*sic*] del tratado y teniendo ella características esenciales"[135] for the former rather than, as regards the latter, a "violación grave."[136] In *Eureko BV v. Poland*, furthermore, a 2005 arbitral award decided under United Nations Commission on International Trade Law arbitration rules in response to a dispute between the Netherlands and Poland, the tribunal defined *exceptio non adimpleti contractus* as the "exception of non performance"[137] and noted that this legal principle relates to "simultaneous performance of particular obligations, i.e. mutuality,"[138] and could only in theory apply to cases of "simultaneous or conditional performance."[139] This careful language suggests that *exceptio non adimpleti contractus* requires

130 Interim Accord, *supra* note 35, at 745 (Roucounas, J. *ad hoc*, dissenting). *See* Diversion of Water from the Meuse, 1937 P.C.I.J. (ser. A/B) No. 70, at 77 (June 28) (Hudson, J., individual). *See also* Articles on State Responsibility, *supra* note 84, at 72. *But see* Crawford & Olleson, *supra* note 120, at 73. Henkin, though not mentioning *exceptio non adimpleti contractus* by name, recognizes that "garden variety" violations of certain bilateral treaty obligations can justify suspension of such treaties in certain circumstances. *See* Henkin, *supra* note 104.

131 *See* Namibia, *supra* note 78, at 213 (De Castro, J., separate) (describing it as the "manifestation of a general principle").

132 *See* Klöckner Industrie-Anlagen GmbH & Others v. Cameroon (1983), 114 I.L.R. 152, 210–12 (1999) (recognizing the existence of *exceptio non adimpleti contractus* in international law, French law, and English law).

133 *See, e.g.*, Alain Pellet & Alina Miron, *Sanctions*, *in* MAX PLANCK ENCYCLOPEDIA OF PUBLIC INTERNATIONAL LAW ¶ 4 (last updated July 2011); Jan Peter Schmidt, *MERCOSUR*, *in* MAX PLANCK ENCYCLOPEDIA OF PUBLIC INTERNATIONAL LAW ¶ 32 (last updated Oct. 2008).

134 International Law Commission, Third Report on State Responsibility, at 35, U.N. Doc. A/CN.4/507/Add.3 (2000) (citing supporting authority).

135 Laudo del Tribunal Arbitral *Ad Hoc* del Mercosur Constituido para Decidir en la Controversia Entre la República del Paraguay a la República Oriental del Uruguay Sobre la Aplicación del "Imesi" (Impueso Específico Interno) a la Comercialización de Cigarrillos (2002), *in* LAUDOS, ACLARACIONES, Y OPINIONES CONSULTIVAS DE LOS TRIBUNALES DEL MERCOSUR 208, 213 (2007).

136 On the material breach regime of article 60 of the VCLT, see *infra* refer to 137–39.

137 Eureko BV v. Poland, I.I.C. 98, at ¶ 176 (2005).

138 *Id.* at ¶ 179.

139 *Id.* at ¶ 177. It should be noted that, as the ICJ would do in Interim Accord, the arbitral tribunal here refused to even acknowledge the existence of *exceptio non adimpleti contractus* in contemporary international law. *See id.*

two elements, reciprocity and non-performance, and that the latter of these two elements need not necessarily rise to the level of a material breach as understood by article 60 of the VCLT.[140]

A final response that a party to a dispute can potentially take if it has suffered an injury under the international law of negotiation lies in the material breach regime of article 60 of the VCLT. "Only a material breach justifies termination or suspension of the treaty, whereas in the context of State responsibility any breach of a treaty gives rise to responsibility irrespective of its gravity."[141] Elagab, in his treatise on the legality of non-forcible countermeasures in international law, refers to the material breach regime as a "very specific form of counter-measures which deals only with the issue of material breach."[142] This is a truly radical option in that it allows the victim party to potentially sever treaty relations with the responsible party, though a party that has suffered a material breach and wishes to invoke this regime must be careful to observe such related modalities as not expressly condoning or by its conduct acquiescing in the continued validity of the treaty.[143]

Analogous to the limits beyond which permissible countermeasures must not transgress, the material breach regime does not apply to "provisions relating to the protection of the human person contained in treaties of a humanitarian character, in particular to provisions prohibiting any form of reprisals against persons protected by such treaties."[144] The Supreme Court of Cyprus, in its 1987 judgment in *Malachtou v. Armefti & Armefti*, suggested that the function, nature, and objective of certain treaties can be such that considerations of reciprocity and subjectivity are inapposite.[145] Such treaties create objective rights that operate independently of treaty compliance and include treaties for the "protection of human rights and the improvements [*sic*] and formulation of common rules and the achievement of social justice."[146] This concern reflects a naturalist impulse in the law of treaties,

[140] It is worth noting that in a commentary to article 60 of the VCLT that he co-authored in 2011 with Tams, Judge Simma conceded that the material breach regime deviated from the concept of reciprocity that is inherent to *exceptio non adimpleti contractus*. *See* Bruno Simma & Christian J. Tams, *Article 60*, *in* 2 The Vienna Convention on the Law of Treaties: A Commentary 1351, 1377–78 (Olivier Corten & Pierre Klein eds., 2011).

[141] Articles on State Responsibility, *supra* note 84, at 117. *See* Gabčíkovo-Nagymaros, *supra* note 102, at 65 (stating that "it is only a material breach of the treaty itself, by a State party to that treaty, which entitles the other party to rely on it as a ground for terminating the treaty. The violation of other treaty rules or of rules of general international law may justify the taking of certain measures, including countermeasures, by the injured State, but it does not constitute a ground for termination under the law of treaties"). There are also, of course, other grounds for terminating or suspending the operation of a treaty. *See* VCLT, *supra* note 63, at arts 54–64.

[142] Elagab, *supra* note 113, at 164. *See* Bruno Simma & Christian J. Tams, *Reacting Against Treaty Breaches*, *in* The Oxford Guide to Treaties 576 (Duncan B. Hollis ed., 2012) (comparing and contrasting the material breach regime of article 60 of the VCLT and the regime of countermeasures within the context of reactions to treaty breaches).

[143] *See* VCLT, *supra* note 63, at art. 45. Article 60(1) and (2) of the VCLT draw certain distinctions between material breaches of bilateral treaties and material breaches of multilateral treaties.

[144] *Id.* at art. 60(5). *See* Namibia, *supra* note 78, at 47. *See also* Aust, *supra* note 63, at 260.

[145] *See* Malachtou v. Armefti & Armefti (1987) (Cyprus), 88 I.L.R. 199, 210–11 (1992).

[146] *Id.* at 211.

but as with countermeasures, what precisely is meant by these exclusions is not altogether clear.[147]

In cases in which a treaty sets forth detailed provisions that seek to regulate the negotiation process, the violation of the treaty-based negotiation obligation will take on added significance as compared with a more generalized treaty that only deals with the modalities of negotiation in cases of dispute as but one aspect of the overall treaty. Given the subject matter, it is more likely that a party's violation of its negotiation obligation under the former type of treaty could be considered a material breach in the sense of article 60 of the VCLT, that is, in the context of a bilateral treaty, a "repudiation of the treaty not sanctioned by the present Convention; or [...] the violation of a provision essential to the accomplishment of the object or purpose of the treaty,"[148] thus allowing the victim party to terminate or suspend the treaty. Of course, this is not to say that a party's violation of its negotiation obligation under the latter type of treaty could not rise to the level of a material breach. Indeed, it very well could, as long as it meets the material breach test.[149] This raises the obvious point that it is difficult to make general conclusions as to material breach, and the significant consequences that can potentially flow from this, *in abstracto*.[150]

A useful analogy can perhaps be drawn here between the material breach regime of article 60 of the VCLT and the rules with respect to serious breaches of *jus cogens* norms in the Articles on State Responsibility.[151] Setting aside the context of repudiation of treaties not sanctioned by the VCLT[152] and the fact that the serious breach regime only applies to *jus cogens* norms, both instruments require the identification of breaches of a certain gravity: either breaches of a material nature (as in the case of the VCLT) or breaches of a serious nature (as in the case of the Articles on State Responsibility). Both instruments also have formal tests to determine the circumstances in which a breach rises to the requisite level of concern: either a "violation of a provision essential to the accomplishment of the object or purpose of the treaty"[153] (as in the case of the VCLT) or a breach that is "gross or systematic"[154] (as in the case of the Articles on State Responsibility). Although the VCLT does not define what is meant by object or purpose, the Commentaries

[147] *See* Simma & Tams, *supra* note 140, at 1366–70.

[148] VCLT, *supra* note 63, at art. 60(3)(a)–(b).

[149] It should also be pointed out that the material breach regime is itself not without what seem to be its own internal inconsistencies in logic. *See* Simma & Tams, *supra* note 140, at 1359 (pointing out, quite accurately, that a textual analysis of the article supports the view that "Article 60 does not legitimize responses to grave breaches of treaty provisions which are not essential, but [...] that trivial breaches of essential provisions can constitute material breaches in the sense of Article 60, paragraph 3(b)").

[150] On article 60 of the VCLT in the jurisprudence of the ICJ, see Interim Accord, *supra* note 35, at 705–706 (Simma, J., separate).

[151] On the latter, see Articles on State Responsibility, *supra* note 84, at 110–16, arts 40–41.

[152] *See* VCLT, *supra* note 63, at art. 60(3)(a).

[153] *Id.* at art. 60(3)(b).

[154] Articles on State Responsibility, *supra* note 84, at 112, art. 40(2).

to the Articles on State Responsibility provide some sense of what is meant by gross or systematic, though they also acknowledge that these criteria will often run into each other when applied in practice.[155] In other words, the material breach regime of article 60 of the VCLT and the rules with respect to serious breaches of *jus cogens* norms in the Articles on State Responsibility are both fact-specific and require more than a breach *simpliciter*.

As a way of bringing together these rather complex thoughts about the interlocking nature of countermeasures and other responses, consider the 1997 Euro-Mediterranean Interim Association Agreement on Trade and Cooperation Between the European Community, of the One Part, and the Palestine Liberation Organization (PLO) for the Benefit of the Palestinian Authority of the West Bank and the Gaza Strip, of the Other Part (Agreement).[156] Article 70(2) of this instrument allows the victim party to respond to "garden variety" violations with "appropriate measures." The victim party must first make recourse to the Joint Committee for European Community–Palestinian Authority Trade and Cooperation, a body established by the Agreement, in all cases but those of "special urgency."[157] In a nod to proportionality, article 70(2) requires that the appropriate measures taken must prioritize those that "least disturb the functioning of the Agreement."[158] The text does not suggest that the legal relationship that the Agreement embodies can be severed on the basis of a violation as such, even in cases of special urgency; and the "least disturb[ance]" standard is quite clearly meant to induce the wrongdoer to comply with its (violated) international legal obligation. Interestingly, the Joint Declaration on Article 70 of the Agreement equates cases of special urgency with cases of "substantial violation" and defines a substantial violation in a way that differs from the material breach definition in article 60 of the VCLT.[159] This means that a concept of material breach analogous to article 60 of the VCLT can only operate as a remedy *external to* the Agreement itself. The responses to internationally wrongful acts are truly multi-layered and nuanced.

[155] *See id.* at 113.

[156] Council Decision 97/430/EC, Euro-Mediterranean Interim Association Agreement on Trade and Cooperation Between the European Community, of the One Part, and the Palestine Liberation Organization (PLO) for the Benefit of the Palestinian Authority of the West Bank and the Gaza Strip, of the Other Part, Annex, 1997 O.J. (L187) 1, 3. *See* Firma Brita GmbH v. Hauptzollamt Hamburg-Hafen, Case C-386/08, 2010 E.C.R. I-1289 (*Brita*). On *Brita*, see Jed Odermatt, *The Court of Justice of the European Union: International or Domestic Court?*, 3(3) CAMBRIDGE J. INT'L & COMP. L. 696, 711–12 (2014).

[157] Agreement, *supra* note 156, at 16, art. 70(2). Article 67 sets forth the functions of the Joint Committee for European Community-Palestinian Authority Trade and Cooperation (Joint Committee) in this respect.

[158] Article 70(2) also requires victim parties that take such appropriate measures to immediately notify the Joint Committee and engage in consultations with the other party under the Joint Committee's auspices if the other party so requests.

[159] *See id.* at 131. *See also id.* at 4, art. 2.

V. Conclusion

When the parties to a dispute exercise their freedom to choose by deciding to negotiate, they are making a tangible contribution to the peaceful settlement of disputes. This is to be encouraged. To facilitate this, international law has developed such that certain modalities govern when it can be said as a matter of law that negotiation has been tried and has been exhausted. Unsurprisingly, the international law of negotiation in this regard is extraordinarily fact-specific, and it involves considerations of both procedural and substantive law. What is clear is that the non-arbitral and non-judicial nature of negotiation in no way detracts from the seriousness of legal obligation for the negotiating parties as they attempt to peacefully settle their dispute. *Ubi jus ibi officium.*

That international law empowers a party to a dispute that has suffered an injury under the law of negotiation to potentially resort to countermeasures and other responses when a negotiation breaks down need not be a particularly alarming proposition. Indeed, in the words of Jessup, a year before he was to become Judge Jessup of the ICJ, these may be "necessary as a safety-valve lest national feelings be strained to a point at which the state yields to the temptation blatantly to violate international law."[160] Just as it is true that any response by the victim party to a violation of the international law of negotiation could inflame a dispute in certain contexts, so a victim party's failure to respond at all could doom the prospects of a settlement in other contexts. As long as the victim party acts reasonably on the particular facts and circumstances, however, then it does not need to fear the law, nor need the law in this area risk being hopelessly compromised.[161]

Let us now apply this body of law to the Palestinian people's unsuccessful attempt to join the United Nations as a Member State in autumn 2011 and its successful attempt to join the same institution as a non-member observer State in autumn 2012.

[160] Philip C. Jessup, *A Half-Century of Efforts to Substitute Law for War*, *in* 99 Collected Courses of The Hague Academy of International Law 1, 17 (1960). *See* Rogoff, *supra* note 89, at 174.

[161] As the arbitral tribunal in Air Service Agreement put it, such responses are a "wager on the wisdom, not on the weakness of the other Party." Air Service Agreement, *supra* note 91, at 445 (making this point within the specific context of countermeasures).

6

The International Law of Negotiation and Palestinian Applications for Admission to the United Nations: Sword or Shield?

I. Introduction

The Exchange of Letters between Israeli Prime Minister Yitzhak Rabin and Palestine Liberation Organization (PLO) Chairman Yasser Arafat on September 9, 1993 (Exchange of Letters) and the Declaration of Principles on Interim Self-Government Arrangements (Declaration of Principles) less than a week later, were important for two main reasons. Firstly, they inaugurated a legal relationship between Israel and the PLO that both parties intended to be governed by international law. Secondly, these instruments provided international law's reference point for assessing the Israeli–Palestinian dispute. They also enabled a process of dispute settlement, an "agenda for negotiations, governed by a tight timetable, rather than a full-blown agreement."[1] This legal relationship would undergo further change and nuance in subsequent years due to the acts and omissions of Israel and the PLO.

Although the precise nature of the bilateral negotiation imperative remained complex in the run-up to the Palestinians' unsuccessful attempt to join the United Nations as a Member State in autumn 2011 and its successful attempt to join the same institution as a non-member observer State in autumn 2012, one constant of this legal relationship was, and has remained, the need for any settlement between the two sides to be reached through consent, in particular, to be negotiated. Indeed, a negotiated settlement has remained the dominant paradigm of peacemaking efforts between Israel and the PLO to the present. That the parties have chosen negotiations means that either side's failure to comply with its obligation to negotiate can result in an internationally wrongful act and, in response,

[1] Avi Shlaim, *The Rise and Fall of the Oslo Peace Process*, *in* International Relations of the Middle East 268, 272 (Louise Fawcett ed., 3d ed. 2013) (referring to the Declaration of Principles in particular).

countermeasures and other responses. Describing the obligation to negotiate in *Affaire du Lac Lanoux*, the arbitral tribunal noted that it would be violated, "par exemple, en cas de rupture injustifiée des entretiens, de délais anormaux, de mépris des procedures prévues, de refus systématiques de prendre en considération les propositions ou les intérêts adverses, plus généralement en cas d'infraction aux règles de la bonne foi."[2]

This chapter brings to bear the international law of negotiation to the Palestinian attempts to join the United Nations in autumn 2011 and autumn 2012. The legal consequences of these applications are not merely of historical interest because they inform the *present* rights and obligations of Israel and the Palestinian people. This chapter proceeds in three sections. Firstly, it takes stock of the bundle of rights and obligations that emerged between the time of the Exchange of Letters and the Declaration of Principles, and the events of autumn 2011 and autumn 2012. It then examines the factual and legal technicalities of these Palestinian applications before setting forth the key issues that arise when assessing their legal consequences. This chapter's analysis raises a number of challenges attendant to applying the international law of negotiation as a framework of legal evaluation.

II. The Bilateral Negotiation Imperative: Bundles of Rights and Obligations

In one sense, to say that the Exchange of Letters and the Declaration of Principles grounded the legal relationship between Israel and the PLO is to simplify the matter. The relationship between the two sides has remained multi-layered and multi-textured, with Israel and the PLO contesting both interpretations of law and the precise legal basis upon which rights and obligations rest. This is made all the more challenging given that what Shehadeh notes with respect to the PLO seems to equally apply to Israel: a side that "utilizes law and legal premises rather inconsistently, primarily as declarations to accompany its political statements."[3] In order to clarify this landscape, it is necessary to engage with the cacophony of interactions that influenced the legal relationship between the two sides between September 1993 and autumn 2011 and autumn 2012, with particular focus on the period after May 4, 1999.

This is not the place to methodically list the many instruments that Israel and the PLO adopted between September 1993 and the Palestinian applications of autumn 2011 and autumn 2012. Primarily, this is because other texts and anthologies,

[2] Affaire du Lac Lanoux (Spain v. Fr.) (1957), 12 R. Int'l Arb. Awards 281, 307 (1963) (internal citation omitted).

[3] Raja Shehadeh, From Occupation to Interim Accords: Israel and the Palestinian Territories 158 (1997).

from various disciplinary perspectives, discuss these in considerable detail,[4] and an inundation of descriptive legalese is seldom helpful to the clarification of law. Yet, because history moves through law and law reflects history,[5] it is instructive to look at two of the more salient of these instruments, in particular the 1994 Israel-Palestine Liberation Organization Agreement on the Gaza Strip and the Jericho Area (Cairo Agreement)[6] and the 1997 Interim Agreement on the West Bank and the Gaza Strip (Interim Agreement).[7]

It will be recalled that the Declaration of Principles stipulated that a five-year transitional period would begin when the Israel Defense Forces (IDF) redeployed from the Gaza Strip and the Jericho Area.[8] The Cairo Agreement, which Israel and the PLO adopted in the Egyptian capital on May 4, 1994, sought to effectuate this.[9] It situated itself within a process that began with the Middle East Peace Conference in Madrid and that would unfold until the objectives that the Exchange of Letters and the Declaration of Principles had articulated were realized.[10] The basic idea was that a Palestinian governance structure would replace the IDF and the Civil Administration as Israeli forces redeployed from Gaza and Jericho.[11] This would effectively separate Israelis from Palestinians, though both sides were guaranteed freedom of movement in the territories, with the only limitation being that Palestinians could only use public roads crossing settlements and not enter the settlements themselves.[12] The IDF would remain in a Military Installation Area.[13] Settlements in Gaza were left unaffected.[14]

According to the Cairo Agreement, the Palestinian Authority would be the agent of internal self-determination for the Palestinians during the transitional period. Its territorial jurisdiction covered Gaza and Jericho but excluded the Military

[4] *See, e.g.*, ISRAEL IN THE MIDDLE EAST: DOCUMENTS AND READINGS ON SOCIETY, POLITICS, AND FOREIGN RELATIONS, PRE-1948 TO THE PRESENT (Itamar Rabinovich & Jehuda Reinharz eds., 2d ed. 2008); THE ISRAEL-ARAB READER: A DOCUMENTARY HISTORY OF THE MIDDLE EAST CONFLICT (Walter Laqueur & Barry Rubin eds., 7th ed. 2008). *See also* United Nations, Information System on the Question of Palestine, http://unispal.un.org/unispal.nsf/udc.htm.

[5] Crawford has described international law as "normativity in collision with history." JAMES CRAWFORD, THE CREATION OF STATES IN INTERNATIONAL LAW 711 (2d ed. 2007) (continuing by stating that, "if it is to be of any value[,] it [i.e., international law] must give guidance to persons at the time of the events and, prima facie at least, acts which were valid or produced legal effects at a particular time should not retroactively be treated as void").

[6] Israel-Palestine Liberation Organization Agreement on the Gaza Strip and the Jericho Area, 33(3) I.L.M. 622 (1994).

[7] Israel-Palestine Liberation Organization: Interim Agreement on the West Bank and the Gaza Strip, with Selected Annexes, 36(3) I.L.M. 551 (1997).

[8] *See* Letter Dated 8 October 1993 from the Permanent Representatives of the Russian Federation and the United States of America to the United Nations Addressed to the Secretary-General, Annex at 4, 5, art. 5(1), U.N. Doc. A/48/486 (Oct. 11, 1993) (Declaration of Principles on Interim Self-Government Arrangements).

[9] Egypt, Russia, and the United States acted as witnesses to the Cairo Agreement.

[10] *See* Cairo Agreement, *supra* note 6, at 626, pmbl.

[11] *See id.* at 627–28, art. 3.

[12] *See id.* at 627, art. 2(5).

[13] *See id.* at 627, art. 1(c).

[14] *See id.* at 627, art. 2(3).

Installation Area and the settlements.[15] The Palestinian Authority's subject-matter jurisdiction excluded matters related to the Military Installation Area and the settlements, external security, and foreign relations but covered "all powers and responsibilities as specified in this Agreement."[16] These specified powers and responsibilities were extensive and numbered over three dozen, ranging from legal administration and education to religious affairs and public works.[17] The Palestinian Authority's *in personam* jurisdiction covered all persons in Gaza and Jericho, with the exception of Israelis.[18]

With its trifurcated jurisdiction and legislative, executive, and judicial functions,[19] the Cairo Agreement created in the Palestinian Authority the most extensive governing body for the Palestinians in history.[20] It is critical to recognize, however, that the Palestinian Authority was not sovereign. For example, while the Cairo Agreement required the Palestinians to create a "strong police force,"[21] the IDF retained its authority with respect to Israelis, air and sea defense, and "external threats."[22] The Palestinian Authority could not engage in foreign relations, including establishing embassies abroad and allowing foreign missions to operate in Gaza and Jericho,[23] and as with every other provision in the Cairo Agreement, the PLO (as well as Israel) was bound to comply with this obligation or risk being responsible for an internationally wrongful act.

The Cairo Agreement allowed the PLO to enter into "agreements with states or international organizations for the benefit of the Palestinian Authority,"[24] but these were to be limited to certain economic arrangements, agreements related to cultural, scientific, and educational matters, relationships of assistance with donor states, and agreements related to regional development projects and multilateral negotiations.[25] A "shall not be considered foreign relations"[26] provision was inserted to dispel, or at least to undermine, any notion that the Palestinian Authority could be construed as a proto-State body during the transitional period (as, in many respects, the Jewish Agency had been during the Mandate for Palestine). Joel Singer, who acted as Legal Advisor for the Israel Ministry of Foreign Affairs at this time, notes that this language had an "added effect on the very nature of the

[15] *See id.* at 629, art. 5(1)(a).

[16] *Id.* at 629, art. 5(1)(b).

[17] *See id.* at Annex II, 667–81, art. 2.

[18] *See id.* at 629, art. 5(1)(c).

[19] *See id.* at 628, art. 4(1).

[20] *Cf.* Joel Singer, *Aspects of Foreign Relations Under the Israeli-Palestinian Agreements on Interim Self-Government Arrangements for the West Bank and Gaza*, 28(2–3) Isr. L. Rev. 268, 277–80 (1994) (analogizing to the self-governing authority, or administrative council, that the Camp David Accords had envisaged for the Palestinians in the territories). On the relationship between the PLO and the Palestinian Authority, see Palestinian Academic Society for the Study of International Affairs, PLO v. PA (Sept. 2014).

[21] Cairo Agreement, *supra* note 6, at 631, art. 8(1).

[22] *Id.*

[23] *See id.* at 630, art. 6(2)(a).

[24] *Id.* at 630, art. 6(2)(b).

[25] *See id.* at 630, art. 6(2)(b)(1)–(4).

[26] *Id.* at 630, art. 6(2)(c).

autonomous entity itself, because full capacity to conduct foreign relations is one of the accepted indicia of sovereignty and statehood."[27]

While the Cairo Agreement extended internal self-determination to the Palestinians, the link between this and potential (future) external self-determination rights was unclear, and in no way predetermined. As with the Exchange of Letters and the Declaration of Principles before it, the Cairo Agreement reaffirmed the commitment of Israel and the PLO to negotiations and contained a "without prejudice" clause that was meant to facilitate a negotiated settlement.[28] According to article 23(3) of the Cairo Agreement, the five-year transitional period that the Declaration of Principles had alluded to would begin with the signing of the Cairo Agreement.[29] This meant that both sides anticipated reaching a final settlement by May 4, 1999, and they were bound to act in good faith during this process to effectuate this end.

Just as Israel and the PLO created the Palestinian Authority as a way to implement their obligations under the Declaration of Principles,[30] so the two sides adopted the Interim Agreement with a view to, *inter alia*, "establish[ing] a Palestinian Interim Self-Government Authority, the elected Council (the 'Council'), for the Palestinian people in the West Bank and the Gaza Strip, for a transitional period not exceeding five years, leading to a permanent settlement based on Security Council resolutions 242 (1967) and 338 (1973)."[31] The Interim Agreement has been described as the "constitutional document defining the PA [i.e., the Palestinian Authority] and its official powers and functions."[32] By reinforcing and extending the Palestinian Authority's powers, the Interim Agreement built upon the Palestinians' internal self-determination.[33] The aim was an overhauled Palestinian Authority composed of a Council with a *Ra'ees*, or "chairman," as head of the Council's Executive Authority.[34]

Article 17 of the Interim Agreement set forth the territorial, functional, and *in personam* jurisdiction of the overhauled Palestinian Authority and recognized its legislative, executive, and judicial competence.[35] The most significant aspect of this was geographical in nature. The Interim Agreement divided the territories into three (jurisdictional) Areas (Areas A, B, and C), with each of these Areas reflecting

[27] Singer, *supra* note 20, at 269.

[28] *See* Cairo Agreement, *supra* note 6, at 637, art. 23(5).

[29] *See id.* at 637, art. 23(3).

[30] *See* Letter, *supra* note 8, at Annex at 5–6, art. 6 (Declaration of Principles on Interim Self-Government Arrangements).

[31] *Id.* at 4, art. 1. *See id.* at 6, art. 7. Egypt, the European Union, Jordan, Norway, Russia, and the United States acted as witnesses to the Interim Agreement. On the technicalities of the Interim Agreement, see Joel Singer, *The West Bank and Gaza Strip: Phase Two*, 7 JUST. 5 (Dec. 1995).

[32] Knox v. Palestine Liberation Organization, 306 F. Supp. 2d 424, 433 (2004).

[33] *See* Interim Agreement, *supra* note 7, at 559, art. 2(1) ("In order that the Palestinians people of the West Bank and the Gaza Strip may govern themselves according to democratic principles").

[34] *See id.* at 559–60, art. 3. The PLO had already agreed to use the phrase *Ra'ees* for its chief executive in a letter attached to the Cairo Agreement.

[35] *See id.* at 564, art. 17.

decreasing levels of authority for the Palestinian Authority. With respect to Areas A and B, for example, civil powers and responsibilities would be transferred from Israel to the Palestinian Authority, and such civil powers and responsibilities unrelated to territory would be transferred to the Palestinian Authority in Area C during the first phase of the IDF's redeployment, with the balance of powers and responsibilities related to territory being transferred to the Palestinian Authority in Area C during the second and third phases of redeployment.[36] Although extensive, none of the civil powers and responsibilities so transferred permitted the Palestinian Authority to act with respect to permanent status issues—indeed, these were expressly excluded from the Palestinian Authority's mandate[37]—and the Interim Agreement was particularly clear on point with respect to Area C, where Israeli interests were most pronounced.[38] *Inter alia*, this meant that Israel and the PLO agreed to defer, and to refrain from asserting, sovereign claims to the territories during the transitional period. The Interim Agreement also set forth modalities according to which the Palestinian Authority would assume powers and responsibilities for internal security and public order in Areas A and B, though it is important to note that in Area B the IDF would have an "overriding responsibility for security for the purpose of protecting Israelis and confronting the threat of terrorism."[39] In Area C, Israel would retain its "continued authority to exercise its powers and responsibilities with regard to internal security and public order, as well as with regard to other powers and responsibilities not transferred."[40]

Although the Interim Agreement extended increased forms of internal self-determination to the Palestinians, it did not create, or somehow deterministically foresee the creation of, a sovereign Palestinian entity. The PLO agreed that the Palestinian Authority would not engage in foreign relations,[41] consented to the IDF's continuing authority with respect to external security for the territories,[42] and assented to modalities of passage that could scarcely be reconciled with sovereignty.[43] While the PLO had sufficient international legal personality at this time to enter into legally-binding agreements with Israel, there was little to indicate that it, or the Palestinian Authority (or the Palestinian people that the PLO represented),

[36] *See id.* at 561–62, art. 11. *See also id.* at Annex III, 604, art. 4. For the detailed listing of civil powers and responsibilities, see *id.* at Annex III, 603.

[37] *See id.* at 564, art. 17. The permanent status issues were listed as settlements, Jerusalem, Palestinian refugees, specified military locations, borders, foreign relations, and Israelis. *See id.* at 564, art. 17(1)(a). *Cf. id.* at 567, art. 31(5) (listing the permanent status issues somewhat differently, as *including* "Jerusalem, refugees, settlements, security arrangements, borders, relations and cooperation with other neighbors, and other issues of common interest").

[38] *See, e.g., id.* at Annex III, 604, art. 4.

[39] *Id.* at 562, art. 13(2)(a). *See id.* at 562–63, art. 13.

[40] *Id.* at Annex III, 604, art. 4(2).

[41] *See id.* at 561, art. 9(5)(a).

[42] *See id.* at 561, art. 10(4). *See also id.* at 562, art. 12(1).

[43] *See id.* at Annex I, 579–82, art. 8.

was a State.[44] As Allain describes it, the Palestinians simply did not have the attributes of sovereignty, namely "the ability of a State to dictate what undertakings it will adopt both inside its own territory, and what obligations, if any, it will take on vis-à-vis other States."[45] The PLO certainly hoped to establish a Palestinian State in the territories, but this was not the present reality.

It is well known that Israel and the PLO failed to reach a final settlement by May 4, 1999, as stipulated by the Interim Agreement,[46] and that they have still not done so. This raises the question of the precise nature of the legal relationship between the two sides between May 5, 1999, and the events of autumn 2011 and autumn 2012. Did it collapse entirely after May 4, or did it continue to remain in force? If it continued to remain in force, did its texture remain the same throughout this period, in whole or in part? Did its integrity remain intact, that is, did the norms and processes that the Interim Agreement had set forth continue on throughout this period, unadulterated and undiluted? Were the rights and obligations of Israel and the PLO the same during this period as they had been during the transitional period? Did the Interim Agreement remain in force *qua* Interim Agreement after May 4, or did the legal relationship between the two sides take on a less tangible, and perhaps less determinate, form? These are difficult questions, to be sure, but without attempting to clarify them, it is difficult to assess the legal consequences of the events of autumn 2011 and autumn 2012.

Consider the official perspectives of Israel and the PLO. In a fact sheet that its Ministry of Foreign Affairs issued a few weeks before May 4, 1999, Israel put on record its position that the transitional period, and its legal content, would continue in force until a final settlement had been reached. "[T]he intention of the parties was not to gamble all the agreed arrangements on the conclusion of negotiations by May 4, 1999,"[47] and the legal relationship between the two sides would continue, so Israel argued, based "not only [on] the language and logic of the accords, but also the practice of the two sides to date."[48] The PLO saw the post-May 4 environment as conducive to a wide variety of political options that, in its view, were not as such foreclosed by international law. According to the PLO's Nasser Al-Kidwa, after May 4, the PLO could react by doing nothing, postpone doing anything as a matter of strategic decision, agree to an extension of the

[44] *See* Ungar v. Palestine Liberation Organization, 402 F.3d 274 (1st Cir. 2005).

[45] Jean Allain, *On Achieving Palestinian Statehood: Concepts, Ends and Means from the Perspective of International Law*, Lectures Delivered at the Ibrahim Abu-Lughod Institute of International Studies, at 11 (Apr. 2002), http://ialiis.birzeit.edu/fmru/userfiles/Achieving-Palestinian-Statehood.pdf. *See* Singer, *supra* note 31, at 13 (making the point that what the Interim Agreement created, or reified, was an autonomy regime, not a sovereign State).

[46] *See* Interim Agreement, *supra* note 7, at 558, pmbl.

[47] Israel Ministry of Foreign Affairs, May 4, 1999: Some Frequently Asked Questions (Apr. 19, 1999), http://mfa.gov.il/MFA/MFA-Archive/1999/Pages/May%204-%201999%20-%20Some%20Frequently%20Asked%20Questions%20-%2019.aspx.

[48] *Id. See* Tal Becker, International Recognition of a Unilaterally Declared Palestinian State: Legal and Policy Dilemmas, Jerusalem Center for Public Affairs, www.jcpa.org/art/becker1.htm.

transitional period for a set period of time, or "take concrete action toward the realization of statehood and independence."[49]

One view, which might be said to be the dominant view, is that the Interim Agreement continued to remain in force *qua* Interim Agreement after May 4, 1999. In the most recent edition of his international law treatise, for example, Shaw makes the point that: "Since neither side [i.e., neither Israel nor the PLO] has to date denounced the Oslo Accords and succeeding instruments, they remain in effect."[50] Watson takes the view that Israeli and PLO acquiescence and waiver had the effect of continuing the bargain in force after May 4.[51] Writing in 2000, he argued that:

> [T]he Oslo Accords remain in force. They did not automatically terminate on 4 May 1999, and neither party has invoked the other's breach as a basis for terminating the Accords outright. Indeed, the parties have acquiesced in the continuation in force of the Accords as they have moved into final-status negotiations.[52]

A difficulty with this view—and it should be pointed out that Shaw and Watson disagree as to whether the "Oslo Accords and succeeding instruments" or simply the "Oslo Accords" remain the operative legal framework, with Shaw preferring the former and Watson focusing on the latter—is that there is no legally-binding instrument (or instruments) called the "Oslo Accords." Is "Oslo Accords" simply meant to be an imprecise reference to all of the instruments concluded between Israel and the PLO since the Exchange of Letters and the Declaration of Principles? If one proceeds on the basis of Shaw's argument, furthermore, how does one identify the Oslo Accords' "succeeding instruments"? Aust suggests that the form, terminology, and express provisions of an instrument, the circumstances surrounding its adoption, and the practice and subsequent acts of relevant actors allow one to determine whether a particular instrument is legally-binding.[53] Which instruments are legally-binding (as if international law were such a binary

[49] Nasser Al-Kidwa, *Re-Declaring Palestinian Statehood: Fears and Expectations, in* May 4, 1999: Implications of Declaring the State 11, 13 (1999). *See* Press Release, Settlement Will Not Be Reached by End of Transitional Period on 4 May, Palestinian Observer Tells Palestinian Rights Committee, U.N. Doc. GA/PAL/797 (Apr. 8, 1999), http://unispal.un.org/UNISPAL.nsf/fd807e46661e36898 52570d00069e918/f38980ab2a50ac0a85256cae00707fe1?OpenDocument.

[50] Malcolm N. Shaw, International Law 173 (7th ed. 2014). *See id.* at 172–74.

[51] *See* Geoffrey R. Watson, The Oslo Accords: International Law and the Israeli-Palestinian Peace Agreements 246–51 (2000).

[52] *Id.* at 309. *Cf.* Mohammed Hussain K.S., *Palestine and International Law: An Overview, in* Essays on Contemporary Issues in International Law 129, 153 (Asian-African Legal Consultative Org. ed., 2009) (arguing that "Israel and the PLO can be viewed as being under a legal obligation to continue with their negotiations on permanent status even if not all issues have been solved by the deadline set in 1999").

[53] *See* Anthony Aust, Modern Treaty Law and Practice 33–34 (3d ed. 2013) (making this point within the specific context of memoranda of understanding). *See also* Philippe Gautier, *Non-Binding Agreements, in* Max Planck Encyclopedia of Public International Law ¶¶ 11–13 (last updated Dec. 2006) (focusing on the parties' intention and conduct, the form of the instrument, and content and context).

proposition), and which are not, or at least not "sufficiently"? Might it be preferable to reorient the discussion to those texts that are "of legal import in the relations between their authors,"[54] as the Institut de Droit International did in its 1983 Resolution on International Texts of Legal Import in the Mutual Relations of Their Authors and Texts Devoid of Such Import, rather than, perhaps too simplistically, to focus simply on those texts that are legally-binding and those that are not? In many ways, it might be said that "Oslo" has become a rather imprecise shorthand for a discourse of dispute settlement, an incantation of aspiration to "peace," rather than a precise legal instrument or instruments as such.

The International Court of Justice (ICJ) had an opportunity to comment upon the Israeli–Palestinian legal relationship well after May 4, 1999, in July 2004, when it handed down its *Legal Consequences of the Construction of a Wall in the Occupied Palestinian Territory* (*Wall*) advisory opinion.[55] After it concluded that it had *prima facie* jurisdiction in *Wall*, the ICJ considered whether "compelling reasons" dictated that it not then proceed to the merits. In finding that there were no such reasons,[56] it referred to the 2003 Quartet Performance-Based Roadmap to a Permanent Two-State Solution to the Israeli-Palestinian Conflict (Roadmap) as the negotiation framework *du jour* for Israel and the PLO[57] and ended by imploring all involved to comply with their Roadmap obligations.[58] Judge Higgins' separate opinion and Judge Al-Khasawneh's separate opinion also referenced the Roadmap as the operative legal framework.[59] The written statements that Israel and the PLO, or "Palestine" (to use the United Nations' nomenclature), submitted to the ICJ also stressed the operative nature of the Roadmap.[60] Had the Roadmap "overridden"

[54] Institut de Droit International, Resolution on International Texts of Legal Import in the Mutual Relations of Their Authors and Texts Devoid of Such Import, Cambridge, at ¶ 1 (1983). Consider, as well, the concept of "tacit conventionality." *See* Jean d'Aspremont, *The International Court of Justice and Tacit Conventionality*, (18) QUEST. INT'L L. 3 (2015).

[55] Legal Consequences of the Construction of a Wall in the Occupied Palestinian Territory, Advisory Opinion, 2004 I.C.J. 136 (July 9). For a recent critical commentary on *Wall*, see Matthijs de Blois, *Bad Law and a Hard Case? The Impact of the* Wall *Advisory Opinion of the ICJ*, *in* WHAT'S WRONG WITH INTERNATIONAL LAW? LIBER AMICORUM A.H.A. SOONS 94 (Cedric Ryngaert et al. eds., 2015).

[56] *See* Wall, *supra* note 55, at 156–64. *See also* KAREL WELLENS, NEGOTIATIONS IN THE CASE LAW OF THE INTERNATIONAL COURT OF JUSTICE: A FUNCTIONAL ANALYSIS 74–76 (2014).

[57] *See* Wall, *supra* note 55, at 160. For the text of the Roadmap, see Letter Dated 7 May 2003 from the Secretary-General Addressed to the President of the Security Council, Annex at 2, U.N. Doc. S/2003/529 (May 7, 2003) (Performance-Based Roadmap to a Permanent Two-State Solution to the Israeli-Palestinian Conflict). The Security Council endorsed the Roadmap on November 19, 2003. *See* S.C. Res. 1515, U.N. Doc. S/RES/1515 (Nov. 19, 2003).

[58] *See* Wall, *supra* note 55, at 200–201. The ICJ also referred to Resolutions 242 and 338, but it predominantly emphasized the Roadmap. The Quartet, the sponsor of the Roadmap, consists of the European Union, Russia, the United Nations, and the United States.

[59] *See id.* at 211–12 (Higgins, J., separate), 238–39 (Al-Khasawneh, J., separate). By contrast, Judge Elaraby only referred to Resolutions 242 and 338. *See id.* at 259 (Elaraby, J., separate).

[60] *See, e.g.*, Letter Dated 29 January 2004 from the Deputy Director General and Legal Advisor of the Ministry of Foreign Affairs, Together with the Written Statement of the Government of Israel, Legal Consequences of the Construction of a Wall in the Occupied Palestinian Territory, Advisory Opinion, 2004 I.C.J., at 3 (Jan. 30); Written Statement Submitted by Palestine, Legal Consequences of the Construction of a Wall in the Occupied Palestinian Territory, Advisory Opinion, 2004 I.C.J., at 171 (Jan. 30).

the "Oslo Accords"? While the former shared in common with the latter a focus on negotiations, it differed in a number of important respects, particularly in that the Roadmap expressly called for a Palestinian State, set up a performance-based process of three phases through which the parties' efforts would be channeled (or so it was hoped), and attempted to deal with (certain aspects of) such permanent status issues as settlements before a final settlement would be reached.[61]

Of course, the Roadmap was not the only legally relevant instrument that Israel and the PLO agreed to between May 5, 1999, and autumn 2011 and autumn 2012. There were many others. Some of the most important of these include the Sharm El-Sheikh Memorandum (1999),[62] the Trilateral Statement on the Middle East Peace Summit at Camp David (Trilateral Statement) (2000),[63] the Joint Statement at the End of the Taba Negotiations (2001),[64] and the Joint Understanding Read by President Bush at the Annapolis Conference (2007).[65] Except for the Trilateral Statement, which the United States also endorsed, these instruments were essentially bilateral in nature, and they were all legally-binding because they articulated sufficiently precise commitments and were concluded within the context of negotiations.[66]

On March 12, 2002, at the height of the second *intifada*, or "uprising," the United Nations Security Council "[a]ffirm[ed] a vision of a region where two States, Israel and Palestine, live side by side within secure and recognized borders,"[67] and it framed this view within the context of a bilateral negotiation imperative.[68] That morning, United Nations Secretary-General Kofi Annan implored Israeli Prime Minister Ariel Sharon and PLO Chairman Arafat to "lead your peoples away from disaster. You have accepted the Tenet [U]nderstandings and the Mitchell [R]ecommendations as the basis for negotiations."[69] While the Secretary-General does not

[61] *See* Roadmap, *supra* note 57.

[62] Israel-Palestine Liberation Organization: The Sharm El-Sheikh Memorandum, 38(6) I.L.M. 1465 (1999).

[63] Trilateral Statement on the Middle East Peace Summit at Camp David, July 25, 2000, http://unispal.un.org/unispal.nsf/9a798adbf322aff38525617b006d88d7/a27b8f698499976f85256e37005b1674?OpenDocument#sthash.fDx6goy0.dpuf.

[64] Joint Statement at the End of the Taba Negotiations, Jan. 27, 2001, http://unispal.un.org/unispal.nsf/9a798adbf322aff38525617b006d88d7/badaa58661cc084f85256e37006fc44d?OpenDocument.

[65] Joint Understanding Read by President Bush at the Annapolis Conference, Annapolis, Nov. 27, 2007, http://georgewbush-whitehouse.archives.gov/news/releases/2007/11/20071127.html.

[66] Instruments that articulate sufficiently precise commitments and are concluded within the context of negotiations are, according to Gautier, presumptively binding, though this can be rebutted when "there are convincing reasons to the contrary." Gautier, *supra* note 53, at ¶ 13.

[67] S.C. Res. 1397, at pmbl., U.N. Doc. S/RES/1397 (Mar. 12, 2002) (italics omitted).

[68] *See id.* at ¶ 2 ("Call[ing] upon the Israeli and Palestinian sides and their leaders to cooperate in the implementation of the Tenet work plan and Mitchell Report recommendations with the aim of resuming negotiations on a political settlement") (italics omitted).

[69] U.N. SCOR, at 3, U.N. Doc. S/PV.4488 (Mar. 12, 2002). *See* Palestinian-Israeli Security Implementation Work Plan (Tenet cease-fire plan), June 14, 2001 (as published in *Ha'aretz*, June 14, 2001), http://unispal.un.org/unispal.nsf/9a798adbf322aff38525617b006d88d7/798c5b335068ebba85256cf00075cb6e?OpenDocument#sthash.NYzAyydp.dpuf; Report of the Sharm El-Sheikh Fact-Finding Committee, Apr. 30, 2001, http://unispal.un.org/unispal.nsf/9a798adbf322aff38525617b006d88d7/6e61d52eaacb860285256d2800734e9a?OpenDocument#sthash.XjpLyur6.dpuf.

have the legal authority to bind Israel and the PLO as to a particular means of dispute settlement, it is worth noting the argument, at least at the time, that the Tenet Understandings and the Mitchell Recommendations formed *the* basis for negotiations. Other United Nations actors also called for the dispute to be settled on the basis of instruments that, taken together, added more confusion to these discussions than coherence.[70] The only baseline consistency that seems to emerge across these scattered instruments is that they reaffirm a *process of negotiation.*[71]

Grappling with these instruments is an extraordinarily technical exercise that requires a granular level of analysis.[72] Textually, there are varying degrees of specificity and generality, clarity and vagueness, both within and between these instruments. How do they relate to one another? What is the relationship between their procedural and substantive provisions? If one refers to the 1969 Vienna Convention on the Law of Treaties (VCLT) by analogy, subsequent agreement and practice with respect to the interpretation and application of these instruments and special rules of law between the parties would need to be taken into account (as a general rule of interpretation).[73] The VCLT's rules related to successive treaties dealing

[70] *See, e.g.,* U.N. Hum. Rts. Council, at ¶ 10, U.N. Doc. A/HRC/RES/16/31 (Mar. 25, 2011) ("Urg[ing] the parties to give renewed impetus to the peace process in line with the Annapolis Peace Conference and the Paris International Donors' Conference for the Palestinian State, and to implement fully the road map endorsed by the Security Council in its resolution 1515 (2003) of 19 November 2003, with the aim of reaching a comprehensive political settlement in accordance with the resolutions of the Security Council, including resolutions 242 (1967) of 22 November 1967, 338 (1973) of 22 October 1973 and 1850 (2008) of 16 December 2008. [*sic*] and other relevant United Nations resolutions, the principles of the Peace Conference on the Middle East, held in Madrid on 30 October 1991, the Oslo Accords, the Arab Peace initiative and subsequent agreements, which will allow two States, Israel and Palestine, to live in peace and security") (italics omitted).

[71] *See, e.g.,* Sharm El-Sheikh Memorandum, *supra* note 62, at 1465, ¶ 1; Trilateral Statement, *supra* note 63 ("Both sides agree that negotiations based on UN Security Council Resolutions 242 and 338 are the only way to achieve such an agreement and they undertake to create an environment for negotiations free from pressure, intimidation and threats of violence"); Joint Statement, *supra* note 64 ("The sides declare that they have never been closer to reaching an agreement and it is thus our shared belief that the remaining gaps could be bridged with the resumption of negotiations following the Israeli elections"); Sharm El-Sheikh Report, *supra* note 69 (calling for an end to violence and the rebuilding of confidence (in addition to the resumption of negotiations) but noting that "none of these steps will long be sustained absent a return to serious negotiations"); Joint Understanding, *supra* note 65 ("In furtherance of the goal of two states, Israel and Palestine, living side by side in peace and security, we agree to immediately launch good-faith bilateral negotiations in order to conclude a peace treaty, resolving all outstanding issues, including all core issues without exception, as specified in previous agreements"). Given its technical nature, it is unsurprising that the Tenet Understandings do not address non-security matters, such as the modalities of negotiation, or any other details, of either a procedural or substantive nature.

[72] The way in which these instruments were produced and the nature of the actors that produced them suggest that this was an exercise in "document-rattling," a sort of strategically created conflict that Ranganathan would argue opens the way to "legality claims." *See* SURABHI RANGANATHAN, STRATEGICALLY CREATED TREATY CONFLICTS AND THE POLITICS OF INTERNATIONAL LAW 29–30 (2014).

[73] *See* Vienna Convention on the Law of Treaties, Vienna, May 23, 1969, art. 31(3). In its 2004 judgment in *Avena and Other Mexican Nationals*, the ICJ noted that article 31 of the VCLT reflects customary international law. *See* Avena and Other Mexican Nationals (Mex. v. U.S.), 2004 I.C.J. 12, 48 (Mar. 31). *See also* Text of the Draft Conclusions and Commentaries Thereto Provisionally Adopted by the Commission at Its Sixty-Fifth Session, *in* Report of the International Law Commission, 65th Sess.,

with the same subject matter would also conceivably be relevant when grappling with this hodgepodge of instruments.[74]

These interpretive devices do not "interpret themselves," of course. They admit of (at least a certain degree of) indeterminacy when applied *in concreto*, and the questions that they raise seem to be as contested as the maxim *lex specialis derogat legi generali* that is undoubtedly involved in these discussions.[75] Yet, at least with respect to *lex specialis derogat legi generali*, the room for debate may be somewhat less.[76] This is because the general international law of negotiation (and its emphasis on such considerations as good faith and meaningful engagement) largely mirrors (in general terms) the specificities of the bilateral negotiation imperative that has developed over the years between the two sides. A somewhat different way of putting this would be to say that while Israel and the PLO remain obliged not to act prejudicially with respect to such permanent status issues as the final status of the territories and settlements, they remain free to make claims with respect to them when doing so cannot reasonably be said to preclude a final settlement and when the assertion of such claims takes place within the context of negotiations. Clearly, however: "Any unilateral declaration of statehood by the Palestinians in the occupied territories or annexation of territory on the part of Israel would, arguably, not only constitute a direct violation of the agreements but contradict the international law of self-determination."[77]

If, as this analysis suggests, a bilateral negotiation imperative was firmly rooted as *the* legal principle between the two sides in the run-up to autumn 2011 and

May 6–June 7, July 8–Aug. 9, 2013, at 12, 13, draft concl. 1(1), U.N. Doc. A/68/10; GAOR, 68th Sess., Supp. No. 10 (2013) (holding that articles 31 and 32 of the VCLT "set forth, respectively, the general rule of interpretation and the rule on supplementary means of interpretation. These rules also apply as customary international law").

[74] *See* VCLT, *supra* note 73, at art. 30. The International Law Commission is currently studying Subsequent Agreements and Subsequent Practice in Relation to Interpretation of Treaties. *See* International Law Commission, Treaties over Time/Subsequent Agreements and Subsequent Practice in Relation to Interpretation of Treaties, http://legal.un.org/ilc/summaries/1_11.shtml.

[75] According to the maxim *lex specialis derogat legi generali*, "whenever two or more norms deal with the same subject matter, priority should be given to the norm that is more specific." Conclusions of the Work of the Study Group on the Fragmentation of International Law: Difficulties Arising from the Diversification and Expansion of International Law, *in* Report of the International Law Commission, 58th Sess., May 1–June 9, July 3–Aug. 11, 2006, at 407, 408, ¶ 5, U.N. Doc. A/61/10; GAOR, 61st Sess., Supp. No. 10 (2006). *See* RANGANATHAN, *supra* note 72, at 11–12. *See, e.g.*, Hassan v. U.K., Eur. Ct. Hum. Rts., at ¶¶ 96–107, No. 29750/09 (2014). There are, of course, other doctrinal approaches to (treaty) conflict. On some of these, see RANGANATHAN, *supra* note 72, at 8–13.

[76] On the series of Israeli–Palestinian instruments as having created a "special independent regime—a *lex specialis*—that governs all aspects of the relationship between them [i.e., Israel and the PLO], including the respective status of each party *vis-à-vis* the territory," see Alan Baker, *International Humanitarian Law, ICRC, and Israel's Status in the Territories*, 94(888) INT'L REV. RED CROSS 1, 5 (2012). *See also* Anne Herzberg, *When International Law Blocks the Flow: The Strange Case of the Kidron Valley Sewage Plant,* 10(2) REGENT J. INT'L L. 71, 106–107 (2014) (making the same point).

[77] Tal Becker, *Self-Determination in Perspective: Palestinian Claims to Statehood and the Relativity of the Right to Self-Determination*, 32(2) ISR. L. REV. 301, 348 (1998). *See* Singer, *supra* note 31, at 8 (making a similar point, with specific reference to the Interim Agreement, by arguing that an Israeli annexation of the territories or a unilateral declaration of statehood by the Palestinians "may be considered a material breach and a ground for terminating the agreement").

autumn 2012, it is important to distinguish between the nature of this framework and other negotiation frameworks. Consider, for example, the 1968 Treaty on the Non-Proliferation of Nuclear Weapons (NPT), which requires States Parties to "pursue negotiations in good faith on effective measures relating to cessation of the nuclear arms race at an early date and to nuclear disarmament, and on a treaty on general and complete disarmament under strict and effective international control."[78] According to the ICJ, this provision of the NPT reflects an "obligation to achieve a precise result—nuclear disarmament in all its aspects—by adopting a particular course of conduct, namely, the pursuit of negotiations on the matter in good faith."[79] Put differently, it points to a specific end, nuclear disarmament, which can be objectively verified.[80]

The Israeli–Palestinian instruments, by contrast, reaffirm negotiation as a means to an end, "peace," the contours of which, both juridically and philosophically, are by no means settled, and that cannot with certainty be predicted *ex ante*.[81] In other words, a final settlement will necessarily reflect the outcome of "horsetrading" between the two sides as to their respective rights and obligations. It will reflect a Vattelian compromise in which, "without precisely deciding on the justice of the jarring pretensions, the parties recede on both sides, and determine what share each shall have of the thing in dispute, or agree to give it entirely to one of the claimants on condition of certain indemnifications granted to the other."[82]

III. Palestinian Applications for Admission to the United Nations: The Events of Autumn 2011 and Autumn 2012

Before turning to the events of autumn 2011 and autumn 2012, it is helpful to briefly review the law that regulates applications for admission to the United Nations.[83] Member State status is open to "all other peace-loving states which

[78] Treaty on the Non-Proliferation of Nuclear Weapons, London/Moscow/Washington, DC, July 1, 1968, art. 6.

[79] Legality of the Threat or Use of Nuclear Weapons, Advisory Opinion, 1996 I.C.J. 226, 264 (July 8). For some criticism of the ICJ's interpretation of the NPT in this regard, see Daniel H. Joyner, *The Legal Meaning and Implications of Article VI of the Non-Proliferation Treaty, in* Nuclear Weapons Under International Law 397, 404–405 (Gro Nystuen et al. eds., 2014). *See also* Marco Roscini, *The Cases Against the Nuclear Weapons States*, 19(10) Am. Soc'y Int'l L. Insights (May 12, 2015).

[80] *See generally* Joyner, *supra* note 79.

[81] Franck, no doubt, would argue that the parameters of what this might involve would "concretize" over time. *See* Thomas M. Franck, *On Proportionality of Countermeasures in International Law*, 102(4) Am. J. Int'l L. 715 (2008) (making this point within the context of international law's principle of proportionality).

[82] Emer de Vattel, The Law of Nations 450 (Béla Kapossy & Richard Whatmore eds., 2008).

[83] On admission to international organizations generally, see Philippe Sands & Pierre Klein, Bowett's Law of International Institutions 538–45 (6th ed. 2009).

accept the obligations contained in the present Charter [of the United Nations (Charter)] and, in the judgment of the Organization, are able and willing to carry out these obligations."[84] To be successful, applications must be approved by the United Nations General Assembly after the Security Council has recommended admission.[85] Whether the conditions of admission have been satisfied in a particular case is a "problem of interpretation and consequently a legal question."[86] It is a question of legal interpretation.

Yet, while assessing applications is undoubtedly a question of law, assessments do not, and need not, occur in a context wholly devoid of political considerations. In other words, the conditions of admission contained in article 4(1) of the Charter do not preclude an accounting of extratextual considerations. In its 1948 *Admission of a State to the United Nations (Charter, Art. 4) (Admission)* advisory opinion, for example, the ICJ made clear that factors that can reasonably and in good faith be connected to the criteria contained in article 4(1) can be considered, so much so, in fact, that "no relevant political factor—that is to say, none connected with the conditions of admission—is excluded."[87] Member States, in this respect, are to be afforded a "wide liberty of appreciation."[88]

A number of the opinions appended to *Admission* supported this appreciation of political judgment in admission decisions. Judge Azevedo, for example, stressed the flexible nature of the conditions of admission and counseled that "all political considerations may intervene in determining the judgment of the organs of the United Nations regarding the qualifications laid down in Article 4 of the Charter."[89] Judge Krylov's dissenting opinion saw both article 4(1) and the entirely consequential and wide-sweeping Purposes and Principles of the United Nations as acting as the proper guides for admission decisions.[90] For Judges Basdevant, Winiarski, McNair, and Read, article 4(1) was essential but not sufficient,[91] and Member States voting on applications for admission were free to entertain

[84] U.N. Charter art. 4(1). *See* P.O. Humber, *Admission to the United Nations,* 24 BRIT. Y.B. INT'L L. 90 (1947). The use of the word "other" in this provision is meant to distinguish between (future) United Nations Member States and the original Member States. For a list of United Nations Member States, with dates of admission, see United Nations, Member States of the United Nations, www.un.org/en/members/index.shtml.

[85] *See* U.N. Charter art. 4(2). *See also* Provisional Rules of Procedure of the Security Council, at arts 58–60, U.N. Doc. S/96/Rev.7 (1983). A Security Council recommendation is a condition predicate to the General Assembly's consideration of an application for admission. *See* Competence of Assembly Regarding Admission to the United Nations, Advisory Opinion, 1950 I.C.J. 4 (Mar. 3). The admission of new Member States is deemed to be an "important question[]" that requires a two-thirds majority vote in the General Assembly of those present and voting. *See* U.N. Charter art. 18(2).

[86] Admission of a State to the United Nations (Charter, Art. 4), Advisory Opinion, 1948 I.C.J. 57, 61 (May 28).

[87] *Id.* at 63.

[88] *Id.* at 64.

[89] *Id.* at 78 (Azevedo, J., individual).

[90] *See id.* at 115 (Krylov, J., dissenting). The Purposes and Principles of the United Nations are listed in, respectively, articles 1 and 2 of the Charter.

[91] *See id.* at 90 (J. Basdevant et al., dissenting).

political considerations.[92] Thus, it can be said that applications for admission trigger a process of legal evaluation that allows for the use of discretion grounded in policy.[93]

With this as background, one can now turn to the events of autumn 2011. The consensus view at the time was that Israel and the PLO needed to settle their dispute through negotiation. The speeches delivered by a variety of States in a Security Council meeting in late July 2011 were perhaps the clearest evidence of this.[94] Nigeria, for example, called for the two sides to "immediately re-enter into direct negotiations on all permanent status issues, including borders, Jerusalem, refugees and security,"[95] and South Africa urged Israel and the PLO to negotiate without preconditions and to avoid prejudicing permanent status issues.[96] Gabon pressed for the parties to resume negotiations,[97] as did Uganda,[98] and the Arab States of Lebanon,[99] Egypt (speaking for the Non-Aligned Movement (NAM)),[100] Jordan,[101] and Morocco[102] also made pleas for negotiations. The Latin American States in the Security Council favored negotiations,[103] as did States ranging from Russia,[104] China,[105] and India[106] to Turkey,[107] Indonesia,[108] and Japan.[109] The European Union put on record its support for negotiations,[110] as did (speaking in their national capacities) France,[111] Portugal,[112] the United Kingdom,[113] and Germany.[114] The United States' call for negotiations was unsurprising: it insisted that Israel and the PLO engage in "serious and responsible negotiations."[115]

[92] *See id.* at 92 (J. Basdevant et al., dissenting) (continuing by stating that, in exercising this power, each Member State is "legally bound to have regard to the principle of good faith, to give effect to the Purposes and Principles of the United Nations and to act in such a manner as not to involve any breach of the Charter").

[93] As Sands and Klein put it, admission to the United Nations allows for "subjective appreciation." SANDS & KLEIN, *supra* note 83, at 542.

[94] *See* U.N. SCOR, U.N. Doc. S/PV.6590 (July 26, 2011); U.N. SCOR, U.N. Doc. S/PV.6590 (Resumption 1) (July 26, 2011).

[95] U.N. SCOR, U.N. Doc. S/PV.6590, *supra* note 94, at 12.

[96] *See id.* at 16–17.

[97] *See id.* at 18–19.

[98] *See* U.N. SCOR, U.N. Doc. S/PV.6590 (Resumption 1), *supra* note 94, at 6.

[99] *See* U.N. SCOR, U.N. Doc. S/PV.6590, *supra* note 94, at 13–15.

[100] *See id.* at 28–30.

[101] *See* U.N. SCOR, U.N. Doc. S/PV.6590 (Resumption 1), *supra* note 94, at 5.

[102] *See id.* at 13–14.

[103] *See* U.N. SCOR, U.N. Doc. S/PV.6590, *supra* note 94, at 20–21 (Brazil), 25–26 (Colombia). Cuba attached itself to the speech of Egypt (on behalf of the NAM). *See id.* at 30–31.

[104] *See id.* at 22–23.

[105] *See id.* at 15–16.

[106] *See id.* at 24–25.

[107] *See* U.N. SCOR, U.N. Doc. S/PV.6590 (Resumption 1), *supra* note 94, at 2–4.

[108] *See* U.N. SCOR, U.N. Doc. S/PV.6590, *supra* note 94, at 31–32.

[109] *See* U.N. SCOR, U.N. Doc. S/PV.6590 (Resumption 1), *supra* note 94, at 4–5.

[110] *See* U.N. SCOR, U.N. Doc. S/PV.6590, *supra* note 94, at 33–34.

[111] *See id.* at 17–18.

[112] *See id.* at 19–20.

[113] *See id.* at 23–24.

[114] *See id.* at 26–28.

[115] *Id.* at 11.

To be sure, while these States would offer strikingly different views as to whether the Palestinian applications of autumn 2011 and autumn 2012 reinforced or undermined the bilateral negotiation imperative, in principle, they all supported a negotiated settlement.

The Palestinians sent their application package to United Nations Secretary-General Ban Ki-moon on September 23, 2011, and this consisted of a formal application for admission and an explanatory memorandum.[116] According to its terms, it would seem that the application was justified based not upon anything that had transpired between Israel and the PLO since the Exchange of Letters and the Declaration of Principles; rather, for the Palestinians' part, everything seemed to be justified on the basis of the General Assembly's partition resolution of 1947,[117] the PLO's Declaration of Independence[118] and General Assembly Resolution 43/177[119] (both from late 1988), and the Palestinian people's "natural, legal and historic rights."[120] It almost seemed as if everything that had taken place after late 1988 could be cast aside as being legally irrelevant to an application for admission to the United Nations.

Looking forward, the "State of Palestine affirm[ed] its commitment to the achievement of a just, lasting and comprehensive resolution of the Israeli-Palestinian conflict based on the vision of two-States living side by side in peace and security."[121] This was hardly a clear vision of a negotiated settlement, however, given that the Palestinians based this commitment upon a hodgepodge of instruments and that which is perhaps the most question-begging concept of all: "international law."[122] President Mahmoud Abbas' explanatory memorandum provided no greater clarity as to a discernible way forward.[123] His reference to the Roadmap,

[116] *See* Application of Palestine for Admission to Membership in the United Nations, U.N. Doc. A/66/371 (Sept. 23, 2011). The application package also contained the required pro forma declaration. *See* Provisional Rules, *supra* note 85, at art. 58. For an official defense of the application in light of criticism that it jeopardized Palestinian rights, see Memorandum Prepared by the Permanent Observer Mission of Palestine to the United Nations—New York: Response to Arguments that the "September Initiative" Regarding Statehood Will Harm the Status of the Palestine Liberation Organization (PLO) and the Rights of the Palestine Refugees (Sept. 2011). On the Palestinians' autumn 2011 bid generally, see John Cerone, *The UN and the Status of Palestine—Disentangling the Legal Issues*, 15(26) AM. SOC'Y INT'L L. INSIGHTS (Sept. 13, 2011); Khaled Elgindy, *Palestine Goes to the UN: Understanding the New Statehood Strategy*, 90(5) FOREIGN AFF. 102 (2011).

[117] *See* G.A. Res. 181, U.N. Doc. A/RES/181 (Nov. 29, 1947).

[118] *See* Letter Dated 18 November 1988 from the Permanent Representative of Jordan to the United Nations Addressed to the Secretary-General, Annex II at 13, U.N. Doc. A/43/827 (Nov. 18, 1988) (Declaration of Independence).

[119] *See* G.A. Res. 43/177, U.N. Doc. A/RES/43/177 (Dec. 15, 1988).

[120] Admission Application, *supra* note 116, at Annex I at 2, 2 (Application of the State of Palestine for Admission to Membership in the United Nations).

[121] *Id.* (Application of the State of Palestine for Admission to Membership in the United Nations).

[122] *Id.* (Application of the State of Palestine for Admission to Membership in the United Nations) (affirming this commitment "as endorsed by the United Nations Security Council and General Assembly and the international community as a whole and based on international law and all relevant United Nations resolutions").

[123] *See id.* at Annex II at 4, 4 (Letter Dated 23 September 2011 from the President of Palestine to the Secretary-General) (putting forward a negotiation paradigm in the open-ended language of "the internationally endorsed terms of reference, including the relevant United Nations resolutions, the

for example, ignored the fact that Israel had lodged fourteen reservations to it when Prime Minister Sharon's Cabinet accepted it.[124]

A few hours after he submitted his application package to Secretary-General Ban, President Abbas turned to address the General Assembly.[125] His narrative of peacemaking efforts was a particular one, of course, as was Israeli Prime Minister Benjamin Netanyahu's shortly thereafter.[126] President Abbas described Israel as, *inter alia*, an apartheid State that operated according to a "logic of ruthless force"[127] and engaged in a "multi-pronged policy of ethnic cleansing aimed at pushing them [i.e., the Palestinians] away from their ancestral homeland."[128] The "occupation" was decried—President Abbas even referred to it, no doubt for dramatic effect but clearly inaccurately from a juridical point of view, as "the only occupation in the world"[129]—and the presence of Israelis (mostly Jews, in practice) beyond the 1949 armistices lines was pinpointed as the "root cause" of the failure of Israel and the PLO to settle their dispute.[130]

President Abbas ended his address by hailing his homeland as the "land of divine messages, ascension of the Prophet Muhammad (peace be upon him) and the birthplace of Jesus Christ (peace be upon him)."[131] In and of itself, this reference to (East) Jerusalem (revered site of the "Farthest Mosque")[132] and Bethlehem[133] was not particularly objectionable. Israel and the PLO, after all, have long agreed that Jerusalem is a permanent status issue, and Bethlehem falls squarely within Area A. What was remarkable, and deeply objectionable (from Israel's perspective), was the absence of any reference to a Jewish connection to the land, be it of a religious or national nature.[134] It was as if Judaism as a religion had been "eclipsed" by

Madrid principles, including the principle of land for peace, the Arab Peace Initiative and the Quartet Roadmap, which specifically requires a freeze of all Israeli settlement activities").

[124] *See* Israel's Response to the Roadmap (May 25, 2003),www.mfa.gov.il/mfa/foreignpolicy/peace/mfadocuments/pages/israel%20response%20to%20the%20roadmap%2025-may-2003.aspx. *See also* Elliot Abrams, Tested by Zion: The Bush Administration and the Israeli-Palestinian Conflict 67–69 (2013); Gideon Alon et al., *Sharon, Abbas to Meet as Cabinet Approves Road Map*, Haaretz, May 26, 2003.

[125] *See* Statement by H.E. Mr. Mahmoud Abbas, President of the State of Palestine, Chairman of the Executive Committee of the Palestine Liberation Organization, President of the Palestinian National Authority, New York (Sept. 23, 2011), http://gadebate.un.org/sites/default/files/gastatements/66/PS_en.pdf.

[126] *See* Statement by H.E. Mr. Benjamin Netanyahu, Prime Minister of the State of Israel, New York (Sept. 23, 2011), http://gadebate.un.org/sites/default/files/gastatements/66/IL_en.pdf.

[127] Abbas Statement, *supra* note 125, at 5.

[128] *Id.* at 2.

[129] *Id.* at 6.

[130] *See id.* at 2 (calling Israel's settlement policy the "primary cause for the failure of the peace process, the collapse of dozens of opportunities, and the burial of the great hopes that arose from the signing of the Declaration of Principles in 1993 between the Palestine Liberation Organization and Israel to achieve a just peace that would begin a new era for our region").

[131] *Id.* at 6.

[132] Koran 17:1.

[133] *See, e.g.*, Matthew 2.

[134] *See* Netanyahu Statement, *supra* note 126, at 7–8 (articulating this Israeli objection). President Abbas' most recent address to the General Assembly, in September 2015, also failed to mention any Jewish connection to the land, stressing only the links of Christians and Muslims: "Palestine is a

Christianity, which in turn had been "eclipsed" by Islam, and as if the PLO had yet to recognize Jewish "peoplehood."

Shortly after President Abbas made his remarks to the General Assembly, Prime Minister Netanyahu took the podium to denounce the Palestinian initiative. This came as a surprise to no one, as Israel had long opposed extending United Nations Member State status to the Palestinians in the absence of a final settlement reached through negotiation.[135] Prime Minister Netanyahu began by castigating the United Nations as a "theater of the absurd. It [i.e., the United Nations] doesn't only cast Israel as the villain; it often casts real villains in leading roles."[136] He countered those advocating the unflinching application of "land for peace" with a skepticism borne out of historical experience. This experience included rejected offers of a Palestinian State by Israel, in 2000 (under Prime Minister Ehud Barak) and 2008 (under Prime Minister Ehud Olmert), which undermined Israeli confidence in the PLO's good faith, and the ascent to power of Hezbollah and Hamas after the IDF had withdrawn from, respectively, southern Lebanon and Gaza. Prime Minister Netanyahu mocked President Abbas' insistence that the Palestinians had come to the United Nations "armed only with their dreams, courage, hope and slogans."[137] In Israel's reckoning, this overlooked the geopolitically much more pressing element: "Yeah, hopes, dreams and 10,000 missiles and Grad rockets supplied by Iran, not to mention the river of lethal weapons now flowing into Gaza from the Sinai, from Libya, and from elsewhere."[138] Despite this, Prime Minister Netanyahu insisted that Israel did not oppose the creation of a Palestinian State as such and would support a Palestinian application for admission to the United Nations within the context of a negotiated final settlement.[139]

country of holiness and peace. It is the birthplace of Christ, the messenger of love and peace, and the *Isra'* and *Mi'raj* (ascension to heaven and night journey) of Mohammed, peace be upon him, who was sent as a mercy unto the world." Statement by H.E. Mr. Mahmoud Abbas, President of the State of Palestine, New York, at 4 (Sept. 30, 2015), http://gadebate.un.org/sites/default/files/gastatements/70/70_PS_en.pdf. In his address to the General Assembly the next day, Prime Minister Netanyahu stressed the ancient pedigree of the Jewish people, as a nation and as a religious community, in Jerusalem. *See* Prime Minister's Office, Address by Prime Minister Benjamin Netanyahu at the UN General Assembly, New York, at 13 (Oct. 1, 2015), http://gadebate.un.org/sites/default/files/gastatements/70/IL_EN.pdf.

[135] In the Security Council meeting of late July 2011 referred to above, see *supra*, 155–56. Israeli Ambassador Ron Prosor had disparaged the idea as being "akin to picking out a chimney-pot for one's house before laying its foundation." U.N. SCOR, U.N. Doc. S/PV.6590, *supra* note 94, at 9. A few minutes later, Ambassador Prosor called for a "road of solutions not resolutions, dialogue not monologue and direct negotiations not unilateral declarations." *Id.* at 11.

[136] Netanyahu Statement, *supra* note 126, at 1.

[137] Abbas Statement, *supra* note 125, at 5. These were President Abbas' actual words. Prime Minister Netanyahu had paraphrased them in his speech as "armed only with their hopes and dreams." Netanyahu Statement, *supra* note 126, at 4.

[138] Netanyahu Statement, *supra* note 126, at 4.

[139] *See id.* at 6. Prime Minister Netanyahu, and Likud, first endorsed the idea of a Palestinian State in a speech that Prime Minister Netanyahu delivered at Bar-Ilan University in June 2009. *See* Israel Ministry of Foreign Affairs, Address by PM Netanyahu at Bar-Ilan University (June 4, 2009), http://mfa.gov.il/MFA/PressRoom/2009/Pages/Address_PM_Netanyahu_Bar-Ilan_University_14-Jun-2009.aspx ("If we receive this guarantee regarding demilitirization [*sic*] and Israel's security needs, and if the

Clearly, the speeches by President Abbas and Prime Minister Netanyahu revealed significant gaps in understanding between the two sides. Consider, for example, the refugee issue. What the two leaders said with respect to this, and *how* they said what they said, suggests that the fears that the Exchange of Letters and the Declaration of Principles were meant to have alleviated some twenty years earlier continued to plague the parties. As part of a final settlement, President Abbas insisted upon the "achievement of a just and agreed upon solution to the Palestine refugee issue in accordance with resolution 194, as stipulated in the Arab Peace Initiative which presented the consensus Arab vision to resolve the core [of] the Arab-Israeli conflict and to achieve a just and comprehensive peace."[140] Prime Minister Netanyahu, by contrast, channeled Israeli angst on the refugee issue to the Palestinians directly: "[W]e want them [i.e., the Palestinians] to give up the fantasy of flooding Israel with millions of Palestinians."[141] It was hardly reassuring to Israelis that PLO Executive Committeeperson Hanan Ashrawi had just days earlier referred to the Israeli "occupation for [*sic*] 63 years,"[142] thus seeming to cast as suspect and "occupation" *any* Israeli presence in what had been the Palestine Mandate.

President Abbas' speech framed the refugee issue within the context of the Arab Peace Initiative. The Arab Peace Initiative, which the League of Arab States had adopted in Beirut in 2002, "call[ed] upon it [i.e., Israel … t]o arrive at a just and agreed solution to the Palestine refugee problem in accordance with United Nations General Assembly resolution 194(III)."[143] Jordanian foreign minister Marwan Muasher, who was heavily involved in the drafting of the Arab Peace Initiative, saw in the use of the word "agreed" a significant concession to Israel,[144] but even Muasher had to admit that "surrendering the right of return altogether was something no Arab was prepared to do. The door could not be closed to *any* number of people to return, a number that can be *agreed* to as per the Arab [Peace] Initiative provisions."[145] Indeed, though often overlooked, three other resolutions

Palestinians recognize Israel as the State of the Jewish people, then we will be ready in a future peace agreement to reach a solution where a demilitarized Palestinian state exists alongside the Jewish state"). *See also* Jodi Rudoren, *Netanyahu's History on Palestinian Statehood*, N.Y. TIMES, Mar. 20, 2015.

[140] Abbas Statement, *supra* note 125, at 4. *See* Saeb Erekat, *The Returning Issue of Palestine's Refugees*, GUARDIAN, Dec. 10, 2010.

[141] Netanyahu Statement, *supra* note 126, at 6. *See* U.N. SCOR, at 9–11, U.N. Doc. S/PV.6706 (Jan. 24, 2012) (Israel).

[142] Natasha Mozgovaya & Reuters, *Palestinians Disappointed by Obama's UN Speech*, HAARETZ, Sept. 21, 2011.

[143] Letter Dated 24 April 2002 from the Chargé d'Affaires a.i. of the Permanent Mission of Lebanon to the United Nations Addressed to the Secretary-General, Annex II at 6, 6, ¶ 2(b), U.N. Doc. A/56/1026 (2002) (Arab Peace Initiative).

[144] *See* MARWAN MUASHER, THE ARAB CENTER: THE PROMISE OF MODERATION 102–33 (2008).

[145] *Id.* at 204. *See* Bruce Maddy-Weitzman, *Arabs vs. the Abdullah Plan*, 17(3) MID. E. Q. 3, 9 (2010). *See also* Asher Susser, *Looking Straight at the Initiative*, HAARETZ, Dec. 18, 2008. It has been suggested that the PLO does not have the international legal authority to waive a "right of return" that adheres to individual Palestinians directly. *See* Mutaz M. Qafisheh, *Bases for the Palestinian Refugees' Right of*

that the Arab League adopted in Beirut seemed to further justify Israeli concerns, expressly calling for a "right of return" without using the word "agreed."[146]

The Palestinian perspective is less surprising, however, when one recalls that the Arab League recognizes "Palestine" as a State Party to the 2004 Arab Charter on Human Rights, a treaty that itself rejects "racism and zionism[,] which constitute a violation of human rights and pose a threat to international peace and security,"[147] and condemns and calls for the elimination of Zionism.[148] Insisting upon a Palestinian "right of return," then, would seem to be consistent with this treaty-based obligation to eliminate Zionism.[149] Arguably, the "only equation in political science with mathematical certainty is that the so-called right of return equals the destruction of the State of Israel."[150] This can hardly be reconciled with Jewish self-determination.

The Security Council released the Report of the Committee on the Admission of New Members Concerning the Application of Palestine for Admission to Membership in the United Nations (Admission Report) on November 11, 2011.[151] In examining the 2011 Palestinian application, the Admission Report looked at the five conditions of admission contained in article 4(1) of the Charter: the criterion of statehood (paragraphs 9–14);[152] the requirement that applicants be "peace-loving" (paragraphs 15–16); the requirement that applicants accept (what would be) their Charter obligations (paragraph 17); the requirement that applicants be able to carry out (what would be) their Charter obligations (paragraph 17);

Return under International Law: Beyond General Assembly Resolution 194, CAMBRIDGE J. INT'L & COMP. L. ONLINE, Nov. 26, 2012, http://cjicl.org.uk/2012/11/26/bases-for-the-palestinian-refugees-right-of-return-under-international-law-beyond-general-assembly-resolution-194-2/. *See also* Mutaz M. Qafisheh, *An Ongoing Anomaly: Pre- and Post-Second World War Palestinian Refugees*, 27(1) INT'L J. Refugee L. 52 (2015).

146 *See* Letter, *supra* note 143, at Annex II at 8, 8, ¶ 2(c) (Question of Palestine, and Recent Developments in the Arab-Israeli Conflict: Support for the Intifadah and Steadfastness of the Palestinian People), Annex II at 9, 9, ¶ 4 (Question of Palestine, and Recent Developments in the Arab-Israeli Conflict: Solidarity with and Support for Lebanon), Annex II at 23, 25, ¶ 12 (Final Communiqué), Annex II at 23, 25, ¶ 13 (Final Communiqué).

147 Arab Charter on Human Rights, Tunis, May 22, 2004, 24(2) B.U. INT'L L.J. 147, 150, pmbl. (2006) (Mohammed Amin Al-Midani & Mathilde Cabanettes trans., Susan M. Akram rev.).

148 *See id.* at 151, art. 2(3) ("All forms of racism, zionism, occupation and foreign domination pose a challenge to human dignity and constitute a fundamental obstacle to the realization of the basic rights of peoples. There is a need to condemn and endeavour to eliminate all such practices").

149 It could be argued that the 2004 Arab Charter on Human Rights is void because it conflicts with the *jus cogens* norm of self-determination, Zionism being the embodiment of the Jewish people's self-determination. This assumes, *arguendo*, the existence of self-determination as a *jus cogens* norm. See fn 39, Chapter 4 in this volume. "A treaty is void if, at the time of its conclusion, it conflicts with a peremptory norm of general international law." VCLT, *supra* note 73, at art. 53.

150 U.N. SCOR, at 10, U.N. Doc. S/PV.6636 (Oct. 24, 2011) (Israel).

151 Report of the Committee on the Admission of New Members Concerning the Application of Palestine for Admission to Membership in the United Nations, U.N. Doc. S/2011/705 (Nov. 11, 2011).

152 Unsurprisingly, the Admission Report referred to the 1933 Montevideo Convention on the Rights and Duties of States for the criteria of statehood. "The state as a person of international law should possess the following qualifications: (a.) a permanent population; (b.) a defined territory; (c.) government; and (d.) capacity to enter into relations with the other states." Montevideo Convention on the Rights and Duties of States, Montevideo, Dec. 26, 1933, art. 1.

and the requirement that applicants be willing to carry out (what would be) their Charter obligations (paragraphs 17–18).[153] Member States in the Security Council fundamentally differed as to whether these conditions, considered individually and in their totality, had been met, and the Committee on the Admission of New Members concluded its deliberations without being able to make a unanimous recommendation to the Security Council as a whole.[154] It seemed that Member States were as divided on the merits of the Palestinian application as were President Abbas and Prime Minister Netanyahu.[155] It is no less important to note that Hamas and Palestinian Prime Minister Salam Fayyad also opposed President Abbas' initiative, though they did so for fundamentally different reasons.[156]

Although the Security Council's failure to recommend the Palestinian application in 2011 precluded the application from proceeding to the General Assembly, the Palestinians succeeded in a simultaneous application that they had made to join the United Nations Educational, Scientific and Cultural Organization (UNESCO) as a Member State. The Constitution of UNESCO provides that: "[S]tates not members of the United Nations Organization may be admitted to membership of the Organization, upon recommendation of the Executive Board, by a two-thirds majority vote of the General Conference."[157] By resolution adopted

[153] "The requisite conditions are five in number: to be admitted to membership in the United Nations, an applicant must (1) be a State; (2) be peace-loving; (3) accept the obligations of the Charter; (4) be able to carry out these obligations; and (5) be willing to do so." Admission, *supra* note 86, at 62 (May 28).

[154] *See* Admission Report, *supra* note 151, at ¶¶ 21–23.

[155] Scholarly opinion was also divided. Although scholars examined each of the conditions of admission in turn, most of the focus was on the criterion of statehood, and even those most sympathetic to Palestinian statehood found it difficult to square the Montevideo criteria of statehood with the present reality of the Palestinians in the territories and beyond. *See, e.g.*, Guy S. Goodwin-Gill, Opinion re the Palestine Liberation Organization, the Future State of Palestine, and the Question of Popular Representation, at ¶ 9 (Aug. 10, 2011) (asserting that: "Until such a time as a final settlement is agreed, the putative State of Palestine will have no territory over which it exercises effective sovereignty, its borders will be indeterminate or disputed, its population, actual and potential, undetermined and many of them continuing to live under occupation or in States of refuge"). For other scholarly views on the Montevideo criteria in light of the events of autumn 2011 (and autumn 2012), see Paul Eden, *Palestinian Statehood: Trapped Between Rhetoric and* Realpolitik, 62(1) INT'L & COMP. L.Q. 225, 230–33 (2013); Srinivas Burra, *Palestine and the Belated UN Non-Member Observer State Status*, 52(4) INDIAN J. INT'L L. 591, 593–94 (2012).

[156] On Hamas' opposition to the application, see Elior Levy, *Hamas' Haniyeh Slams Abbas over UN Bid*, YNETNEWS, Sept. 18, 2011, www.ynetnews.com/articles/0,7340,L-4123918,00.html. On Prime Minister Fayyad's opposition, see *Spiegel Interview with Palestinian Prime Minister: "An Independent Palestine Will Be Inevitable,"* SPIEGEL ONLINE, Sept. 19, 2011, www.spiegel.de/international/world/spiegel-interview-with-palestinian-prime-minister-an-independent-palestine-will-be-inevitable-a-787165.html. Prime Minister Fayyad had put forward an ambitious two-year plan in August 2009 that would have seen the establishment of Palestine as an "independent, democratic, progressive, and modern Arab state, with full sovereignty over its territory in the West Bank and Gaza, on the 1967 borders, with East Jerusalem as its capital." Palestinian National Authority, Palestine, "Ending the Occupation, Establishing the State," Programme of the Thirteenth Government, at 4 (Aug. 2009). For more on Prime Minister Fayyad's project, see Robert M. Danin, *A Third Way to Palestine: Fayyadism and Its Discontents*, 90(1) FOREIGN AFF. 94 (2011); *A Palestinian State in Two Years: Interview with Salam Fayyad, Palestinian Prime Minister*, 39(1) J. PAL. STUD. 58 (2009).

[157] Constitution of the United Nations Educational, Scientific, and Cultural Organization, London, Nov. 16, 1945, art. 2(1).

by its General Conference on October 31, 2011, UNESCO accepted the Palestinian application for admission.[158]

Admission to UNESCO only requires that the applicant entity satisfy a single condition: statehood.[159] Although the Palestinian application to join UNESCO passed with 107 votes in favor, fourteen against, and fifty-two abstentions, admission to UNESCO did not mean that "Palestine" had somehow become a State from an international law perspective. For one, admission to an international organization does not, in and of itself, a State make. To be sure, it is not completely irrelevant, but the question of admission is formally separate and distinct from the question of statehood.[160] None of the concerns that the Admission Report would express with respect to Palestinian statehood shortly after the UNESCO vote were any less salient immediately after the UNESCO vote.[161] The debate as to statehood had not gone away: it had simply moved to a different forum of adjudication.[162]

The Palestinian application for admission to the United Nations in autumn 2011 reflected Palestinian frustration with the bilateral negotiation imperative. Given the politics involved in securing Security Council recommendations in such cases, politics that, to be sure, are no less "apparent" or "real" than when the General Assembly makes decisions for admission, few were surprised when the Palestinian application failed at the Security Council. The Quartet responded

[158] *See* John Cerone, *Introductory Note to the Admission of Palestine to UNESCO and Related Documents*, 51(3) I.L.M. 606, 616 (2012) (UNESCO Res. 36/76 (Oct. 31, 2011)). *See also* Kathleen Claussen, *What Effect of Palestine's Membership in UNESCO?*, CAMBRIDGE J. INT'L & COMP. L. ONLINE, Nov. 4, 2011, http://cjicl.org.uk/2011/11/04/what-effect-of-palestines-membership-in-unesco-2/. On the potential consequences within the United Nations system for the Palestinians after their admission to UNESCO, see Larry D. Johnson, *Palestine's Admission to UNESCO: Consequences Within the United Nations?*, 40(1–3) DENV. J. INT'L L. & POL'Y 118 (2012).

[159] Although statehood is the only condition of admission to UNESCO, UNESCO, in the Palestinians' case, did refer to the Palestinians' previous application to join UNESCO in 1989 and the expectation that the Palestinians would shortly thereafter ratify the UNESCO Constitution, which, in the event, ended up happening on November 23, 2011. For the text of the Palestinians' 1989 application to UNESCO, see Application for the Admission of Palestine as a Member State of UNESCO, Doc. 131 EX/45 (May 18, 1989). *See also* Explanatory Note Concerning the Request for the Admission of the State of Palestine to UNESCO, Doc. 131 EX/43 (May 12, 1989) (making the legal case for the Palestinians' 1989 application to UNESCO); "PLO/Palestine" and the Criteria for Statehood in International Law, Doc. 131 EX/INF.7 (May 26, 1989) (making the legal case against the Palestinians' 1989 application to UNESCO).

[160] *See* Cerone, *supra* note 158, at 607. *See also* Joseph Weiler, *Editorial*, 22(3) EUR. J. INT'L L. 621, 621–23 (2011) (making this point within the context of the Palestinians' 2011 application for admission to the United Nations as a Member State). "Recognition and UN membership are two different matters, one does not imply the other—neither is UN membership a requirement for statehood, nor does the General Assembly have the powers to constitute a State." Al-Haq, Al-Haq's Questions & Answers on Palestine's September Initiatives at the United Nations, No. 249/2011, at 6 (July 20, 2011).

[161] *See* Admission Report, *supra* note 151, at ¶¶ 9–14.

[162] *Cf.* Martti Koskenniemi, *The Fate of Public International Law: Between Technique and Politics*, 70(1) M.L.R. 1 (2007). "Even where the applicant is required to be a 'state,'" it should also be noted, "it does not inexorably follow that this means the traditional definition of a state. The meaning of a term or concept in one context is not necessarily its meaning in all contexts." Frederic L. Kirgis, *Admission of "Palestine" as a Member of a Specialized Agency and Withholding Payment of Assessments in Response*, 84(1) AM. J. INT'L L. 218, 220 n.17 (1990). *See id.* at 220–21.

by scrambling, issuing a statement that appealed for calm on the same day that President Abbas submitted his application package to Secretary-General Ban. The Quartet's statement referred to nearly every conceivable instrument that had been reached between Israel and the PLO, as well as those instruments that had been put forward by the international community generally. Considered as a whole, these background norms (if "background norms" is a proper description of this cacophony of instruments) were more of a "kitchen sink" approach to dispute settlement than a clear and discernible way forward for the parties.

In its statement of September 23, 2011, the Quartet "urgent[ly] appeal[ed] to the parties to overcome the current obstacles and resume direct bilateral Israeli-Palestinian negotiations without delay or preconditions."[163] It set forth a fairly detailed set of deadlines for progress between the parties: an agenda-setting meeting within a month's time that would set working methods and a time frame for final settlement that would be no later than December 31, 2012; and benchmarks for "comprehensive proposals"[164] on security and territory (within three months) and "substantial progress"[165] (within six months). The Quartet also envisaged a Donors Conference, expressed support for Prime Minister Fayyad's state-building efforts, and called for an international conference, to be held in Moscow and with the consultation of Israel and the PLO, at the "appropriate time."[166] Finally, the Quartet pleaded with Israel and the PLO to avoid "provocative actions."[167]

Given the "heat" that the Palestinian application of autumn 2011 had generated, it was perhaps to be expected that Israel and the PLO would respond to the Quartet's call differently. Prime Minister Netanyahu's Office issued a statement in early October 2011 that, though expressing some reservations, welcomed the Quartet's insistence upon direct negotiations without preconditions.[168] This showed a particular level of good faith in light of the fact that senior Palestinian negotiator Nabil Shaath had a week earlier charged Israel with being in "full occupation of our [i.e., the Palestinian people's] country for years, 62 years and we have been in negotiations now for 20 years of these 62 years,"[169] thus suggesting, at least on one interpretation, that non-Arab life in the former Palestine Mandate was itself "settlement." The PLO's response to the Quartet's call was to precondition a return to negotiations on Israeli acceptance of a settlement freeze beyond the 1949 armistice

[163] Statement by Middle East Quartet, Sept. 23, 2011, U.N. Doc. SG/2178.

[164] *Id.*

[165] *Id.*

[166] *Id.*

[167] *Id.*

[168] *See* Israel Ministry of Foreign Affairs, Israel Welcomes Quartet Call for Direct Negotiations (Oct. 2, 2011), http://mfa.gov.il/mfa/pressroom/2011/pages/israel_welcomes_quartet_call_direct_negotiations_2-oct-2011.aspx.

[169] Australian Broadcasting Corporation, Shaath Discusses Palestinian Push for Recognition (Sept. 26, 2011), www.abc.net.au/lateline/content/2011/s3326307.htm. *See also Interview: "Bringing in the International Community as a Major Factor in the Solution": An Interview with Dr. Nabil Shaath*, 20(2–3) PAL.-ISR. J. 126, 126–27 (2015).

lines and recognition that these same lines would become the borders that would ultimately separate Israel and the State of Palestine.[170]

The Quartet held a series of intensive meetings with each of the two sides in Jerusalem in late 2011.[171] In early 2012, Jordanian King Abdullah II hosted talks in Amman, with Israel and the PLO meeting face-to-face for the first time in well over a year.[172] Chief Palestinian negotiator Saeb Erekat insisted that these talks did "not constitute a return to negotiations,"[173] but if they did not, one wonders exactly what they did represent, and precisely why one side to the dispute saw fit to "gloat" that it was not negotiating with the other side when bilateral negotiations lay at the heart of its legal obligation. Israel and the PLO exchanged proposals (as required by the Quartet's statement of September 23),[174] but the talks broke down after the fifth meeting.[175] The Quartet issued a statement in mid March that "reiterate[d] its call on the parties to remain engaged and to refrain from provocative actions"[176] and made a similar call a month later.[177] Late spring 2012 brought a letter from President Abbas to Prime Minister Netanyahu,[178] followed by a reply from the latter that the PLO regarded as a "non-starter."[179] By the summer, the Quartet-led process had effectively broken down. Israel remained willing, and insisted upon, negotiating with the PLO without preconditions, but the Palestinians refused to negotiate without Israel having already agreed to its conditions.

[170] *See* Herb Keinon & Khaled Abu Toameh, *Israeli Call to Resume Direct Talks Rebuffed by PA*, Jerusalem Post, Dec. 11, 2011; DPA, *Palestinians Rebuff Quartet's Calls to Return to Table*, Haaretz, Oct. 27, 2011.

[171] *See* Office of the Quartet Representative Tony Blair, Quartet Envoys and Tony Blair Call on Israelis and Palestinians to Hold Direct Talks (Dec. 14, 2011), www.tonyblairoffice.org/quartet/news-entry/quartet-envoys-and-tony-blair-urge-parties-to-return-to-direct-talks/; UN Calls for Immediate Resumption of Direct Israeli-Palestinian Talks (Nov. 14, 2011), http://unispal.un.org/unispal.nsf/9a798adbf322aff38525617b006d88d7/7800c2d91e2f29a285257948006b1d00?OpenDocument; Office of the Quartet Representative Tony Blair, Tony Blair and Quartet Envoys Meet with Israeli and Palestinian Negotiators (Oct. 26, 2011), www.tonyblairoffice.org/quartet/news-entry/tony-blair-and-quartet-envoys-meet-with-israeli-and-palestinian-negotiators/.

[172] *See* Office of the Quartet Representative Tony Blair, Israeli and Palestinian Negotiators Hold Their First Meeting in More than a Year (Jan. 3, 2012), www.tonyblairoffice.org/quartet/news-entry/israeli-and-palestinian-negotiators-hold-their-first-meeting/.

[173] Attila Somfalvi, *Erekat: No Negotiations Yet*, Ynetnews, Jan. 2, 2012, www.ynetnews.com/articles/0,7340,L-4169882,00.html.

[174] *See* Herb Keinon, *PA Officials: Israeli Border Proposal a Non-Starter*, Jerusalem Post, Jan. 27, 2012; Barak Ravid & Natasha Mozgovaya, *Israel Presents the Palestinians with its Stance on Borders*, Haaretz, Jan. 26, 2012; Herb Keinon, "*Document Israel Gave PA Was Just an Outline*," Jerusalem Post, Jan. 5, 2012; Herb Keinon & Khaled Abu Toameh, *Israel, PA Agree to Meet Again Next Week*, Jerusalem Post, Jan. 3, 2012.

[175] For details of each of the five meetings in Amman, see Barak Ravid, *Netanyahu's Border Proposal: Israel to Annex Settlement Blocs, but Not Jordan Valley*, Haaretz, Feb. 19, 2012.

[176] Middle East Quartet Holds Informal Consultations, Mar. 12, 2012, U.N. Doc. SG/2181.

[177] *See* Statement by Middle East Quartet, Apr. 11, 2012, U.N. Doc. SG/2182.

[178] *See* Dan Ephron, *Palestinian President Mahmoud Abbas Threatens Legal Action Against Israel*, Daily Beast, Apr. 17, 2012, www.thedailybeast.com/articles/2012/04/17/palestinian-president-mahmoud-abbas-threatens-legal-action-against-israel.html.

[179] *See* Ron Friedman, *Netanyahu's Letter to Abbas Offers Nothing New, PLO Says*, Times of Israel, May 13, 2012, www.timesofisrael.com/plo-netanyahus-letter-to-abbas-offers-nothing-new/.

President Abbas' letter to Prime Minister Netanyahu of April 17, 2012, had warned Israel that if the Palestinians' conditions were not met that the Palestinians would "seek the full and complete implementation of international law as it pertains to the powers and responsibilities of Israel as occupying power in all of the occupied Palestinian territory."[180] Precisely what this meant was perhaps deliberately left vague, but President Abbas seemed to be implying that the Palestinians would again approach the United Nations. They did so in autumn 2012, but this time, the Palestinians were under no illusion as to the feasibility of applying for admission as a Member State. Instead, President Abbas approached the General Assembly directly in an application for non-member observer State status.

The Charter does not mention non-member observer State status as such, but it is a status that has developed as a matter of practice.[181] Non-member observer State status, as its name suggests, implies that the applicant entity is, or asserts to be, a *State*. Hence, when President Abbas approached the United Nations in autumn 2012, he did so, in his reckoning, as President of the *State* of Palestine, *not* as President of an *aspiring State* of Palestine.[182] His view was that this would make a "significant step towards fulfilling the Palestinian people's natural, historical, and legal rights to self-determination and independence."[183] Shortly thereafter, on November 29, 2012, the General Assembly voted 138 votes to nine, with forty-one abstentions, to adopt Resolution 67/19, which accorded non-member observer State status to the Palestinians.[184]

As with the Quartet's statement of September 23, 2011, Resolution 67/19 did little to clarify precisely how Israel and the PLO were to arrive at a final settlement. It "purport[ed] to establish a new state of legal relations, or at least declare a fact that carries legal consequences."[185] In Resolution 67/19, the General Assembly referenced nearly every conceivable instrument on the subject of the Israeli–Palestinian

[180] Ephron, *supra* note 178.

[181] *See* Camille Mansour, *Palestinian Options at the United Nations, in* ABORTED STATE? THE UN INITIATIVE AND NEW PALESTINIAN JUNCTURES 35, 35–36 (Noura Erakat & Mouin Rabbani eds., 2013); Johnson, *supra* note 158, at 119–22; Al-Haq, *supra* note 160, at 6.

[182] *See* Statement by H.E. Mr. Mahmoud Abbas, President of the State of Palestine, Chairman of the Executive Committee of the Palestine Liberation Organization, President of the Palestinian National Authority, New York (Sept. 27, 2012), http://gadebate.un.org/sites/default/files/gastatements/67/PS_en.pdf.

[183] Palestine Liberation Organization, Negotiations Affairs Department, Position Paper: Enhancement of Palestine's Status at the UN (Nov. 26, 2012), www.nad-plo.org/print.php?id=357.

[184] *See* G.A. Res. 67/19, U.N. Doc. A/RES/67/19 (Nov. 29, 2012). *See also* John Cerone, *Legal Implications of the UN General Assembly Vote to Accord Palestine the Status of Observer State*, 16(37) AM. SOC'Y INT'L L. INSIGHTS (Dec. 7, 2012); Daniel Costelloe, *The Status of Palestine at the General Assembly*, CAMBRIDGE J. INT'L & COMP. L. ONLINE, Nov. 29, 2012, http://cjicl.org.uk/2012/11/29/the-status-of-palestine-at-the-general-assembly-2/. On how the adoption of Resolution 67/19 affected Palestinian participation in the work of the General Assembly and other United Nations organs, as well as in United Nations conferences, see Status of Palestine in the United Nations: Report of the Secretary-General, at 2–3, U.N. Doc. A/67/738 (Mar. 8, 2013).

[185] Yaël Ronen, *Recognition of the State of Palestine: Still Too Much Too Soon?*, at 3 (Hebrew University of Jerusalem Faculty of Law International Law Forum Research Paper No. 15-13, 2013).

dispute in what, to be blunt, read as a position paper for the Palestinian side.[186] Its vision of an "independent, sovereign, democratic, contiguous and viable State of Palestine living side by side in peace and security with Israel on the basis of the pre-1967 borders,"[187] for example, reaffirmed Palestinian self-determination five times but made no express reference to Jewish self-determination. What is more, the General Assembly conflated the 1949 armistice lines with "pre-1967 borders." Resolution 67/19 also called for a "just resolution of the problem of the Palestine refugees in conformity with resolution 194(III) of 11 December 1948"[188] in such a way that seemed to challenge Jewish self-determination. In according "Palestine non-member observer *State* status in the United Nations,"[189] the General Assembly was clearly persuaded by the large number of international organizations and United Nations Member States that recognized the existing reality of a "State of Palestine."[190] Resolution 67/19 ended with an urgent call for the "resumption and acceleration of negotiations within the Middle East peace process,"[191] thus recognizing that the "peace process" between Israel and the PLO was fledgling at best.

The General Assembly vigorously debated what was to become Resolution 67/19, both before and after the vote. President Abbas spoke just after Sudan.[192] Although he claimed that he did not seek to "delegitimize a State established decades ago, that is, Israel,"[193] he did charge it with being an apartheid regime that had institutionalized racism and systemic oppression. 1948 was politicized as "one of the most dreadful campaigns of ethnic cleansing and dispossession in modern history,"[194] thus absolving the Arabs, and specifically the Arabs of Palestine, of

[186] Given that many of the States that voted in favor of Resolution 67/19 were States Parties to treaties that condemned and called for the elimination of Zionism, this is not particularly surprising. *See, supra* nn 147–50, on Arab Charter; African Charter on Human and Peoples' Rights, Nairobi, June 27, 1981, pmbl. (calling for the "eliminat[ion of] colonialism, neo-colonialism, apartheid, zionism and [... the] dismantl[ing of] aggressive foreign military bases and all forms of discrimination, particularly those based on race, ethnic group, color, sex, language, religion or political opinions").

[187] G.A. Res. 67/19, *supra* note 184, at ¶ 4.

[188] *Id.* at pmbl.

[189] *Id.* at ¶ 2 (emphasis added).

[190] *See id.* at pmbl. In a position paper that it circulated shortly before the adoption of Resolution 67/19, the PLO stated that "132 countries, including 9 of the 10 most populous countries in the world, already recognize Palestine. Combined, these countries represent over 75% of the world's population." Palestine Liberation Organization, Palestine Initiative to Seek an Enhanced Status as an Observer State at the United Nations: Frequently Asked Questions, at 2 (Oct. 2012), www.nad-plo.org/userfiles/file/FAQ/%2828%20October%202012%29%20UNGA%20bid%20QA%20_Final.pdf.

[191] G.A. Res. 67/19, *supra* note 184, at ¶ 5 (continuing by stating that this was to be "based on the relevant United Nations resolutions, the terms of reference of the Madrid Conference, including the principle of land for peace, the Arab Peace Initiative and the Quartet road map to a permanent two-State solution to the Israeli-Palestinian conflict for the achievement of a just, lasting and comprehensive peace settlement between the Palestinian and Israeli sides that resolves all outstanding core issues, namely the Palestine refugees, Jerusalem, settlements, borders, security and water").

[192] Khartoum had introduced the draft resolution and called it a "qualitative addition along the path to achieving the international will to establish a real peace in the Middle East based on the two-State solution." U.N. GAOR, at 2, U.N. Doc. A/67/PV.44 (Nov. 29, 2012).

[193] *Id.* at 4. *See* Palestine Liberation Organization, *supra* note 183. *See also* Nabil Shaath, The Time is Now: Support Palestine's UN Bid (Nov. 29, 2012), www.nad-plo.org/print.php?id=367.

[194] U.N. GAOR, *supra* note 192, at 3.

any role in what followed their rejection of the General Assembly's call for two States for two peoples, one majority Jewish, one majority Arab.[195] President Abbas proposed a settlement that added nothing new to the debate,[196] since it had been articulated in various forms, and fora, previously.

To no one's surprise, Israel castigated the Palestinian application. It argued that the General Assembly was not a proper forum for adjudicating the Israeli–Palestinian dispute and implored the General Assembly to impress upon President Abbas that "peace can be achieved only through negotiations by recognizing Israel as a Jewish State."[197] Without recognizing Jewish self-determination, which is to say, without accepting Jewish "peoplehood," Israeli Ambassador Ron Prosor insisted, a final settlement with a Palestinian State would never be achieved.[198] Prime Minister Netanyahu would later tell *Die Welt* that President Abbas' was "not the speech of a man who wants peace. It was terrible incitement, full of venom. It wasn't the way that a leader speaks to his people preparing them for peace."[199]

IV. Assessing the Palestinian Applications for Admission to the United Nations: Key Issues and Legal Consequences

The Palestinian applications raise a number of legal questions. This section addresses a few of them. Firstly, it assesses whether the applications can be reconciled with the PLO's substantive obligation of law to negotiate status issues with Israel. Did they challenge and undermine this body of law or complement and facilitate it? Taking the view that there was at least some degree of *prima facie* disconnect between the applications and international law, this section then enquires whether they might nevertheless have been justifiable on the basis that they were countermeasures in response to an internationally wrongful act by Israel. Finally, this section asks whether the applications might be seen as permissible measures by virtue of the legal principle *exceptio non adimpleti contractus* or in light of a material breach by Israel. The answers to these questions are by no means straightforward, and Israel can perhaps just as plausibly argue that the Palestinian applications allowed it to take countermeasures and, indeed, may even have triggered the

195 *See* G.A. Res. 181, U.N. Doc. A/RES/181 (Nov. 29, 1947).

196 *See* U.N. GAOR, *supra* note 192, at 4 (calling for "no less than the independence of the State of Palestine, with East Jerusalem as its capital, on all the Palestinian territory occupied in 1967, living in peace and security alongside the State of Israel, as well as a solution to the refugee issue on the basis of resolution 194(III), in line with the operative part of the Arab Peace Initiative").

197 *Id.* at 5.

198 *See id.* at 6.

199 Cornelius Tittel & Clemens Wergin, *The Palestinians Want a State Without Peace*, Die Welt, Dec. 5, 2012.

application of *exceptio non adimpleti contractus* or amounted to a material breach of the PLO's legal commitments to the Jewish State.

It will be recalled that parties to a dispute have a number of means at their disposal when they seek a peaceful settlement. When they choose to negotiate, whether as a precondition to jurisdiction or as a substantive obligation of law (the violation of which would amount to an internationally wrongful act), the international law of negotiation frames the legal evaluation. Parties' acts and omissions will then be evaluated on a case-by-case basis. To draw from a case currently pending before the ICJ, one can refer to *Obligation to Negotiate Access to the Pacific Ocean (Obligation to Negotiate).*[200] Bolivia, in its application of April 24, 2013, instituting proceedings against Chile, alleges that it has a dispute with Chile that involves the latter's obligation to "negotiate in good faith and effectively with Bolivia in order to reach an agreement granting Bolivia a fully sovereign access to the Pacific Ocean."[201] That part of Bolivia's application that requests the ICJ to adjudge and declare that Chile has an obligation to negotiate "in good faith, promptly, formally, within a reasonable time and effectively,"[202] reflects a common standard of interpretation as to the meaning of negotiation under international law.

Bearing this in mind, it is clear that Israel and the PLO took different views as to how exactly the Palestinian applications related to the bilateral negotiation imperative. The PLO acknowledged that it had chosen negotiation as a means of dispute settlement, but it was unclear exactly what it understood by this obligation, how it sought to comply with it, and what good faith steps it was taking at the time of the applications that might reasonably be said to contribute to a successful outcome. The PLO's Negotiations Affairs Department concluded that the "Palestinian initiative at the United Nations does not contradict, nor is it a substitute for, negotiations. These are parallel paths that complement one another."[203] Yet it is difficult to see how this might be the case given that the PLO was, by its own admission and also in practice, refusing to negotiate with Israel in any meaningful sense.

[200] *See* International Court of Justice, Obligation to Negotiate Access to the Pacific Ocean (Bol. v. Chile), www.icj-cij.org/docket/index.php?p1=3&p2=1&code=bch&case=153&k=f3. On *Obligation to Negotiate* in an "era of transforming sovereignty," see Solon Solomon, *The Case of* Bolivia v. Chile *in an Era of Transforming Sovereignty*, 25(3) FLA. J. INT'L L. 331 (2013).

[201] Application Instituting Proceedings of Bolivia, Obligation to Negotiate Access to the Pacific Ocean (Bol. v. Chile), 2013 I.C.J., at ¶ 1 (Apr. 24). In late-September 2015, the ICJ rejected Chile's preliminary objection and found that it had jurisdiction, on the basis of article 31 of the 1948 Pact of Bogotá, to entertain Bolivia's application. *See* Obligation to Negotiate Access to the Pacific Ocean (Bol. v. Chile) (Preliminary Objection), 2015 I.C.J. (Sept. 24).

[202] Obligation to Negotiate Application, *supra* note 201, at ¶ 32(c).

[203] Palestine Liberation Organization, *supra* note 183. *See* Neve Gordon & Yinon Cohen, *Western Interests, Israeli Unilateralism, and the Two-State Solution,* 41(3) J. PAL. STUD. 6, 8 (2012) (arguing that applying to the United Nations was an attempt by the Palestinians to "alter the existing power imbalance so as to make room for meaningful negotiations"). For Burgis-Kasthala, a Palestinian application represented "one last desperate attempt at re-igniting a more balanced approach to negotiations that would result in a final settlement rather than serve as a cover for continued settlements, fragmentation, and internal political polarization." Michelle Leanne Burgis-Kasthala, *Over-Stating Palestine's UN Membership Bid? An Ethnographic Study on the Narratives of Statehood*, 25(3) EUR. J. INT'L L. 677, 685 (2014). *See* Elgindy, *supra* note 116.

President Abbas, in his address to the General Assembly on September 23, 2011, affirmed "the *option* of negotiating a lasting solution to the conflict in accordance with resolutions of international legitimacy"[204] and conditioned the exercise of this *option* on certain preconditions. The Palestinians were unwilling to negotiate with Israel as a matter of course and did not seem to view this as legally problematic.[205] To be sure, the PLO was "ready to return immediately to the negotiating table on the basis of the adopted terms of reference based on international legitimacy and a complete cessation of settlement activities,"[206] but it would not negotiate with Israel at the present moment. The PLO, then, acted as if negotiations were aspirational (and subject to its preconditions) rather than a substantive obligation of law.

The Palestinian applications seemed to have had two main aims. Firstly, they sought to reorient the legal discourse away from the bilateral negotiation imperative to one that was international in orientation, one that could, the Palestinians hoped, "internationaliz[e ...] the conflict as a legal matter, not only a political one."[207] Consider that both Palestinian applications took place after January 21, 2009, which was when the PLO had lodged a declaration with the International Criminal Court (ICC) that would have recognized ICC jurisdiction over "acts committed on the territory of Palestine since 1 July 2002."[208] When ICC Prosecutor Luis Moreno-Ocampo rejected the Palestinians' ICC declaration in April 2012, he indicated that United Nations recognition of Palestinian statehood would "inform[] the current legal status of Palestine for the interpretation and application of article 12 [of the 1998 Rome Statute of the International Criminal Court]."[209] Admission to the United Nations as a non-member observer State does not as such create a State, but it is undoubtedly a "diplomatic nuance emphasizing

[204] Abbas Statement, *supra* note 125, at 4 (emphasis added).

[205] *See* Saeb Erakat, *Palestine Liberation Organization Legal Brief in Support of Recognition of the State of Palestine, in* PALESTINE MEMBERSHIP IN THE UNITED NATIONS: LEGAL AND PRACTICAL IMPLICATIONS 14, 27 (Mutaz Qafisheh ed., 2013) (contending that Palestinian applications were "consistent with agreements signed between Israel and Palestine, as those agreements envisioned an end to the Israeli occupation of Palestinian land consistent with UN Security Council resolutions 242 and 338").

[206] Abbas Statement, *supra* note 125, at 4.

[207] Mahmoud Abbas, *The Long Overdue Palestinian State*, N.Y. TIMES, May 16, 2011 (continuing by stating that this would "pave the way for us [i.e., the Palestinians] to pursue claims against Israel at the United Nations, human rights treaty bodies and the International Court of Justice"). *See* Valentina Azarov, *An International Legal Demarche for Human Rights? Perils and Prospects of the Palestinian UN Bid*, 18(4–5) INT'L J. HUM. RTS. 527 (2014); Adam G. Yoffie, *The Palestine Problem: The Search for Statehood and the Benefits of International Law*, 36(2) YALE J. INT'L L. 497 (2011).

[208] Palestine, Declaration Recognizing the Jurisdiction of the International Criminal Court, Jan. 21, 2009. On this, see Yaël Ronen, *ICC Jurisdiction over Acts Committed in the Gaza Strip: Article 12(3) of the ICC Statute and Non-State Entities*, 8(1) J. INT'L CRIM. JUST. 3 (2010); Yuval Shany, *In Defence of Functional Interpretation of Article 12(3) of the Rome Statute: A Response to Yaël Ronen*, 8(2) J. INT'L CRIM. JUST. 329 (2010); Alain Pellet, *The Palestinian Declaration and the Jurisdiction of the International Criminal Court*, 8(4) J. INT'L CRIM. JUST. 981 (2010).

[209] International Criminal Court, Situation in Palestine, at ¶ 7, Apr. 3, 2012. *See* Rome Statute of the International Criminal Court, Rome, July 17, 1998, art. 12 (articulating a State-centric understanding of "Preconditions to the Exercise of Jurisdiction").

statehood,"[210] and the Palestinians clearly viewed Moreno-Ocampo's language as an invitation to "internationalize" the dispute, reorienting it away from the negotiation table with Israel so that the PLO could "break bread" with the international community at the ICC, and other international institutions.

The second aim of the Palestinian applications was instrumental. The Palestinians viewed their applications as tactics that would increase their ability to achieve their sought-after objectives without having to negotiate with Israel. The PLO saw the 2011 application as a "positive factor in creating the serious constructive negotiation conditions to bring about fruitful results"[211] and framed the 2012 application as a way to "enhance the chances for peace [... and] salvag[e] the chances for a just peace."[212] By the Palestinians' own admission, then, the applications took place outside of the bilateral negotiation imperative rather than, as international law would have required, necessarily embedded within it. The purpose of these efforts, Schanzer has argued, has been to "force the Israelis to relinquish territory or other meaningful concessions, and to do so outside the scope of bilateral negotiations."[213]

Israel's view of the applications was unmistakable and clear, particularly given that the Palestinians had failed to negotiate status issues with it for an extended period of time when they made their applications. "Israel wants peace with a Palestinian state," Prime Minister Netanyahu proclaimed before the General Assembly on September 23, 2011, "but the Palestinians want a state without peace."[214] In that the bilateral negotiation imperative required Israel to negotiate status issues with the Palestinians, that Israel had already "conceded" a Palestinian State as part of a final settlement, and that the PLO was attempting to achieve some formal trappings of statehood outside of negotiations, there is a good deal of truth in this. It is difficult to see how a party that has agreed to negotiate a dispute can be said to be in compliance with the international law of negotiation when it, in this case, the PLO, openly refuses to engage with this body of law. Some would see this as the open flouting of law.

In his speech to the General Assembly, Prime Minister Netanyahu recognized the salience of settlements (to the Palestinians) but argued that the issue of security

[210] Martin Wählisch, *Beyond a Seat in the United Nations: Palestine's U.N. Membership and International Law*, 53 HARV. INT'L L.J. ONLINE 226, 253 (2012).

[211] Speech by His Excellency President Mahmoud Abbas to the Parliamentary Assembly of the Council of Europe (Oct. 6, 2011), http://unispal.un.org/unispal.nsf/9a798adbf322aff38525617b006d88d7/76dbbd49e69df4ad85257921004624c3?OpenDocument#sthash.0TItkJiK.dpuf (though noting that the PLO would only return to bilateral negotiations "in accordance with a clear reference to international legitimacy and on the basis of a complete cessation of settlement activities").

[212] Abbas Statement, *supra* note 182, at 6. Admission to the United Nations as a non-member observer State would "realign the political process and discourse with international law and lay to rest any questions on the issue of Palestinian statehood." Palestine Liberation Organization, *supra* note 190, at 4.

[213] *The Palestinian Authority's International Criminal Court Gambit: A True Partner for Peace?*, S. Comm. Mid. E. & N. Afr., 114th Cong., at 1 (2015) (Statement of Jonathan Schanzer, Vice President for Research, Foundation for Defense of Democracies).

[214] Netanyahu Statement, *supra* note 126, at 2.

was just as pressing (to Israel). He made the case that both of these issues, *inter alia*, needed to be addressed within negotiations rather than outside of them. Rather than setting preconditions to the resumption of negotiations, as President Abbas had done, Prime Minister Netanyahu pointedly suggested: "We have to stop negotiating about the negotiations. Let's just get on with it. Let's negotiate peace."[215] Arguably, Israel's talk of "painful compromises"[216] was an indication of *prima facie* Israeli good faith with respect to the bilateral negotiation imperative.[217]

The Palestinians, by contrast, insisted upon the end of settlement activities as a precondition to negotiation. They could no more lawfully do this, however, than Israel could do so with respect to its security concerns. Having agreed to settle their dispute through negotiation, both parties were under a substantive obligation of law to engage with this body of law in good faith, and violation of this obligation would amount to an internationally wrongful act. For one party to precondition the resumption of negotiations upon its prior positions having been addressed would be to fall foul of the international law of negotiation. It would be to violate the obligation of ensuring that negotiations are "meaningful, which will not be the case when either of them [i.e., either party to a dispute] insists upon its own position without contemplating any modification of it."[218] Apart from this, there is also a sense that permanent status issues are inherently interrelated and interdependent, which often means that isolating a single one of the issues can make it exceedingly difficult to resolve the dispute as a whole.[219]

States' views as to how the Palestinian applications could be reconciled with the obligation to negotiate ranged from unequivocal support of the applications to a sense of panic and unease, with a majority of statements in the General Assembly in 2012 having been "drafted in a[n] elusive manner, whether due to failure to comprehend the complexities of the matter or in an attempt to appease all sides without undertaking any commitment."[220] At one end of the spectrum was Russia, which fully supported the Palestinians and saw in the 2012 application an "important milestone in reinstating historical equality."[221] Djibouti, speaking for the Organization of Islamic Cooperation, stressed past Israeli–Palestinian negotiations, accused Israel of having acted in bad faith, and lauded the 2012 application

[215] *Id.* at 8.

[216] *Id.* at 7.

[217] "A definite offer to negotiate for the purpose of reaching a settlement or of concluding a Special Agreement certainly testifies to the good will of the party extending such an invitation." Wellens, *supra* note 56, at 259.

[218] North Sea Continental Shelf (F.R.G./Den.) (F.R.G./Neth.), 1969 I.C.J. 3, 47 (Feb. 20).

[219] *See* Manfred Lachs, *The Law and the Settlement of International Disputes, in* Dispute Settlement Through the United Nations 283, 287–88 (K. Venkata Raman ed., 1977) (making this point generally about negotiated settlements).

[220] Ronen, *supra* note 185, at 13. The international community's split as to how the Palestinian application of 2012 could be reconciled with the PLO's obligation to negotiate largely mirrored the debates in the Security Council of less than a year earlier. The Admission Report addressed this dynamic. *See* Admission Report, *supra* note 151, at ¶¶ 6–7.

[221] U.N. GAOR, at 5, U.N. Doc. A/67/PV.45 (Nov. 29, 2012).

as a "step closer to achieving a sustainable solution on the basis of two States living side by side in peace and security."[222] Namibia rejected the idea that the Palestinian application was counterproductive, particularly given that substantive negotiations had not taken place in recent years.[223] Brazil threw its support behind President Abbas and saw him as acting as "part of a peaceful and multilateral approach, one that is fully consistent with Security Council and General Assembly resolutions."[224] China supported Resolution 67/19,[225] as did the United Arab Emirates, which interpreted the Palestinian move as an "important step towards settling the Palestinian question and consolidating Palestinians' right to self-determination [...] an historic opportunity to overcome the political crisis and the no-peace situation that has resulted from Israel's continued occupation of Palestinian lands."[226] Other States saw the Palestinian application as "help[ing] to preserve the two-State solution"[227] and "provid[ing] a vigorous impetus, in the end, to make the long yearned-for comprehensive solution to the conflict on the basis of two States a reality."[228] Iran conveyed the NAM's view that Resolution 67/19 would "positively contribute to salvaging the prospects for peace."[229] Norway, which had played such a crucial role in the process that began in Oslo, explained its affirmative vote as follows: Resolution 67/19 "does not prejudge the outcomes of final status negotiations between the parties. Neither does it violate the Oslo Accords. The Palestinians have a legitimate right to take this step, based on the right of the Palestinian people to self-determination."[230]

The European Union struggled to coherently respond to the Palestinian application in 2012 given its Member States' deep divisions. France argued that its affirmative vote on Resolution 67/19 was a vote in favor of "two States for two peoples,"[231] but the idea that the Palestinians had accepted Jewish "peoplehood" and self-determination is difficult to sustain, a point that Israel made quite clear a few minutes earlier in the General Assembly.[232] The United Kingdom had sought

[222] *Id.* at 12.
[223] *See id.* at 26.
[224] *Id.* at 18.
[225] *See id.* at 13.
[226] *Id.* at 16–17.
[227] *Id.* at 3 (Costa Rica).
[228] *Id.* at 4 (Mexico).
[229] *Id.* at 10.
[230] U.N. GAOR, *supra* note 192, at 21.
[231] *Id.* at 13.
[232] Ambassador Prosor put it thus: "In fact, I did not hear President Abbas use the phrase 'two States for two peoples' this afternoon. In fact, I have never heard him say the phrase 'two States for two peoples', because the Palestinian leadership has never recognized that Israel is the nation State of the Jewish people. They have never been willing to accept what this very body recognized 65 years ago—Israel is the Jewish State. In fact, today he asked the world to recognize a Palestinian State, but he still refused to recognize the Jewish State. Not only does he not recognize the Jewish State, he is also trying to erase Jewish history. This year, he even tried to erase the connection between the Jewish people and Jerusalem. He said that Jews were trying to alter the historical character of Jerusalem. He said that we are trying to 'Judaize Jerusalem.'" U.N. GAOR, *supra* note 192, at 6.

a Palestinian assurance that it would resume negotiations with Israel without preconditions after the vote, but not having received this assurance, it abstained.[233] The Netherlands worried that Resolution 67/19 "could complicate efforts to resume direct negotiations between the parties."[234] Bulgaria and Hungary both abstained, the former out of concern for the "possible adverse impact of the resolution on the prospect for an early resumption of negotiations,"[235] the latter due to its sense of "possible negative consequences that could result from the adoption of today's resolution."[236] The Czech Republic voted against Resolution 67/19, for similar reasons,[237] and Germany abstained out of fear that the Palestinian application would be deleterious to the bilateral negotiation imperative.[238] By contrast, Greece and Austria saw their votes in favor of Resolution 67/19 as facilitative of a two-State solution and the resumption of negotiations without preconditions.[239] Given these deep divisions in the European Union, it is not altogether surprising that High Representative Catherine Ashton's statement shortly before the vote merely reiterated the European Union's readiness to recognize a State of Palestine "when appropriate."[240]

A number of States outside of the European Union objected to the 2012 application primarily due to its timing: the application had been lodged in the absence of a final peace settlement, or even, some would argue, a reasonable prospect of one. Japan, which voted in favor of Resolution 67/19, warned the Palestinians against acceding to international organizations since this "might negatively affect the prospects for the resumption of negotiations."[241] South Korea explained its abstention on the vote out of a concern for potentially adverse consequences for the bilateral negotiation imperative,[242] a view that Australia also shared.[243] Canada opposed Resolution 67/19 "in the strongest of terms"[244] because, in its view, the Palestinian application challenged the bilateral negotiation imperative and undermined the chances of a successful settlement.[245] The United States' view on the

[233] *See id.* at 14–15.
[234] U.N. GAOR, *supra* note 221, at 2.
[235] U.N. GAOR, *supra* note 192, at 16.
[236] *Id.* at 19.
[237] *See id.* at 19–20.
[238] *See id.* at 15.
[239] *See id.* at 19 (Greece), 19 (Austria).
[240] Declaration by the High Representative on Behalf of the European Union on the Middle East Peace Process, Brussels, No. 16079/12, Nov. 29, 2012 (recalling the Berlin Declaration on the Middle East Peace Process of March 1999). The actual language in the Berlin Declaration on the Middle East Peace Process of March 1999 was that the European Union "declare[d] its readiness to consider the recognition of a Palestinian State in due course in accordance with the basic principles referred to above." Letter Dated 26 March 1999 from the Permanent Representative of Germany to the United Nations Addressed to the Secretary-General, Annex at 2, 2, U.N. Doc. A/54/76 (Mar. 26, 1999) (Berlin Declaration on the Middle East Peace Process).
[241] U.N. GAOR, *supra* note 221, at 3.
[242] *See id.* at 6.
[243] *See* U.N. GAOR, *supra* note 192, at 20.
[244] *Id.* at 8.
[245] *See id.* at 8–9.

Palestinian application was well known, and its statement in the General Assembly immediately after the adoption of Resolution 67/19 stunned no one.[246] In voting against Resolution 67/19, Ambassador Susan Rice made the case that the Palestinian application was both prejudicial and "unfortunate and counterproductive."[247] Thus, the international community was split as to how the Palestinian application of 2012 could be reconciled with the PLO's obligation to negotiate status issues with Israel.

Those in favor of the Palestinian applications might be tempted to refer to *Wall* to support their argument that the applications did not offend the obligation to negotiate. In *Wall*, the ICJ had to address the view that its exercise of jurisdiction would impede, undermine, or complicate the chances of a successful negotiated settlement between Israel and the PLO.[248] It rejected this objection, finding that the potential effect of an advisory opinion, be it favorable or unfavorable, was unclear and speculative and that the argument against the ICJ's exercise of jurisdiction on this basis was not "compelling."[249] The ICJ held that it was "not clear [...] what influence the Court's opinion might have on those negotiations [i.e., the Roadmap negotiations]: participants in the present proceedings have expressed differing views in this regard."[250] That the ICJ equivocated in favor of exercising jurisdiction in *Wall* is not to say that PLO support for the request for an advisory opinion did not impede, undermine, or complicate the bilateral negotiation imperative. It could very well be said to have done so and, what is more, to have breached the PLO's substantive obligation of law to negotiate with Israel, but this was not at issue in the case. In moving forward with the request for an advisory opinion, the ICJ was merely concluding that, in its view, the procedural objection to its exercise of jurisdiction had not been met.

Since the Palestinian applications of 2011 and 2012—which, it will be recalled, President Abbas had lodged purportedly and assertedly as the leader of a *State*—took place outside of negotiations with Israel and in such a way that it might reasonably have been predicted would have had a preclusive effect on a final settlement or (at the very least) to have made the achievement of such a settlement more difficult to attain, there appears to have been at least some degree of *prima facie* disconnect between the applications and the PLO's substantive obligation of law to negotiate with Israel. Former ICJ Judge Bedjaoui, speaking within the context of good faith negotiations with a view to nuclear disarmament, made the point in 2008 that a "manifestly unjustified breaking off of negotiations is radically incompatible with good faith,"[251] and it would seem that the same can be said of

[246] *See id.* at 13.
[247] *Id.*
[248] *See* Wall, *supra* note 55, at 159–60.
[249] *Id.* at 160.
[250] *Id.*
[251] Judge Mohammed Bedjaoui, Keynote Address at Good Faith, International Law, and Elimination of Nuclear Weapons Conference, Geneva, at 24 (May 1, 2008), http://lcnp.org/disarmament/2008May01eventBedjaoui.pdf.

the Palestinian applications. The conclusion, then, is that the Palestinian applications were internationally wrongful.

This raises the question whether the wrongfulness of the Palestinian applications vis-à-vis the international law of negotiation (as *lex generalis*) and the bilateral negotiation imperative (as *lex specialis*) was nonetheless precluded on some legal basis. Theoretically, there would seem to have been three potential bases for this, namely that the applications amounted to: countermeasures in response to an internationally wrongful act by Israel; actions taken within the context of *exceptio non adimpleti contractus*; or a suspension or termination of the bilateral negotiation imperative in light of a material breach by Israel.[252] Although these three potential justifications are distinct, they would all have required that the applications had been a response to an Israeli internationally wrongful act, with the caveat that the "materiality of the breach is a threshold [for the material breach regime], implying that suspension (or termination) is simply not allowed for non-material breaches."[253]

There is no question that the PLO framed the applications within the context of what it argued were ongoing internationally wrongful acts by Israel. Palestinian Ambassador Riyad H. Mansour, for example, speaking in the Security Council at the time of the 2011 application, argued that bilateral negotiations had been "undermined, obstructed and stalled as a direct result of Israel's intransigence, its egregious violations of international law and human rights and its refusal to commit to the most basic principles and parameters essential for the achievement of a just and lasting peace."[254] In his address to the General Assembly in autumn 2012, President Abbas charged Israel with "emptying the Oslo Accords of their meaning,"[255] making their implementation "extremely difficult if not completely impossible,"[256] and engaging in "violations of international law and covenants."[257] The PLO Negotiations Affairs Department, which has completed numerous studies documenting alleged Israeli violations of the bilateral negotiation imperative,[258] released a study in July 2011 that concluded that while the Palestinians had fully complied with their international legal obligations "Israel [had] systematically

[252] *See* Chapter 5, section IV.

[253] Filippo Fontanelli, *The Invocation of the Exception of Non-Performance: A Case-Study on the Role and Application of General Principles of International Law of Contractual Origin*, 1(1) CAMBRIDGE J. INT'L & COMP. L. 119, 133 (2012).

[254] U.N. SCOR, *supra* note 150, at 6.

[255] Abbas Statement, *supra* note 182, at 3.

[256] *Id.*

[257] *Id.* at 4.

[258] *See, e.g.*, Palestine Liberation Organization, Negotiations Affairs Department, Oslo Process: 20 Years of Oslo: 1993–2013 (Sept. 12, 2013), www.nad-plo.org/userfiles/file/New%20Publications/OSLOPROCESS_PUBLICATION_2013.pdf. The general tenor of these studies was more or less along the lines of what Palestinian Ambassador Nasser Al-Kidwa stated in the General Assembly a decade and a half before the 2011 and 2012 applications: "The Israeli Government has violated everything: international law, relevant Security Council resolutions, resolutions of the tenth special session of the General Assembly, the agreements reached between the two parties and, finally, the very bases of the peace process." U.N. GAOR, at 32, U.N. Doc. A/52/PV.16 (Sept. 29, 1997).

violated its obligations by undertaking unilateral actions that violate all signed agreements."[259] PLO position papers from October 2011 and November 2012 also contended that Israel had violated its legal obligations to the Palestinian people.[260] Ashrawi condemned Israeli actions by stating that "Israel treats Oslo selectively, like a box of chocolates: it picks and chooses what it wants, and totally disregards the rest."[261] Erekat put forward the official Palestinian view that Israel's actions amounted to the "denial of a clearly recognized right of self-determination and gross violations of internationally recognized human rights and humanitarian law."[262] Clearly, then, the Palestinians viewed Israel as being in violation of international law at the time of the 2011 and 2012 applications.[263]

To have qualified as permissible countermeasures, however, the Palestinian applications would also have had to have complied with, *inter alia*, the object and limits of countermeasures[264] (in particular the requirement that countermeasures can only be taken as inducements to compliance[265] and must, "as far as possible, be taken in such a way as to permit the resumption of performance of the obligations in question")[266] and have been "commensurate with the injury suffered, taking into account the gravity of the internationally wrongful act and the rights in question."[267] The PLO did provide notice to Israel in the run-up to the Palestinian applications of 2011 and 2012, but it did not offer to negotiate with it as the law requires,[268] and it is doubtful that the Palestinian applications could have qualified as "urgent countermeasures [...] necessary to preserve its [i.e., the PLO's] rights"[269] since these must involve immediate threats to rights comparable to the electronic withdrawal of funds from a bank.[270] Israel's acts in the run-up to

[259] Palestine Liberation Organization, Negotiations Office, Recognizing the Palestinian State on the 1967 Border & Admission of Palestine as a Full Member of the United Nations, at 3 (July 2011), www.nad-plo.org/userfiles/file/fact%20sheet/who%20and%20why%20recognize%20Palestine%20 Factsheet%20-%20english%20July%202011_pdf.pdf.

[260] *See* Palestine Liberation Organization, Negotiations Affairs Department, Palestine's Application for UN Membership (Oct. 2011), www.nad-plo.org/etemplate.php?id=303; Palestine Liberation Organization, Negotiations Affairs Department, Palestine's Enhancement of Status at the UN (Nov. 2012), www.nad-plo.org/print.php?id=365.

[261] Rashid Khalidi, *Interview with Hanan Ashrawi: Oslo, the PA, and Reinventing the PLO,* 44(1) J. PAL. STUD. 76, 76 (2014).

[262] Erakat, *supra* note 205, at 24.

[263] This section assumes, *arguendo*, that Israel was in violation of international law at the time of the 2011 and 2012 applications. It is not necessary to reach a definitive conclusion on this point, however, since, as this section suggests, the Palestinian applications otherwise seemed to have failed as permissible responses under international law. *Cf.* Archer Daniels Midland Co. and Tate & Lyle Ingredients Americas, Inc. v. Mex., at ¶¶ 181–84, I.C.S.I.D. Case No. ARB(AF)/04/05 (2007).

[264] *See* Articles on Responsibility of States for Internationally Wrongful Acts, With Commentaries, *in* International Law Commission, 2(2) Y.B. Int'l L. Comm'n 30, 129, art. 49, U.N. Doc. A/CN.4/ SER.A/2001/Add.1 (Part 2) (2001).

[265] *See id.* at 129, art. 49(1).

[266] *Id.* at 129, art. 49(3).

[267] *Id.* at 134, art. 51.

[268] *See id.* at 135, art. 52(1)(b).

[269] *Id.* at 135, art. 52(2).

[270] *See id.* at 136.

the 2011 and 2012 applications did not immediately threaten Palestinian rights in a way that was temporally comparable to the electronic withdrawal of funds from a bank. Indeed, the PLO went to great lengths to stress the extended nature of Israel's alleged violations of international law.

At this point, it may be useful to refer to *Archer Daniels Midland Co. (ADM) and Tate & Lyle Ingredients Americas, Inc., (TLIA) v. Mexico (ADM and TLIA)* (2007), an arbitral award that found that a Mexican excise tax on certain syrups and soft drinks was an impermissible countermeasure to an allegedly internationally wrongful act by the United States.[271] The Arbitral Tribunal in *ADM and TLIA* held that "substantial evidence supporting inducement [on the part of Mexico, in adopting the particular tax at issue,]"[272] was absent and looked at Mexican statements issued just prior to the tax's adoption to get a sense of context and an indication of Mexican intent.[273] Apart from the question of inducement, the Arbitral Tribunal also concluded that the tax was disproportionate to the allegedly internationally wrongful act.[274] A similar train of thought can be applied to the argument that the Palestinian applications were permissible countermeasures.

Because they were lodged, quite calculatedly, in defiance of negotiations with Israel, it is difficult to see how the Palestinian applications can be properly seen as inducements to Israeli compliance. Hence, Palestinian insistence that the applications would "safeguard the internationally-endorsed two-State solution and provide a framework for negotiations with clear parameters, so that all final status issues can be resolved through direct negotiations with Israel,"[275] rings rather hollow. Furthermore, if the Palestinian applications were meant to have made Palestinian self-determination more meaningful, which is itself quite doubtful,[276] they effectively did so, it could be argued, by making Jewish self-determination more tenuous, and a final settlement less likely.

Israel, of course, saw the Palestinian applications as affronts to international legality and rejected the notion that their wrongfulness could be precluded on the basis that they were permissible countermeasures.[277] Israel responded to the two

[271] ADM and TLIA, *supra* note 263. This conclusion was rendered on the basis of customary international law. *See id.* at ¶¶ 113–23.

[272] *Id.* at ¶ 150.

[273] *See id.* at ¶¶ 134–51.

[274] *See id.* at ¶¶ 152–60.

[275] Palestine Liberation Organization, *supra* note 190, at 2.

[276] *See* Richard Falk, *Foreword, in* Aborted State?, *supra* note 181, at 10, 16–17. Writing within the context of the 2011 application, Khalidi commented that "the state of Palestine is not now and will not soon become a real state in any meaningful sense of that word." Rashid Khalidi, *On the Possible Recognition of a Palestinian State at the United Nations, in* Aborted State?, *supra* note 181, at 25, 25. United States Ambassador Rice argued in the General Assembly on the day of Resolution 67/19's adoption that: "Progress towards a just and lasting two-State solution cannot be made by pressing a green voting button here in this Hall, nor does adopting any resolution create a State where none indeed exists or change the reality on the ground." U.N. GAOR, *supra* note 192, at 13.

[277] "Palestinian unilateral action in the United Nations breaches the Oslo Accords, the Interim Agreements, the Paris Protocol and other bilateral agreements that form the basis of 40 spheres of Israeli-Palestinian cooperation, all of which could be jeopardized by unilateral action at the United

applications by withholding tax revenue that it was otherwise required to have transferred to the Palestinian Authority.[278] At a meeting on November 21, 2011, United Nations Special Coordinator for the Middle East Peace Process and Personal Representative of the Secretary-General Robert Serry informed the Security Council that Israel was withholding some $100 million of tax revenue per month, amounting to two-thirds of the Palestinian Authority's annual revenue, in response to the 2011 application (to UNESCO).[279] Special Coordinator and Personal Representative Serry worried that this would undermine the Palestinian Authority's ability to provide services to the Palestinian people and uphold the rule of law,[280] and Quartet Representative Tony Blair expressed a similar concern two days later.[281] Oscar Fernandez-Taranco, United Nations Assistant Secretary-General for Political Affairs, reported to the Security Council a month later that Israel had decided to transfer the frozen tax revenue to the Palestinian Authority.[282]

In response to the adoption of Resolution 67/19, Israel froze just over $100 million of tax revenue (in December 2012 and January 2013), though it did eventually release these funds.[283] There were also developments with respect to planning permission and zoning for settlements.[284] At his weekly Cabinet meeting on December 2, 2012, Prime Minister Netanyahu made clear Israel's response to Resolution 67/19: "Today we are building and we will continue to build in Jerusalem and in all areas that are on the map of the strategic interests of the State of Israel."[285] Since Israel has always viewed settlements as a permanent status issue, however, and not as such unlawful in the absence of a final settlement, it is difficult to see how these developments might be interpreted as a countermeasure *stricto sensu*. In summary, rather than having "compell[ed] its [i.e., Israel's] compliance with

Nations." U.N. SCOR, *supra* note 150, at 11 (Israel). *See* Israel Ministry of Foreign Affairs, Behind the Headlines: The Dangers of Premature Recognition of a Palestinian State (June 8, 2011), www.mfa.gov.il/mfa/foreignpolicy/issues/pages/the%20dangers%20of%20premature%20recognition%20of%20a%20palestinian%20state-15-jun-2011.aspx. The Israelis viewed Resolution 67/19, and the Palestinian application that had led the way to it, as a "gross violation of the Palestinian's [*sic*] commitment not to go to the UN and to resolve issues through peace negotiations. This now has all been swept aside and of course we have to protect our vital interests, and so we're doing that. But the fact that the Palestinians tore to shreds their commitments under the Oslo Accords and went to the UN unilaterally is somehow dismissed." "*The Palestinians,*" *supra* note 199.

278 *See* Eden, *supra* note 155, at 234–39.

279 *See* U.N. SCOR, at 3, U.N. Doc. S/PV.6662 (Nov. 21, 2011). *See also* Barak Ravid, *Israel to Keep Holding Palestinian Authority Funds, Against Advice of Security Officials*, HAARETZ, Nov. 14, 2011.

280 *See* U.N. SCOR, *supra* note 279.

281 *See* Office of the Quartet Representative, Quartet Rep Tony Blair Urges the Israeli Government to Release Palestinian Tax Revenue Without Delay, Nov. 23, 2011, www.tonyblairoffice.org/news/entry/tony-blair-urges-the-israeli-government-to-release-palestinian-funds/.

282 *See* U.N. SCOR, at 2, U.N. Doc. S/PV.6692 (Dec. 20, 2011). *See also* Joel Greenberg, *Israel to Release Withheld Tax Funds to Palestinians*, WASH. POST, Nov. 30, 2011.

283 *See* Status of Palestine, *supra* note 184, at 4. *See also id.* at 6.

284 *See* British Israel Communications & Research Centre, *Israel Announces Response to Palestinian UN Vote*, Dec. 3, 2012, www.bicom.org.uk/news-article/10649/?print.

285 Israel Ministry of Foreign Affairs, Cabinet Communique (Dec. 2, 2012), http://mfa.gov.il/MFA/PressRoom/2012/Pages/Cabinet-communiqu%C3%A9-2-December%202012.aspx.

international law"[286] or acted as a "source of positive pressure to steer the peace process back in the right direction,"[287] the Palestinian applications only seemed to have exacerbated the gap between the two sides.[288]

As to whether the Palestinian applications amounted to actions taken within the context of *exceptio non adimpleti contractus*, this is a rather complicated matter. It will be recalled that *exceptio non adimpleti contractus* focuses on "non-performance of an obligation inscribed in a framework of reciprocal obligations."[289] At root, the bilateral negotiation imperative requires good faith. Without it, it is unlikely that Israel and the PLO will adopt the reciprocal trade-offs necessary to move the dispute to sustainable peace. The problem that arises when analyzing the Palestinian applications within this context, however, is that the Palestinians never argued that their applications were the non-performance of a legal obligation. Quite to the contrary, in fact, the PLO consistently argued that its applications fully complied with international law and were supported by it. Hence, it is difficult to be persuaded by *exceptio non adimpleti contractus* in the case of the Palestinian applications since the Palestinians themselves did not even view their conduct as the non-performance of a legal obligation.

Despite assertions at the time of the Palestinian applications (by the PLO) that "Israel ha[d] violated all of the agreements that it ha[d] signed with the PLO, including the DOP [i.e., the Declaration of Principles] and the Interim Agreement,"[290] and (by Israel) that Resolution 67/19 "violate[d] fundamental binding commitments,"[291] neither side claimed that the other had materially breached the bilateral negotiation imperative, and this is significant.[292] Neither side, in other words, claimed that the other party's actions had amounted to a material breach in the sense of article 60 of the VCLT, that is, in the context of a bilateral treaty, a "repudiation of the treaty not sanctioned by the present Convention; or [... t]he violation of a provision essential to the accomplishment of the object or purpose of the treaty."[293]

[286] Palestine Liberation Organization, *supra* note 183. *See* Howard LaFranchi, *Israeli Envoy Calls Divisive Settlement Plan a Politically Necessary Reprisal*, Christian Sci. Monitor, Dec. 11, 2012.

[287] Palestine Liberation Organization, Enhancement of Status, *supra* note 260.

[288] Of course, Israel's response to the Palestinian applications, assuming that the Palestinian applications were unlawful in the first place, would also have had to have complied with the requirements for permissible countermeasures. *See, e.g.*, Articles on State Responsibility, *supra* note 264, at 131, art. 50(1)(b) (stating that countermeasures "shall not affect [...] obligations for the protection of fundamental human rights").

[289] Fontanelli, *supra* note 253, at 128.

[290] Erakat, *supra* note 205, at 28.

[291] U.N. GAOR, *supra* note 192, at 7.

[292] To be sure, there were rumblings on both sides in the run-up to the applications to the effect that they would mark the end of the bilateral negotiation imperative, but these ceased in official circles in the actual wake of the applications. *See* Khaled Abu Toameh, *Fatah: Oslo Accords Will Cease to Exist After UN Bid*, Jerusalem Post, Nov. 8, 2012; Harriet Sherwood, *Israel Warns Palestinians All Deals Are Off if UN Vote Goes Ahead*, Guardian, June 17, 2011.

[293] VCLT, *supra* note 73, at art. 60(3)(a)–(b). This is not to say that Israel could not have pressed a plausible case with respect to material breach. *See, e.g.*, Alan Baker, Ten Points Regarding the

Given its sweeping implications, international law is reluctant to recognize material breach in the first place, and it categorically rejects the application of the material breach regime when a party that could potentially raise it does not do so, whether expressly or by implication. Conduct can imply suspension or termination, but there is a considerable threshold that must be met, and "conduct may be construed as an implicit denunciation only if it clearly demonstrates the intent of the party concerned to [suspend or] terminate the treaty."[294] Thus, it is doubtful that the Palestinian applications can be interpreted as either permissible responses to an Israeli material breach or the PLO's suspension or termination of the bilateral negotiation imperative.[295] Watson's point retains its validity: "although each side claims the other has violated Oslo, neither side has purported to terminate Oslo, and indeed each claims to be abiding by the Accords. The parties have continued with Oslo because it is, ultimately, in their interests to do so."[296]

Fundamental Breach by the Palestinians of the Oslo Accords, Jerusalem Center for Public Affairs (Jan. 5, 2015), http://jcpa.org/ten-points-breach-palestinians-oslo-accords/#sthash.tuC7Z8fB.dpuf; Dan Diker, *Palestinian Unilateralism and Israel's Rights in Arab-Israeli Diplomacy*, in ISRAEL'S RIGHTS AS A NATION-STATE IN INTERNATIONAL DIPLOMACY 115 (Alan Baker ed., 2011). In fact, in a leaked confidential memorandum dated March 2009 from the PLO's Negotiations Affairs Department, the Palestinians' legal team seemed to be well aware of this possibility, at least with respect to the Palestinian Declaration Recognizing the Jurisdiction of the International Criminal Court of January 21, 2009. *See* Memorandum from the Negotiations Support Unit of the Negotiations Affairs Department, Palestine Liberation Organization, to Palestinian Leadership on Legal Approaches to be Advanced at the ICC in Order to Protect Overall Palestinian Strategy and Realize Palestinian Rights and Interests, at 4 (Mar. 25, 2009), http://thepalestinepapers.com/files/4494.pdf. The same argument would seem to apply, *mutatis mutandis*, to Resolution 67/19.

294 Amoco Int'l Fin. Corp. v. Iran et al., Case No. 56 (Partial Award) (1987) (Iran-U.S. Cl. Trib.), 83 I.L.R. 500, 537 (1990).

295 That the Chair of the Ad Hoc Liaison Committee maintained in September 2014 that outside economic cooperation with Israel and the Palestinian Authority would continue as long as neither side materially breached its obligations, which, of course, implies that neither side was then in material breach of its obligations, may be seen as further evidence of the absence of material breach associated with the Palestinian applications. *See* Norway Ministry of Foreign Affairs, Opening Address at the AHLC Meeting in New York (Sept. 22, 2014), www.regjeringen.no/en/aktuelt/ahlc-meeting/id2001147/.

296 WATSON, *supra* note 51, at 250 (though articulating this over a decade before the Palestinian applications). *See also* Office of the Quartet, Report for the Meeting of the Ad-Hoc Liaison Committee on Action in Support of Palestinian State-Building, at 4 (Sept. 30, 2015) (making the point that, "with successive negotiations falling short of a final status agreement, the parties continued to apply this agreement [i.e., the Interim Agreement], albeit selectively, inconsistently, and often poorly. Presently, more than two decades since the start of the Oslo process and in the absence of an achievable alternative, the parties remain tied to this framework"). Of course, whether it is ultimately in the interests of Israel and the PLO to continue with "Oslo" is a debatable point. Despite some speculation to the contrary, President Abbas' September 2015 address to the General Assembly was arguably too equivocal to have amounted to a renunciation of the Oslo bargain, though it did go "to the brink." *See* Abbas Statement, *supra* note 134. *See also* Rick Gladstone & Jodi Rudoren, *Mahmoud Abbas, at U.N., Says Palestinians Are No Longer Bound by Oslo Accords*, N.Y. TIMES, Sept. 30, 2015; Elliott Abrams, *Abbas's "Bombshell,"* WEEKLY STANDARD, Sept. 30, 2015; Barak Ravid, *Was It a Bombshell or Stink Bomb that Abbas Dropped in His UN Speech?*, HAARETZ, Sept. 30, 2015. Prime Minister Netanyahu issued a statement shortly after President Abbas' speech that condemned it and reiterated Israel's call for negotiations without preconditions. *See* Prime Minister's Office, Response of PM Netanyahu's Office to Abu Mazen's Speech (Sept. 30, 2015), http://www.pmo.gov.il/English/MediaCenter/Spokesman/Pages/spokeResponse300915.aspx.

V. Conclusion

Given the fact that negotiation involves colorable claims in competition, it is perhaps to be expected that this chapter's evaluation leads to conclusions that are partial and indecisive in the absence of a final settlement. This is the case, as well, with respect to countermeasures and other responses, not least because "clear statements explaining which unilateral self-help measure a state actually relies on in a particular instance are rarely advanced at the time."[297] The bilateral negotiation imperative may be too much for Israel and the PLO to bear, or it may not. At least in part, one's view of this reflects one's policy preference, and it would probably be asking too much to think that the law could fully insulate itself from this.[298]

Despite this interplay between law and politics, it would be wise to recall an important point that Judge Higgins made in *Wall*. She observed that it was not the separation barrier as such that stymied Palestinian self-determination. Rather, the "real impediment is[, or was,] the apparent inability and/or unwillingness of both Israel and Palestine to move in parallel to secure the necessary conditions."[299] Similarly, the Palestinian applications of autumn 2011 and autumn 2012 no more facilitate a sustainable settlement than Israel's withholding of tax revenue to the Palestinian Authority or the presence of Jews beyond the 1949 armistices lines impedes it. It is the failure to engage with the bilateral negotiation imperative that does this, as much for reasons of policy as for considerations of law.

[297] James Crawford, State Responsibility: The General Part 676 (2014) (making this point with respect to countermeasures in particular).

[298] *Cf.* Edward W. Said, *The Burdens of Interpretation and the Question of Palestine,* 16(1) J. Pal. Stud. 29, 30 (1986) (claiming that "there is no neutrality, there can be no neutrality or objectivity about Palestine. This is not to say, on the other hand, that all positions are equal, or that all perspectives are as heavily or as lightly invested. But it is to say that so ideologically saturated is the question of Palestine, so manifestly present is it to most people who come to deal with it, that even a superficial or cursory apprehension of it involves a position taken, an interest defended, a claim or a right asserted. There is no indifference, no objectivity, no neutrality because there is simply no room for them in a space that is as crowded and overdetermined as this one").

[299] Wall, *supra* note 55, at 214 (Higgins, J., separate) (identifying these "necessary conditions" as, "at one and the same time, for Israel to withdraw from Arab occupied territory and for Palestine to provide the conditions to allow Israel to feel secure in so doing").

7

Conclusion

For all of international law's focus on the peaceful settlement of disputes, it is not altogether clear how the intervention of outside actors actually contributes to peace settlements. This is not only the case with respect to the Israeli–Palestinian dispute. Consider remarks that a number of MPs recently made in the House of Commons about the 1998 Agreement Reached in the Multi-Party Negotiations (Belfast Agreement).[1] The debate related to a motion, adopted on a majority of 274 to 12, which resolved that "the Government should recognise the state of Palestine alongside the state of Israel, as a contribution to securing a negotiated two state solution."[2] Mark Durkan MP, who lauded the international community's role in bringing together nationalist and unionist parties in Northern Ireland, argued that "it is not in the parties' gift to do all the giving; that is where responsible international input can create some givens and new realities."[3] By contrast, the MP Ian Paisley, Jr, warned against the conceit of outside arrogance, cautioning Parliament (or, in the case of the Israeli–Palestinian dispute, one might say the international community) not to "assume that it has the right to tell people how to sort out their peace processes, when it knows that there is a better way."[4] "[P]articipants," he continued, "have to find their way; they cannot be told, lectured or dictated to on what is the best way."[5] The practical effect of "good intentions," in other words, might not always be as planned, or as effective as anticipated.

Over the years, for over a century now, the international community has adopted a number of approaches to the Palestine question. Nearly every body of the United Nations (and related international organizations), many non-governmental organizations, and certainly every State have attempted, in ways both significant and slight, to steer the conversation in particular directions. Between the two world wars, the Mandate for Palestine acted as the international community's endorsed dispensation. The United Kingdom's administration of it was roundly criticized, for either fulfilling the Mandate's terms or ignoring them. It was during this time, too, that self-determination and a distinct national identity for Palestinian Arabs *qua* Palestinian Arabs remained *in statu nascendi*, though the International Court

[1] *See* Agreement Reached in the Multi-Party Negotiations, Belfast, Apr. 10, 1998.

[2] 586(40) HANSARD, at col. 130 (Oct. 13, 2014).

[3] *Id.* at col. 117.

[4] *Id.* at col. 89.

[5] *Id.*

of Justice (ICJ) would come to recognize the former as being of an "*erga omnes* character [... and] one of the essential principles of contemporary international law"[6] and observe in 2004 that "the existence of a 'Palestinian people' is no longer in issue."[7] A variety of means of dispute settlement were attempted between the 1948 War and the 1973 War, ranging from inquiry to mediation to conciliation, with the United Nations Security Council deciding in 1973 that, "immediately and concurrently with the cease-fire, negotiations shall start between the parties concerned under appropriate auspices aimed at establishing a just and durable peace in the Middle East."[8] By 1993, this generalized negotiation imperative had evolved to include a specifically bilateral negotiation imperative between Israel and the Palestine Liberation Organization (PLO). Nearly two decades later, the PLO approached the United Nations in a series of admission applications (in autumn 2011 and autumn 2012). As with all other acts and omissions of Israel and the PLO *inter se* since 1993, these applications can be evaluated according to negotiation as a substantive obligation of law. The dispute remains ongoing, seemingly unabated.

One of the challenges that an international lawyer faces when evaluating an ongoing dispute such as the one between Israel and the PLO is that neither the law as applied nor the acts and omissions of the parties to it are static. When parties choose to negotiate their dispute, as in the Israeli–Palestinian case, a process of dynamic communication ensues, with disagreements being resolved, or so it might be hoped, through "agreed adjustments or unilateral acquiescences."[9] As a general matter, international law looks favorably upon negotiated settlements (absent a conflict with *ordre public international*),[10] but during the actual process of negotiation, it can be difficult to draw dispositive conclusions with respect to legal rights and wrongs. And it hardly clarifies matters to point out, as the ICJ recently did, that "the absence of a court or tribunal with jurisdiction to resolve disputes about compliance with a particular obligation under international law does not affect the existence and binding force of that obligation."[11] The absence of such a court or tribunal "merely" reorients the discussion to questions of who, or what, speaks *for* international law.[12]

[6] East Timor (Port. v. Austl.), 1995 I.C.J. 90, 102 (June 30).

[7] Legal Consequences of the Construction of a Wall in the Occupied Palestinian Territory, Advisory Opinion, 2004 I.C.J. 136, 182–83 (July 9).

[8] S.C. Res. 338, at ¶ 3, U.N. Doc. S/RES/338 (Oct. 22, 1973).

[9] W. Michael Reisman, *The Diversity of Contemporary International Dispute Resolution: Functions and Policies*, 4(1) J. INT'L DISP. SETTLEMENT 47, 47 (2013) (making this point within the context of commercial disputes).

[10] *Cf.* R.P. ANAND, INTERNATIONAL COURTS AND CONTEMPORARY CONFLICTS 372 (1974) (noting that: "As is well known, in the international field the will of the parties is law, and the courts will give effect to it even if it is in derogation of customary principles of law unless, of course, it is of an immoral character or runs counter to universally recognized principles of international law of an absolutely binding character").

[11] Application of the Convention on the Prevention and Punishment of the Crime of Genocide (Croat. v. Serb.), 2015 I.C.J., at ¶ 86 (Feb. 3).

[12] Not to mention what international law is *for*. *See* Martti Koskenniemi, *What Is International Law For?*, *in* INTERNATIONAL LAW 29 (Malcolm D. Evans ed., 4th ed. 2014).

Although this difficulty in drawing dispositive conclusions during ongoing negotiations applies to international law norms generally (ranging from, in the Israeli–Palestinian context, self-determination and respect for the territorial integrity and political independence of States to considerations of international peace and security and the law of statehood), it is particularly to be stressed, given the focus of this study, when applying the international law of negotiation to the Israeli–Palestinian dispute. Part of this has to do with the subjective nature of the international law of negotiation, a body of law that is itself tied up with considerations of due diligence and case-by-case evaluation. In theory, judgments can be made during ongoing negotiations—the Institut de Droit International, for example, has insisted that "obligations to co-operate, to negotiate, to consult or even simply to take into consideration a possible future occurrence with a view to an equally possible action, are legal obligations which a third party may determine, within certain limits, as having been or not having been performed in good faith"[13]—but to say this is really a much more basic jurisprudential defense of law *as law* in the absence of a court or tribunal with jurisdiction in the instant case than a commentary on the international law of negotiation as such.

A number of equitable devices, such as estoppel, acquiescence, and unilateral declarations, can further complicate legal evaluation during ongoing negotiations.[14] Although often not given its proper due in the literature, ICJ Judge Ajibola's separate opinion appended to *Territorial Dispute* considers a number of these.[15] For Judge Ajibola, estoppel stabilizes the law, reinforces its reliability, consistency, and finality, and acts to further the principle of good faith, while acquiescence can be defined as "tacit or implied consent, which may constitute an admission or recognition."[16] When a party acquiesces in a particular state of affairs, estoppel reinforces the "reformed" legal terrain, precluding the estopped party from later being able to rely upon prior rights and obligations that its earlier conduct had modified.[17] Judge Ajibola suggests that estoppel and acquiescence are militating factors, meaning that they cut against an estopped party later being able to disavow conduct in which it had earlier acquiesced.[18] There is nuance in this

[13] Institut de Droit International, Resolution on International Texts of Legal Import in the Mutual Relations of Their Authors and Texts Devoid of Such Import, Cambridge, at ¶ 3 (1983) (continuing by noting that "[t]he violation of such obligations entails the same consequences as that of any other legal obligation").

[14] "Equity" is used here in its "loosest" sense, understanding it, as Anand does, as a "'catalytic force' to mitigate the harshness of law and keep its principles in harmony with justice." ANAND, *supra* note 10, at 366. Somewhat relatedly, on inaction as practice and/or evidence of acceptance as law, see International Law Commission, Third Report on Identification of Customary International Law, at 9–14, U.N. Doc. A/CN.4/682 (2015).

[15] *See* Territorial Dispute (Libya/Chad), 1994 I.C.J. 6, 77–83 (Feb. 3) (Ajibola, J., separate).

[16] *Id.* at 78 (Ajibola, J., separate).

[17] In *Delimitation of the Maritime Boundary in the Gulf of Maine Area*, the ICJ stressed the exceptional nature of acquiescence, stating that relevant conduct must be "sufficiently clear, sustained and consistent." Delimitation of the Maritime Boundary in the Gulf of Maine Area (Can./U.S.), 1984 I.C.J. 246, 309 (Oct. 12).

[18] *See* Territorial Dispute, *supra* note 15, at 81 (Ajibola, J., separate) ("All these legal, judicial as well as arbitral references fortify my view, based on the principle of estoppel, that the silence or

point. Framed as militating factors, estoppel and acquiescence factor into assessments of legality. They can be used to "massage" outcomes, but they do not predetermine them. They are not conclusive. They are considerations.[19]

The classic ICJ cases on estoppel are the *North Sea Continental Shelf* cases.[20] In *North Sea Continental Shelf*, the ICJ rejected the notion that the then Federal Republic of Germany was estopped from denying the applicability of the 1958 Geneva Convention on the Continental Shelf on the basis of past conduct and statements that had "not only clearly and consistently evinced acceptance of that régime, but also had caused Denmark or the Netherlands, in reliance on such conduct, detrimentally to change position or suffer some prejudice."[21] While the ICJ has spoken elsewhere of estoppel and acquiescence,[22] numerous other courts and tribunals have also relied upon these principles when engaging with international law, such as the International Tribunal for the Law of the Sea[23] and the Swiss Federal Tribunal.[24]

The 1969 Vienna Convention on the Law of Treaties (VCLT) also reflects the principles of estoppel and acquiescence. It prohibits States from invoking the VCLT's material breach regime when, after they have become aware of a ground for material breach, they have expressly agreed to a treaty's continuing validity or acquiesced in it by virtue of conduct.[25] If one applies this understanding of estoppel

acquiescence of Libya from the date of signing the 1955 Treaty to the present time, without any protest whatsoever, clearly militates against its claim").

[19] *See* Gulf of Maine, *supra* note 17, at 305 (referring to estoppel and acquiescence as "different aspects of one and the same institution"). *See also* Institut de Droit International, *supra* note 13 (referring to estoppel and acquiescence within the context of international texts of legal import in the mutual relations of their authors and texts devoid of such import).

[20] *See* North Sea Continental Shelf (F.R.G./Den.) (F.R.G./Neth.), 1969 I.C.J. 3 (Feb. 20).

[21] *Id.* at 26. *See* Land, Island, and Maritime Frontier Dispute, Application to Intervene (El Sal./Hond.), 1990 I.C.J. 92, 118 (Sept. 13) (indicating as "some essential elements required by estoppel [...] a statement or representation made by one party to another and reliance upon it by that other party to his detriment or to the advantage of the party making it").

[22] *See, e.g.,* Sovereignty over Pedra Branca/Pulau Batu Puteh, Middle Rocks and South Ledge (Malay./Sing.), 2008 I.C.J. 12, 51 (May 23) (stating, with respect to acquiescence, that "silence may also speak, but only if the conduct of the other State calls for a response"). "The absence of reaction may well amount to acquiescence." *Id.* at 50. On estoppel and acquiescence in the case law of the ICJ, see Ian Sinclair, *Estoppel and Acquiescence, in* FIFTY YEARS OF THE INTERNATIONAL COURT OF JUSTICE: ESSAYS IN HONOUR OF SIR ROBERT JENNINGS 104 (Vaughan Lowe & Malgosia Fitzmaurice eds., 1996). *See also* Andreas Kulick, *About the Order of Cart and Horse, Among Others—Estoppel in the Jurisprudence of International Investment Arbitration Tribunals,* EUR. J. INT'L L. (forthcoming); Megan L. Wagner, *Jurisdiction by Estoppel in the International Court of Justice,* 74(5) CAL. L. REV. 1777, 1784–89 (1986).

[23] *See* Dispute Concerning Delimitation of the Maritime Boundary Between Bangladesh and Myanmar in the Bay of Bengal (Bangl./Myan.), 2012 I.T.L.O.S., at ¶ 124 (Mar. 14). In the recent arbitral award in *Chagos Marine Protected Area*, estoppel was said to require the following four factors: "(a) a State has made clear and consistent representations, by word, conduct, or silence; (b) such representations were made through an agent authorized to speak for the State with respect to the matter in question; (c) the State invoking estoppel was induced by such representations to act to its detriment, to suffer a prejudice, or to convey a benefit upon the representing State; and (d) such reliance was legitimate, as the representation was one on which that State was entitled to rely." Chagos Marine Protected Area (Mauritius v. U.K.), at ¶ 438 (Mar. 18, 2015).

[24] *See* Canton of Valais v. Canton of Tessin (1980), 75 I.L.R. 114 (1987) (Switz.).

[25] *See* Vienna Convention on the Law of Treaties, Vienna, May 23, 1969, art. 45.

and acquiescence to the bilateral negotiation imperative and the Palestinian applications of autumn 2011 and autumn 2012, the conclusions reached in the previous chapter would only seem to be reinforced. This is because Israel and the PLO expressly agreed (in both autumn 2011 and autumn 2012) that the bilateral negotiation imperative continued to remain in force (even though they attached radically different interpretations to it); and neither party acquiesced in the suspension or termination of the bilateral negotiation imperative by virtue of conduct (in a way that the other party recognized).

Unilateral declarations, though exceptional and to be interpreted restrictively, have a similar effect as estoppel and acquiescence as equitable devices. Like estoppel and acquiescence, they alter how international law applies in given situations by creating, or recognizing, new legal situations.[26]

> When it is the intention of the State making the declaration that it should become bound according to its terms, that intention confers on the declaration the character of a legal undertaking, the State being thenceforth legally required to follow a course of conduct consistent with the declaration.[27]

Unilateral declarations, like estoppel and acquiescence, are to be assessed on a case-by-case basis and are rooted in good faith.[28] The International Law Commission (ILC), in Special Rapporteur Víctor Rodríguez Cedeño's Eighth Report on Unilateral Acts of States in 2005, cited the Jordanians' waiver of claims to the West Bank in 1988 as an example of a unilateral declaration,[29] and in the Commentary to its 2006 Guiding Principles Applicable to Unilateral Declarations of States Capable of Creating Legal Obligations, the ILC referred to this as being "represent[ative of] an important indication of their authors' intention to commit themselves."[30] Since 1993, both Israel and the PLO have taken a number of unilateral acts that have qualified as unilateral declarations and, as such, have had legal effect.[31]

[26] *See* Nuclear Tests (Austl. v. Fr.), 1974 I.C.J. 253, 267–68 (Dec. 20); Nuclear Tests (N.Z. v. Fr.), 1974 I.C.J. 457, 472–73 (Dec. 20). On the *Nuclear Tests* cases and unilateral acts as inchoate treaties, see Hugh Thirlway, The Sources of International Law 44–52 (2014).

[27] Nuclear Tests (Austl. v. Fr.), *supra* note 26, at 267; Nuclear Tests (N.Z. v. Fr.), *supra* note 26, at 472.

[28] *See* Questions Relating to the Seizure and Detention of Certain Documents and Data (E. Timor v. Austl.) (Provisional Measures) (Order), 2014 I.C.J., at ¶ 44 (Mar. 3).

[29] *See* International Law Commission, Eighth Report on Unilateral Acts of States, at 11–12, U.N. Doc. A/CN.4/557 (2005).

[30] Guiding Principles Applicable to Unilateral Declarations of States Capable of Creating Legal Obligations, With Commentaries, *in* International Law Commission, 2(2) Y.B. Int'l L. Comm'n 161, 162, U.N. Doc. A/CN.4/SER.A/2006/Add.1 (Part 2) (2006). The ILC finished its work on unilateral acts of States in 2006. *See generally id. See also* Eva Kassoti, *Unilateral Legal Acts Revisited: Common Law v. Civil Law Approaches and Lessons from the International Law Commission's (Failed) Attempt to Codify Unilateral Acts of States,* 26 Hague Y.B. Int'l L. 168 (2013); Duncan B. Hollis, *Defining Treaties, in* The Oxford Guide to Treaties 11, 31–33 (Duncan B. Hollis ed., 2012).

[31] *See, e.g.,* Israel Ministry of Foreign Affairs, Statement by PM Netanyahu on the Cabinet Decision to Suspend New Construction in Judea and Samaria (Nov. 25, 2009), http://mfa.gov.il/MFA/PressRoom/2009/Pages/Statement%20by%20PM_Netanyahu_suspend_new_construction_Judea_Samaria_25-Nov-2009.aspx.

It should be borne in mind that Israel and the PLO have resolved that agreements reached during the transitional period will not prejudice or preempt the outcome of permanent status negotiations.[32] Can the same be said for those equitable devices that have arisen between Israel and the PLO during the transitional period? In other words, can the two sides choose to overlook, or (re)interpret the legal consequences of, for example, instances of estoppel, acquiescence, or unilateral declarations during the transitional period if they decide that to do so would facilitate a final settlement? If the purpose, or at least *a* purpose, of "without prejudice" clauses is to ensure that parties have maximally robust menus of options when negotiating final settlements,[33] then the answer to this would seem to be in the affirmative. Of course, considerations of *jus cogens* will influence how, and the extent to which, a final settlement reflects Jewish and Palestinian self-determination, but as the representatives of the Jewish and Palestinian people, respectively, the State of Israel and the PLO can largely interpret self-determination as they see fit. They "merely" have to ensure that a final settlement reflects international law's flexible notion of the "free and genuine expression of the will of the people[ ]."[34] Assuming that they stay within the international law of self-determination, *how* Israel and the PLO choose do this, is not particularly a concern of international law.

Given that the promise of the bilateral negotiation imperative remains unfulfilled, it is difficult to speak definitively about the dispute's legalities (and illegalities) at the present moment. Israel and the PLO have agreed that questions of law vis-à-vis their dispute will be settled during permanent status negotiations, and not before. This suggests that conclusions of law reached prior to this time will be partial and fleeting, and in any event, they are destined to be overridden by a final settlement. Of course, this has not stopped Israel and the PLO, and other interested parties (in the juridical and descriptive senses), from opining about the dispute. Background "chatter" about the Israeli–Palestinian dispute dominates the headlines and debating chambers of the world, with the languages of "law" and "legitimacy" having been appropriated for strategic advantage. In his final report to the United Nations Human Rights Council as Special Rapporteur on the Situation of Human Rights in the Palestinian Territories Occupied Since 1967, Richard Falk spoke of this dynamic as a (Palestinian) "'legitimacy war', which involves a worldwide struggle to gain control over the debate about legal entitlements and moral proprieties in the conflict supported by a global solidarity movement that

[32] *See, e.g.*, Letter Dated 8 October 1993 from the Permanent Representatives of the Russian Federation and the United States of America to the United Nations Addressed to the Secretary-General, Annex at 4, 5, art. 5(4), U.N. Doc. A/48/486 (Oct. 11, 1993) (Declaration of Principles on Interim Self-Government Arrangements).

[33] "Without prejudice" clauses can also act as gap fillers, or residual legal frameworks. *See* Responsibilities and Obligations of States with Respect to Activities in the Area, Advisory Opinion, 2011 I.T.L.O.S. 10, 65–66 (Feb. 1).

[34] Western Sahara, Advisory Opinion, 1975 I.C.J. 12, 68 (Oct. 16).

has begun to sway public opinion."[35] "[G]ain[ing] control over the debate" by "speaking truth to power" only goes so far, however, since it is not the activists on the barricades who will have to reach, and then implement, a final settlement but, rather, Israel and the Palestinian people.

The Israeli author Amos Oz has written of his belief that a final settlement will require "[c]ompromise, not capitulation. A compromise means that the Palestinian people should never go down on their knees; neither should the Israeli Jewish people."[36] Vattel refers to compromise in peace agreements as each side's "extinction of all his pretensions."[37] "Were the rules of strict and rigid justice to be observed in it," he suggests of a peace agreement, "so that each party should precisely receive every thing to which he has a just title, it would be impossible ever to make a peace."[38] For Vattel, peace agreements reflect compromise and are instrumental to it. Compromise involves the waiver of (maximalist) rights and obligations. At least juridically, compromise cures all.

International law may be naive in thinking that all disputes can be settled by peaceful means, or that they can be settled at all. It certainly gives parties to disputes myriad means of settlement, but it is not obvious why the breadth of these modalities should somehow make the reaching of a final settlement a foregone conclusion. Game theory, for example, would counsel to the contrary, at least as Robert J. Aumann laid it out in his 2005 Nobel Lecture in Economic Sciences: "Wanting peace now may cause you never to get it—not now, and not in the future. But if you can wait, maybe you will get it now."[39] Might the unthinkable be entertained, that it might be counterproductive to insist upon an Israeli–Palestinian "peace process" by rote? Mere incantations of the desirable, after all, do not make that which is desired inherently more likely to be obtained.

What does seem clear is that Israel and the PLO will have to forgo certain claims and cure certain breaches if they are to reach a final settlement. Unless both sides are willing to do this, to negotiate with one another without preconditions and according to the exacting international law of negotiation, it is unlikely that there will be a settlement of the Israeli–Palestinian dispute, at least one reached consensually. For international law to insist otherwise, or for those who engage with the language of law to imagine otherwise, does not bring a final peace any closer. But it certainly makes it more distant.

[35] Report of the Special Rapporteur on the Situation of Human Rights in the Palestinian Territories Occupied Since 1967, at 4, U.N. Doc. A/HRC/25/67 (Jan. 13, 2014).

[36] AMOS OZ, *Between Right and Right*, *in* HOW TO CURE A FANATIC 1, 8 (2010).

[37] EMER DE VATTEL, THE LAW OF NATIONS 663 (Béla Kapossy & Richard Whatmore eds., 2008).

[38] *Id.* at 662.

[39] Robert J. Aumann, Nobel Prize in Economic Sciences Lecture, War and Peace (Dec. 8, 2005), http://www.nobelprize.org/nobel_prizes/economic-sciences/laureates/2005/aumann-lecture.pdf.

ANNEX: MAPS

"To your descendants I will give this land from the river of Egypt to the Euphrates River" with Illustration of Map of Greater Israel, New Zionist Organization, Tel Hai Fund, No. PS-164 (1936–37). Courtesy of the Jabotinsky Institute, Tel Aviv.

The Jewish national home provisions of the Palestine Mandate originally extended to both banks of the Jordan River. Through the (first) partition of Palestine in mid 1922, these provisions were disapplied to those parts of Palestine east of the Jordan.

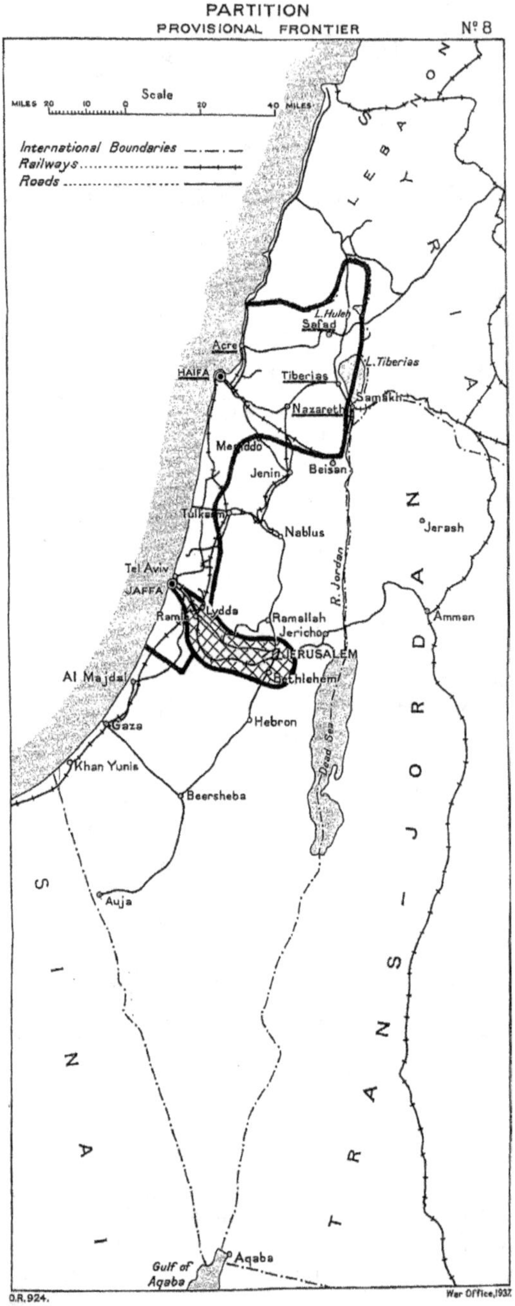

Partition: Provisional Frontier
Palestine Royal Commission Report, at 411, cmd. 5479 (1937)

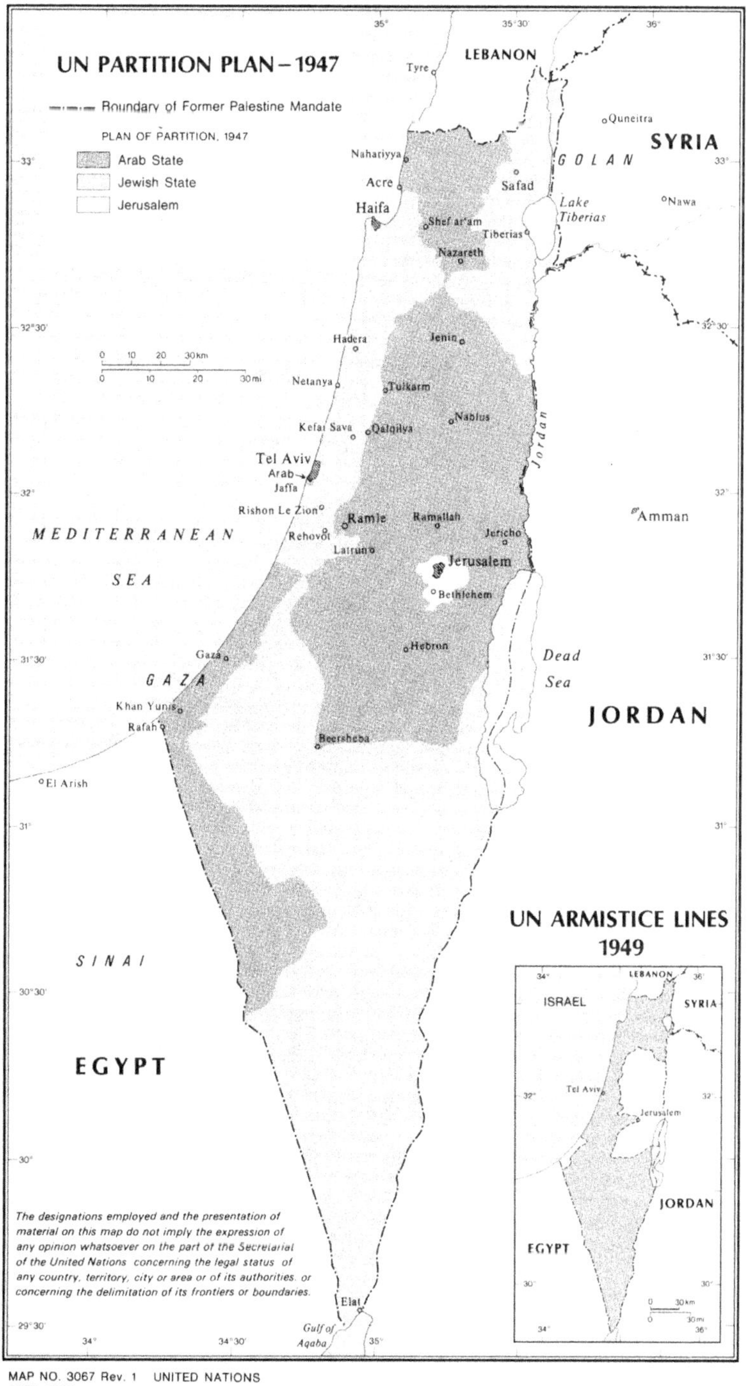

MAP NO. 3067 Rev. 1 UNITED NATIONS
APRIL 1983

Reprinted with permission of the United Nations.

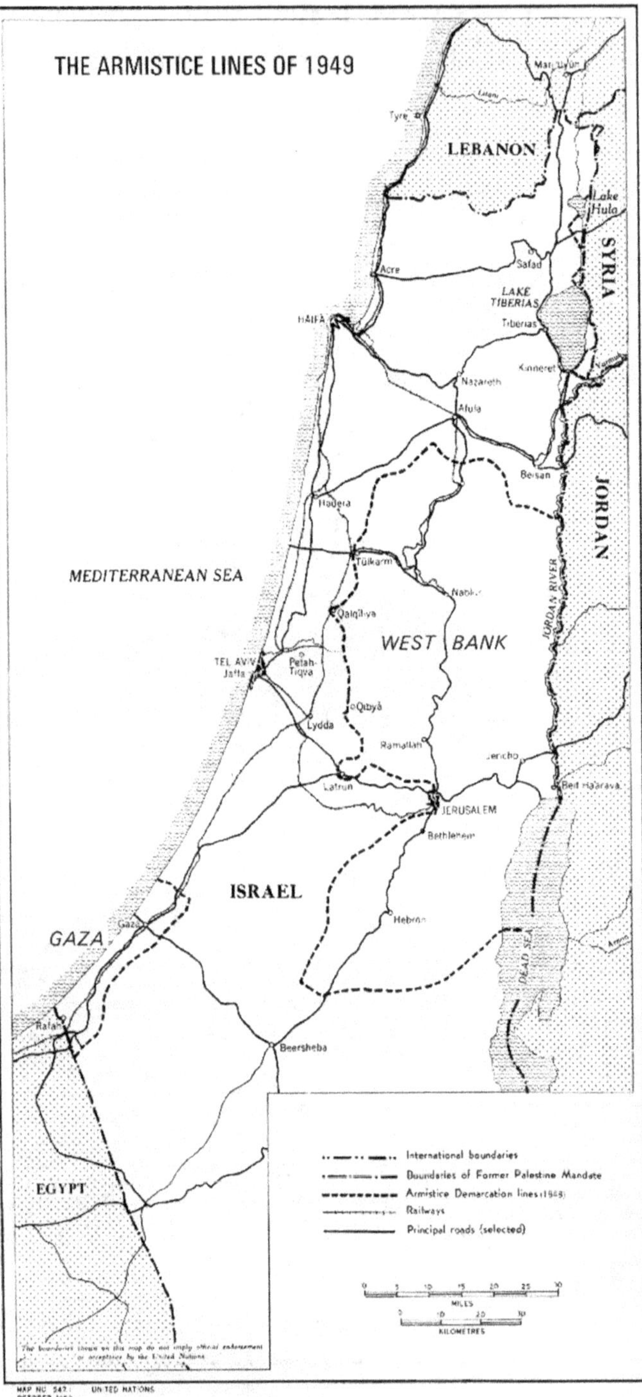

Reprinted with permission of the United Nations.

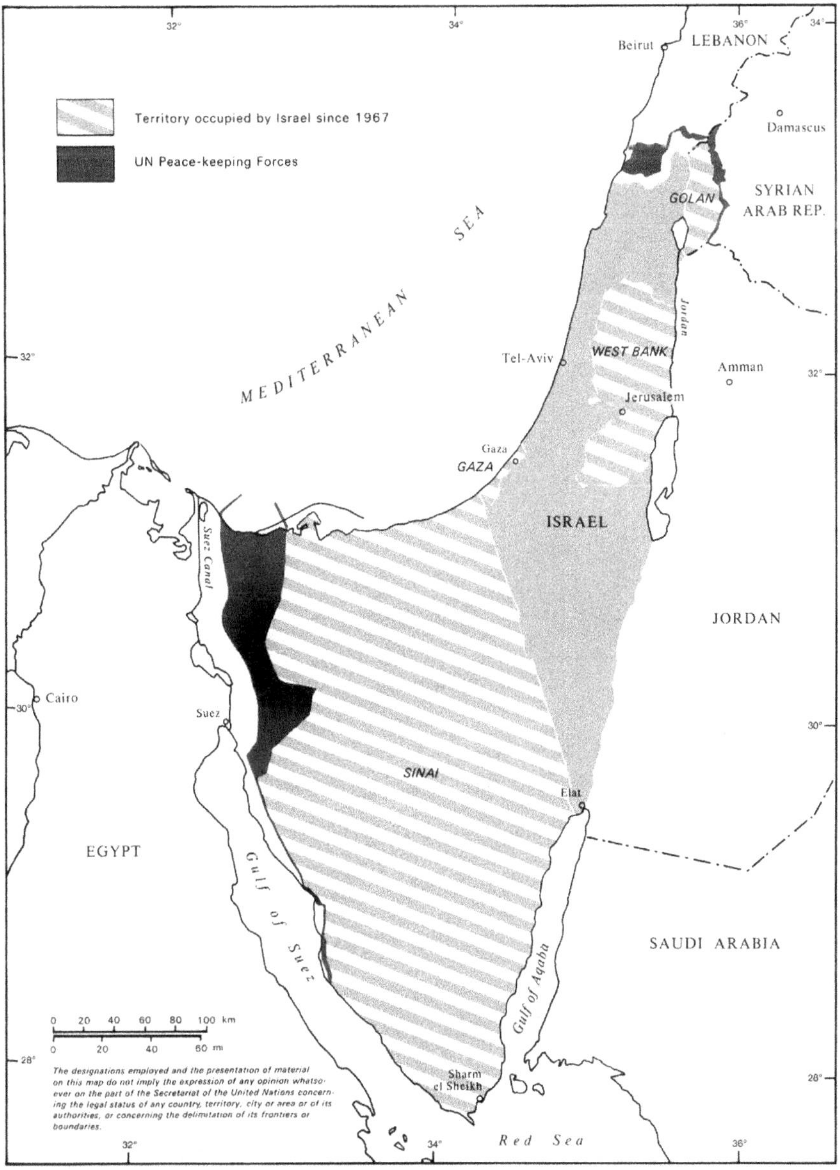

MAP NO. 3014 UNITED NATIONS
NOVEMBER 1978

Reprinted with permission of the United Nations.

Map No. 3243 Rev.4 UNITED NATIONS
June 1997

Department of Public Information
Cartographic Section

Reprinted with permission of the United Nations.

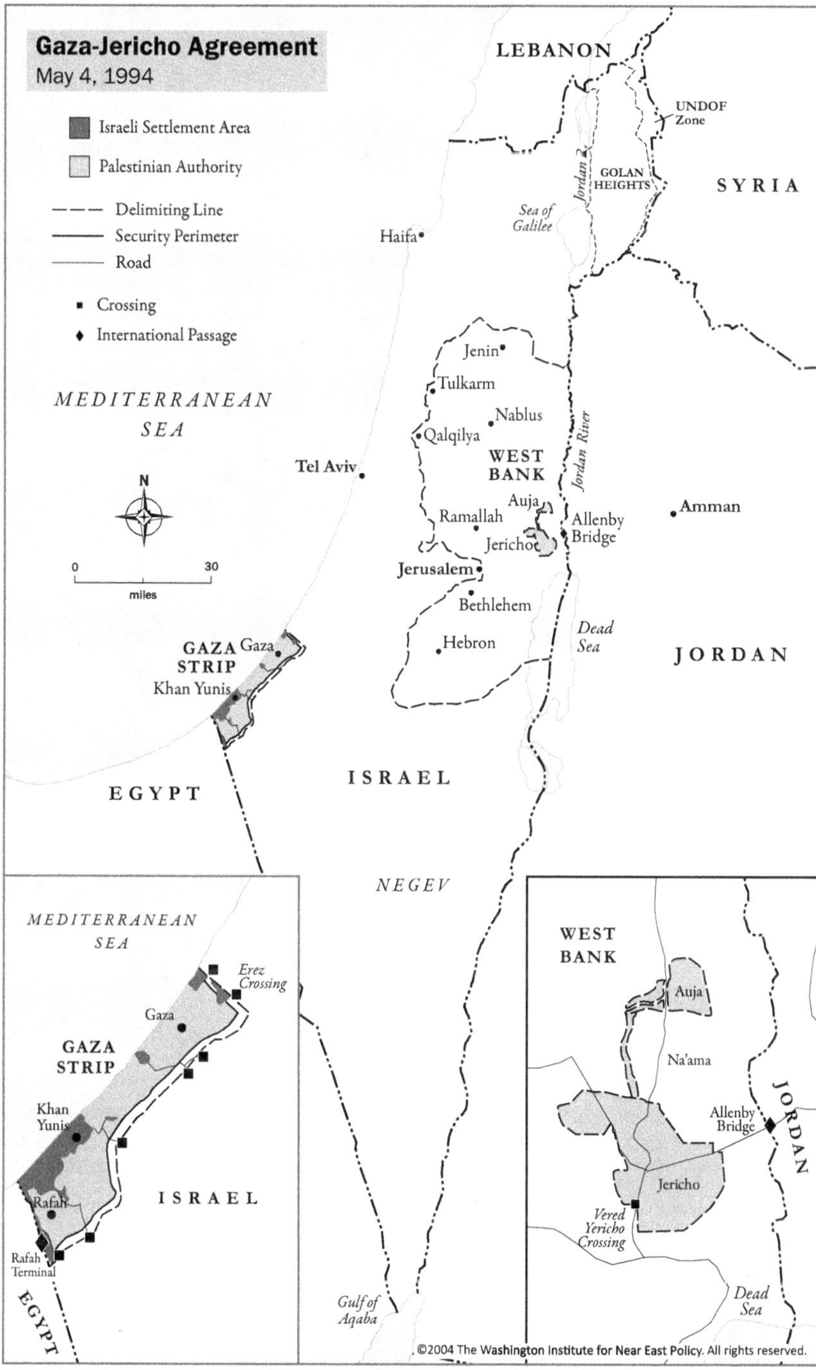
Gaza-Jericho Agreement
May 4, 1994
Israeli Settlement Area
Palestinian Authority
Delimiting Line
Security Perimeter
Road
Crossing
International Passage
MEDITERRANEAN SEA
N
0
30
miles
LEBANON
UNDOF Zone
GOLAN HEIGHTS
SYRIA
Jordan
Sea of Galilee
Haifa
Jenin
Tulkarm
Nablus
Qalqilya
WEST BANK
Jordan River
Tel Aviv
Auja
Ramallah
Allenby Bridge
Amman
Jericho
Jerusalem
Bethlehem
Dead Sea
Hebron
GAZA STRIP
Gaza
Khan Yunis
JORDAN
EGYPT
ISRAEL
NEGEV
MEDITERRANEAN SEA
Erez Crossing
Gaza
GAZA STRIP
Khan Yunis
ISRAEL
Rafah
Rafah Terminal
EGYPT
Gulf of Aqaba
WEST BANK
Auja
Na'ama
Allenby Bridge
JORDAN
Jericho
Vered Yericho Crossing
Dead Sea

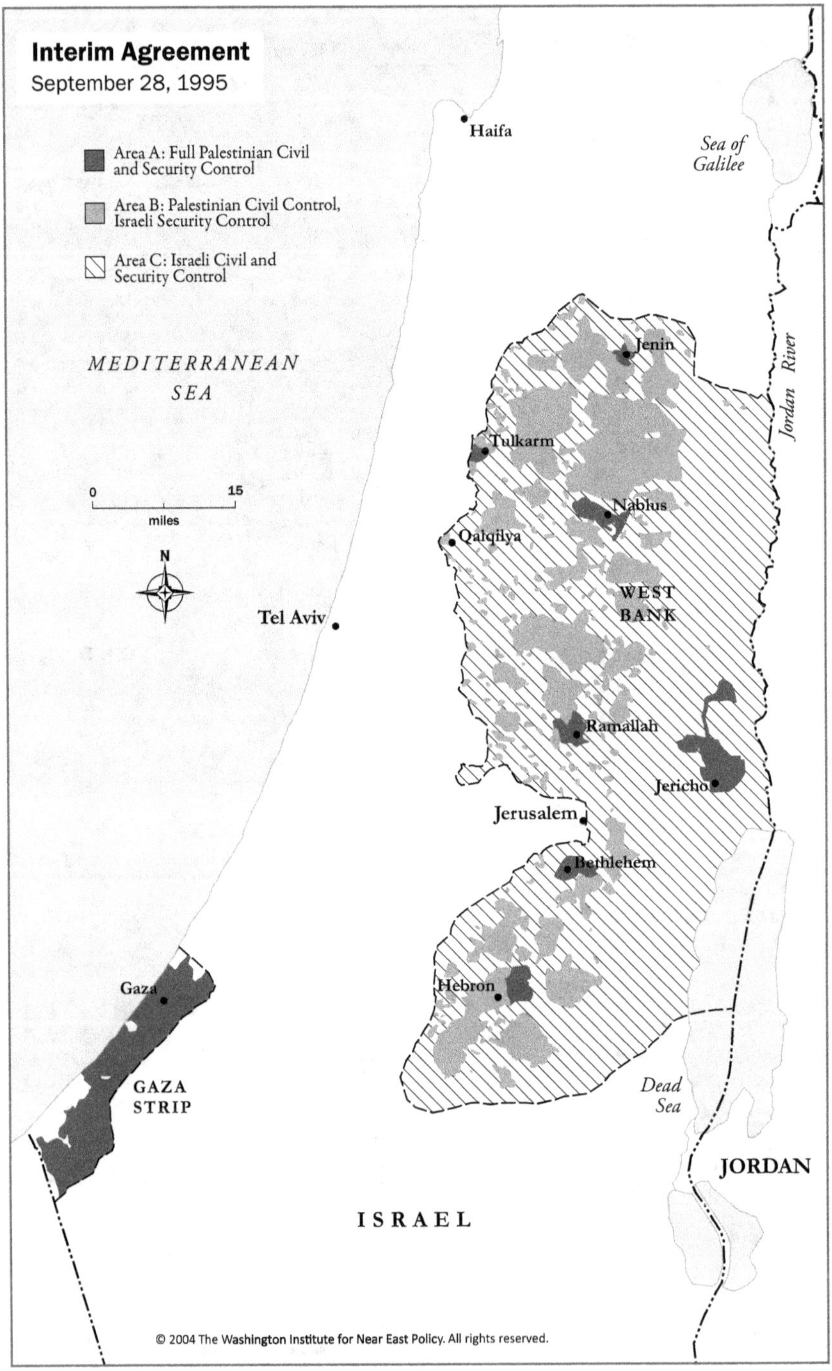
Interim Agreement
September 28, 1995
Area A: Full Palestinian Civil and Security Control
Area B: Palestinian Civil Control, Israeli Security Control
Area C: Israeli Civil and Security Control
MEDITERRANEAN SEA
0 15 miles
N
Haifa
Sea of Galilee
Jordan River
Jenin
Tulkarm
Nablus
Qalqilya
WEST BANK
Tel Aviv
Ramallah
Jericho
Jerusalem
Bethlehem
Hebron
Gaza
GAZA STRIP
Dead Sea
JORDAN
ISRAEL
© 2004 The Washington Institute for Near East Policy. All rights reserved.

BIBLIOGRAPHY

Books, Book Reviews, Journal Articles, Religious Texts, and Works in Collection

ABBAS, MAHMOUD (ABU MAZEN), THROUGH SECRET CHANNELS: THE ROAD TO OSLO: SENIOR PLO LEADER ABU MAZEN'S REVEALING STORY OF THE NEGOTIATIONS WITH ISRAEL (1995)

Address of the Palestinian Delegation to the Madrid Middle East Peace Conference, Presented by Dr. Haider Abdul Shafi, Head of the Palestinian Delegation, Oct. 31, 1991, 6 PAL. Y.B. INT'L L. 296 (1990)

ABRAMS, ELLIOT, TESTED BY ZION: THE BUSH ADMINISTRATION AND THE ISRAELI-PALESTINIAN CONFLICT (2013)

Ahmad, Jawad, *The Indus Waters Kishenganga Arbitration and State-to-State Disputes*, 29(3) ARB. INT'L 507 (2013)

Ajami, Fouad, *The End of Pan-Arabism*, 57(2) FOREIGN AFF. 355 (1978)

Ajibola, Bola A., *Dispute Resolution by the International Court of Justice*, 11(1) LEIDEN J. INT'L L. 123 (1998)

Aksentijević, Mirko, *Reflections on the Palestinian Resistance*, 2(1) J. PAL. STUD. 111 (1972)

Akzin, Benjamin, *The Palestine Mandate in Practice*, 25(1) IOWA L. REV. 32 (1939)

Alami, Musa, *The Lesson of Palestine*, 3(4) MID. E. J. 373 (1949)

Al-Husayni, Haj Amin, *The Goal of the Zionist Movement: To Establish a Jewish State in Palestine and in the Neighbouring Arab Countries and to Build a Jewish Temple in Place of the Dome of the Rock at the al-Aqsa Mosque*, *in* THROUGH THE EYES OF THE MUFTI 98 (Zvi Elpeleg ed., Rachel Kessel trans., 2009)

Al-Kidwa, Nasser, *Re-Declaring Palestinian Statehood: Fears and Expectations*, *in* May 4, 1999: IMPLICATIONS OF DECLARING THE STATE 11 (1999)

Allon, Yigal, *Israel: The Case for Defensible Borders*, 55(1) FOREIGN AFF. 38 (1976)

AL MADFAI, MADIHA RASHID, JORDAN, THE UNITED STATES AND THE MIDDLE EAST PEACE PROCESS, 1974–1991 (2007)

Al-Shuaibi, Issa, *The Development of Palestinian Entity Consciousness: Part III*, 9(3) J. PAL. STUD. 99 (1980)

AMERASINGHE, CHITTHARANJAN F., DIPLOMATIC PROTECTION (2008)

ANAND, R.P., CONFRONTATION OR COOPERATION? INTERNATIONAL LAW AND THE DEVELOPING COUNTRIES (2d rev. ed. 2011)

——, INTERNATIONAL COURTS AND CONTEMPORARY CONFLICTS (1974)

——, *The Formation of International Organizations and India: A Historical Study*, 23(1) LEIDEN J. INT'L L. 5 (2010)

ANDERSON, BENEDICT, IMAGINED COMMUNITIES: REFLECTIONS ON THE ORIGIN AND SPREAD OF NATIONALISM (2006)

ANGHIE, ANTHONY, IMPERIALISM, SOVEREIGNTY AND THE MAKING OF INTERNATIONAL LAW (2007)

Antonius, George, *Syria and the French Mandate*, 13(4) INT'L AFF. 523 (1934)

ANTONIUS, GEORGE, THE ARAB AWAKENING: THE STORY OF THE ARAB NATIONAL MOVEMENT (1938)

Arab League, 2(2) INT'L ORG. 378 (1948)

ARAB OFFICE, THE FUTURE OF PALESTINE (reprint 1976) (1947)

ARABS AND ISRAELIS: CONFLICT AND PEACEMAKING IN THE MIDDLE EAST (Abdel Monem Said Aly et al. eds., 2013)

AS-SA'ID, NURI, ARAB INDEPENDENCE AND UNITY (1943)

AUST, ANTHONY, MODERN TREATY LAW AND PRACTICE (3d ed. 2013)

AZARIA, DANAE, TREATIES ON TRANSIT OF ENERGY VIA PIPELINES AND COUNTERMEASURES (2015)

Azarov, Valentina, *An International Legal Demarche for Human Rights? Perils and Prospects of the Palestinian UN Bid*, 18(4–5) INT'L J. HUM. RTS. 527 (2014)

Baker, Alan, *International Humanitarian Law, ICRC, and Israel's Status in the Territories*, 94(888) INT'L REV. RED CROSS 1 (2012)

BAKER, JAMES A., III, THE POLITICS OF DIPLOMACY: REVOLUTION, WAR AND PEACE: 1989–1992 (1995)

Barbour, Nevill, *The White Paper of 1939, in* FROM HAVEN TO CONQUEST: READINGS IN ZIONISM AND THE PALESTINE PROBLEM UNTIL 1948 461 (Walid Khalidi ed., 2005)

Barnett, David, & Efraim Karsh, *Azzam's Genocidal Threat*, 18(4) MID. E. Q. 85 (2011)

Barnidge, Robert P., Jr, *The Due Diligence Principle Under International Law*, 8(1) INT'L CMTY. L. REV. 81 (2006)

——, *Neocolonialism and International Law, With Specific Reference to Customary Counterterrorism Obligations and the Principle of Self-Defence*, 49(1) INDIAN J. INT'L L. 21 (2009)

——, *Questioning the Legitimacy of* Jus Cogens *in the Global Legal Order*, 38 Isr. Y.B. HUM. RTS. 199 (2008)

——, *The United Nations and the African Union: Assessing a Partnership for Peace in Darfur*, 14(1) J. CONFLICT & SEC. L. 93 (2009)

——, *John Quigley, The Six-Day War and Israeli Self-Defense: Questioning the Legal Basis for Preventive War* (2013), 1 J. USE FORCE & INT'L L. 190 (2014)

——, *Jonathan Schanzer, State of Failure: Yasser Arafat, Mahmoud Abbas, and the Unmaking of the Palestinian State* (2013), 5(1) J. MID. E. & AFR. 91 (2014)

Bartal, Shaul, *The Palestinian Refugee Problem Resolved*, 20(4) MID. E. Q. 29 (2013)

Bassiouni, M. Cherif, & Eugene M. Fisher, *The Arab-Israeli Conflict—Real and Apparent Issues: An Insight into Its Future from the Lessons of the Past*, 44(3) ST. JOHN'S L. REV. 399 (1970)

Becker, Tal, *Self-Determination in Perspective: Palestinian Claims to Statehood and the Realty of the Right to Self-Determination*, 32(2) ISR. L. REV. 301 (1998)

Bederman, David J., *Counterintuiting Countermeasures*, 96(4) AM. J. INT'L L. 817 (2002)

Beker, Avi, *The Forgotten Narrative: Jewish Refugees from Arab Countries*, 17(3–4) JEWISH POL. STUD. REV. 3 (2005)

Bentwich, Norman, *Mandated Territories: Palestine and Mesopotamia (Iraq)*, 2 BRIT. Y.B. INT'L L. 48 (1921)

——, *The Mandate for Palestine*, 10 BRIT. Y.B. INT'L L. 137 (1929)

——, THE MANDATES SYSTEM (1930)

Benvenisti, Eyal, *The Israeli-Palestinian Declaration of Principles: A Framework for Future Settlement*, 4(1) EUR. J. INT'L L. 542 (1993)

BERNADOTTE, FOLKE, TO JERUSALEM (Joan Bulman trans., 1951)

BIGER, GIDEON, THE BOUNDARIES OF MODERN PALESTINE, 1840–1947 (2005)
BIN TALAL, HASSAN, PALESTINIAN SELF-DETERMINATION: A STUDY OF THE WEST BANK AND GAZA STRIP (1981)
Blum, Yehuda Z., *From Camp David to Oslo*, 28(2–3) ISR. L. REV. 211 (1994)
Bobrov, R.L., *Basic Principles of Present-Day International Law, in* CONTEMPORARY INTERNATIONAL LAW 36 (Grigory Tunkin ed., G. Ivanov-Mumjiev trans., 1969)
Bowett, D.W., *Contemporary Developments in Legal Techniques in the Settlement of Disputes, in* 180 COLLECTED COURSES OF THE HAGUE ACADEMY OF INTERNATIONAL LAW 169 (1983)
Boyle, Francis A., *The Creation of the State of Palestine*, 1(1) EUR. J. INT'L L. 301 (1990)
——, *The Interim Agreement and International Law*, 22(3) ARAB STUD. Q. 1 (2000)
"Bringing in the International Community as a Major Factor in the Solution": An Interview with Dr. Nabil Shaath, 20(2–3) PAL.-ISR. J. 126 (2015)
Brown, Philip Marshall, *The Aaland Islands Question*, 15(2) AM J. INT'L L. 268 (1921)
BUBER, MARTIN, *Nationalism, in* A LAND OF TWO PEOPLES: MARTIN BUBER ON JEWS AND ARABS 47 (Paul Mendes-Flohr ed., 2005)
Burgis-Kasthala, Michelle Leanne, *Over-Stating Palestine's UN Membership Bid? An Ethnographic Study on the Narratives of Statehood*, 25(3) EUR. J. INT'L L. 677 (2014)
Burra, Srinivas, *Palestine and the Belated UN Non-Member Observer State Status*, 52(4) INDIAN J. INT'L L. 591 (2012)

Caradon, Lord, *An Interview with Lord Caradon*, 5(3–4) J. PAL. STUD. 142 (1976)
Cassese, Antonio, *The Israel-PLO Agreement and Self-Determination*, 4(1) EUR. J. INT'L L. 564 (1993)
——, SELF-DETERMINATION OF PEOPLES: A LEGAL REAPPRAISAL (2008)
CATTAN, HENRY, PALESTINE AND INTERNATIONAL LAW: THE LEGAL ASPECTS OF THE ARAB-ISRAELI CONFLICT (1974)
——, PALESTINE AND INTERNATIONAL LAW: THE LEGAL ASPECTS OF THE ARAB-ISRAELI CONFLICT (2d ed. 1976)
——, *Recollections on the United Nations Resolution to Partition Palestine*, 4 PAL. Y.B. INT'L L. 260 (1987)
Cerone, John, *Introductory Note to the Admission of Palestine to UNESCO and Related Documents*, 51(3) I.L.M. 606, 616 (2012)
——, *Legal Implications of the UN General Assembly Vote to Accord Palestine the Status of Observer State*, 16(37) AM. SOC'Y INT'L L. INSIGHTS (Dec. 7, 2012)
——, *The UN and the Status of Palestine—Disentangling the Legal Issues*, 15(26) AM. SOC'Y INT'L L. INSIGHTS (Sept. 13, 2011)
Chowdhury, S., *The Status and Norms of Self-Determination in Contemporary International Law, in* THIRD WORLD ATTITUDES TOWARD INTERNATIONAL LAW: AN INTRODUCTION 87 (Frederick E. Snyder & Surakiart Sathirathai eds., 1987)
CLAPHAM, ANDREW, BRIERLY'S LAW OF NATIONS: AN INTRODUCTION TO THE ROLE OF INTERNATIONAL LAW IN INTERNATIONAL RELATIONS (7th ed. 2014)
Claussen, Kathleen, *What Effect of Palestine's Membership in UNESCO?*, CAMBRIDGE J. INT'L & COMP. L. ONLINE, Nov. 4, 2011
COLLIER, JOHN, & VAUGHAN LOWE, THE SETTLEMENT OF DISPUTES IN INTERNATIONAL LAW: INSTITUTIONS AND PROCEDURES (2000)
Costelloe, Daniel, *The Status of Palestine at the General Assembly*, CAMBRIDGE J. INT'L & COMP. L. ONLINE, Nov. 29, 2012
CRAWFORD, JAMES, BROWNLIE'S PRINCIPLES OF PUBLIC INTERNATIONAL LAW (6th ed. 2012)

——, THE CREATION OF STATES IN INTERNATIONAL LAW (2d ed. 2007)

——, *The Creation of the State of Palestine: Too Much Too Soon?*, 1(1) EUR. J. INT'L L. 307 (1990)

——, *Introduction* to THE INTERNATIONAL LAW COMMISSION'S ARTICLES ON STATE RESPONSIBILITY: INTRODUCTION, TEXT, AND COMMENTARIES 1 (James Crawford ed., 2003)

——, STATE RESPONSIBILITY: THE GENERAL PART (2014)

——, & Simon Olleson, *The Exception of Non-Performance: Links Between the Law of Treaties and the Law of State Responsibility*, 21 AUSTL. Y.B. INT'L L. 55 (2000)

CROSSMAN, RICHARD H.S., A NATION REBORN: A PERSONAL REPORT ON THE ROLES PLAYED BY WEIZMANN, BEVIN AND BEN-GURION IN THE STORY OF ISRAEL (1960)

CUNNINGHAM, KATHLEEN GALLAGHER, INSIDE THE POLITICS OF SELF-DETERMINATION (2014)

Curtis, Michael, *International Law and the Territories*, 32(2) HARV. INT'L L.J. 457 (1991)

Dajani, Burhan, *The September 1993 Israeli-PLO Documents: A Textual Analysis*, 23(3) J. PAL. STUD. 5 (1994)

Dajani, Omar M., *Forty Years Without Resolve: Tracing the Influence of Security Council Resolution 242 on the Middle East Peace Process*, 37(1) J. PAL. STUD. 24 (2007)

——, *Stalled Between Seasons: The International Legal Status of Palestine During the Interim Period*, 26(1) DENV. J. INT'L L. & POL'Y 27 (1997)

Danin, Robert M., *A Third Way to Palestine: Fayyadism and Its Discontents*, 90(1) FOREIGN AFF. 94 (2011)

Darwish, Mahmoud, Those Who Pass Between Fleeting Words, *in* INTIFADA: THE PALESTINIAN UPRISING AGAINST ISRAELI OCCUPATION 26 (Zachary Lockman & Joel Beinin eds., 1989)

D'Aspremont, Jean, *The International Court of Justice and Tacit Conventionality*, (18) QUEST. INT'L L. 3 (2015)

De Blois, Matthijs, *Bad Law and a Hard Case? The Impact of the* Wall *Advisory Opinion of the ICJ*, *in* WHAT'S WRONG WITH INTERNATIONAL LAW? LIBER AMICORUM A.H.A. SOONS 94 (Cedric Ryngaert et al. eds., 2015)

Degan, Vladimir-Djuro, *The Value of the Manila Declaration on International Dispute Settlement in a Case in Which the Philippines Is a Party*, 11(1) CHIN. J. INT'L L. 5 (2012)

DE WAART, PAUL J.I.M., DYNAMICS OF SELF-DETERMINATION IN PALESTINE: PROTECTION OF PEOPLES AS A HUMAN RIGHT (1994)

Dhokalia, R.P., *International Recognition of the Human Right of Collective Self-Determination*, 11(1–2) BAN. L.J. 20 (1975)

Diker, Dan, *Palestinian Unilateralism and Israel's Rights in Arab-Israeli Diplomacy*, *in* ISRAEL'S RIGHTS AS A NATION-STATE IN INTERNATIONAL DIPLOMACY 115 (Alan Baker ed., 2011)

Dinstein, Yoram, *Collective Human Rights of Peoples and Minorities*, 25(1) INT'L & COMP. L.Q. 102 (1976)

6 DOCUMENTS OF THE UNITED NATIONS CONFERENCE ON INTERNATIONAL ORGANIZATION, SAN FRANCISCO, 1945 (1945)

18(2) DOCUMENTS OF THE UNITED NATIONS CONFERENCE ON INTERNATIONAL ORGANIZATION, SAN FRANCISCO, 1945 (1954)

DOWTY, ALAN, ISRAEL/PALESTINE (3d ed. 2012)

——, *Much Ado About Little: Ahad Ha'am's "Truth from Eretz Yisrael," Zionism, and the Arabs*, 5(2) ISR. STUD. 154 (2000)

——, *"A Question That Outweighs All Others": Yitzhak Epstein and Zionist Recognition of the Arab Issue*, 6(1) ISR. STUD. 34 (2001)

DUGARD, JOHN, THE SOUTH WEST AFRICA/NAMIBIA DISPUTE: DOCUMENTS AND SCHOLARLY WRITINGS ON THE CONTROVERSY BETWEEN SOUTH AFRICA AND THE UNITED NATIONS (1973)

Dumberry, Patrick, *Is Turkey the "Continuing" State of the Ottoman Empire Under International Law?*, 59(2) NETH. INT'L L. REV. 235 (2012)

Eden, Paul, *Palestinian Statehood: Trapped Between Rhetoric and* Realpolitik, 62(1) INT'L & COMP. L.Q. 225 (2013)

ELAGAB, OMER YOUSIF, THE LEGALITY OF NON-FORCIBLE COUNTER-MEASURES IN INTERNATIONAL LAW (1988)

Elaraby, Nabil, *Some Legal Implications of the 1947 Partition Resolution and the 1949 Armistice Agreements*, 33(1) LAW & CONTEMP. PROBS. 97 (1968)

Elgindy, Khaled, *Palestine Goes to the UN: Understanding the New Statehood Strategy*, 90(5) FOREIGN AFF. 102 (2011)

El-Sadat, Anwar, *Where Egypt Stands*, 51(1) FOREIGN AFF. 114 (1972)

Emerson, Rupert, *Self-Determination*, 65(3) AM. J. INT'L L. 459 (1971)

Erakat, Saeb, *Palestine Liberation Organization Legal Brief in Support of Recognition of the State of Palestine, in* PALESTINE MEMBERSHIP IN THE UNITED NATIONS: LEGAL AND PRACTICAL IMPLICATIONS 14 (Mutaz Qafisheh ed., 2013)

Falk, Richard, *Foreword, in* Aborted State? THE UN INITIATIVE AND NEW PALESTINIAN JUNCTURES 10 (Noura Erakat & Mouin Rabbani eds., 2013)

——, *Forty Years After 242: A "Canonical" Text in Disrepute?*, 37(1) J. PAL. STUD. 39 (2007)

——, *Some International Law Implications of the Oslo/Cairo Framework for the PLO/Israeli Peace Process, in* HUMAN RIGHTS, SELF-DETERMINATION AND POLITICAL CHANGE IN THE OCCUPIED PALESTINIAN TERRITORIES 1 (Stephen Bowen ed., 1997)

Fallaci, Oriana, *Hussein of Jordan, in* INTERVIEW WITH HISTORY 140 (John Shepley trans., 1977)

Firmage, Edwin Brown, *The Treaty on the Non-Proliferation of Nuclear Weapons*, 63(4) AM. J. INT'L L. 711 (1969)

Fishman, Joel, *The Jewish Nation-State Bill: Is There a Contradiction Between Judaism and Democracy?*, 26(1–2) JEWISH POL. STUD. REV. 6 (2014)

Fontanelli, Filippo, *The Invocation of the Exception of Non-Performance: A Case-Study on the Role and Application of General Principles of International Law of Contractual Origin*, 1(1) CAMBRIDGE J. INT'L & COMP. L. 119 (2012)

Forlati, Serena, *Reactions to Non-Performance of Treaties in International Law*, 25(3) LEIDEN J. INT'L L. 759 (2012)

Franck, Thomas M., *On Proportionality of Countermeasures in International Law*, 102(4) AM. J. INT'L L. 715 (2008)

Frankfurter, Felix, *The Palestine Situation Restated*, 9(3) FOREIGN AFF. 409 (1931)

Gabay, Mayer, *Legal Aspects of the Camp David Framework for Peace in Relation to the Autonomy Proposal, in* MODELS OF AUTONOMY 255 (Yoram Dinstein ed., 1981)

Garfinkle, Adam M., *On the Origin, Meaning, Use and Abuse of a Phrase*, 27(4) MID. E. STUD. 539 (1991)

GARVEY, MARCUS, *Declaration of the Rights of the Negro Peoples of the World, in* SELECTED WRITINGS AND SPEECHES OF MARCUS GARVEY 16 (Bob Blaisdell ed., 2004)

Gavison, Ruth, *The Jews' Right to Statehood: A Defense*, 15 AZURE 70 (2003)

General Assembly, 1(3) INT'L ORG. 488 (1947)

Ghandhi, Sandy, *Human Rights and the International Court of Justice: The* Ahmadou Sadio Diallo *Case*, 11(3) HUM. RTS. L. REV. 527 (2011)

——, *The International Court of Justice and the Provisional Measures Order in the* Georgia v. Russian Federation *Case, in* CONFLICT IN THE CAUCASUS: IMPLICATIONS FOR INTERNATIONAL LEGAL ORDER 80 (James A. Green & Christopher P.M. Waters eds., 2010)

Ghanem, As'ad, *Palestinian Nationalism: An Overview*, 18(2) ISR. STUD. 11 (2013)

Gilbert, Martin, *"An Overwhelmingly Jewish State"—From the Balfour Declaration to the Palestine Mandate, in* ISRAEL'S RIGHTS AS A NATION-STATE IN INTERNATIONAL DIPLOMACY 23 (Alan Baker ed., 2011)

GLENDON, MARY ANN, RIGHTS TALK: THE IMPOVERISHMENT OF POLITICAL DISCOURSE (1991)

Glozman, Edy, et al., *False Negotiations: The Art and Science of Not Reaching an Agreement*, 59(4) J. CONFLICT RESOL. 671 (2015)

Goldberg, Arthur J., *United Nations Security Council Resolution 242 and the Prospects for Peace in the Middle East*, 12(2) COLUM. J. TRANSNAT'L L. 187 (1973)

Gordon, Neve, & Yinon Cohen, *Western Interests, Israeli Unilateralism, and the Two-State Solution*, 41(3) J. PAL. STUD. 6 (2012)

Grant, Tom, *Who Can Make Treaties? Other Subjects of International Law, in* THE OXFORD GUIDE TO TREATIES 125 (Duncan B. Hollis ed., 2012)

Green, James A., *Persistent Objector Teflon? Customary International Human Rights Law and the United States in International Adjudicative Proceedings, in* ADJUDICATING INTERNATIONAL HUMAN RIGHTS: ESSAYS IN HONOUR OF SANDY GHANDHI 167 (James A. Green & Christopher P.M. Waters eds., 2015)

Harkabi, Yehoshafat, *Arab Positions on Zionism, in* ZIONISM AND THE ARABS 187 (Shmuel Almog ed., 1983)

——, *The Palestinian Covenant and Its Meaning, in* ISRAEL, THE MIDDLE EAST, AND THE GREAT POWERS 219 (Israel Stockman-Shomron ed., 1984)

HASKINS, CHARLES HOMER, & ROBERT HOWARD LORD, SOME PROBLEMS OF THE PEACE CONFERENCE (1920)

HASSOUNA, HUSSEIN A., THE LEAGUE OF ARAB STATES AND REGIONAL DISPUTES: A STUDY OF MIDDLE EAST CONFLICTS (1975)

HELLER, MARK A., A PALESTINIAN STATE: THE IMPLICATIONS FOR ISRAEL (1983)

Henkin, Louis, *International Law: Politics, Values and Functions: General Course on Public International Law, in* 216 COLLECTED COURSES OF THE HAGUE ACADEMY OF INTERNATIONAL LAW 9 (1989)

Herzberg, Anne, *When International Law Blocks the Flow: The Strange Case of the Kidron Valley Sewage Plant*, 10(2) REGENT J. INT'L L. 71 (2014)

HERZL, THEODOR, THE JEWISH STATE (2010)

Higgins, Rosalyn, *International Law and the Avoidance, Containment and Resolution of Disputes: General Course on Public International Law, in* 230 COLLECTED COURSES OF THE HAGUE ACADEMY OF INTERNATIONAL LAW 9 (1991)

HITLER, ADOLF, MEIN KAMPF (2013)

HITTI, PHILIP K., HISTORY OF SYRIA INCLUDING LEBANON AND PALESTINE (1951)

——, *The Possibility of Union Among the Arab States*, 48(4) AM. HIST. REV. 722 (1943)

Hollis, Duncan B., *Defining Treaties, in* THE OXFORD GUIDE TO TREATIES 11 (Duncan B. Hollis ed., 2012)

THE HOLY BIBLE (Dom Bernard Orchard & R.C. Fuller eds., rev. standard version, Catholic ed. 2004)

Hourani, Albert, *Near Eastern Nationalism Yesterday and Today*, 42(1) FOREIGN AFF. 123 (1963)
Humber, P.O., *Admission to the United Nations*, 24 BRIT. Y.B. INT'L L. 90 (1947)
HUPP, CLEA LUTZ, THE UNITED STATES AND JORDAN: MIDDLE EAST DIPLOMACY DURING THE COLD WAR (2014)
HUSSAIN, IJAZ, KASHMIR DISPUTE: AN INTERNATIONAL LAW PERSPECTIVE (2d ed. 2004)
Hussain, Mohammed, K.S., *Palestine and International Law: An Overview, in* Essays on Contemporary Issues in International Law 129 (Asian-African Legal Consultative Org. ed., 2009)

International Law and Solutions to the Arab-Israeli Conflict, 83 AM. SOC'Y INT'L L. PROC. 121 (1989) (Francis Boyle), (Malvina Halberstam)
THE ISRAEL-ARAB READER: A DOCUMENTARY HISTORY OF THE MIDDLE EAST CONFLICT (Walter Laqueur & Barry Rubin eds., 7th ed. 2008)
Iwasawa, Yuji, & Naoki Iwatsuki, *Procedural Conditions, in* THE LAW OF INTERNATIONAL RESPONSIBILITY 1149 (James Crawford et al. eds., 2010)

Jabotinsky, Vladimir, *Evidence Submitted to the Palestine Royal Commission (1937), in* THE ZIONIST IDEA: A HISTORICAL ANALYSIS AND READER 559 (Arthur Hertzberg ed., 1997)
Jessup, Philip C., *A Half-Century of Efforts to Substitute Law for War, in* 99 COLLECTED COURSES OF THE HAGUE ACADEMY OF INTERNATIONAL Law 1 (1960)
Johnson, Larry D., *Palestine's Admission to UNESCO: Consequences Within the United Nations?*, 40(1–3) DENV. J. INT'L L. & POL'Y 118 (2012)
JOYNER, DANIEL H., INTERPRETING THE NUCLEAR NON-PROLIFERATION TREATY (2011)
Joyner, Daniel H., *The Legal Meaning and Implications of Article VI of the Non-Proliferation Treaty, in* NUCLEAR WEAPONS UNDER INTERNATIONAL LAW 397 (Gro Nystuen et al. eds., 2014)

KARAYANNI, MICHAEL, CONFLICTS IN A CONFLICT: A CONFLICT OF LAWS CASE STUDY ON ISRAEL AND THE PALESTINIAN TERRITORIES (2014)
Karsh, Efraim, *Israel, the Hashemites and the Palestinians: The Fateful Triangle*, 9(3) ISR. AFF. 1 (2003)
——, PALESTINE BETRAYED (2011)
Kassim, Anis F., *Legal Systems and Developments in Palestine*, 1 PAL. Y.B. INT'L L. 19 (1984)
Kassoti, Eva, *Unilateral Legal Acts Revisited: Common Law v. Civil Law Approaches and Lessons from the International Law Commission's (Failed) Attempt to Codify Unilateral Acts of States*, 26 HAGUE Y.B. INT'L L. 168 (2013)
KATSELLI PROUKAKI, ELENA, THE PROBLEM OF ENFORCEMENT IN INTERNATIONAL LAW: COUNTERMEASURES, THE NON-INJURED STATE AND THE IDEA OF INTERNATIONAL COMMUNITY (2010)
KATTAN, VICTOR, FROM COEXISTENCE TO CONQUEST: INTERNATIONAL LAW AND THE ORIGINS OF THE ARAB-ISRAELI CONFLICT, 1891–1949 (2009)
Kaur, Satpal, *Self-Determination in International Law*, 10 INDIAN J. INT'L L. 479 (1970)
20 KEESING'S CONTEMPORARY ARCHIVES (1974)
Keith, K.J., *Resolving International Disputes: The Role of the Courts*, 7 N.Z. Y.B. INT'L L. 255 (2009)
Kelman, Herbert C., *Some Determinants of the Oslo Breakthrough*, 2(2) INT'L NEGOT. 183 (1997)
Kent, Andrew, *Evaluating the Palestinians' Claimed Right of Return*, 34(1) U. PA. J. INT'L L. 149 (2012)

Khalidi, Rashid, *Interview with Hanan Ashrawi: Oslo, the PA, and Reinventing the PLO*, 44(1) J. PAL. STUD. 76 (2014)

——, *On the Possible Recognition of a Palestinian State at the United Nations, in* ABORTED STATE? THE UN INITIATIVE AND NEW PALESTINIAN JUNCTURES 25 (Noura Erakat & Mouin Rabbani eds., 2013)

——, PALESTINIAN IDENTITY: THE CONSTRUCTION OF MODERN NATIONAL CONSCIOUSNESS (2010)

Kirgis, Frederic L., *Admission of "Palestine" as a Member of a Specialized Agency and Withholding Payment of Assessments in Response*, 84(1) AM. J. INT'L L. 218 (1990)

KLABBERS, JAN, INTERNATIONAL LAW (2013)

——, *The Right to Be Taken Seriously: Self-Determination in International Law*, 28(1) HUM. RTS. Q. 186 (2006)

KNOP, KAREN, DIVERSITY AND SELF-DETERMINATION IN INTERNATIONAL LAW (2008)

Kolatt, Israel, *The Zionist Movement and the Arabs, in* ESSENTIAL PAPERS ON ZIONISM 617 (Jehuda Reinharz & Anita Shapira eds., 1996)

Kolb, Robert, *Principles as Sources of International Law (With Special Reference to Good Faith)*, 53(1) NETH. INT'L L. REV. 1 (2006)

Koskenniemi, Martti, *The Fate of Public International Law: Between Technique and Politics*, 70(1) M.L.R. 1 (2007)

——, *National Self-Determination Today: Problems of Legal Theory and Practice*, 43(2) INT'L & COMP. L.Q. 241 (1994)

——, *What Is International Law For?, in* INTERNATIONAL LAW 29 (Malcolm D. Evans ed., 4th ed. 2014)

Kulick, Andreas, *About the Order of Cart and Horse, Among Others—Estoppel in the Jurisprudence of International Investment Arbitration Tribunals*, EUR. J. INT'L L. (forthcoming)

Lachs, Manfred, *The Law and the Settlement of International Disputes, in* DISPUTE SETTLEMENT THROUGH THE UNITED NATIONS 283 (K. Venkata Raman ed., 1977)

——, *The Law in and of the United Nations (Some Reflections on the Principle of Self-Determination)*, 1 INDIAN. J. INT'L L. 429 (1960)

LAJPAT RAI, LALA, *Self-Determination for India, in* 7 THE COLLECTED WORKS OF LALA LAJPAT RAI 239 (B.R. Nanda ed., 2005)

LANSING, ROBERT, THE PEACE NEGOTIATIONS: A PERSONAL NARRATIVE (1921)

LAPIDOTH, RUTH, AUTONOMY: FLEXIBLE SOLUTIONS TO ETHNIC CONFLICTS (1997)

——, *The Peace Process, in* ISRAEL, THE MIDDLE EAST, AND THE GREAT POWERS 197 (Israel Stockman-Shomron ed., 1984)

LASSNER, JACOB, & S. ILAN TROEN, JEWS AND MUSLIMS IN THE ARAB WORLD: HAUNTED BY PASTS REAL AND IMAGINED (2007)

Lauterpacht, Hersch, *The Absence of an International Legislature and the Compulsory Jurisdiction of International Tribunals*, 11 BRIT. Y.B. INT'L L. 134 (1930)

Lawrence, T.E., *Syria: The Raw Material, in* SECRET DESPATCHES FROM ARABIA AND OTHER WRITINGS 101 (Malcolm Brown ed., 1991) (Arab Bulletin, Mar. 12, 1917, Fragmentary Notes Written Early in 1915, But Not Circulated)

Lenin, V.I., *The Right of Nations to Self-Determination, in* THE LENIN ANTHOLOGY 153 (Robert C. Tucker ed., 1975)

——, *Socialism and War, in* LENIN ON WAR AND PEACE: THREE ARTICLES 1 (1966)

Lesaffre, Hubert, *Circumstances Precluding Wrongfulness in the ILC Articles on State Responsibility: Countermeasures, in* THE LAW OF INTERNATIONAL RESPONSIBILITY 469 (James Crawford et al. eds., 2010)

Lewis, Bernard, *The Anti-Zionist Resolution*, 55(1) FOREIGN AFF. 54 (1976)
——, *Palestine: On the History and Geography of a Name*, 2(1) INT'L HIST. REV. 1 (1980)
LIE, TRYGVE, IN THE CAUSE OF PEACE: SEVEN YEARS WITH THE UNITED NATIONS (1954)
Lieblich, Eliav, & Yoram Shachar, *Cosmopolitanism at a Crossroads: Hersch Lauterpacht and the Israeli Declaration of Independence*, 84 BRIT. Y.B. INT'L L. 1 (2014)
Lorca, Arnulf Becker, *Petitioning the International: A "Pre-History" of Self-Determination*, 25(2) EUR. J. INT'L L. 497 (2014)
Lundström, Aage, *The Death of Count Folke Bernadotte, September 17, 1948*, *in* FROM HAVEN TO CONQUEST: READINGS IN ZIONISM AND THE PALESTINE PROBLEM UNTIL 1948 789 (Walid Khalidi ed., 2005)

Maddy-Weitzman, Bruce, *Arabs vs. the Abdullah Plan*, 17(3) MID. E. Q. 3 (2010)
Malanczuk, Peter, *Some Basic Aspects of the Agreements Between Israel and the PLO from the Perspective of International Law*, 7(4) EUR. J. INT'L L. 485 (1996)
Mallison, W. Thomas, & Sally V. Mallison, *The National Rights of the People of Palestine*, 9(4) J. PAL. STUD. 119 (1980)
Mansour, Camille, *Palestinian Options at the United Nations*, *in* ABORTED STATE? THE UN INITIATIVE AND NEW PALESTINIAN JUNCTURES 35 (Noura Erakat & Mouin Rabbani eds., 2013)
McCorquodale, Robert, *The Individual and the International Legal System*, *in* International Law 280 (Malcolm D. Evans ed., 4th ed. 2014)
——, *Self-Determination: A Human Rights Approach*, 43(4) INT'L & COMP. L.Q. 857 (1994)
——, & Kristin Hausler, *Caucuses in the Caucasus: The Application of the Right of Self-Determination*, *in* CONFLICT IN THE CAUCASUS: IMPLICATIONS FOR INTERNATIONAL LEGAL ORDER 26 (James A. Green & Christopher P.M. Waters eds., 2010)
THE MEANING OF THE HOLY QUR'ĀN ('Abdullāh Yūsuf 'Alī trans., 2002)
Meir, Golda, *Israel in Search of Lasting Peace*, 51(3) FOREIGN AFF. 447 (1973)
MERRILLS, J.G., INTERNATIONAL DISPUTE SETTLEMENT (5th ed. 2011)
——, *The Mosaic of International Dispute Settlement Procedures: Complementary or Contradictory?*, 54(2) NETH. INT'L L. REV. 361 (2007)
Morris, Benny: *The 1948 War Was an Islamic Holy War*, 17(3) MID. E. Q. 63 (2010)
MUASHER, MARWAN, THE ARAB CENTER: THE PROMISE OF MODERATION (2008)
Muñoz, Edgardo, *Right to Withhold Performance Under Ibero-American Law*, 1 CUADERNOS DE LA MAESTRÍA EN DERECHO 379 (2011)
Murphy, John F., *Beyond Camp David*, 74 AM. SOC'Y INT'L L. PROC. 117 (1980)

Nawaz, M.K., *The Meaning and Range of the Principle of Self-Determination*, 14(1) DUKE L.J. 82 (1965)
Nirmal, B.C., *The Right of Self-Determination of the Tibetan People, Approaches and Modalities*, *in* TIBETAN PEOPLE'S RIGHT OF SELF-DETERMINATION 44 (1996)
——, THE RIGHT TO SELF-DETERMINATION IN INTERNATIONAL LAW (1999)
NISAN, MORDECHAI, ONLY ISRAEL WEST OF THE RIVER: THE JEWISH STATE AND THE PALESTINIAN QUESTION (2011)
——, *The Palestinian Features of Jordan*, *in* JUDEA, SAMARIA, AND GAZA: VIEWS ON THE PRESENT AND FUTURE 191 (Daniel J. Elazar ed., 1982)
NUSSEIBEH, SARI, WHAT IS A PALESTINIAN STATE WORTH? (2011)

Öberg, Marko Divac, *The Legal Effects of Resolutions of the UN Security Council and General Assembly in the Jurisprudence of the ICJ*, 16(5) EUR. J. INT'L L. 879 (2005)

O'BRIEN, CONOR CRUISE, THE SIEGE: THE SAGA OF ISRAEL AND ZIONISM (1986)
Odermatt, Jed, *The Court of Justice of the European Union: International or Domestic Court?*, 3(3) Cambridge J. Int'l & Comp. L. 696 (2014)
Ofuatey-Kodjoe, W., *Self-Determination, in* 1 UNITED NATIONS LEGAL ORDER 349 (Oscar Schachter & Christopher C. Joyner eds., 1995)
Okowa, Phoebe, *The International Court of Justice and the Georgia/Russia Dispute*, 11(4) HUM. RTS. L. REV. 739 (2011)
ORAKHELASHVILI, ALEXANDER, PEREMPTORY NORMS IN INTERNATIONAL LAW (2008)
ORWELL, GEORGE, *Notes on Nationalism, in* ESSAYS 300 (2014)
The Oslo Agreement: An Interview with Nabil Shaath, 23(1) J. PAL. STUD. 5 (1993)
Oz, Amos, *Between Right and Right, in* HOW TO CURE A FANATIC 1 (2010)
——, HOW TO CURE A FANATIC (2010)

A Palestinian State in Two Years: Interview with Salam Fayyad, Palestinian Prime Minister, 39(1) J. PAL. STUD. 58 (2009)
Paulus, Andreas, *Whether Universal Values Can Prevail over Bilateralism and Reciprocity, in* REALIZING UTOPIA: THE FUTURE OF INTERNATIONAL LAW 89 (Antonio Cassese ed., 2012)
Pearlman, Wendy, *The Palestinian National Movement, in* THE 1967 ARAB-ISRAELI WAR: ORIGINS AND CONSEQUENCES 126 (William Roger Louis & Avi Shlaim eds., 2012)
Pellet, Alain, *The Palestinian Declaration and the Jurisdiction of the International Criminal Court*, 8(4) J. INT'L CRIM. JUST. 981 (2010)
Peretz, Don, *Arab Palestine: Phoenix or Phantom?*, 48(2) FOREIGN AFF. 322 (1970)
Peters, Anne, *International Dispute Settlement: A Network of Cooperational Duties*, 14(1) EUR. J. INT'L L. 1 (2003)
Philby, H.St.J.B., *The Arabs and the Future of Palestine*, 16(1) FOREIGN AFF. 156 (1937)
Pinsker, Leo, *Auto-Emancipation: An Appeal to His People by a Russian Jew (1882), in* THE ZIONIST IDEA: A HISTORICAL ANALYSIS AND READER 181 (Arthur Hertzberg ed., 1997)
PIPES, DANIEL, GREATER SYRIA: THE HISTORY OF AN AMBITION (1992)
PORTMANN, ROLAND, LEGAL PERSONALITY IN INTERNATIONAL LAW (2010)

Qafisheh, Mutaz M., *Bases for the Palestinian Refugees' Right of Return under International Law: Beyond General Assembly Resolution 194*, CAMBRIDGE J. INT'L & COMP. L. ONLINE, Nov. 26, 2012
——, *An Ongoing Anomaly: Pre- and Post-Second World War Palestinian Refugees*, 27(1) INT'L J. REFUGEE L. 52 (2015)
Quigley, John, *Displaced Palestinians and a Right of Return*, 39(1) HARV. INT'L L.J. 171 (1998)
——, *The Israel-PLO Interim Agreements: Are They Treaties?*, 30(3) CORNELL INT'L L.J. 717 (1997)
——, THE SIX-DAY WAR AND ISRAELI SELF-DEFENSE: QUESTIONING THE LEGAL BASIS FOR PREVENTIVE WAR (2013)
——, THE STATEHOOD OF PALESTINE: INTERNATIONAL LAW IN THE MIDDLE EAST CONFLICT (2010)
Qureshi, Zainab, *Self Determination, International Law & the Indigenous*, 1(3–4) PAK. J. INT'L L. 121 (2011)

RABINOVICH, ITAMAR, WAGING PEACE: ISRAEL AND THE ARABS, 1948–2003 (2004)
ISRAEL IN THE MIDDLE EAST: DOCUMENTS AND READINGS ON SOCIETY, POLITICS, AND FOREIGN RELATIONS, PRE-1948 TO THE PRESENT (Itamar Rabinovich & Jehuda Reinharz eds., 2d ed. 2008)

RAIČ, DAVID, STATEHOOD AND THE LAW OF SELF-DETERMINATION (2002)

RANGANATHAN, SURABHI, STRATEGICALLY CREATED TREATY CONFLICTS AND THE POLITICS OF INTERNATIONAL LAW (2014)

Reisman, W. Michael, *The Diversity of Contemporary International Dispute Resolution: Functions and Policies*, 4(1) J. INT'L DISP. SETTLEMENT 47 (2013)

Renan, Ernest, *What Is a Nation?*, *in* NATION AND NARRATION 8 (Homi K. Bhabha ed., 2008)

A Review of the Present Position of the Arab Countries, *in* MEMOIRS OF KING ABDULLAH OF TRANSJORDAN, app. 1 at 243 (Philip P. Graves ed., 1950)

Rogoff, Martin A., *The Obligation to Negotiate in International Law: Rules and Realities*, 16(1) MICH. J. INT'L L. 141 (1994)

Ronen, Yaël, *ICC Jurisdiction over Acts Committed in the Gaza Strip: Article 12(3) of the ICC Statute and Non-State Entities*, 8(1) J. INT'L CRIM. JUST. 3 (2010)

Roscini, Marco, *The Cases Against the Nuclear Weapons States*, 19(10) AM. SOC'Y INT'L L. INSIGHTS (May 12, 2015)

ROSENNE, SHABTAI, BREACH OF TREATY (1985)

——, *Directions for a Middle East Settlement—Some Underlying Legal Problems*, 33(1) LAW & CONTEMP. PROBS. 44 (1968)

——, *Israel and the United Nations: Changed Perspectives, 1945–1976*, 78 AM. JEWISH Y.B. 3 (1978)

——, ISRAEL'S ARMISTICE AGREEMENTS WITH THE ARAB STATES (1951)

Rostow, Eugene, *"Palestinian Self-Determination": Possible Futures for the Unallocated Territories of the Palestine Mandate*, 5 YALE STUD. WORLD PUB. ORD. 147 (1979)

Said, Edward W., *The Burdens of Interpretation and the Question of Palestine*, 16(1) J. PAL. STUD. 29 (1986)

——, *From Intifadah to Independence*, (158) MID. E. REP. 12 (1989)

——, PEACE AND ITS DISCONTENTS: GAZA-JERICHO 1993–1995 (1995)

——, THE QUESTION OF PALESTINE (1992)

SAMUEL, KATJA L.H., THE OIC, THE UN, AND COUNTER-TERRORISM LAW-MAKING: CONFLICTING OR COOPERATIVE LEGAL ORDERS? (2013)

SANDS, PHILIPPE, & PIERRE KLEIN, BOWETT'S LAW OF INTERNATIONAL INSTITUTIONS (6th ed. 2009)

Sayapin, Sergey, *The United Nations General Assembly Resolution 68/262 in the Context of General International Law*, 2(1) EUR. POL. & L. DISC. 19 (2015)

SAYEGH, FAYEZ A., ARAB UNITY: HOPE AND FULFILLMENT (1958)

——, *The Camp David Agreement and the Palestine Problem*, 8(2) J. PAL. STUD. 3 (1979)

Schachter, Oscar, *Dispute Settlement and Countermeasures in the International Law Commission*, 88(3) AM. J. INT'L L. 471 (1994)

——, *International Law in Theory and Practice: General Course in Public International Law*, *in* 178 COLLECTED COURSES OF THE HAGUE ACADEMY OF INTERNATIONAL LAW 9 (1982)

——, *The Invisible College of International Lawyers*, 72(2) NW. U. L. REV. 217 (1977)

SCHANZER, JONATHAN, STATE OF FAILURE: YASSER ARAFAT, MAHMOUD ABBAS, AND THE UNMAKING OF THE PALESTINIAN STATE (2013)

Scharf, Michael P., & Margaux Day, *The International Court of Justice's Treatment of Circumstantial Evidence and Adverse Inferences*, 13(1) CHI. J. INT'L L. 123 (2012)

Schmitt, Michael N., *"Below the Threshold" Cyber Operations: The Countermeasures Response Option and International Law*, 54(3) VA. J. INTL L. 697 (2014)

Schwebel, Stephen M., *What Weight to Conquest?*, 64(2) AM. J. INT'L L. 344 (1970)

Seabury, Paul, *The League of Arab States: Debacle of a Regional Arrangement*, 3(4) INT'L ORG. 633 (1949)

Self-Determination: The Case of Palestine, 82 AM. SOC'Y INT'L L. PROC. 334 (1988) (Yehuda Blum), (Allan Gerson)

SEN, AMARTYA, IDENTITY AND VIOLENCE: THE ILLUSION OF DESTINY (2007)

Senaratne, Kalana, *Internal Self-Determination in International Law: A Critical Third-World Perspective*, 3(2) ASIAN J. INT'L L. 305 (2013)

Shany, Yuval, *Does International Law Grant the People of Crimea and Donetsk a Right to Secede? Revisiting Self-Determination in Light of the 2014 Events in Ukraine*, 21(1) BROWN J. WORLD AFF. 233 (2014)

——, *In Defence of Functional Interpretation of Article 12(3) of the Rome Statute: A Response to Yaël Ronen*, 8(2) J. INT'L CRIM. JUST. 329 (2010)

Sharon, Moshe, *Palestine in the Islamic and Ottoman Period*, *in* THE PALESTINIANS: PEOPLE, HISTORY, POLITICS 9 (Michael Curtis et al. eds., 1975)

SHAW, MALCOLM N., INTERNATIONAL LAW (7th ed. 2014)

SHEHADEH, RAJA, FROM OCCUPATION TO INTERIM ACCORDS: ISRAEL AND THE PALESTINIAN TERRITORIES (1997)

Shihadeh, Raja, *Can the Declaration of Principles Bring About a "Just and Lasting Peace"?*, 4(1) EUR. J. INT'L L. 555 (1993)

Shlaim, Avi, *The Oslo Accord*, 23(3) J. PAL. STUD. 24 (1994)

——, *The Rise and Fall of the All-Palestine Government in Gaza*, 20(1) J. PAL. STUD. 37 (1990)

——, *The Rise and Fall of the Oslo Peace Process*, *in* INTERNATIONAL RELATIONS OF THE MIDDLE EAST 268 (Louise Fawcett ed., 3d ed. 2013)

SHWADRAN, BENJAMIN, JORDAN: A STATE OF TENSION (1959)

Simma, Bruno, & Christian J. Tams, *Article 60*, *in* 2 THE VIENNA CONVENTION ON THE LAW OF TREATIES: A COMMENTARY 1351 (Olivier Corten & Pierre Klein eds., 2011)

——, *Reacting Against Treaty Breaches*, *in* THE OXFORD GUIDE TO TREATIES 576 (Duncan B. Hollis ed., 2012)

Sinanoglou, Penny, *The Peel Commission and Partition, 1936–1938*, *in* BRITAIN, PALESTINE AND EMPIRE: THE MANDATE YEARS 119 (Rory Miller ed., 2010)

Sinclair, Ian, *Estoppel and Acquiescence*, *in* FIFTY YEARS OF THE INTERNATIONAL COURT OF JUSTICE: ESSAYS IN HONOUR OF SIR ROBERT JENNINGS 104 (Vaughan Lowe & Malgosia Fitzmaurice eds., 1996)

Singer, Joel, *Aspects of Foreign Relations Under the Israeli-Palestinian Agreements on Interim Self-Government Arrangements for the West Bank and Gaza*, 28(2–3) ISR. L. REV. 268 (1994)

——, *The West Bank and Gaza Strip: Phase Two*, 7 JUST. 5 (Dec. 1995)

SINGH, KHUSHWANT, TRAIN TO PAKISTAN (2012)

Skordas, Achilles, *Self-Determination of Peoples and Transnational Regimes: A Foundational Principle of Global Governance*, *in* TRANSNATIONAL CONSTITUTIONALISM: INTERNATIONAL AND EUROPEAN MODELS 207 (Nicholas Tsagourias ed., 2007)

Skouteris, Thomas, *Engaging History in International Law*, *in* NEW APPROACHES TO INTERNATIONAL LAW 99 (J.M. Beneyto & D. Kennedy eds., 2012)

Sluglett, Peter, *An Improvement on Colonialism? The "A" Mandates and Their Legacy in the Middle East*, 90(2) INT'L AFF. 413 (2014)

Smith, Charles D., *The United States and the 1967 War*, *in* THE 1967 ARAB-ISRAELI WAR: ORIGINS AND CONSEQUENCES 165 (William Roger Louis & Avi Shlaim eds., 2012)

Solomon, Solon, *The Quest for Self-Determination: Defining International Law's Inherent Interstate Limits*, 11(2) SANTA CLARA J. INT'L L. 397 (2013)

——, *The Case of* Bolivia v. Chile *in an Era of Transforming Sovereignty*, 25(3) FLA. J. INT'L L. 331 (2013)

Spoerl, Joseph S., *Palestinians, Arabs, and the Holocaust*, 26(1–2) JEWISH POL. STUD. REV. 14 (2014)

Srnská, Milena, *On the Principle of Equal Rights and Self-Determination of Nations*, *in* THE LEGAL PRINCIPLES GOVERNING FRIENDLY RELATIONS AND CO-OPERATION AMONG STATES IN THE SPIRIT OF THE UNITED NATIONS CHARTER 115 (1966)

Stein, Leonard, *The Jews in Palestine*, 4(3) FOREIGN AFF. 415 (1926)

Stepanowa, Anna, *International Law and Legality of Secession in Crimea*, CAMBRIDGE J. INT'L & COMP. L. ONLINE, Apr. 20, 2014

St. John, Ronald Bruce, *Chile, Peru and the Treaty of 1929: The Final Settlement*, 8(1) BOUNDARY & SEC. BULL. 91 (2000)

STONE, JULIUS, ISRAEL AND PALESTINE: ASSAULT ON THE LAW OF NATIONS (1981)

SUMMERS, JAMES, PEOPLES AND INTERNATIONAL LAW: HOW NATIONALISM AND SELF-DETERMINATION SHAPE A CONTEMPORARY LAW OF NATIONS (2007)

Susser, Asher, *Partition and the Arab Palestinian Minority in Israel*, 14(2) ISR. STUD. 105 (2009)

Tarre Moser, Patricia, *Non-Recognition of State Immunity as a Judicial Countermeasure to* Jus Cogens *Violations: The Human Rights Answer to the ICJ Decision on the* Ferrini *Case*, 4(3) GOETTINGEN J. INT'L L. 809 (2012)

THIRLWAY, HUGH, THE SOURCES OF INTERNATIONAL LAW (2014)

Troen, S. Ilan, *Israeli Views of the Land of Israel/Palestine*, 18(2) ISR. STUD. 100 (2013)

Tunkin, G.I., *Coexistence and International Law*, *in* 95 COLLECTED COURSES OF THE HAGUE ACADEMY OF INTERNATIONAL LAW 1 (1958)

——, THEORY OF INTERNATIONAL LAW (William E. Butler ed. & trans., 2003)

——, LAW AND FORCE IN THE INTERNATIONAL SYSTEM (1985)

TWAIN, MARK, THE INNOCENTS ABROAD (2002)

UMOZURIKE, U.O., INTERNATIONAL LAW AND COLONIALISM IN AFRICA (1979)

UNITED NATIONS, TREATY HANDBOOK, U.N. Sales No. E.12.V.1 (rev. ed. 2012)

1946–47 U.N.Y.B.

1948–49 U.N.Y.B.

VATTEL, EMER DE, THE LAW OF NATIONS (Béla Kapossy & Richard Whatmore eds., 2008)

Verhoeven, Joe, *The Law of Responsibility and the Law of Treaties*, *in* THE LAW OF INTERNATIONAL RESPONSIBILITY 105 (James Crawford et al. eds., 2010)

Wagner, Megan L., *Jurisdiction by Estoppel in the International Court of Justice*, 74(5) CAL. L. REV. 1777 (1986)

Waibel, Michael, *The Diplomatic Channel*, *in* THE LAW OF INTERNATIONAL RESPONSIBILITY 1085 (James Crawford et al. eds., 2010)

WATSON, GEOFFREY R., THE OSLO ACCORDS: INTERNATIONAL LAW AND THE ISRAELI-PALESTINIAN PEACE AGREEMENTS (2000)

Wählisch, Martin, *Beyond a Seat in the United Nations: Palestine's U.N. Membership and International Law*, 53 HARV. INT'L L.J. ONLINE 226 (2012)

Weiler, Joseph, *Editorial*, 22(3) EUR. J. INT'L L. 621 (2011)
Weiner, Justus R., *The Palestinian Refugees' "Right to Return" and the Peace Process*, 20(1) B.C. INT'L & COMP. L. REV. 1 (1997)
Weitz, Eric D., *Self-Determination: How a German Enlightenment Idea Became the Slogan of National Liberation and a Human Right*, 120(2) AM. HIST. REV. 462 (2015)
WELLENS, KAREL, NEGOTIATIONS IN THE CASE LAW OF THE INTERNATIONAL COURT OF JUSTICE: A FUNCTIONAL ANALYSIS (2014)
Whelan, Anthony, *Wilsonian Self-Determination and the Versailles Settlement*, 43(1) INT'L & COMP. L.Q. 99 (1994)
WILDE, RALPH, INTERNATIONAL TERRITORIAL ADMINISTRATION: HOW TRUSTEESHIP AND THE CIVILIZING MISSION NEVER WENT AWAY (2008)
Wright, Quincy, *The Bombardment of Damascus*, 20(2) AM. J. INT'L L. 263 (1926)
——, MANDATES UNDER THE LEAGUE OF NATIONS (1930)
——, *Recognition and Self-Determination*, 48 AM. SOC'Y INT'L L. PROC. 23 (1954)
——, *Sovereignty of the Mandates*, 17(4) AM. J. INT'L L. 691 (1923)
——, *The Tacna-Arica Arbitration*, 10(1) MINN. L. REV. 28 (1925)

Yoffie, Adam G., *The Palestine Problem: The Search for Statehood and the Benefits of International Law*, 36(2) YALE J. INT'L L. 497 (2011)
Yusuf, Abdulqawi A., *The Role that Equal Rights and Self-Determination of Peoples Can Play in the Current World Community, in* REALIZING UTOPIA: THE FUTURE OF INTERNATIONAL LAW 375 (Antonio Cassese ed., 2012)

Zahran, Mudar, *Jordan Is Palestinian*, 19(1) MID. E. Q. 3 (2012)
Ziegler, Reuven (Ruvi), *Protecting Recognized Geneva Convention Refugees Outside Their States of Asylum*, 25(2) INT'L J. REFUGEE L. 235 (2013)
ZIFF, WILLIAM B., THE RAPE OF PALESTINE (1948)

Newspaper Articles

Abbas, Mahmoud, *The Long Overdue Palestinian State*, N.Y. TIMES, May 16, 2011
Abrams, Elliott, *Abbas's "Bombshell,"* WEEKLY STANDARD, Sept. 30, 2015
Abu Toameh, Khaled, *Fatah: Oslo Accords Will Cease to Exist After UN Bid*, JERUSALEM POST, Nov. 8, 2012
Alon, Gideon, et al., *Sharon, Abbas to Meet as Cabinet Approves Road Map*, HAARETZ, May 26, 2003

Bin Talal, Crown Prince Hassan (Jordan), *Palestine: Might Versus Rights*, TIMES, Sept. 3, 1982
British Israel Communications & Research Centre, *Israel Announces Response to Palestinian UN Vote*, Dec. 3, 2012
Browne, Mallory, *Jews in Grave Danger in All Moslem Lands: Nine Hundred Thousand in Africa and Asia Face Wrath of Their Foes*, N.Y. TIMES, May 16, 1948

DPA, *Palestinians Rebuff Quartet's Calls to Return to Table*, HAARETZ, Oct. 27, 2011

Ephron, Dan, *Palestinian President Mahmoud Abbas Threatens Legal Action Against Israel*, DAILY BEAST, Apr. 17, 2012
Erekat, Saeb, *The Returning Issue of Palestine's Refugees*, GUARDIAN, Dec. 10, 2010

Friedman, Ron, *Netanyahu's Letter to Abbas Offers Nothing New, PLO Says*, TIMES OF ISRAEL, May 13, 2012

Gladstone, Rick & Jodi Rudoren, *Mahmoud Abbas, at U.N., Says Palestinians Are No Longer Bound by Oslo Accords*, N.Y. TIMES, Sept. 30, 2015
Greenberg, Joel, *Israel to Release Withheld Tax Funds to Palestinians*, WASH. POST, Nov. 30, 2011

Hammami, Said, *The Palestinian Way to Middle East Peace*, TIMES, Nov. 16, 1973

Keinon, Herb, *"Document Israel Gave PA Was Just an Outline,"* JERUSALEM POST, Jan. 5, 2012
——, *PA Officials: Israeli Border Proposal a Non-Starter*, JERUSALEM POST, Jan. 27, 2012
——, & Khaled Abu Toameh, *Israel, PA Agree to Meet Again Next Week*, JERUSALEM POST, Jan. 3, 2012
——, *Israeli Call to Resume Direct Talks Rebuffed by PA*, JERUSALEM POST, Dec. 11, 2011

LaFranchi, Howard, *Israeli Envoy Calls Divisive Settlement Plan a Politically Necessary Reprisal*, CHRISTIAN SCI. MONITOR, Dec. 11, 2012
Levy, Elior, *Hamas' Haniyeh Slams Abbas over UN Bid*, YNETNEWS, Sept. 18, 2011

Meir, Golda, *On the Palestinians*, N.Y. TIMES, Jan. 14, 1976
——, *"Who Can Blame Israel?,"* SUN. TIMES, June 15, 1969
Mozgovaya, Natasha, & Reuters, *Palestinians Disappointed by Obama's UN Speech*, HAARETZ, Sept. 21, 2011
M. Rabin: Le Dialogue Avec l'O.L.P. n'est Possible que Sur le Champ de Bataille, LE MONDE, Mar. 22, 1977

Ravid, Barak, *Israel to Keep Holding Palestinian Authority Funds, Against Advice of Security Officials*, HAARETZ, Nov. 14, 2011
——, *Netanyahu's Border Proposal: Israel to Annex Settlement Blocs, but Not Jordan Valley*, HAARETZ, Feb. 19, 2012
——, *Was It a Bombshell or Stink Bomb that Abbas Dropped in His UN Speech?*, HAARETZ, Sept. 30, 2015
——, & Natasha Mozgovaya, *Israel Presents the Palestinians with its Stance on Borders*, HAARETZ, Jan. 26, 2012
Rudoren, Jodi, *Netanyahu's History on Palestinian Statehood*, N.Y. TIMES, Mar. 20, 2015

Schmidt, Dana Adams, *Aim to Oust Jews Pledged by Sheikh; Head of Moslem Brotherhood Says U.S., British "Politics" Has Hurt Palestine Solution*, N.Y. TIMES, Aug. 2, 1948
Selden, Charles A., *Prince of Hedjaz Welcomes Zionists*, N.Y. TIMES, Mar. 5, 1919
Sherwood, Harriet, *Israel Warns Palestinians All Deals Are Off if UN Vote Goes Ahead*, GUARDIAN, June 17, 2011
Sokol, Sam, *The Catastrophe Called Israel?*, JERUSALEM POST, May 10, 2012

Somfalvi, Attila, *Erekat: No Negotiations Yet*, YNETNEWS, Jan. 2, 2012
Spiegel Interview with Palestinian Prime Minister: "An Independent Palestine Will Be Inevitable," SPIEGEL ONLINE, Sept. 19, 2011
Susser, Asher, *Looking Straight at the Initiative*, HAARETZ, Dec. 18, 2008

Tittel, Cornelius & Clemens Wergin, *The Palestinians Want a State Without Peace*, DIE WELT, Dec. 5, 2012

Entries in Encyclopedia

Gautier, Philippe, *Non-Binding Agreements, in* MAX PLANCK ENCYCLOPEDIA OF PUBLIC INTERNATIONAL LAW (last updated Dec. 2006)
Giegerich, Thomas, *Retorsion, in* MAX PLANCK ENCYCLOPEDIA OF PUBLIC INTERNATIONAL LAW (last updated Mar. 2011)

Pellet, Alain, & Alina Miron, *Sanctions, in* MAX PLANCK ENCYCLOPEDIA OF PUBLIC INTERNATIONAL LAW (last updated July 2011)

Schmidt, Jan Peter, *MERCOSUR, in* MAX PLANCK ENCYCLOPEDIA OF PUBLIC INTERNATIONAL LAW (last updated Oct. 2008)
Stone, Julius, *International Conflict Resolution, in* INTERNATIONAL ENCYCLOPEDIA OF THE SOCIAL SCIENCES (1968)
Thürer, Daniel, & Thomas Burri, *Self-Determination, in* MAX PLANCK ENCYCLOPEDIA OF PUBLIC INTERNATIONAL LAW (last updated Dec. 2008)

Reports, Statements, and Memoranda

Address by King Hussein on Jordan's Disengagement from the West Bank, 31 July, 1988, *in* THE ISRAELI-PALESTINIAN CONFLICT: A DOCUMENTARY RECORD: 1967–1990 520 (Yehuda Lukacs ed., 1992)
Address by King Hussein to the 17th Session of the Palestine National Council, Amman, 22 November, 1984 [Excerpts], *in* THE ISRAELI-PALESTINIAN CONFLICT: A DOCUMENTARY RECORD: 1967–1990 485 (Yehuda Lukacs ed., 1992)
Address to the Knesset by Prime Minister Rabin Presenting his Government, July 13, 1992, 13–14 Documents on the Foreign Policy of Israel (1992–94)
Addresses at the Opening Meeting of the Geneva Peace Conference, Dec. 21, 1973, *in* Israel's Foreign Relations: Volumes I–II: 1947–1974
Al-Haq, Al-Haq's Questions & Answers on Palestine's September Initiatives at the United Nations, No. 249/2011 (July 20, 2011)
Allain, Jean, *On Achieving Palestinian Statehood: Concepts, Ends and Means from the Perspective of International Law*, Lectures Delivered at the Ibrahim Abu-Lughod Institute of International Studies (Apr. 2002)

Al Madfai, Madiha Rashid, Jordan, the United States and the Middle East Peace Process, 1974–1991, app. B at 222 (2007) (Jordan-US Exchange of Questions and Answers on the Camp David Accords, September 1978)

Amir Abdallah, Proposal for the Solution of the Palestine Problem Submitted to the Woodhead Commission, May 1938, *in* 1 DOCUMENTS ON PALESTINE 357 (Mahdi Abdul Hadi ed., 2007)

Amir Faysal's Memorandum to the Paris Peace Conference, Jan. 1, 1919, *in* 2 THE ARAB STATES AND THE ARAB LEAGUE: A DOCUMENTARY RECORD 302 (Muhammad Khalil ed., 1962)

Analysis of Paragraph 11 of the General Assembly's Resolution of 11 December 1948, U.N. Doc. W/45 (May 15, 1950)

Application for the Admission of Palestine as a Member State of UNESCO, Doc. 131 EX/45 (May 18, 1989)

Application of Palestine for Admission to Membership in the United Nations, Annex I at 2, U.N. Doc. A/66/371 (Sept. 23, 2011) (Application of the State of Palestine for Admission to Membership in the United Nations)

Application of Palestine for Admission to Membership in the United Nations, Annex II at 4, U.N. Doc. A/66/371 (Sept. 23, 2011) (Letter Dated 23 September 2011 from the President of Palestine to the Secretary-General)

ARAB REACTIONS IN PALESTINE TO THE REPORT OF THE ANGLO-AMERICAN COMMITTEE OF ENQUIRY, June 6, 1946, No. CAB/129/10

The Attitude of the Arab States Towards International Conferences and Organizations in Which Israel Participates, May 19, 1951, *in* 2 THE ARAB STATES AND THE ARAB LEAGUE: A DOCUMENTARY RECORD 168 (Muhammad Khalil ed., 1962)

Aumann, Robert J., Nobel Prize in Economic Sciences Lecture, War and Peace (Dec. 8, 2005)

Australian Broadcasting Corporation, Shaath Discusses Palestinian Push for Recognition (Sept. 26, 2011)

Baker, Alan, Ten Points Regarding the Fundamental Breach by the Palestinians of the Oslo Accords, Jerusalem Center for Public Affairs (Jan. 5, 2015)

Becker, Tal, International Recognition of a Unilaterally Declared Palestinian State: Legal and Policy Dilemmas, Jerusalem Center for Public Affairs

Bedjaoui, Mohammed, Keynote Address at Good Faith, International Law, and Elimination of Nuclear Weapons Conference, Geneva (May 1, 2008)

Begin Addresses Jewish Leaders in New York, Sept. 20, 1978, *in* PEACE IN THE MAKING: THE MENACHEM BEGIN-ANWAR EL SADAT PERSONAL CORRESPONDENCE 83 (Harry Hurwitz & Yisrael Medad eds., 2011)

Begin Addresses the Knesset on the Peace Treaty, Mar. 21, 1979, *in* PEACE IN THE MAKING: THE MENACHEM BEGIN-ANWAR EL SADAT PERSONAL CORRESPONDENCE 117 (Harry Hurwitz & Yisrael Medad eds., 2011)

The Boycott of Zionist Goods and Products, Dec. 2, 1945, *in* 2 THE ARAB STATES AND THE ARAB LEAGUE: A DOCUMENTARY RECORD 161 (Muhammad Khalil ed., 1962)

Boycott of Zionist Products and Goods, June 12, 1946, *in* 2 THE ARAB STATES AND THE ARAB LEAGUE: A DOCUMENTARY RECORD 162 (Muhammad Khalil ed., 1962)

CABINET, REPORT OF PALESTINE ROYAL COMMISSION, app. II at 7, No. CAB/24/270 (1937) (Letter from Professor Reginald Coupland to the Secretary of State for the Colonies, June 23, 1937)

Cablegram Dated 18 May 1948 from the President of the Security Council Addressed to the Foreign Minister of Egypt, and Reply Thereto Submitted by the Representative of Egypt at the Three Hundred and First Meeting of the Security Council, U.N. Doc. S/767 (May 22, 1948)

Cablegram Dated 18 May 1948 from the President of the Security Council Addressed to the Foreign Minister of Iraq, and Reply Thereto Submitted by the Representative of Iraq at the 301st Meeting of the Security Council, U.N. Doc. S/769 (May 22, 1948)

Cablegram Dated 18 May 1948 from the President of the Security Council Addressed to the Foreign Minister of Lebanon, and Reply Thereto Submitted by the Representative of Lebanon at the 301st Meeting of the Security Council, U.N. Doc. S/770 (May 22, 1948)

Cablegram Dated 18 May 1948 from the President of the Security Council Addressed to the Foreign Minister of Saudi Arabia, and Reply Thereto Submitted by the Representative of Saudi Arabia on 22 May 1948, U.N. Doc. S/772 (May 22, 1948)

Cablegram Dated 18 May 1948 from the President of the Security Council Addressed to the Foreign Minister of Syria, and Reply Thereto Submitted by the Representative of Syria at the 301st Meeting of the Security Council, U.N. Doc. S/768 (May 22, 1948)

Cablegram Dated 18 May 1948 from the President of the Security Council Addressed to the Foreign Minister of Transjordan, and Reply Thereto Dated 20 May 1948, U.N. Doc. S/760 (May 20, 1948)

Cablegram Dated 18 May 1948 from the President of the Security Council Addressed to the Foreign Minister of Yemen, and Reply Thereto Submitted by the Foreign Minister of Yemen on 23 May 1948, U.N. Doc. S/774 (May 24, 1948)

Cablegram Dated 27 September 1948 from Ralph Bunche to the Secretary-General Transmitting Report Regarding the Assassination of the United Nations Mediator, U.N. Doc S/1018 (Sept. 28, 1948)

Conclusions of the Work of the Study Group on the Fragmentation of International Law: Difficulties Arising from the Diversification and Expansion of International Law, *in* Report of the International Law Commission, 58th Sess., May 1–June 9, July 3–Aug. 11, 2006, at 407, U.N. Doc. A/61/10; GAOR, 61st Sess., Supp. No. 10 (2006)

CRISTESCU, AURELIU, THE RIGHT TO SELF-DETERMINATION: HISTORICAL AND CURRENT DEVELOPMENT ON THE BASIS OF UNITED NATIONS INSTRUMENTS, U.N. Doc. E/CN.4/Sub.2/404/Rev.1 (1981)

Declaration Approved by the Council of the League of Nations, London, July 24, 1922, 17(3) AM. J. INT'L L. SUPP. 193 (1922) (1923)

Declaration by the High Representative on Behalf of the European Union on the Middle East Peace Process, Brussels, No. 16079/12, Nov. 29, 2012

Declaration of the Establishment of the State of Israel, 14 May 1948, *in* THE ARAB-ISRAEL CONFLICT AND ITS RESOLUTION: SELECTED DOCUMENTS 61 (Ruth Lapidoth & Moshe Hirsch eds., 1992)

Defending Palestine, Oct. 9, 1947, *in* 2 THE ARAB STATES AND THE ARAB LEAGUE: A DOCUMENTARY RECORD 164 (Muhammad Khalil ed., 1962)

Despatch from Secretary of State for the Colonies to High Commissioner, Palestine, No. 1223, Oct. 4, 1923, *in* FUTURE OF PALESTINE, app. 1 at 2, No. CAB/24/162 (1923)

Embassy of Israel, Background Paper, Aug. 15, 1979, *in* RECORDS OF THE PRIME MINISTER'S OFFICE: CORRESPONDENCE AND PAPERS, 1979–1997. MIDDLE EAST. SITUATION IN THE MIDDLE EAST; PART 1 at 62, No. PREM/19/92 (1979)

Explanatory Note Concerning the Request for the Admission of the State of Palestine to UNESCO, Doc. 131 EX/43 (May 12, 1989)

GANDHI, MAHATMA, *Speech at Public Meeting, Jaffna, in* 35 THE COLLECTED WORKS OF MAHATMA GANDHI (SEPTEMBER 1927–JANUARY 1928) 320 (Publ'n Dep't, Gov't of India ed., 1969)

Goodwin-Gill, Guy S., Opinion re the Palestine Liberation Organization, the Future State of Palestine, and the Question of Popular Representation (Aug. 10, 2011)

HANDBOOK ON THE PEACEFUL SETTLEMENT OF DISPUTES BETWEEN STATES, U.N. Doc. OLA/COD/2394 (1992)

An Interim Report on the Civil Administration of Palestine, During the Period 1st July 1920–30th June 1921, *in* PALESTINE AND TRANSJORDAN ADMINISTRATION REPORTS: 1918–1948: VOLUME I: 1918–1924 169 (R. Jarman ed., 1995)

International Criminal Court, Situation in Palestine, Apr. 3, 2012

International Law Association, Sofia Conference Report: Non-State Actors (2012)

International Law Commission, Eighth Report on Unilateral Acts of States, U.N. Doc. A/CN.4/557 (2005)

International Law Commission, Third Report on Identification of Customary International Law, U.N. Doc. A/CN.4/682 (2015)

International Law Commission, Third Report on State Responsibility, U.N. Doc. A/CN.4/507/Add.3 (2000)

International Meeting of Experts on Further Study of the Concept of the Rights of Peoples, Final Report and Recommendations, SHS-89/CONF.602/7 (1990)

Ismailia Summit, Dec. 26, 1977, *in* PEACE IN THE MAKING: THE MENACHEM BEGIN-ANWAR EL SADAT PERSONAL CORRESPONDENCE 51 (Harry Hurwitz & Yisrael Medad eds., 2011)

Israeli Foreign Minister Abba Eban, Statement to the Knesset Regarding the "Legitimate Rights of the Palestinian People," Jerusalem, July 18, 1973, *in* 2 DOCUMENTS ON PALESTINE 403 (Mahdi Abdul Hadi ed., 2007)

Israel Knesset Statement, Prime Minister, Yitzhak Rabin, Following the Rabat Conference, 5 November, 1974 [Excerpts], *in* THE ISRAELI-PALESTINIAN CONFLICT: A DOCUMENTARY RECORD, 1967–1990 188 (Yehuda Lukacs ed., 1992)

Israel Ministry of Foreign Affairs, Address by PM Netanyahu at Bar-Ilan University (June 4, 2009)

Israel Ministry of Foreign Affairs, Behind the Headlines: The Dangers of Premature Recognition of a Palestinian State (June 8, 2011)

Israel Ministry of Foreign Affairs, Cabinet Communique (Dec. 2, 2012)

Israel Ministry of Foreign Affairs, Israel Welcomes Quartet Call for Direct Negotiations (Oct. 2, 2011)

Israel Ministry of Foreign Affairs, May 4, 1999: Some Frequently Asked Questions (Apr. 19, 1999)

Israel Ministry of Foreign Affairs, Special Report on the Issue of Jewish Refugees from Arab Countries (Apr. 3, 2012)

Israel Ministry of Foreign Affairs, Statement by PM Netanyahu on the Cabinet Decision to Suspend New Construction in Judea and Samaria (Nov. 25, 2009)

Israel's Response to the Roadmap (May 25, 2003)

Jabotinsky, Zeev, *The Ethics of the Iron Wall*, Jabotinsky Institute, Tel AVIV, No. A1-7/14 (Nov. 4–Dec. 31, 1923)

The Jewish National Home in Palestine, Committee on Foreign Affairs, U.S. House of Representatives, 78th Congress, 2d Sess., H. Res. 418 and H. Res. 419 1 (1944)

Jewish Terrorism in Palestine, Dec. 12, 1946, *in* 2 THE ARAB STATES AND THE ARAB LEAGUE: A DOCUMENTARY RECORD 163 (Muhammad Khalil ed., 1962)

Karsh, Efraim, *The Myth of Palestinian Centrality* (Begin-Sadat Center for Strategic Studies Mideast Security and Policy Studies No. 108, 2014)

King Hussein's Plan for a Federation, 15 Mar. 1972, *in* THE ARAB-ISRAEL CONFLICT AND ITS RESOLUTION: SELECTED DOCUMENTS 143 (Ruth Lapidoth & Moshe Hirsch eds., 1992)

Lapidoth, Ruth, *Israel and the Palestinians: Some Legal Issues* (Jerusalem Institute for Israel Studies Series No. 94, 2003)

League of Arab States, Khartoum Resolution, Sept. 1, 1967

League of Arab States, Seventh Arab Summit Conference, Rabat Resolutions, Oct. 29, 1974, *in* ISRAEL IN THE MIDDLE EAST: DOCUMENTS AND READINGS ON SOCIETY, POLITICS, AND FOREIGN RELATIONS, PRE-1948 TO THE PRESENT 342 (Itamar Rabinovich & Jehuda Reinharz eds., 2d ed. 2008)

League of Arab States, Sixth Arab Summit Conference, Algiers, Overview and Resolutions, Nov. 28, 1973, *in* ISRAEL IN THE MIDDLE EAST: DOCUMENTS AND READINGS ON SOCIETY, POLITICS, AND FOREIGN RELATIONS, PRE-1948 TO THE PRESENT 334 (Itamar Rabinovich & Jehuda Reinharz eds., 2d ed. 2008)

Letter Dated 29 April 1976 from the Permanent Representative of the Union of Soviet Socialist Republics to the United Nations Addressed to the Secretary-General, Annex at 1, U.N. Doc. A/31/84 (Apr. 29, 1976)

Letter Dated 31 August 1977 from the Permanent Representative of Israel to the United Nations Addressed to the Secretary General, Annex I at 1, U.N. Doc. A/32/202 (Aug. 31, 1977) (Statement Issued After a Meeting of the Palestinian Central Council, Held at Damascus on 25 and 26 August 1977)

Letter Dated 31 August 1977 from the Permanent Representative of Israel to the United Nations Addressed to the Secretary General, Annex II at 1, U.N. Doc. A/32/202 (Aug. 31, 1977) (Fifteen-Point Programme Adopted at the Thirteenth Session of the Palestinian National Council, Held at Cairo from 12 to 20 March 1977)

Letter Dated 1 December 1948 from the Acting Mediator to the Secretary-General Transmitting a Communication from the Syrian Government Concerning the Security Council Resolution of 16 November (S/1080), U.N. Doc. S/1097 (Dec. 2, 1948)

Letter Dated 3 December 1982 from the Permanent Representative of Morocco to the United Nations Addressed to the Secretary-General, U.N. Doc. A/37/696 (Dec. 15, 1982)

Letter Dated 5 December 1977 from the Permanent Representative of the Libyan Arab Jamahiriya to the United Nations Addressed to the Secretary-General, U.N. Doc. A/32/411 (Dec. 6, 1977)

Letter Dated 3 December 1979 from the Permanent Representative of Tunisia to the United Nations Addressed to the Secretary-General, Annex at 1, U.N. Doc. A/34/763 (Dec. 10, 1979) (Final Declaration of the Tenth Arab Summit Conference)

Letter Dated 18 December 1973 from the Secretary-General to the President of the Security Council, U.N. Doc. S/11161 (Dec. 18, 1973)

Letter Dated 20 February 1976 from the Chargé d'Affairs a.i. of the Permanent Mission of the United States of America to the United Nations Addressed to the Secretary-General, U.N. Doc. A/31/54 (Feb. 23, 1976)

Letter Dated 29 January 2004 from the Deputy Director General and Legal Advisor of the Ministry of Foreign Affairs, Together with the Written Statement of the Government of Israel, Legal Consequences of the Construction of a Wall in the Occupied Palestinian Territory, Advisory Opinion, 2004 I.C.J. (Jan. 30)

Letter Dated 18 May 1948 from the Assistant Secretary-General for Security Council Affairs Addressed to the Arab Higher Committee, and Reply Dated 24 May 1948 Addressed to the Secretary-General Concerning the Questions Submitted by the Security Council, U.N. Doc. S/775 (May 24, 1948)

Letter Dated 18 May 1948 from the Assistant Secretary-General for Security Council Affairs Addressed to the Jewish Agency for Palestine, and Reply Dated 22 May 1948 Addressed to the Secretary-General Concerning the Questions Submitted by the Security Council, U.N. Doc. S/766 (May 22, 1948)

Letter Dated 22 November 1973 from the Permanent Representative of Algeria to the United Nations Addressed to the Secretary-General, U.N. Doc. A/9330 (Nov. 22, 1973)

Letter Dated 8 November 1978 from the Permanent Representative of Iraq to the United Nations Addressed to the Secretary-General, Annex at 1 U.N. Doc. A/33/400 (Nov. 29, 1978) (Statement Dated 6 November 1978 Issued by the Ninth Arab Summit Conference)

Letter Dated 18 November 1988 from the Permanent Representative of Jordan to the United Nations Addressed to the Secretary-General, Annex I at 8, U.N. Doc. A/43/827 (Nov. 18, 1988) (Political Communiqué)

Letter Dated 18 November 1988 from the Permanent Representative of Jordan to the United Nations Addressed to the Secretary-General, Annex II at 13, U.N. Doc. A/43/827 (Nov. 18, 1988) (Declaration of Independence)

Letter Dated 10 October 1973 from the Permanent Representative of Algeria to the United Nations Addressed to the Secretary-General, U.N. Doc. S/11019 (Oct. 10, 1973)

Letter Dated 28 October 1964 from the Permanent Representative of the United Arab Republic to the United Nations Addressed to the Secretary-General, U.N. Doc. A/5763 (Oct. 29, 1964)

Letter from President Johnson to King Faisal, Washington, September 25, 1967, *in* 19 FOREIGN RELATIONS OF THE UNITED STATES, 1964–1968 Doc. 447, 846

Letter from the Chairman of the United Nations Palestine Commission to the President of the Security Council Dated 16 February 1948, Annex at 1 U.N. Doc. S/676 (Feb. 16, 1948) (First Special Report to the Security Council: The Problem of Security in Palestine)

Letter from the Higher Arab Committee for Palestine, Presented to the Heads of Arab Governments, Foreign Ministers, Secretariat-General of the Arab League, and to Leaders of Political Parties and Parliamentary Blocs, Concerning Mr. Eric Johnston's Scheme, Aug. 18, 1955, *in* 2 THE ARAB STATES AND THE ARAB LEAGUE: A DOCUMENTARY RECORD 634 (Muhammad Khalil ed., 1962)

Letters Following Begin's Hospitalization, Aug. 2–27, 1980, *in* PEACE IN THE MAKING: THE MENACHEM BEGIN-ANWAR EL SADAT PERSONAL CORRESPONDENCE 186 (Harry Hurwitz & Yisrael Medad eds., 2011)

ICJ Commemorative Speech: ICJ Lead Attorney Vaughan Lowe, Speech on the Occasion of the First Anniversary of the International Court of Justice's Advisory Opinion on Israel's Wall (July 9, 2005)

Mansfield, Telegram Number 946 of 24 August 1979, *in* RECORDS OF THE PRIME MINISTER'S OFFICE: CORRESPONDENCE AND PAPERS, 1979–1997. MIDDLE EAST. SITUATION IN THE MIDDLE EAST; PART 1 at 38, No. PREM/19/92 (1979)

Memorandum by the British Representative, 17(3) AM. J. INT'L L. SUPP. 172 (1922) (1923)

Memorandum from the Negotiations Support Unit of the Negotiations Affairs Department, Palestine Liberation Organization, to Palestinian Leadership on Legal Approaches to be Advanced at the ICC in Order to Protect Overall Palestinian Strategy and Realize Palestinian Rights and Interests (Mar. 25, 2009)

Memorandum of Agreement Between the United States and Israel Regarding the Geneva Peace Conference, Sept. 17, 1975, *in* ISRAEL IN THE MIDDLE EAST: DOCUMENTS AND READINGS ON SOCIETY, POLITICS, AND FOREIGN RELATIONS, PRE-1948 TO THE PRESENT 348 (Itamar Rabinovich & Jehuda Reinharz eds., 2d ed. 2008)

Memorandum Prepared by the Permanent Observer Mission of Palestine to the United Nations—New York: Response to Arguments that the "September Initiative" Regarding Statehood Will Harm the Status of the Palestine Liberation Organization (PLO) and the Rights of the Palestine Refugees (Sept. 2011)

Memorandum Submitted by the Arab Higher Committee to the Permanent Mandates Commission and the Secretary of State for the Colonies, July 23, 1937

Memorial of Georgia, Application of the International Convention on the Elimination of All Forms of Racial Discrimination (Geor. v. Russ.), vol. 1, 2009 I.C.J. (Sept. 2)

Middle East Quartet Holds Informal Consultations, Mar. 12, 2012, U.N. Doc. SG/2181

National Covenant of the Palestine Liberation Organization, May 28, 1964, HAARETZ, May 14, 2002

Norway Ministry of Foreign Affairs, Opening Address at the AHLC Meeting in New York (Sept. 22, 2014)

Note Verbale Dated 15 November 1978 from the Permanent Representative of Iraq to the United Nations Addressed to the Secretary-General, at app. I, U.N. Doc. A/33/380 (Nov. 20, 1978) (Declaration Concerning the Israeli "Self-Rule" Plan, Signed in Mid-August; Declaration by the Administrative Board of the Arab Graduates' Union, Jerusalem, 21 September 1978)

Note Verbale Dated 15 November 1978 from the Permanent Representative of Iraq to the United Nations Addressed to the Secretary-General, at app. II, U.N. Doc. A/33/380 (Nov. 20, 1978) (Declaration by the Administrative Board of the Arab Graduates' Union, Jerusalem, 21 September 1978)

Note Verbale Dated 15 November 1978 from the Permanent Representative of Iraq to the United Nations Addressed to the Secretary-General, at app. III, U.N. Doc. A/33/380 (Nov. 20, 1978) (Declaration from the Professional Unions, Jerusalem, 24 September 1978)

Note Verbale Dated 15 November 1978 from the Permanent Representative of Iraq to the United Nations Addressed to the Secretary-General, at app. IV, U.N. Doc. A/33/380 (Nov. 20, 1978) (Declaration from the Occupied Territories (Circulated Clandestinely During the Last Week of September 1978))

Note Verbale Dated 15 November 1978 from the Permanent Representative of Iraq to the United Nations Addressed to the Secretary-General, at app. V, U.N. Doc. A/33/380 (Nov. 20, 1978) (Declaration by the Arab Graduates' Union, Jerusalem, 28 September 1978)

Note Verbale Dated 15 November 1978 from the Permanent Representative of Iraq to the United Nations Addressed to the Secretary-General, at app. VI, U.N. Doc. A/33/380

(Nov. 20, 1978) (Declaration by the Conference of the Popular Organizations in the Occupied Land, Held at Beit Hanina (Jerusalem) on 1 October 1978)

Note Verbale Dated 15 November 1978 from the Permanent Representative of Iraq to the United Nations Addressed to the Secretary-General, at app. VII, U.N. Doc. A/33/380 (Nov. 20, 1978) (Declaration Submitted on 3 October 1978 to the Ramallah Municipality by the Students of the UNRWA Men's Teachers' Training Centre in Support of the Resolution Adopted at the Meeting on 1 October at Jerusalem)

Office of the Quartet, Report for the Meeting of the Ad-Hoc Liaison Committee on Action in Support of Palestinian State-Building (Sept. 30, 2015)

Office of the Quartet Representative, Quartet Rep Tony Blair Urges the Israeli Government to Release Palestinian Tax Revenue Without Delay, Nov. 23, 2011

Office of the Quartet Representative Tony Blair, Israeli and Palestinian Negotiators Hold Their First Meeting in More than a Year (Jan. 3, 2012)

Office of the Quartet Representative Tony Blair, Quartet Envoys and Tony Blair Call on Israelis and Palestinians to Hold Direct Talks (Dec. 14, 2011)

Office of the Quartet Representative Tony Blair, Tony Blair and Quartet Envoys Meet with Israeli and Palestinian Negotiators (Oct. 26, 2011)

PALESTINE, No. CAB/24/237 (1937)

Palestine, Declaration Recognizing the Jurisdiction of the International Criminal Court, Jan. 21, 2009

The Palestine Arab Case: A Statement by The Arab Higher Committee (The Body Representing the Palestine Arabs) (1947)

Palestine Liberation Organization, Palestine Initiative to Seek an Enhanced Status as an Observer State at the United Nations: Frequently Asked Questions (Oct. 2012)

Palestine Liberation Organization, Political Program, June 9, 1974, *in* ISRAEL IN THE MIDDLE EAST: DOCUMENTS AND READINGS ON SOCIETY, POLITICS, AND FOREIGN RELATIONS, PRE-1948 TO THE PRESENT 344 (Itamar Rabinovich & Jehuda Reinharz eds., 2d ed. 2008)

Palestine Liberation Organization, Negotiations Affairs Department, Oslo Process: 20 Years of Oslo: 1993–2013 (Sept. 12, 2013)

Palestine Liberation Organization, Negotiations Affairs Department, Palestine's Application for UN Membership (Oct. 2011)

Palestine Liberation Organization, Negotiations Affairs Department, Palestine's Enhancement of Status at the UN (Nov. 2012)

Palestine Liberation Organization, Negotiations Affairs Department, Position Paper: Enhancement of Palestine's Status at the UN (Nov. 26, 2012)

Palestine Liberation Organization, Negotiations Office, Recognizing the Palestinian State on the 1967 Border & Admission of Palestine as a Full Member of the United Nations (July 2011)

Palestine National Council, Political Program, 12 January, 1973, *in* THE ISRAELI-PALESTINIAN CONFLICT: A DOCUMENTARY RECORD: 1967–1990 303 (Yehuda Lukacs ed., 1992)

The Palestine National Covenant, 1968, *in* THE ISRAELI-PALESTINIAN CONFLICT: A DOCUMENTARY RECORD: 1967–1990 291 (Yehuda Lukacs ed., 1992)

Palestine Royal Commission Report, cmd. 5479 (1937)

Palestinian Academic Society for the Study of International Affairs, PLO v. PA (Sept. 2014)

Palestinian National Authority, Palestine, "Ending the Occupation, Establishing the State," Programme of the Thirteenth Government (Aug. 2009)

Paper by the Foreign Office Research Department, Sept. 30, 1948, FO 371/68382, *in* 6 THE ARAB LEAGUE: BRITISH DOCUMENTARY SOURCES: 1943–1963 153 (Anita L.P. Burdett ed., 1995)

Peace with Israel, Apr. 1, 1950, *in* 2 THE ARAB STATES AND THE ARAB LEAGUE: A DOCUMENTARY RECORD 165 (Muhammad Khalil ed., 1962)

Permanent Delegation of the Russian Federation to UNESCO, Legal Argumments [*sic*] for Russia's Position on Crimea and Ukraine (Nov. 7, 2014)

"PLO/Palestine" and the Criteria for Statehood in International Law, Doc. 131 EX/INF.7 (May 26, 1989)

The Policy of the Arab States Towards the Question of Palestine, *in* 2 THE ARAB STATES AND THE ARAB LEAGUE: A DOCUMENTARY RECORD 166 (Muhammad Khalil ed., 1962)

President Sadat's Address to the Egyptian Parliament, Nov. 9, 1977, *in* PEACE IN THE MAKING: THE MENACHEM BEGIN-ANWAR EL SADAT PERSONAL CORRESPONDENCE 4 (Harry Hurwitz & Yisrael Medad eds., 2011)

Press Release, Secretary-General Says Reported Statements by Palestine National Conference Offer "Fresh Opportunities for Progress Towards Peace," U.N. Doc. SG/SM/4219 (Nov. 15, 1988)

Press Release, Settlement Will Not Be Reached by End of Transitional Period on 4 May, Palestinian Observer Tells Palestinian Rights Committee, U.N. Doc. GA/PAL/797 (Apr. 8, 1999)

Press Release, Transjordan Notifies UN of Armed Entry into Palestine, U.N. Doc. PAL/167 (May 16, 1948)

Prime Minister's Office, At the Cabinet Meeting (Nov. 23, 2014)

Prime Minister's Office, Response of PM Netanyahu's Office to Abu Mazen's Speech (Sept. 30, 2015)

Prime Minister's Office, Address by Prime Minister Benjamin Netanyahu at the UN General Assembly, New York (Oct. 1, 2015)

The Problem of Palestine, Evidence Submitted by the Arab Office, Jerusalem, to the Anglo-American Committee of Inquiry, March 1946 (1946)

Progress Report of the United Nations Conciliation Commission for Palestine Covering the Period from 23 January to 19 November 1951, U.N. Doc. A/1985 (1951)

Progress Report of the United Nations Mediator on Palestine Submitted to the Secretary-General for Transmission to the Members of the United Nations, U.N. Doc. A/648 (1948)

Public Hearings Before the Anglo-American Committee of Inquiry, Jerusalem (Palestine), Mar. 25, 1946

Questionnaire by UN Special Representative Gunnar Jarring to the Governments of Egypt, Jordan, Israel, and Lebanon, With Replies, March 1969, *in* THE ISRAELI-PALESTINIAN CONFLICT: A DOCUMENTARY RECORD: 1967–1990 2 (Yehuda Lukacs ed., 1992)

Questions Addressed to the Governments of Egypt, Saudi Arabia, Transjordan, Iraq, Yemen, Syria and Lebanon, to the Arab Higher Committee and to the Jewish Authorities in Palestine Pursuant to the Decision of the Security Council Taken at the 295th Meeting Held on 18 May 1948, U.N. Doc. S/753 (May 18, 1948)

The Reagan Peace Plan—U.S. Involvement in Mideast Peace Effort, "A Moral Imperative." President Ronald Reagan, 1 September, 1982, *in* THE ISRAELI-PALESTINIAN CONFLICT: A DOCUMENTARY RECORD: 1967–1990 72 (Yehuda Lukacs ed., 1992)

Recommendations of the King-Crane Commission with Regard to Syria-Palestine and Iraq (Aug. 29, 1919)

Record of a Discussion Between the Prime Minister and King Hussein of Jordan at 10 Downing Street on 20 September 1979 at 1800 Hours, *in* RECORDS OF THE PRIME MINISTER'S OFFICE: CORRESPONDENCE AND PAPERS, 1979–1997, No. PREM/19/92 4 (1979)

Regional Conferences Attended by Israel, Sept. 23, 1952, *in* 2 THE ARAB STATES AND THE ARAB LEAGUE: A DOCUMENTARY RECORD 171 (Muhammad Khalil ed., 1962)

Reinhold, Steven, *Good Faith in International Law* (Bonn Research Paper on Public International Law No. 2/2013, 2013)

Rejection of Palestine Partition Plan, Dec. 12, 1946, *in* 2 THE ARAB STATES AND THE ARAB LEAGUE: A DOCUMENTARY RECORD 164 (Muhammad Khalil ed., 1962)

Reply of the Arab Higher Committee for Palestine to the White Paper Issued by the British Government of May 17, 1939

Report of the Committee on the Admission of New Members Concerning the Application of Palestine for Admission to Membership in the United Nations, U.N. Doc. S/2011/705 (Nov. 11, 2011)

Report of the International Committee of Jurists Entrusted by the Council of the League of Nations with the Task of Giving an Advisory Opinion upon the Legal Aspects of the Aaland Islands Question, L.N.O.J. 3 (Special Supp. No. 3 1920)

Report of the International Law Commission, 58th Sess., May 1–June 9, July 3–Aug. 11, 2006, at 13-100, U.N. Doc. A/61/10; GAOR, 61st Sess., Supp. No. 10 (2006)

Report of the Secretary-General, U.N. Doc. A/31/270 (Oct. 18, 1976)

Report of the Secretary-General, U.N. Doc. A/43/691 (Sept. 30, 1988)

Report of the Secretary-General on the Activities of the Special Representative to the Middle East, U.N. Doc. A/8815 (Sept. 15, 1972)

Report of the Secretary-General Submitted in Pursuance of Security Council Resolution 344 (1973), U.N. Doc. S/11169 (Dec. 24, 1973)

Report of the Secretary-General Submitted Under General Assembly Resolution 31/62 Concerning the Peace Conference on the Middle East, U.N. Doc. S/12290 (Feb. 28, 1977)

Report of the Sharm El-Sheikh Fact-Finding Committee, Apr. 30, 2001

Report of the Special Rapporteur on the Situation of Human Rights in the Palestinian Territories Occupied Since 1967, U.N. Doc. A/HRC/25/67 (Jan. 13, 2014)

REPORT ON MIDDLE EAST CONFERENCE HELD IN CAIRO AND JERUSALEM, MARCH 12TH TO 30TH, 1921, WITH APPENDICES, No. CAB/24/126 (1921)

Report Presented to the Council of the League of Nations by the Commission of Rapporteurs, L.N. Doc. B7 21/68/106 (1921)

Research-Based Progress Report of the Human Rights Council Advisory Committee Containing Recommendations on Mechanisms to Assess the Negative Impact of Unilateral Coercive Measures on the Enjoyment of Human Rights and to Promote Accountability, U.N. Doc. A/HRC/28/74 (Feb. 10, 2015)

THE RIGHT OF SELF-DETERMINATION OF THE PALESTINIAN PEOPLE, U.N. Doc. ST/SG/SER.F/3 (1979)

Rights Brought Home: The Human Rights Bill, cmd. 3782 (1997)

Ronen, Yaël, *Recognition of the State of Palestine: Still Too Much Too Soon?* (Hebrew University of Jerusalem Faculty of Law International Law Forum Research Paper No. 15-13, 2013)

Sadat Addresses the Knesset in Jerusalem, Nov. 20, 1977, *in* PEACE IN THE MAKING: THE MENACHEM BEGIN-ANWAR EL SADAT PERSONAL CORRESPONDENCE 15 (Harry Hurwitz & Yisrael Medad eds., 2011)

Sadat Receives an Honorary Degree, May 26, 1979, *in* PEACE IN THE MAKING: THE MENACHEM BEGIN-ANWAR EL SADAT PERSONAL CORRESPONDENCE 146 (Harry Hurwitz & Yisrael Medad eds., 2011)

Separate Peace with Israel, Apr. 13, 1950, *in* 2 THE ARAB STATES AND THE ARAB LEAGUE: A DOCUMENTARY RECORD 166 (Muhammad Khalil ed., 1962)

Shaath, Nabil, The Time is Now: Support Palestine's UN Bid (Nov. 29, 2012)

Ships Carrying Contraband Goods and Immigrants to Israel, Apr. 8, 1950, *in* 2 THE ARAB STATES AND THE ARAB LEAGUE: A DOCUMENTARY RECORD 166 (Muhammad Khalil ed., 1962)

Speech by His Excellency President Mahmoud Abbas to the Parliamentary Assembly of the Council of Europe (Oct. 6, 2011)

Speech by President J. 'Abd an-Nasir at the Officers' Club, Cairo, Apr. 25, 1959, *in* 2 THE ARAB STATES AND THE ARAB LEAGUE: A DOCUMENTARY RECORD 975 (Muhammad Khalil ed., 1962)

Statement by H.E. Mr. Benjamin Netanyahu, Prime Minister of the State of Israel, New York (Sept. 23, 2011)

Statement by H.E. Mr. Mahmoud Abbas, President of the State of Palestine, Chairman of the Executive Committee of the Palestine Liberation Organization, President of the Palestinian National Authority, New York (Sept. 23, 2011)

Statement by H.E. Mr. Mahmoud Abbas, President of the State of Palestine, Chairman of the Executive Committee of the Palestine Liberation Organization, President of the Palestinian National Authority, New York (Sept. 27, 2012)

Statement by H.E. Mr. Mahmoud Abbas, President of the State of Palestine, New York (Sept. 30, 2015)

State of Palestine, Palestine Liberation Organization, Negotiations Affairs Department, Statement by PLO Executive Committee Member Dr. Saeb Erekat on Palestine's Accession to International Treaties (Dec. 31, 2014), http://unispal.un.org/UNISPAL.NSF/0/6AC3115500C569E985257DC100552B95

Statement by Middle East Quartet, Sept. 23, 2011, U.N. Doc. SG/2178

Statement by Middle East Quartet, Apr. 11, 2012, U.N. Doc. SG/2182

Statement by President Ronald Reagan on Relations with the PLO, 14 December, 1988, *in* THE ISRAELI-PALESTINIAN CONFLICT: A DOCUMENTARY RECORD: 1967–1990 120 (Yehuda Lukacs ed., 1992)

Statement by State Department Spokesman Charles Redman on the Resolutions of the 19th Palestine National Council, 16 November, 1988, *in* THE ISRAELI-PALESTINIAN CONFLICT: A DOCUMENTARY RECORD: 1967–1990 115 (Yehuda Lukacs ed., 1992)

Statement by the Arab Governments Condemning the Palestine Partition Resolution, Dec. 17, 1947, *in* 2 THE ARAB STATES AND THE ARAB LEAGUE: A DOCUMENTARY RECORD 550 (Muhammad Khalil ed., 1962)

Statement Issued by the Governments of the Arab League States on the Occasion of the Entry of the Arab Armies into Palestine, May 15, 1948, *in* 2 THE ARAB STATES AND THE ARAB LEAGUE: A DOCUMENTARY RECORD 557 (Muhammad Khalil ed., 1962)

Statement Issued by the Palestine Liberation Organization Rejecting U.N. Resolutions [*sic*] 242, Cairo, 23 November, 1967, *in* THE ISRAELI-PALESTINIAN CONFLICT: A DOCUMENTARY RECORD: 1967–1990 290 (Yehuda Lukacs ed., 1992)

Statement to the *Ad Hoc* Committee on the Palestinian Question by the Representative of the Arab Higher Committee, 29 September 1947, *in* The Arab-Israel Conflict and Its Resolution: Selected Documents 57 (Ruth Lapidoth & Moshe Hirsch eds., 1992)

Statements of the Prime Minister David Ben-Gurion Regarding Moving the Capital of Israel to Jerusalem

Status of Palestine in the United Nations: Report of the Secretary-General, U.N. Doc. A/67/738 (Mar. 8, 2013)

Status, Privileges, and Immunities Under International Law of the Permanent Observer Mission of Palestine to the United Nations (May 5, 2000), 2000 U.N. Jurid. Y.B. 359, U.N. Doc. ST/LEG/SER.C/38

2 A Survey of Palestine Prepared in December 1945 and January 1946 for the Information of the Anglo-American Committee of Inquiry (1991)

Trans-Jordania, in Report on Middle East Conference Held in Cairo and Jerusalem, March 12th to 30th, 1921, With Appendices, app. 19 at 107, No. CAB/24/126 (1921)

Two Memoranda Sent by the Political Committee of the Arab League to the U.N. Mediator (Bernadotte) and to the Security Council, Rejecting the Extension of the Truce, First Memorandum, July 8, 1948, *in* 2 The Arab States and the Arab League: A Documentary Record 563 (Muhammad Khalil ed., 1962)

UN Calls for Immediate Resumption of Direct Israeli-Palestinian Talks (Nov. 14, 2011)

United Nations Conciliation Commission for Palestine, Third Progress Report to the Secretary-General of the United Nations (For the Period Extending from 9 April to 8 June 1949 Inclusive), U.N. Doc. A/927 (June 13, 1949)

United Nations Division for Palestinian Rights, Approaches Towards the Settlement of the Arab-Israeli Conflict and the Question of Palestine, no. 7 (Oct. 1991) (Excerpts from the Address of Prime Minister Itzhak Shamir to the Knesset, Jerusalem, Oct. 7, 1991)

United Nations Division for Palestinian Rights, Approaches Towards the Settlement of the Arab-Israeli Conflict and the Question of Palestine, no. 7 (Oct. 1991) (Statement Made at the Opening Session of the Middle East Peace Conference, Madrid, Oct. 30, 1991, United States President George H. Bush)

United Nations Division for Palestinian Rights, Approaches Towards the Settlement of the Arab-Israeli Conflict and the Question of Palestine, no. 7 (Oct. 1991) (Text of the Invitation to the Middle East Peace Conference, Oct. 18, 1991)

United Nations Division for Palestinian Rights, Approaches Towards the Settlement of the Arab-Israeli Conflict and the Question of Palestine, no. 8 (Nov. 1991) (Excerpts from the PLO Chairman's Address Concerning the Intifadah and the Middle East Peace Conference, Nov. 9, 1991)

United Nations Division for Palestinian Rights, Approaches Towards the Settlement of the Arab-Israeli Conflict and the Question of Palestine, no. 10 (Jan. 1992) (Text of Draft "Outline of Model of the Palestinian Interim Self-Government Authority (PISGA)," Washington, DC, Jan. 14, 1992)

United Nations Palestine Commission, Communication from the Representative of the Arab Higher Committee for Palestine, U.N. Doc. A/AC.21/6 (Jan. 19, 1948)

United Nations Palestine Commission, Excerpts from the Arab Press of Palestine, U.N. Doc. P/40 (Apr. 2, 1948)

United Nations Palestine Commission, First Special Report to the Security Council: The Problem of Security in Palestine, U.N. Doc. A/AC.21/9 (Feb. 16, 1948)

United Nations Special Committee on Palestine, Report to the General Assembly: Volume I, U.N. Doc. A/364 (Sept. 3, 1947)
United Nations Special Committee on Palestine, Report to the General Assembly: Volume II: Annexes, Appendix and Maps, U.N. Doc. A/364/Add.I (Sept. 9, 1947)
United Nations Special Committee on Palestine, Report to the General Assembly: Volume III: Annex A: Oral Evidence Presented at Public Meetings, U.N. Doc. A/364/Add.2 (1947)
United Nations Special Committee on Palestine, Report to the General Assembly: Volume IV: Annex B: Oral Evidence Presented at Private Meetings, U.N. Doc. A/364/Add.3 (1947)
United Nations Special Committee on Palestine, Report to the General Assembly: Volume V: Index to the Report and Annexes, U.N. Doc. A/364/Add.4 (Oct. 9, 1947)
U.S. Proposals for a Settlement of the Arab-Israeli Conflict: Address by Secretary Dulles to the Council on Foreign Relations, Aug. 26, 1955, *in* 2 THE ARAB STATES AND THE ARAB LEAGUE: A DOCUMENTARY RECORD 638 (Muhammad Khalil ed., 1962)

Wilson, Woodrow, Fourteen Points, Jan. 8, 1918
Written Statement Submitted by Palestine, Legal Consequences of the Construction of a Wall in the Occupied Palestinian Territory, Advisory Opinion, 2004 I.C.J. (Jan. 30)

Plenary Proceedings

League of Nations

British Mandate for Palestine, Minutes of Meeting of Council Held at Geneva on September 29th, 1923, Oct. 13, 1923

League of Nations, Permanent Mandates Commission, Minutes of the 32d (Extraordinary) Sess. (Aug. 6, 1937)
League of Nations, Permanent Mandates Commission, Minutes of the 32d (Extraordinary) Sess. (Aug. 12, 1937)
League of Nations, Permanent Mandates Commission, Minutes of the 32d (Extraordinary) Sess. (Aug. 13, 1937)

United Nations General Assembly

U.N. GAOR, U.N. Doc. A/C.1/PV.48 (May 7, 1947)
U.N. GAOR, U.N. Doc. A/PV.78 (May 14, 1947)
U.N. GAOR, U.N. Doc. A/PV.135 (May 14, 1948)
U.N. GAOR, U.N. Doc. A/C.1/SR.200 (Nov. 15, 1948)
U.N. GAOR, U.N. Doc. A/C.1/SR.207 (Nov. 22, 1948)
U.N. GAOR, U.N. Doc. A/C.1/402 (Nov. 26, 1948)
U.N. GAOR, U.N. Doc. A/C.1/405 (Nov. 30, 1948)
U.N. GAOR, U.N. Doc. A/C.1/SR.220 (Dec. 1, 1948)
U.N. GAOR, U.N. Doc. A/PV.184 (Dec. 11, 1948)
U.N. GAOR, U.N. Doc. A/PV.185 (Dec. 11, 1948)

U.N. GAOR, U.N. Doc. A/PV.186 (Dec. 11, 1948)
U.N. GAOR, U.N. Doc. A/PV.1526 (June 19, 1967)
U.N. GAOR, U.N. Doc. A/PV.1566 (Sept. 25, 1967)
U.N. GAOR, U.N. Doc. A/PV.1575 (Oct. 2, 1967)
U.N. GAOR, U.N. Doc. A/PV.1582 (Oct. 6, 1967)
U.N. GAOR, U.N. Doc. A/PV.1584 (Oct. 10, 1967)
U.N. GAOR, U.N. Doc. A/PV.2267 (Oct. 14, 1974)
U.N. GAOR, U.N. Doc. A/PV.2282 and Corr. 1 (Nov. 13, 1974)
U.N. GAOR, U.N. Doc. A/PV.2296 (Nov. 22, 1974)
U.N. GAOR, U.N. Doc. A/PV.2390 (Nov. 3, 1975)
U.N. GAOR, U.N. Doc. A/AC.183/2 (Mar. 9, 1976)
U.N. GAOR, U.N. Doc. A/52/PV.16 (Sept. 29, 1997)
U.N. GAOR, U.N. Doc. A/67/PV.44 (Nov. 29, 2012)
U.N. GAOR, U.N. Doc. A/67/PV.45 (Nov. 29, 2012)
U.N. GAOR, U.N. Doc. A/68/PV.80 (Mar. 27, 2014)

United Nations Human Rights Commission

Commission on Human Rights Sub-Commission on the Promotion and Protection of Human Rights, Summary Record of the 14th Meeting, U.N. Doc. E/CN.4/Sub.2/2004/SR.14 (Aug. 11, 2004)

United Nations Human Rights Committee

U.N. Hum. Rts. Comm., U.N. Doc. CCPR/C/SR.1675 (July 21, 1998)
U.N. Hum. Rts. Comm., U.N. Doc. CCPR/C/SR.1676 (Sept. 28, 1998)

United Nations Human Rights Council

U.N. Hum. Rts. Council, U.N. Doc. A/HRC/RES/16/31 (Mar. 25, 2011)

United Nations Palestine Commission

Summary Record of the Sixteenth Meeting of the United Nations Palestine Commission, U.N. Doc. A/AC.21/SR.16 (Jan. 21, 1948)

United Nations Security Council

U.N. SCOR, U.N. Doc. S/PV.1348 (June 6, 1967)
U.N. SCOR, U.N. Doc. S/8227 (Nov. 7, 1967)
U.N. SCOR, U.N. Doc. S/PV.1375 (Nov. 13, 1967)
U.N. SCOR, U.N. Doc. S/PV.1377 (Nov. 15, 1967)
U.N. SCOR, U.N. Doc. S/PV.1382 (Nov. 22, 1967)
U.N. SCOR, U.N. Doc. S/PV.1407 (Mar. 24, 1968)

U.N. SCOR, U.N. Doc. S/PV.1736 (Aug. 13, 1973)
U.N. SCOR, U.N. Doc. S/PV.1744 (Oct. 9, 1973)
U.N. SCOR, U.N. Doc. S/11036 (Oct. 21, 1973)
U.N. SCOR, U.N. Doc. S/PV.1747 (Oct. 21–22, 1973)
U.N. SCOR, U.N. Doc. S/PV.1870 (Jan. 12, 1976)
U.N. SCOR, U.N. Doc. S/13911 (Apr. 28, 1980)
U.N. SCOR, U.N. Doc. S/PV.2220 (Apr. 30, 1980)
U.N. SCOR, U.N. Doc. S/PV.4488 (Mar. 12, 2002)
U.N. SCOR, U.N. Doc. S/PV.6590 (July 26, 2011)
U.N. SCOR, U.N. Doc. S/PV.6590 (Resumption 1) (July 26, 2011)
U.N. SCOR, U.N. Doc. S/PV.6636 (Oct. 24, 2011)
U.N. SCOR, U.N. Doc. S/PV.6662 (Nov. 21, 2011)
U.N. SCOR, U.N. Doc. S/PV.6692 (Dec. 20, 2011)
U.N. SCOR, U.N. Doc. S/PV.6706 (Jan. 24, 2012)

United Kingdom House of Commons

586(40) HANSARD (Oct. 13, 2014)

United States House of Representatives

The Palestinian Authority's International Criminal Court Gambit: A True Partner for Peace?, S. Comm. Mid. E. & N. Afr., 114th Cong. (2015)

Treaties and Instruments

African Charter on Human and Peoples' Rights, Nairobi, June 27, 1981
Agreement Between His Britannic Majesty and His Highness the Amir of Trans-Jordan, *in* LEGISLATION OF TRANSJORDAN: 1918–1930, app. I. at 703 (C.R.W. Seton ed., 1931)
Agreement Between the Government of India and the Government of the Islamic Republic of Pakistan on Bilateral Relations, Simla, July 2, 1972
Agreement Reached in the Multi-Party Negotiations, Belfast, Apr. 10, 1998
Alexandria Protocol, Alexandria, Oct. 7, 1944, *in* 2 THE ARAB STATES AND THE ARAB LEAGUE: A DOCUMENTARY RECORD 53 (Muhammad Khalil ed., 1962) (Special Resolution Concerning Palestine)
Arab Charter on Human Rights, Tunis, May 22, 2004, 24(2) B.U. INT'L L.J. 147 (2006) (Mohammed Amin Al-Midani & Mathilde Cabanettes trans., Susan M. Akram rev.)
Article 25 of the Palestine Mandate, Territory Known as Trans-Jordan, Note by the Secretary-General, Geneva, Sept. 23, 1922, 17(3) AM. J. INT'L L. SUPP. 171 (1922) (1923)
Articles on Prevention of Transboundary Harm from Hazardous Activities, With Commentaries, *in* International Law Commission, 2(2) Y.B. Int'l L. Comm'n 148, U.N. Doc. A/CN.4/SER.A/2001/Add.1 (Part 2) (2001)
Articles on Responsibility of States for Internationally Wrongful Acts, With Commentaries, *in* 2(2) Y.B. Int'l L. Comm'n 30, U.N. Doc. A/CN.4/SER.A/2001/Add.1 (Part 2) (2001)

Balfour Declaration, Foreign Office, Nov. 2, 1917

British Mandate for Palestine, 17(3) AM. J. INT'L L. SUPP. 164 (1922) (1923)

Camp David Accords, Sept. 17, 1978, *in* ISRAEL IN THE MIDDLE EAST: DOCUMENTS AND READINGS ON SOCIETY, POLITICS, AND FOREIGN RELATIONS, PRE-1948 TO THE PRESENT 376 (Itamar Rabinovich & Jehuda Reinharz eds., 2d ed. 2008)

Constitution of the United Nations Educational, Scientific, and Cultural Organization, London, Nov. 16, 1945

Covenant of the League of Arab States, Cairo, Mar. 22, 1945, *in* 2 THE ARAB STATES AND THE ARAB LEAGUE: A DOCUMENTARY RECORD 56 (Muhammad Khalil ed., 1962) (Special Appendix Relating to Palestine)

Covenant of the League of Nations Adopted by the Peace Conference at Plenary Session, Apr. 28, 1919, 13(2) AM. J. INT'L L. SUPP. 128 (1919)

Draft Articles Provisionally Adopted by the Commission on First Reading, *in* International Law Commission, 2(2) Y.B. Int'l L. Comm'n 58, U.N. Doc. A/CN.4/SER.A/1996/Add.l (Part 2) (1996)

Egyptian-Israeli General Armistice Agreement, Rhodes, Feb. 24, 1949

Euro-Mediterranean Interim Association Agreement on Trade and Cooperation Between the European Community, of the One Part, and the Palestine Liberation Organization (PLO) for the Benefit of the Palestinian Authority of the West Bank and the Gaza Strip, of the Other Part, Council Decision 97/430/EC, Annex, 1997 O.J. (L187) 1

General Recommendation 21, *in* Report of the Committee on the Elimination of Racial Discrimination 125, U.N. Doc. A/51/18 (Sept. 30, 1996)

Guiding Principles Applicable to Unilateral Declarations of States Capable of Creating Legal Obligations, With Commentaries, *in* International Law Commission, 2(2) Y.B. Int'l L. Comm'n 161, U.N. Doc. A/CN.4/SER.A/2006/Add.1 (Part 2) (2006)

Hashemite Jordan Kingdom-Israel: General Armistice Agreement, Rhodes, Apr. 3, 1949

I.C.J. STAT.

Indus Waters Treaty, Karachi, Sept. 19, 1960

Institut de Droit International, Resolution on International Texts of Legal Import in the Mutual Relations of Their Authors and Texts Devoid of Such Import, Cambridge (1983)

International Convention on the Elimination of All Forms of Racial Discrimination, New York, Dec. 21, 1965

Israel-Palestine Liberation Organization Agreement on the Gaza Strip and the Jericho Area, 33(3) I.L.M. 622 (1994)

Israel-Palestine Liberation Organization: Interim Agreement on the West Bank and the Gaza Strip, with Selected Annexes, 36(3) I.L.M. 551 (1997)

Israel-Palestine Liberation Organization: The Sharm El-Sheikh Memorandum, 38(6) I.L.M. 1465 (1999)

Israel-PLO Recognition: Exchange of Letters Between PM Rabin and Chairman Arafat (Sept. 9, 1993)

Israeli-Syrian General Armistice Agreement, Hill 232, Near Mahanayim, July 20, 1949

Joint Statement at the End of the Taba Negotiations, Jan. 27, 2001
Joint Understanding Read by President Bush at the Annapolis Conference, Annapolis, Nov. 27, 2007
Jordanian-Palestinian Accord, Amman, 11 February, 1985, *in* THE ISRAELI-PALESTINIAN CONFLICT: A DOCUMENTARY RECORD, 1967–1990 488 (Yehuda Lukacs ed., 1992)

Lebanese-Israeli General Armistice Agreement, Ras En Naqoura, Mar. 23, 1949
Letter Dated 24 April 2002 from the Chargé d'Affaires a.i. of the Permanent Mission of Lebanon to the United Nations Addressed to the Secretary-General, Annex II at 6, U.N. Doc. A/56/1026 (2002) (Arab Peace Initiative)
Letter Dated 24 April 2002 from the Chargé d'Affaires a.i. of the Permanent Mission of Lebanon to the United Nations Addressed to the Secretary-General, Annex II at 8, U.N. Doc. A/56/1026 (2002) (Question of Palestine, and Recent Developments in the Arab-Israeli Conflict: Support for the Intifadah and Steadfastness of the Palestinian People)
Letter Dated 24 April 2002 from the Chargé d'Affaires a.i. of the Permanent Mission of Lebanon to the United Nations Addressed to the Secretary-General, Annex II at 9, U.N. Doc. A/56/1026 (2002) (Question of Palestine, and Recent Developments in the Arab-Israeli Conflict: Solidarity with and Support for Lebanon)
Letter Dated 24 April 2002 from the Chargé d'Affaires a.i. of the Permanent Mission of Lebanon to the United Nations Addressed to the Secretary-General, Annex II at 23, U.N. Doc. A/56/1026 (2002) (Final Communiqué)
Letter Dated 9 January 1995 from the Permanent Representatives of Israel, Jordan, the Russian Federation, and the United States of America to the United Nations Addressed to the Secretary General, Annex at 3, U.N. Doc. A/50/73 (Jan. 27, 1995) (Treaty of Peace Between the State of Israel and the Hashemite Kingdom of Jordan, Oct. 26, 1994, Arava/Araba)
Letter Dated 26 March 1999 from the Permanent Representative of Germany to the United Nations Addressed to the Secretary-General, Annex at 2 U.N. Doc. A/54/76 (Mar. 26, 1999) (Berlin Declaration on the Middle East Peace Process)
Letter Dated 7 May 2003 from the Secretary-General Addressed to the President of the Security Council, Annex at 2, U.N. Doc. S/2003/529 (May 7, 2003) (Performance-Based Roadmap to a Permanent Two-State Solution to the Israeli-Palestinian Conflict)
Letter Dated 8 October 1993 from the Permanent Representatives of the Russian Federation and the United States of America to the United Nations Addressed to the Secretary-General, Annex at 4, U.N. Doc. A/48/486 (Oct. 11, 1993) (Declaration of Principles on Interim Self-Government Arrangements)

Montevideo Convention on the Rights and Duties of States, Montevideo, Dec. 26, 1933

OIC Final Declaration, Fez (May 8–12, 1979)
OIC Res. 1/2-IS, Lahore (Feb. 22–24, 1974)
Order of the High Commissioner for Palestine, Sept. 1, 1922

Palestine Liberation Organization, Political Program, June 9, 1974, *in* ISRAEL IN THE MIDDLE EAST: DOCUMENTS AND READINGS ON SOCIETY, POLITICS, AND FOREIGN RELATIONS, PRE-1948 TO THE PRESENT 344 (Itamar Rabinovich & Jehuda Reinharz eds., 2d ed. 2008)
Palestine Order in Council, Aug. 10, 1922

Palestinian-Israeli Security Implementation Work Plan (Tenet cease-fire plan), June 14, 2001

Peace Treaty Between Israel and Egypt, Mar. 26, 1979, *in* ISRAEL IN THE MIDDLE EAST: DOCUMENTS AND READINGS ON SOCIETY, POLITICS, AND FOREIGN RELATIONS, PRE-1948 TO THE PRESENT 383 (Itamar Rabinovich & Jehuda Reinharz eds., 2d ed. 2008)

Provisional Rules of Procedure of the Security Council, U.N. Doc. S/96/Rev.7 (1983)

Res. 19/15, *in* Report of the Human Rights Council on Its Nineteenth Session 44, U.N. Doc. A/HRC/19/2 (May 24, 2013)

Resolutions of the General Syrian Congress, *in* GEORGE ANTONIUS, THE ARAB AWAKENING: THE STORY OF THE ARAB NATIONAL MOVEMENT, app. G at 440 (1938)

Rome Statute of the International Criminal Court, Rome, July 17, 1998

Sykes-Picot Agreement (May 15–16, 1916), *in* THE ISRAEL-ARAB READER: A DOCUMENTARY HISTORY OF THE MIDDLE EAST CONFLICT 13 (Walter Laqueur & Barry Rubin eds., 7th ed. 2008)

Text of the Draft Conclusions and Commentaries Thereto Provisionally Adopted by the Commission at Its Sixty-Fifth Session, *in* Report of the International Law Commission, 65th Sess., May 6–June 7, July 8–Aug. 9, 2013, at 12 U.N. Doc. A/68/10; GAOR, 68th Sess., Supp. No. 10 (2013)

Treaty Between Australia and the Democratic Republic of Timor-Leste on Certain Maritime Arrangements in the Timor Sea, Sydney, Jan. 12, 2006

Treaty of Peace with Turkey, Lausanne, July 24, 1923

Treaty on the Non-Proliferation of Nuclear Weapons, London/Moscow/Washington, DC, July 1, 1968

Trilateral Statement on the Middle East Peace Summit at Camp David, July 25, 2000

U.N. Charter

United Nations Convention on the Law of the Sea, Montego Bay, Dec. 10, 1982

Vienna Convention on the Law of Treaties, Vienna, May 23, 1969

INDEX